NOI

Haiphong

HANOI
Pages 152–177

inh

CENTRAL
VIETNAM

Hue

Danang

Hoi An

**SOUTH CENTRAL
VIETNAM**
Pages 102–119

Kontum

Pleiku

Buon
Ma Thuot

Nha Trang

Dalat

SOUTH CENTRAL
VIETNAM

HO CHI MINH
CITY

Phan Thiet

HO CHI MINH CITY
Pages 52–83

Vinh Long

n Tho

0 kilometers   200

0 miles   200

asian trails

Journey through lost kingdoms and discover the hidden history of Asia to let Asian Trails be your guide!

CAMBODIA

Asian Trails Ltd. (Phnom Penh Office)

No. 22, Street 294, Sangkat Boeng Keng Kong I

Khan Chamkarmorn, P.O. Box 621, Phnom Penh, Cambodia

Tel: (855 23) 216 555 Fax: (855 23) 216 591

E-mail: res@asiantrails.com.kh

CHINA

Asian Trails China

Rm. 1001, Scitech Tower, No. 22 Jianguomenwai Avenue

Beijing 1401, P.R. China

Tel: (86 10) 6515 9259 & 9279 & 9260 Fax: (86 10) 6515 9293

E-mail: kris.vangoethem@asiantrailschina.com

INDONESIA

P.T. Asian Trails Indonesia

Jl. By Pass Ngurah Rai No. 260 Sanur

Denpasar 80228, Bali, Indonesia

Tel: (62 361) 285 771 Fax: (62 361) 281 515

E-mail: info@asiantrailsbali.com

LAOS

Asian Trails Laos (AT Lao Co., Ltd.)

P.O. Box 5422, Unit 10, Ban Khounta Thong

Sikhottabong District, Vientiane, Lao P.D.R.

Tel: (856 21) 263 936 Fax: (856 21) 262 956

E-mail: vte@asiantrails.laopdr.com

MALAYSIA

Asian Trails (M) Sdn. Bhd.

11-2-B Jalan Manau off Jalan Kg. Attap 50460

Kuala Lumpur, Malaysia

Tel: (60 3) 2274 9488 Fax: (60 3) 2274 9588

E-mail: res@asiantrails.com.my

MYANMAR

Asian Trails Tour Ltd.

73 Pyay Road, Dagon Township, Yangon, Myanmar

Tel: (95 1) 211 212, 223 262 Fax: (95 1) 211 670

E-mail: res@asiantrails.com.mm

THAILAND

Asian Trails Ltd.

9th Floor, SG Tower, 161/1 Soi Mahadlek Luang 3, Rajdamri Road

Lumpini, Pathumwan, Bangkok 10330

Tel: (66 2) 626 2000 Fax: (66 2) 651 8111

E-mail: res@asiantrails.org

VIETNAM

Asian Trails Co., Ltd.

5th Floor, 21 Nguyen Trung Ngan Street, District 1

Ho Chi Minh City, Vietnam

Tel: (84 8) 3 910 2871 Fax: (84 8) 3 910 2874

E-mail: vietnam@asiantrails.com.vn

CONTACT

Contact us for our brochure or log into

www.asiantrails.info   www.asiantrails.net   www.asiantrails.travel

EYEWITNESS TRAVEL

VIETNAM
AND ANGKOR WAT

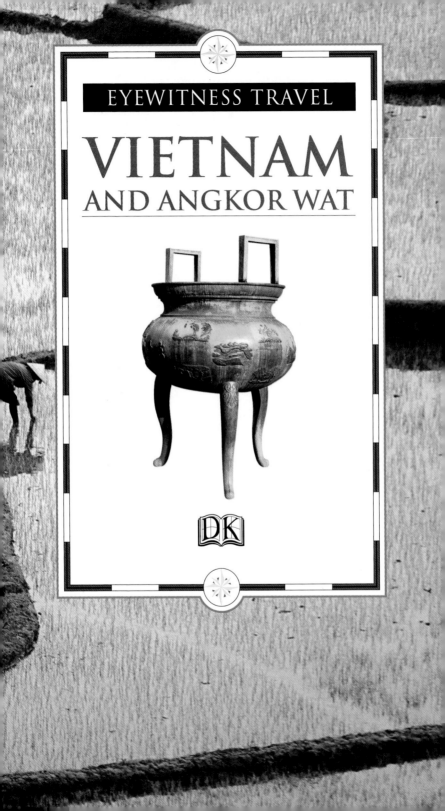

EYEWITNESS TRAVEL

VIETNAM
AND ANGKOR WAT

DK

CONTENTS

LONDON, NEW YORK,
MELBOURNE, MUNICH AND DELHI
www.dk.com

MANAGING EDITOR Aruna Ghose
DESIGN MANAGER Priyanka Thakur
PROJECT EDITOR Shahnaaz Bakshi
PROJECT DESIGNER Kavita Saha
EDITORS Arunabh Borgohain, Jyoti Kumari,
Jayashree Menon, Asavari Singh
DESIGNER Shipra Gupta
CARTOGROPHY MANAGER Uma Bhattacharya
SENIOR PICTURE RESEARCHER Taiyaba Khatoon
PICTURE RESEARCHER Sumita Khatwani
DTP DESIGNER Vinod Harish

CONTRIBUTORS
Claire Boobbyer, Andrew Forbes, Dana Healy, Richard Sterling

CONSULTANTS
Claire Boobbyer, Dana Healy

PHOTOGRAPHERS
Demetrio Carrasco, David Henley, Chris Stowers

ILLUSTRATORS
Gary Cross, Surat Kumar Mantu, Arun Pottirayil,
Gautam Trivedi, Mark Warner

Reproduced in Colourscan (Singapore)
Printed in Malaysia by Vivar Printing Sdn. Bhd.

First Published in Great Britain in 2007
by Dorling Kindersley Limited
80 Strand, London WC2R 0RL

11 12 13 14 10 9 8 7 6 5 4 3 2 1

Reprinted with revisions 2009, 2011
Copyright © 2007, 2011 Dorling Kindersley Limited, London
A Penguin Company

A CIP CATALOGUE RECORD IS AVAILABLE FROM THE BRITISH LIBRARY.

ISBN 978-1-4053-6081-4

Floors are referred to throughout in accordance with American
usage; ie the first floor is at ground level.

Front cover main image: aerial view of Ha Long Bay, North Vietnam

MIX
Paper from
responsible sources
FSC www.fsc.org FSC™ C018179

Spirals of incense burning, Thien
Hau Pagoda *(see p70)*

INTRODUCING VIETNAM

Fishermen working in the
waterways of the Mekong Delta

◁ The green paddy fields of Dien Bien Phu, Northern Vietnam *(see p195)*

Limestone hills in the blue waters of Halong Bay *(see pp182–4)*

Exquisite urn in the courtyard
of Tu Dam Pagoda *(see p139)*

Figurine of a royal
court musician

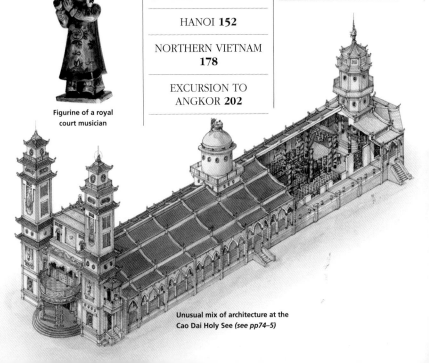

Unusual mix of architecture at the
Cao Dai Holy See *(see pp74–5)*

INTRODUCING VIETNAM

DISCOVERING VIETNAM

Vietnam's fertile S-shaped land, extending from the mountainous north and Red River Delta through to the rich floodplains of the Mekong Delta, offers a wealth of cultural delights. Charming Hanoi in the north, with its distinctive blend of French-colonial influence and Vietnamese character, and fast-moving Ho Chi Minh City, the modern economic capital in the far south, are a thrill to the senses. The diverse country in between offers stunning limestone scenery, ornate temples, heavenly food, villages populated by ethnic minorities, as well as visible reminders of the Vietnam War. These pages outline the regional highlights that will help you make the most of your trip.

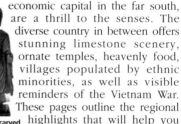

Intricately carved Oc Eo statue

work of art. A day trip out of town are the remarkable **Cu Chi Tunnels** (*see p72*), a monument to the ingenuity of local people during the Vietnam War, and the **Cao Dai Holy See** (*see pp74–5*), a vast complex at the center of the unique Cao Dai religion.

HO CHI MINH CITY

Statue of Ho Chi Minh in front of the People's Committee Building

- **Shopping in Dong Khoi**
- **Ingenious Cu Chi Tunnels**
- **Ornate Cholon Pagodas**

Long celebrated as the "Paris of the Orient," Ho Chi Minh City is a charming blend of the old and new. The shopping hub of the city is **Dong Khoi** (*see pp56–7*), the setting for Graham Greene's famed novel *The Quiet American*, where French-colonial buildings stand alongside smart hotels, restaurants, and shopping centers. The **People's Committee Building** (*see p59*), with its exquisite Parisian-style façade, is an architectural highlight. The excellent **War Remnants Museum** (*see p65*) portrays the horrors of the Vietnam War. To the west, the bustling markets of **Cholon** (*see pp68–9*) sell everything from spices and pickles to silks and herbal medicines, and jostle for space with numerous temples. The **Jade Emperor Pagoda** (*see pp62–3*) has a richly decorated roof, itself a

MEKONG DELTA AND SOUTHERN VIETNAM

- **Experience life on the delta at the floating markets**
- **Boat trips around Vinh Long**
- **Coral reefs at Con Dao**

The Mekong Delta stretches across vast distances of rice fields and mangrove forests. River boat rides from **My Tho** (*see p88*) and **Vinh Long** (*see pp90–91*) carry visitors along narrow waterways to visit traditional craft villages and orchard-filled islands, while the busy floating markets near **Can Tho** (*see p94*) have a lively appeal. Nearby, the towns of **Tra Vinh** (*see p89*) and **Soc Trang** (*see p96*) are home to Vietnam's Khmer minority, and boast some noteworthy

Theravada Buddhist temples, which are quite distinct from the Mahayana pagodas of the ethnic Viet. Just offshore, near charming **Ha Tien** (*see p100*), lies **Phu Quoc Island** (*see p101*), known for its wonderful sunsets and scenic hiking trails. Beyond the delta, the **Con Dao Islands** (*see p98*) are noted for fine beaches, magnificent reefs, and an amazing variety of marine life.

SOUTH CENTRAL VIETNAM

- **Spectacular beaches**
- **Ancient temples**
- **Cool retreat at Dalat**

The South Central coast offers some of the best beaches in the country. **Mui Ne Beach** (*see p106*), the kite-boarding capital of Vietnam, is a relaxed stretch of palm-fringed shores and towering sand dunes, while the coast around **Nha Trang** (*see pp108–11*) features superb diving and island-hopping opportunities. **Phan Rang–Thap Cham** (*see p107*) has three of the best-preserved

Painted fishing boats in the harbor at Ha Tien, Mekong Delta

◁ **Painting of Vinh Tri villagers in the rice fields of Tongking (present-day Tonkin) by a contemporary Vietnamese artist**

Lavish interior of the Tomb of Khai Dinh in Hue, Central Vietnam

Cham temple complexes in Vietnam. The cool climate, great hiking trails, and cascading waterfalls of **Dalat** *(see pp114–16)* make this hill station a popular retreat, and the ethnic minority villages around **Buon Ma Thuot** *(see p117)* and **Kontum** *(see p118)* provide a fascinating insight into a traditional way of life.

Palm-fringed sands at Mui Ne Beach, South Central Vietnam

CENTRAL VIETNAM

- **Shopping in pretty Hoi An**
- **Imperial palaces at Hue**
- **A tour of the DMZ**

The massive ramparts of the World Heritage Site-designated Citadel at **Hue** *(see pp138–45)* and the surrounding area reveal a grand city of ruined temples, royal tombs, and beautiful palaces. A rest-and-recreation center for US soldiers during the Vietnam War, **China Beach** *(see p133)* is still a popular seaside resort. The historic town of **Hoi An** *(see pp124–9)* is a mecca for shopping, where tailors vie to

rustle up a suit within hours. Former French resorts are being overtaken by jungles: **Ba Na Hill Station** *(see p133)* offers splendid views over the South China Sea, while **Bach Ma National Park** *(see p136)* is a bird-watcher's paradise. Tours to the former **DMZ** *(see p149)* are a moving experience, as is revisiting key sites of the Vietnam War.

HANOI

- **Tranquil Temple of Literature**
- **Explore the medieval streets of the Old Quarter**
- **Elegant colonial architecture**

The oldest capital city in the region, Hanoi is home to magnificent indigenous and colonial architecture, a vibrant art scene, and some of the best restaurants in the nation. Nothing, however, beats exploring the historic, narrow streets of the **Old Quarter** *(see pp156–7)*, where craftsmen have plied their wares for centuries. At the heart of the city is the scenic setting of **Hoan Kiem Lake** *(see p160)*, favored by locals for a stroll or a game of chess. The revered **Temple of Literature** *(see pp166–7)* is a calm sanctuary from the bustle of the city, and nearby, the elegant French Quarter features wide leafy boulevards and palatial colonial buildings. Curious visitors can observe the great communist leader's embalmed body at the **Ho Chi Minh Mausoleum** *(see p165)*. Not to be missed is a Water Puppet *(see p159)*

performance, a traditional and mesmerizing art form, which is unique to Hanoi and the Red River Delta.

NORTHERN VIETNAM

- **Cruise Halong Bay**
- **Extraordinary Perfume Pagoda**
- **Ethnic minorities at Sapa**

Both nature and tradition flourish in Northern Vietnam. To the south of Hanoi is the sacred **Perfume Pagoda** *(see p192)*, a pilgrimage site in a hillside grotto reached by an enchanting sampan ride through a flooded valley. To the north are the **Yen Tu Pilgrimage Sites** *(see p185)*, tucked away on mist-covered mountains, offering insights into Vietnamese religious tradition. In the northeast, spectacular mountain scenery and tranquil lakes distinguish the drive to **Ba Be National Park** *(see p200)*. A boat trip around stunning **Halong Bay** *(see pp182–4)*, where dramatic limestone pinnacles rise out of the sea, is an unforgettable experience. In the northwest, hill peoples, such as the Red Dao and Hmong *(see pp198–9)*, congregate at the lively weekend market in **Sapa** *(see pp196–7)*, and families in the **Mai Chau Valley** *(see p194)* offer the chance to stay in an authentic Thai stilt house. The adventurous can attempt the challenging climb up **Mount Fansipan** *(see p197)*, Vietnam's highest peak.

Black Hmong women selling bright cloth in Sapa, Northern Vietnam

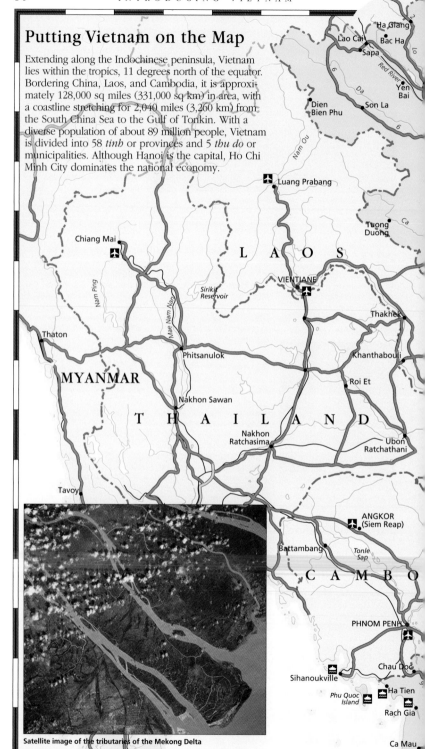

Putting Vietnam on the Map

Extending along the Indochinese peninsula, Vietnam lies within the tropics, 11 degrees north of the equator. Bordering China, Laos, and Cambodia, it is approximately 128,000 sq miles (331,000 sq km) in area, with a coastline stretching for 2,040 miles (3,260 km) from the South China Sea to the Gulf of Tonkin. With a diverse population of about 89 million people, Vietnam is divided into 58 *tinh* or provinces and 5 *thu do* or municipalities. Although Hanoi is the capital, Ho Chi Minh City dominates the national economy.

Ha Giang
Lao Cai Bac Ha
Sapa
Red River
Dien
Bien Phu
Son La
Yen
Bai
Da
Nam Ou
Luang Prabang
Ca
Tuong
Duong
Chiang Mai
L A O S
VIENTIANE
Nam Ping
Sirikit
Reservoir
Mae Nam Nan
Thakhek
Thaton
Phitsanulok
Khanthabouli
MYANMAR
Roi Et
Nakhon Sawan
T H A I L A N D
Nakhon
Ratchasima
Ubon
Ratchathani
Tavoy
ANGKOR
(Siem Reap)
Battambang
Tonle
Sap
C A M B O
PHNOM PENH
Chau Doc
Sihanoukville
Ha Tien
Phu Quoc
Island
Rach Gia
Ca Mau

Satellite image of the tributaries of the Mekong Delta

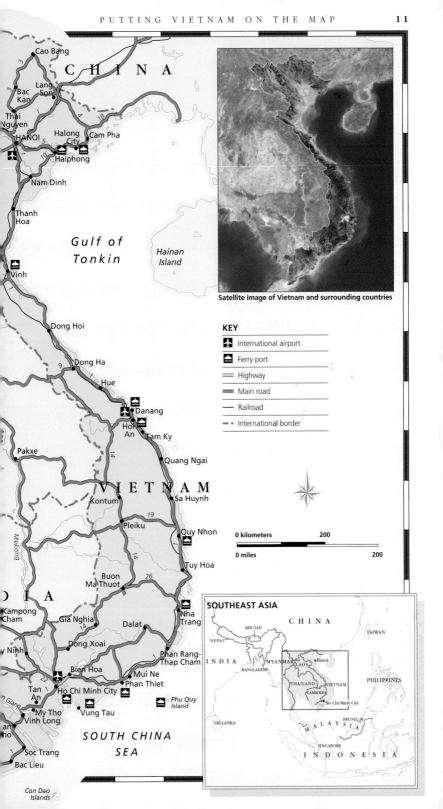

Satellite image of Vietnam and surrounding countries

KEY

✈ International airport

⛴ Ferry port

═══ Highway

━━━ Main road

── Railroad

--- International border

0 kilometers   200

0 miles   200

CHINA

Cao Bang
Lang Son
Bac Kan
Thai Nguyen
HANOI
Halong City
Cam Pha
Haiphong
Nam Dinh
Thanh Hoa

Gulf of Tonkin

Hainan Island

Vinh

Dong Hoi

Dong Ha

Hue

Danang

Hoi An

Tam Ky

Quang Ngai

VIETNAM

Kontum

Sa Huynh

Pakxe

Pleiku

Quy Nhon

Tuy Hoa

Buon Ma Thuot

Gia Nghia

Nha Trang

Dalat

Kampong Cham

Dong Xoai

Ninh

Bien Hoa

Phan Rang-Thap Cham

Mui Ne

Tan An

Ho Chi Minh City

Phan Thiet

Phu Quy Island

My Tho

Vinh Long

Vung Tau

Soc Trang

Bac Lieu

Con Dao Islands

SOUTH CHINA SEA

Mekong

SOUTHEAST ASIA

CHINA

BHUTAN
NEPAL
INDIA
BANGLADESH
MYANMAR
LAOS
THAILAND
VIETNAM
CAMBODIA
Hanoi
Ho Chi Minh City
TAIWAN
PHILIPPINES
SRI LANKA
MALAYSIA
BRUNEI
SINGAPORE
INDONESIA

A PORTRAIT OF VIETNAM

*L*ush *green mountains, scenic beaches, ancient pagodas, and the allure of a fascinating culture attract millions of visitors to Vietnam each year. Today, the country is emerging as an increasingly prosperous nation, with a thriving tourism industry, largely due to economic reforms and a successful effort by its people to emphasize that Vietnam is "a nation, not a war."*

Bounded by the warm waters of the South China Sea, Vietnam is in the southeastern corner of the Indochinese peninsula. To the country's west are Laos and Cambodia, separated from Vietnam by the Annamite Mountains or the Truong Son Range, while to the north lies the great bulk of China. Vietnam itself is long and thin – just 31 miles (50 km) wide at its narrowest – with an extensive coastline stretching from the Gulf of Tonkin in the north to the Gulf of Thailand in the south.

Exhibit in the Museum of Royal Fine Arts, Hue

The Vietnamese generally divide their country into three regions. In the north, dominated by the charming capital Hanoi and hemmed in by mountains on three sides, is the fertile Red River Delta. The long central part of Vietnam is marked by several scenic beaches, the former imperial city of Hue, the mercantile town of Hoi An, and the large port city of Danang, along with remnants of the Demilitarized Zone (DMZ). In its lower half, it broadens and is home to the highlands around Pleiku and Dalat. In the far south lies burgeoning Ho Chi Minh City, Vietnam's commercial hub, and the Mekong Delta. Characterized by palm trees and numerous canals, this bucolic region is the country's largest rice-producing belt.

Vietnam's geographical diversity is reflected in its people, and the nation is home to 54 recognized ethnic groups. The largest, Viet or Kinh, constitute 86 percent of the nation's 86 million people and live mainly on the coastal plains and in the delta

The Yen River winding its way to the Perfume Pagoda *(see pp192–3)*

◁ Street vendors setting up a makeshift kitchen to prepare hot snacks, Hoi An *(see pp124–9)*

Hmong minority of the Northern Highlands

regions. Most of the ethnic minorities inhabit the Northern and Central Highlands and are distinguished by their unique history, culture, and language. The ethnic Chinese, or Hoa, by contrast, are mostly based in the lowlands and major cities, while the Cham and Khmer are settled in the southern coastal plains and the Mekong Delta.

CULTURE

The traditional structure of Vietnamese society has always been hierarchical and patriarchal. Drawing heavily from the Confucian model, family and filial duties are upheld as cardinal virtues. Elders are given respect and education is highly esteemed. The role of women has changed since their emancipation by the Communist regime. Today, although women have gained equality in the public sphere, the home is usually still "run" by a woman.

Vietnam's culture is made more fascinating by the foreign influences it has assimilated over the centuries. Nearly 1,000 years of Chinese occupation has left its mark on the Vietnamese, who have selected and adopted those customs, traditions, beliefs, and architecture most suited to their culture. It is, however, a love-hate relationship, with Vietnam emulating Chinese culture while rejecting any form of political domination by its northern neighbor. The impact of the French, who attacked Saigon after a wave of Catholic executions in the 19th century and went on to conquer the country, is less comprehensive. The colonial power's influence is most visible in the distinctive architecture of the cities and, to some extent, in the food.

Some overseas Vietnamese or *Viet Kieu*, who fled the country as refugees from the communist North in the 1950s and from the South after 1975, are now returning and bringing Western cultural influences with them. While members of the older generation refuse to visit their former homeland, still ruled by the very people who forced them into exile, others are coming back to set up businesses or discover their "roots."

French-style baguettes for sale

Tourism and the media have also played a role in the Westernization of the culture, which is evident among urban youngsters. Everyone is learning English, smartphones are coveted, and jeans and designer clothing are common. Even up to a decade ago, Vietnam was known for its austere fashions, but today, it is an emporium for purchasing clothes, accessories, and homeware in luxurious fabrics and funky designs. Western-style clothing is popular among young women but the traditional *ao dai* or trouser dress is still worn on special occasions, in schools, and in formal settings.

A Vietnamese woman in *ao dai* and scarf

Flamboyantly carved dragon pillars adorning Quan Am Pagoda in Ho Chi Minh City *(see p70)*

RELIGION

During the communist years, atheism was officially promoted, but in the modern era of pragmatism, old faiths and traditions flourish. Vietnam has long embraced a mélange of faiths based on Tam Giao or the Triple Religion of Buddhism, Taoism, and Confucianism, to which has been added ancestor worship, indigenous spirit beliefs, and even Hindu traditions from ancient Champa. The country is also home to a large Catholic population, and idiosyncratic faiths such as Cao Daism *(see p23)* and Hoa Hao. These are all tolerated, provided they do not threaten the Communist Party's hold on power.

Buddhist monk at prayer

LANGUAGE AND LITERATURE

Vietnamese or *tieng Viet* is the national language of Vietnam, spoken by around 87 percent of the population as their first language. Until about AD 1000, there was no written form of Vietnamese, but in the 11th century, a system called *chu nom* was introduced, using adapted Chinese characters. In the 17th century, a Romanized script, *quoc ngu*, was developed by European missionaries, which has become the accepted script. However, there are regional and intra-regional variations in dialect throughout the country.

Vietnam has a rich literary heritage, written in Chinese, *chu nom*, and *quoc ngu*. The epic poem, *The Tale of Kieu*, written by mandarin and scholar Nguyen Du (1766–1820), is a classic morality tale widely regarded as the greatest work in Vietnamese literature. Also famous are the poems of high-ranking concubine, Ho Xuan Huong (1775–1825), known for her witty verse. Today, as a result of gradual political liberalization, a new style of writing has emerged that explores "forbidden issues," and focuses on the plight of the individual. Bao Ninh is a popular writer whose novel *Sorrow of War* is a powerful account of the Vietnam War. Some contemporary names include Pham Thi Hoai, Nguyen Huy Thiep, and Duong Thu Huong.

ECONOMIC DEVELOPMENT

Once among the poorest nations of the world, Vietnam is currently experiencing an unprecedented economic boom. The credit for this initially went to the introduction of *doi moi* (economic reforms) in 1986, which permitted the setting up of free market enterprises, abolished the practice of collectivized farming, and set the stage for political liberalization. Vietnam boasts Asia's fastest-growing economy, with an average growth rate of over 7 percent since 2005. In 1993, the World Bank declared 58 percent of the population to be living in poverty. By 2008, this figure was less than 16 percent. Agriculture remains the most important element of the economy, form-

Motorbikes and modern buildings in Ho Chi Minh City

ing a major portion of the country's exports sector and employing nearly 65 percent of the population. Today, Vietnam is the world's second-largest exporter of rice – an astounding feat for a nation facing famine in the 1980s.

The industrial sector has shown immense improvement and expansion as well. Mining continues to be an integral part of the economy, and oil, gas, and coal production account for more than 25 percent of industrial GDP. The tourism industry is one of the largest earners of foreign currency in the country. Vietnam has also made great strides on the international stage. In 1995, it became a full member of ASEAN, and of the WTO in 2006.

The effects of this new-found prosperity can be seen everywhere. Large, glitzy malls have cropped up in major cities, while streets once filled with bicycles are now overflowing with locally produced Japanese and Korean motorbikes and air-conditioned cars.

GOVERNMENT AND POLITICS

Vietnam is a one-party country run by the Vietnamese Communist Party. In 2006, Nguyen Tan Dung and Nguyen Minh Triet became the prime minister and president of the Republic of Vietnam respectively. They were chosen by the National Congress which meets every five years. Authoritarian in essence, the party opposes political dissent; many who have expressed disagreement with the regime have been punished. However, since the adoption of limited free market capitalism, the party has taken several steps towards reforming. At the same time though, it is plagued with corruption, slowing down the process of any political change. As a result, while economic reform speeds along, political rights and freedoms continue to lag behind. Just before Congress met in 2006, the party canvassed public opinion, a clear sign that it has modernized its approach. The desire for change amongst the Vietnamese is great, and the populace recognizes that an increased say in politics is not only desirable, but essential for continued development.

CONSERVATION

Despite its increasing wealth, Vietnam remains a poor country with a rapidly expanding population and limited land resources. By 2020, Vietnam is projected to have around twice the population of Thailand, but with less than half the arable land. According to the World Conservation Monitoring Center, at present around 74,000 acres (30,000 ha) of forest is lost annually. Both plantlife and wildlife have suffered at the hands of hunters

Farming Vietnam's most important crop, rice

and farmers, but the government's relocation and collectivized farming programs have perhaps had the greatest long-term impact on the environment. In the 1980s, large tracts of arable land were cleared for futile farming efforts that never saw fruition.

Fortunately, the outlook for Vietnam's nature is improving now. Laws protecting forests and endangered species are being introduced every year, in keeping with Ho Chi Minh's 1962 pronouncement that "forest is gold." Tourism has indirectly had a positive impact on the environment by providing a new source of income that can prove far more profitable than hunting and logging.

Shop selling a wide variety of handicrafts, Hoi An

TOURISM

When Vietnam first opened to tourism in the early 1990s, many visitors were drawn by images of a war-torn nation. The Viets have since done their best to change this view, emphasizing the country's beauty instead. Historic pagodas and faded French-colonial buildings have been restored, while most hotels and restaurants have now returned to the private sector, allowing proprietors to strive for excellence in an increasingly competitive industry. The country's road and rail transport infrastructure needs major upgrading, but its airports and national airline now offer a high standard of service.

The tourism industry has grown at almost 20 percent annually, although it began to slow in 2008. Each year, millions of visitors are drawn to the country by its ancient monuments, scenic beaches, sophisticated cuisine, excellent shopping opportunities, and the warmth of the Vietnamese people. Another positive outcome of the tourist boom has been the resurgence of traditional culture, including music, dance, and drama. Old festivals are being re-established, and arts such as water puppetry are flourishing.

Hien Lam Pavilion in the Hue Citadel, one of the country's premier tourist attractions (see p143)

Landscape and Wildlife

Vietnam is one of Asia's most ecologically diverse countries. Habitats range from the cool mountains of the northwest, through the narrow coastal plains and highland plateaus of the center, to the delta regions of the Red and Mekong Rivers. Especially noteworthy for wildlife enthusiasts are the expansive national parks of Northern Vietnam, filled with fascinating flora and fauna *(see p201)*. For sightings of indigenous and migratory birds, the Mekong Delta offers some of the best opportunities *(see p97)*, while offshore are numerous islands, some with pristine coral reefs *(see p190)*.

Phalaenopsis orchid

KEY

The Deltas

Central Highlands

Central Coastline

Northern Mountains

THE DELTAS

The broad and fertile Red River Delta forms the heartland of Northern Vietnam, while Southern Vietnam is dominated by the rich alluvial lands of the Mekong Delta. Most of Vietnam's rice is produced in these belts. However, while the Red River Delta is almost completely given over to agriculture, the Mekong Delta is also home to wildlife-rich marshlands and mangrove forests.

CENTRAL HIGHLANDS

Embracing the southern reaches of the Truong Son Range, the topography of the Central Highlands varies between craggy mountains to the far west, and fertile plateaus towards the interior. The red volcanic soil around Pleiku and Kontum supports coffee, tea, and rubber plantations, while the mountains are home to jungles with many species of flora and fauna.

Red mangroves *are distinctive for their supporting roots, which arch above the water level, providing a secure environment for many species of small fish, birds, and reptiles.*

Asian elephants *were widely used in forestry work, but are increasingly threatened today. Yok Don National Park (see p118) is an important conservation site.*

The endangered red-headed crane, *also known as the Sarus crane, is found almost exclusively in the grasslands of the Mekong Delta, with the largest concentration at the Tam Nong Bird Sanctuary (see p90).*

The paulownia, *a deciduous tree indigenous to Vietnam and southern China, produces a purple, foxglove-like flower during the early spring.*

The big-eyed pit viper *is a small, arboreal predator, which stuns rodents, lizards, and small birds with its toxic venom before eating them.*

The clouded leopard *is named for the ellipses marking its tawny coat. It has short legs, a bushy tail, and is related to the extinct saber-toothed cat.*

BUTTERFLIES OF VIETNAM

Vietnam is filled with the fluttering colors of butterflies – from elegant, broad-winged giants on azaleas in city parks, to the innumerable clouds of multicolored purple sapphires and knights at Cuc Phuong National Park (see p193) each April and May. At Tam Dao National Park (see p200) in the north, more than 300 species have been identified, while at Cat Tien National Park (see p77), the count stands at 440 species. The butterflies' names are generally as evocative and beautiful as their colorful wings. Some of the best-known species are the white dragontail, red lacewing, and jungle queen.

Swallowtail

Red lacewing

Peacock pansy

Red Jezebel

CENTRAL COASTLINE

The upper center comprises a very long and comparatively narrow strip of coastal flatland running along the choppy waters of the South China Sea. While the land is not as productive as the delta regions, it is home to some beautiful beaches, especially around Nha Trang (see p111) in the lower half of the central coastline.

The three-striped box turtle is a critically endangered species, indigenous to the waterways of Central and Northern Vietnam.

The white-breasted kingfisher is twice the size of the common kingfisher and makes its presence known by its loud sharp call. It has a large red beak, and its striking blue wings and tail are set in contrast against a white throat.

The coconut palm is ubiquitous in Vietnam. It provides many products, including food from its nutritious fruit, wood for boat building, palm fronds for thatch, and coir for mats and handicrafts.

THE NORTHERN MOUNTAINS

The northern mountains all but encircle the Red River Delta on three sides. Sharp, jagged peaks rise above long mountain valleys, forming the most inaccessible part of the entire country. The forest-clad slopes of the northwest once provided a safe retreat for flora and fauna, but today new roads, logging, and human settlement pose an increasing threat to the area's natural beauty.

The rhododendron campanulata, a wild plant, flourishes on the stony slopes of the highest and remote reaches of the Truong Son Range. The flowers are beautiful but poisonous.

The Asiatic black bear is a nocturnal omnivore, distinguished by its coat of smooth black fur and the v-shaped patch of white fur on its chest. It is now rarely sighted in Vietnam.

The stump-tail macaque is a sturdily built primate found in Northern Vietnam. It weighs up to 22 lb (10 kg) and can live for more than 30 years.

Peoples of Vietnam

Handwoven bamboo basket

Vietnam is home to a diverse mix of more than 54 officially recognized ethnic groups. Of these, the Kinh or ethnic Viet of southern Chinese origin, make up around 86 percent of the population. Settled along the coast and in the Red River and Mekong Deltas, they share the plains with the Hoa or ethnic Chinese, as well as the Khmer and Cham. A further 50 ethnic groups live scattered across the Northern and Central Highlands, all with their own distinctive customs, clothing, and languages. While the northern groups, such as Thai and Hmong, have mostly migrated from China, those of the Central Highlands are mainly indigenous.

Viet Kinh bride and groom in silk *ao dais,* the traditional Viet costume

The Khmer *are of Cambodian origin and still follow many of their customs such as Prathom Sva Pol or the Monkey Dance, which is performed during the Oc Om Boc Festival (see p33). Dancers don exotic masks and simulate simian behavior during the show.*

The Bahnar *people of the Central Highlands center their cultural activities around* nha rong *or communal houses. With distinctive upward tapering roofs, these buildings are inaugurated with gong music, dancing, and jars of rice wine.*

Baby carriers are used by mothers, almost from the time they give birth, to take their infants everywhere.

DISTRIBUTION OF ETHNIC GROUPS

KEY

1	Khmer		
2	Cham Balamon	**8**	Mnong
3	Cham Bani	**9**	Bru
4	K'ho/ Lat	**10**	Muong
5	Ede/ Rhade	**11**	Black Thai
6	Jarai	**12**	Flower Hmong
7	Bahnar	**13**	Red Dao

Viet Kinh make up around 86 per cent of the country's population

Cham Muslims *or Cham Bani follow an indigenous form of Shiite Islam. Friday prayers are chanted by a group of about 50 priests, who dress in white sarongs and cover their shaved heads with a ceremonial turban.*

The Bru *live in the Central Highlands and belong to the Mon-Khmer group. They rely on wet-rice farming and enjoy lively folk music for entertainment. A common habit among the Bru is smoking tobacco and adults, as well as children, can be seen with a pipe in their mouth.*

Mnong tribesmen, *once acclaimed elephant catchers and trainers, have long enjoyed communal smoking of tobacco through water pipes. Today, both men and women of this matrilineal society are known for their skills at basket weaving, textile printing, and jewelry making.*

The distinctive headgear of Black Thai women consists of a black turban embellished with bright embroidery.

THAI COMMUNITY

The second largest ethnic minority in Vietnam, the Thai are divided into Black, White, and Red subgroups based on the color of their clothing, as well as on the basis of their early settlements around the Black and Red Rivers respectively. The Black Thai are the most industrious and prosperous of all the subgroups, farming rich rice paddies in the uplands of the northwest. Although a high value is set on education, they are faithful to their cultural heritage. They continue to perform spirit worship, and have kept their ancient folk songs and dances alive and unchanged through the centuries.

Flower Hmong women *are among the most distinctive of all minority groups. They dress elaborately with layers of colored cloth, and devote much of their time to the exquisite embroidery for which they are famous* (see pp198–9).

The costume favored by Thai women consists of a narrow tube skirt accompanied by a sash and a tight blouse with silver buttons down the front.

The Muong *are justly celebrated for their weaving skills. They usually place their bamboo loom in the shady space under their thatched stilt houses.*

The Red Dao *subdivision of Northern Vietnam's Dao minority group derives its name from the brilliant red turbans worn by the women, who beautify themselves by shaving off their hair and eyebrows. Arguably the most enterprising of the highland peoples, the Dao make a living farming, weaving, and paper making. They also have a rich literary heritage, which is written in a variation of the Chinese script.*

Religions of Vietnam

The three most prominent strands in Vietnam's religious tradition are Buddhism, Taoism, and Confucianism, known collectively as Tam Giao, Three Teachings, or Triple Religion. Added to this are the indigenous customs of spirit worship, ancestor veneration, and the deification of Vietnam's patriotic heroes – all practiced widely. Cao Dai is a recent syncretic religion based in the south. Vietnam also has a large population of Christians, and a smaller section of Hindu and Muslim Cham.

The yin-yang symbol derives from Taoism

Confucius, the Buddha, and Laozi – three great religious teachers

TAM GIAO

In Vietnam, Mahayana Buddhism has become closely linked with Confucianism, an ethical system originating in China, and Taoism, also from China. The three Sinitic teachings are known as Tam Giao. Vietnamese follow both Mahayana and Theravada Buddhism.

Theravada Buddhism *claims to rely more strictly on the tenets of the Buddha, and was brought to Vietnam by traders from India. The monks wear saffron robes and chant scriptures from the* Tripitika, *which is a part of the Buddhist canon.*

Boddhisattvas *idolized by Mahayana Buddhists include Dai The Chi Bo Tat, God of Power; Thich Ca, the Historical Buddha; and Quan Am, Goddess of Mercy.*

The Chinese sage Confucius *(551–479 BC) has been revered for centuries. His teachings outline a code of ethics that includes loyalty to the state and the family. Confucian ideas have led to complex hierarchies in Vietnamese families, extending respect, co-operation, and submission to even the most distant cousins.*

Incense burning, *originally a Buddhist practice, is an integral part of religious life in the Tam Giao pantheon, ancestor worship, Cao Dai temples, and even in Catholic churches.*

Groups of family tombs *can be seen in paddy fields everywhere. Viet religion is family-oriented and this proximity to ancestors is at once comforting and reassuring of continuity. This custom evolved from Confucianism.*

Laozi, *a Chinese philosopher of 6th century BC, identified Tao or The Way as the natural source of everything in the world and the guarantor of stability. Taoism focuses on following The Way to live in harmony with the universe.*

CAO DAISM

Founded by Ngo Van Chieu, a Vietnamese civil servant, Cao Dai or Supreme Spirit reinterprets aspects of Tam Giao. A cornerstone of this unusual religion is a belief in "Divine Agents" who make contact with priests during seances. Patron saints include Joan of Arc, Louis Pasteur, and Charlie Chaplin. Initially condemned by the Communists, Cao Dai is now tolerated and has about three million followers.

Cao Dai priests *wear yellow, blue, and red robes to symbolize Buddhism, Taoism, and Confucianism, and don tall, square miters bearing the Divine Eye symbol.*

Cao Dai services *at the Holy See (see pp74–5) are remarkably colorful, as the elaborate costumes of the worshippers blend and mingle with dragon-entwined pillars.*

The all-seeing Divine Eye *first appeared to Ngo Van Chieu in a vision and is the iconic symbol of Cao Daism. Framed in a triangle, its image features prominently in all Cao Dai temples.*

ANCESTOR VENERATION AND SPIRIT WORSHIP

Practiced almost universally in Vietnam, ancestor and spirit worship effectively make up a fourth, unacknowledged strand to Tam Giao. While ancestor veneration is derived from Chinese culture, spirit worship is an indigenous Southeast Asian tradition. Buddhism and Confucianism officially disapprove of spirit worship, but have never been able to eliminate it from Viet tradition.

Ancestral tablets, *based on the Confucian tradition of filial devotion, are found in most homes as well as in temple altars. The memorial tablets are complete with pictures and descriptions of the deceased, set alongside offerings of fruit, flowers, incense, tea, and even cigarettes and alcohol.*

Ghost money, *often in the form of fake US dollars, is sent to ancestors in the spirit world by burning it along with other useful items made of paper, such as cars, TV sets, and houses.*

Animism *is based on the belief that guardian spirits exist in stones, fields, forests, and many other inanimate items. The Vietnamese, particularly the hill tribes, make small houses in order to appease these entities, and often leave offerings at shrines.*

OTHER RELIGIONS

Vietnam's ethnic diversity is matched by an equally eclectic range of religions and belief systems. Chiefly through the efforts of European missionaries from the 16th century on, the country is home to about nine million Christians, of which more than 90 percent are Catholics. A more obscure religion is Hoa Hao, which is centered in the Mekong Delta. The sect is based on a puritanical interpretation of Buddhism, and was known for its militant opposition to communism during the Vietnam War. In addition, variations of Hinduism and Islam are followed by the Cham of the central coast and Mekong Delta respectively.

Cathedrals and churches, *found all over Vietnam, cater to the interests of the Christian community.*

Traditional Music and Theater

Bamboo flutes

Vietnam has a long and rich heritage of music and theater, combining both indigenous and foreign influences. Its repertoire of musical traditions plays an intrinsic role in the country's many theater forms, and includes folk songs, classical music, imperial compositions, and the unique courtship melodies of various ethnic minorities. This multifaceted legacy is deeply rooted in Vietnamese culture and forms an integral part of all celebrations and festivals.

Musician playing the *dan bau*, a single-stringed instrument

MUSIC IN VIETNAM

Vietnamese traditional music comprises several genres, including court, religious, ceremonial, chamber, folk, and theater music. Foreign influences have left their mark, with the adoption of operatic traditions from China as well as Indian rhythms through contact with the Cham Empire – all modified to create a distinctive Vietnamese style of music. Another aspect is the use of a five-tone scale in contrast to the eight-tone scale usually used in Western music.

Hat Chau Van *uses rhythmic singing and dancing to induce a state of trance in a person who is believed to be estranged from the spirits. This art form originated in the 16th century as an incantation during religious rituals.*

Quan Ho *are singing contests that originated in the 13th century and are an important part of spring festivals. This popular folk art features groups of young men and women who take turns to sing, alternately challenging and responding to each other in a traditional courtship ritual.*

Dan day, a rectangular, long-necked lute, with three strings.

Trong de, a drum played with a hardwood drumstick.

Phach, a wooden instrument that resembles castanets.

Ca Tru (Hat A Dao) *or singing for reward is a form of chamber music. In this geisha-style entertainment, women sing and play a phach for well-off men. The art flourished in the 15th century, but suffered a fall in popularity during the communist era. Today, it is being revived as part of the nation's cultural heritage.*

Nhac Tai Tu *is a form of chamber music that accompanies* cai luong *theater. Instruments in the picture above are the* dan tranh *(left), a sixteen-stringed zither, the* dan nguyet *(center), and the flute (right).*

MUSICAL INSTRUMENTS

The Vietnamese have a diverse range of indigenous musical instruments manufactured from natural materials such as wood, animal horn, bamboo, stone, and reed. Among the most commonly used are the *dan bau*, in which a single string is stretched over a sound box and plucked by a wooden pick; the *dan nguyet* or moon-shaped lute, used in Vietnam since the 11th century; *dan trung*, a bamboo xylophone; *broh*, a two-stringed bamboo lute; *dan ty ba*, a pear-shaped guitar; and many types of gong (*cong chien*) and drum (*trong*).

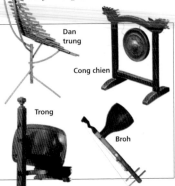

Dan trung

Cong chien

Trong

Broh

THEATER STYLES

Vietnam has a remarkable tradition of performing art genres, with music, singing, and dance as an essential aspect of all theater forms. The presentations vary in style and intended audience – *cheo* is a popular style of theater that traditionally provided moral instruction for rural communities, while *roi nuoc* (water puppetry) delivers spectacular entertainment at the end of the harvest season. *Tuong* or *hat boi*, a more classical form of theater, was developed as entertainment for the king and his court, and *cai luong*, a modernized form of *tuong*, was created for urban intellectuals.

Roi nuoc is a unique art that uses water as a stage (see p159). *Colorful puppets, guided by hidden puppeteers, enact tales from folklore, mythology, history, and everyday life, accompanied by a musical ensemble, drum rolls, and exploding firecrackers.*

Tuong (Hat Boi), *influenced by Chinese opera, uses stylized gestures and symbolism to represent emotion and character. It celebrates Confucian virtues of courage, virtue, and filial piety, and explores themes of loyalty to the king and good overcoming evil.*

Elaborate tuong make-up, *costumes, and stage settings rely on traditional theatrical conventions. For example, make-up helps to define a character. Hence, a face painted red symbolizes loyalty and bravery, while a white face stands for cruelty and villainy.*

Performers in costumes of the court, Hue

ROYAL MUSIC AND DANCE

Entertainment for Vietnam's royal audiences found its main inspiration from the music of the Chinese Imperial Court. *Nha nhac* or court music was introduced in the 13th century and reached its pinnacle under the Nguyen Dynasty *(see p41)*. Performances of this elegant music, accompanied by dances, were held at royal ceremonies, such as coronations and funerals, as well as on religious events and special occasions. With the fall of the monarchy in Vietnam, *nha nhac* was forgotten, but has been revived in recent years. In 1996, it was added to the syllabus of Hue College of Art, and in 2003, it was recognised as a Masterpiece of Oral and Intangible Heritage by UNESCO.

Cai Luong (Reformed Theater) *emerged in south Vietnam in the early 20th century, and incorporates elements of French theater in the form of spoken scenes. Less stylized than traditional theater,* cai luong *tackles social issues such as corruption, alcoholism, and gambling.*

Cheo (Popular Theater) *originated among the rice farmers of the Red River Delta. Performances are usually held outside the village communal house and combine singing, dancing, poetry, and improvisation.*

Traditional dancers

Architecture

Vietnam's long history of foreign invasions has left a legacy in the form of diverse architectural styles found throughout the country. Indigenous architecture in the shape of "tube houses" and single-story pagodas exist alongside buildings that reveal foreign influences. The ancient buildings of the central coast indicate the Cham influence, while Chinese elements are reflected in the pagodas, especially in Hanoi and Hue. French influence is pervasive in the colonial buildings.

Temple bell, Cong Pagoda, Hoi An

Diep Dong Nguyen House – ancient tube house in Hoi An

PAGODAS

Vietnamese pagodas are generally single-story buildings, resting on wooden pillars that support a complex cantilevered structure of timber beams, surmounted by a tiled roof with upswept eaves. The interior consists of a front hall, a central hall, and the main altar hall, usually arranged in ascending levels. Most pagodas have a sacred pond, a bell tower, and a garden. There is elaborate use of symbolism, especially including several Chinese characters.

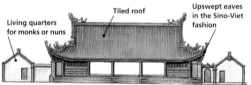

Living quarters for monks or nuns

Tiled roof

Upswept eaves in the Sino-Viet fashion

The Thay Pagoda in Hanoi *rests on a stone platform supporting ironwood columns that carry the entire weight of the building. The low, steep-pitched roof features elaborate upswept eaves with dragon finials. Turned wooden grills admit a flow of fresh air.*

One Pillar Pagoda in Hanoi *was originally built on a single wooden pillar set in a pond, and designed to resemble a lotus flower. Partially burned in 1954, it now rests on a concrete pillar. Fire has long been a hazard for wooden pagodas.*

The Tran Quoc Pagoda in Hanoi *is an eminent example of a single-story pagoda built around many brick stupas. Considered to be Vietnam's oldest pagoda, it was built by Emperor Ly Nam De in the 6th century AD on the banks of the Red River, but due to heavy erosion, the pagoda was shifted to its present site, Ho Tay (see p168).*

Characteristic Chinese-style "flying" eaves

Multi-tiered pagodas *are derived from Chinese tradition. They are usually pointed at the top, and the roofs are made of terra-cotta tiles.*

Thanh long *or dragon is associated in both Vietnamese and Chinese mythology with imperial power, prosperity, longevity, and good fortune. Dragon motifs are used extensively to decorate both pagodas and temples.*

ROYAL CITADELS

Awe-inspiring and imposing, Vietnamese citadels were constructed to provide defense against both physical and spiritual attack. This was achieved by assuming Chinese characteristics of huge, square stone walls topped by battlements, along with elements of *feng shui*. Military architecture under French influence gave rise to citadels with massive, thick walls, ringed by moats, punctuated by towers, with crenellated ramparts and pentagonal bastions.

The Ngo Mon Gate of Hue Citadel, *made of thick stone walls and in accordance with the principles of* feng shui, *has five entrances. The central way, used solely by the emperor, is flanked by openings for mandarins of the royal court.*

Hien Nhon Gate at Hue Citadel *is a fine example of Sino-Viet decorative elements combined with French military genius. This Chinese gate has elaborate turrets, as well as two-story platforms to provide vantage points for soldiers.*

FRENCH ARCHITECTURE

The capital of French Indochina in the 19th century, Hanoi was transformed with the construction of villas in French provincial style, administrative buildings emulating Parisian styles, and even Franco-Gothic structures such as Hanoi Cathedral.

Louvered shutters

Ornate wrought iron work

Hanoi's State Guest House, *once the residence of the French governor, is a beautiful, restored French-colonial building, with an elaborately upswept wrought-iron entrance.*

The Presidential Palace in Hanoi *is a perfect example of the French-colonial style, with a grand staircase, wrought-iron gates, Belle Époque filigree work, and colonnades. Built between 1900 and 1906, it is flanked by extensive gardens and orchards.*

TUBE ARCHITECTURE AND ITS PRESENT ADAPTATION

Interior courtyard for fresh air and to separate work and living areas.

The rear of the house was occupied by the kitchen and bathroom areas.

First built during the Le Dynasty (1428–1788), "tube houses" can be as little as 6.5 ft (2 m) wide, but up to 262 ft (80 m) deep. Behind the shopfront are work areas, courtyards, and living rooms. Today, these houses have soared to create tall, thin "rocket buildings," still limited in their ground area by the original land deeds.

Narrow frontage for shop area

Colorful present-day "rocket buildings" lined up in Hanoi

Tet Nguyen Dan

As the country's single most important festival, Tet Nguyen Dan or Festival of the First Day marks the onset of the lunar new year. Celebrated as a time of rebirth and renewals, this spring festival serves as an opportunity for thanksgiving and paying homage to ancestors. Preparations begin a week before Tet, as people clear their debts, clean the family tombs, decorate homes with peach blossoms or kumquat trees, and make offerings to the Jade Emperor *(see pp62–3)*. The three main days of Tet are a purely domestic affair, as families gather for elaborate meals, exchange gifts, and wish each other a happy new year.

Colorful Tet mask

Houses are traditionally decorated with kumquat trees during Tet

ANCESTOR WORSHIP

The Vietnamese veneration of ancestors finds its greatest expression during Tet, when the spirits of deceased family members are believed to visit the living. The ancestors are invoked with prayers, special foods, and symbolic gifts made of paper, such as false money, clothes, and even watches.

Dazzling colorful displays of flowers *brighten streets and markets all over Vietnam around Tet. Peach blossom sprigs, symbolizing prosperity and well-being, are popular for decorating houses, shops, and temples.*

Offerings of food and drink   Portrait of the deceased

Names of the deceased

Incense sticks

Family chapels or altars *are an integral part of almost every household in the country. They display pictures of ancestors along with tablets listing their names, incense, flowers, and offerings of fruit, rice, and alcohol.*

Incense sticks *play a key role in Tet rites. The scented smoke is said to waft up to the heavens, attracting ancestors to the celebrations on earth. Sticks of all sizes are crafted in small villages and left to dry in the sun before being taken into towns for sale.*

Tombs of ancestors *dotting cultivated fields are common in Vietnam. During Tet, relatives clean the tombs of their ancestors and make many offerings to ensure that the spirits of the deceased are at peace.*

SPECIAL TET FOOD

Tet is a time of indulgence, and festivities are not complete without an array of delicacies. Families may save all year for the necessary luxuries, but the resulting feast is considered well worth it. Pork, duck, and chicken are on the menu, along with rich soups and mounds of sticky rice. Succulent tropical fruits follow meals, especially dragon fruit and watermelon whose pulp is an auspicious red.

Traditional Tet confectionery *consists of candied fruits, coconuts, soursop juice, lotus seeds, or ginger and puffed-rice treats. The markets overflow with bins of sweets the week before Tet.*

Banh tet ingredients ready for wrapping

Banh chung and banh tet *are savory treats most closely associated with Tet. They consist of glutinous rice, mung bean paste, and fatty pork, boiled together in small parcels of banana leaves tied with strips of bamboo.*

TET FESTIVITIES

Lavish, exuberant, and time-honored Tet activities, frowned upon during the years of communist austerity, have made a major comeback in recent years. Entire communities participate in the traditional music, singing, and dancing, as well as fairs, processions, and games played through the centuries. Young people take advantage of this opportunity to meet and flirt.

Human chess, *played only during Tet, is a unique game where local people take the place of pawns. Participants should be young, attractive, and have had no recent instances of bad luck in their lives.*

Bit mat dap nieu or breaking the pots is a traditional game in which revelers, donning flashy Tet masks as blindfolds, try to break clay pots with wooden clubs.

Vibrant firecracker procession

TET FIRECRACKERS

Once an essential part of Tet festivities, firecrackers have been banned in Vietnam since 1994 on grounds of public safety, and replica firecrackers are paraded instead. According to lore, loud noises scare off evil spirits, but for the time being, even playing recordings of bursting crackers is forbidden by law.

The dragon dance *is an age-old tradition originating in China. To welcome the coming year, costumed young men prance vigorously through the streets, accompanied by wild drumming. The dragon symbolizes good luck, and the dance is said to drive away demons.*

VIETNAM THROUGH THE YEAR

Most traditional festivals in Vietnam have close links with Chinese cultural traditions, and follow the lunar calendar, which has only 29.5 days a month. Accordingly, the solar dates change annually, and festivals do not fall on fixed dates. Secular holidays, by contrast, are fixed to the Western calendar, and often associated with the country's recent revolutionary history. Over the past two decades, with the liberalization of the Vietnamese

Branches of peach blossoms at Tet

economy and society, many traditional festivals have also staged a grand comeback, including those related to the imperial dynasties of Vietnam. These are marked by ancestor worship ceremonies, colorful parades, feasts, singing, and dancing. In addition to nationwide events, there are many local festivals as well, especially in the Red River Delta. The ethnic minorities of the north, and the Cham and Khmer of the south celebrate their own festivals.

SPRING (FEB–APR)

A time of renewal and rebirth, spring is the most festive season in Vietnam. Ushered in with the lunar new year, Tet *(see pp28–9)*, it marks a long period of merrymaking all across the country.

1ST LUNAR MONTH

Tet Nguyen Dan *(late Jan–Feb)*. Commonly known as Tet, this is the most important festival in the Vietnamese calendar. Homes and streets are decorated with lights and colorful flowers, stalls selling traditional foods are set up, and families exchange gifts and gather for feasts. Officially a three-day holiday, businesses often shut for a week.
Founding of the Vietnamese Communist Party *(Feb 3)*. Commemorates the day on which Ho Chi Minh established the party in 1930.

Tay Son Festival *(early Feb)*, Tay Son District, Binh Dinh Province. Marking the 18th-century Tay Son Rebellion, this week-long revelry features elephant parades, a drumming competition, and martial arts performances.
Yen Tu Festival *(mid Feb–end Apr)*, Yen Tu Mountain *(see p185)*. Honors the founding of the Truc Lam Buddhist sect. Pilgrims climb to the summit to burn incense and meditate at the pagodas here.
Lim Festival *(mid-Feb)*, Lim Village, Bac Ninh Province. Celebrated 14 days after Tet, this festival is best known for its *quan ho* folk songs. Clad in ethnic garb, both men and women sing improvised lyrics to each other, often in the form of witty repartee. Also features wrestling matches and weaving competitions.
Perfume Pagoda Festival *(Feb–May)*, Perfume Pagoda *(see p192–3)*. The scenic surrounds are said to be the

Traditionally clothed women singing at Lim Festival

Buddha's heaven. Thousands of pilgrims visit the pagoda to celebrate this three-month-long religious festival.

2ND LUNAR MONTH

Hai Ba Trung Festival *(early Mar)*, Den Hai Ba Trung *(see p163)*, Hanoi. Honors the heroic Trung Sisters. A procession takes their statues from the temple to the Red River for a ceremonial bath.
Ba Chua Kho Temple Festival *(Mar)*, Ba Chua Kho Temple, Co Me, Bac Ninh Province. Worshippers congregate at the temple to petition Lady Chua Kho for good fortune and borrow money from her in a symbolic ritual.

3RD LUNAR MONTH

Thay Pagoda Festival *(Apr 5–7)*, Thay Pagoda *(see p173)*, Ha Tay Province. People gather to worship the

Street market festooned with brightly colored flowers during Tet

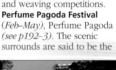

Platters of food offerings to Lady Chua Kho, Ba Chua Kho Temple Festival

patron saint of water puppets, Tu Dao Hanh, who is said to have become a Buddhist at Thay Pagoda. Celebrated over two days, several water puppet shows are staged to mark the occasion.

Hon Chen Festival *(early Apr)*, Hon Chen Temple *(see p148)*, Hue. Based on an old Cham festival, this biannual event, held in the third and seventh lunar months, pays tribute to the Goddess Thien Y A Na. This colorful event features a procession of boats on the Perfume River, as well as the staging of traditional tableaus.

Thanh Minh *(early Apr)*. Dedicated to departed souls, this festival is observed all across Vietnam. Offerings are made to the spirits of the deceased, and ancestral graves are repaired and cleaned properly.

Hung Kings' Temple Festival *(Apr)*, Hung Kings' Temples *(see p173)*, Phu Tho Province. This three-day festival honors the Hung Kings and the celebrations include gaily

Cleaning and decorating a small grave for Thanh Minh

colored parades that take place around the temples. Various cultural events such as classical opera at Den Ha and *xoan* song performances are held at Den Thuong.

Liberation Day *(Apr 30)*. Honors the fall of Saigon to communist forces on April 30, 1975.

SUMMER (MAY–JULY)

With the summer solstice celebrated in early June, this primarily hot and wet season is when the country observes some of its most important national holidays.

4TH LUNAR MONTH

Labor Day *(May 1)*. Legions of workers parade through cities to mark their solidarity with working people throughout the world.

Ho Chi Minh's Birthday *(May 19)*. Supposedly a secular public holiday, this day has become something of a quasi-spiritual event as Ho Chi Minh achieves the status of a deified hero in Vietnam.

The Buddha's Birthday *(May 28)*. Also known as Le Phat Dan. Lanterns are hung outside temples and homes to celebrate the Buddha's birth, enlightenment, and death.

Tra Co Village Festival *(May 30–Jun 7)*, Hai Ninh District, Quang Ninh Province. Held in far northeast Vietnam, this rural festival highlights events such as pig-breeding and cooking contests, traditional games, and dancing.

VIETNAMESE ASTROLOGY

The Vietnamese zodiac runs on a 12-year cycle, each represented by a specific animal. Instead of centuries, the Viet lunar calendar is divided into 60-year cycles known as *hoi*. Each of these consists of five 12-year animal cycles.

Cat *(Meo)* 2011, known for being tranquil, realistic, intelligent, and artistic.

Dragon *(Thin)* 2012, imperial symbol, associated with the male element yang.

Snake *(Ty)* 2013, enigmatic, wise, and likes to live well.

Horse *(Ngo)* 2014, signifies freedom and confidence.

Goat *(Mui)* 2015, associated with creativity and good taste.

Monkey *(Than)* 2016, versatile and mischievous. Associated with inventors, entertainers, and anything ingenious.

Rooster *(Dau)* 2017, brave and resilient, but can also be self-absorbed and pretentious.

Dog *(Tuat)* 2018, is considered lucky, loyal, and likeable.

Pig *(Hoi)* 2019, is honest, patient, and also associated with virility.

Rat *(Ty)* 2020, welcomed as a bringer of good luck.

Buffalo *(Suu)* 2021, associated with riches achieved through hard work.

Tiger *(Dan)* 2022, warmhearted yet fearsome, and brave in the face of danger.

The dragon, a symbol of royalty, adorns many palaces and tombs

Colorful procession celebrating National Day or Quoc Khanh in Hanoi

5TH LUNAR MONTH

Tet Doan Ngo *(early Jun)*. Also known as the "Killing the Inner Insect Festival," Tet Doan Ngo signals the summer solstice. This Taoist festival falls at the hottest time of the year, when fevers caused by insects are at their peak. To ensure good health and well-being, offerings are made to the God of Death.

Chem Temple Festival *(mid-Jun)*, Thuy Phuong Village, Tu Liem District, Hanoi. Held in honor of Ly Ong Trong, a great 3rd-century warrior, this festival features elaborate ceremonies such as a dragon-boat race, the releasing of pigeons, and a ritualized washing of the temple's statues.

6TH LUNAR MONTH

Dad Xa Village Festival *(Jul 9–10)*, Tam Thanh District, Phu Tho Province. Hosted to honor General Ly Thuong Kiet's victory over the Chinese in AD 1075. The festivities include boat racing on the Song Da or Black River.

Tam Tong Festival *(Jul)*, Vinh Loc District, Thanh Hoa Province. With no fixed date, Tam Tong takes place at times of drought.

AUTUMN (AUG–OCT)

While the south remains hot and wet, the north becomes cooler and pleasant. As the leaves change color, autumn is a good time to follow the festivals in the north.

7TH LUNAR MONTH

Hon Chen Festival *(early Aug)*, Hon Chen Temple *(see p31)*.

Trung Nguyen *(mid-Aug)*. The most important festival after Tet, the Taoist Trung Nguyen also has a Buddhist equivalent, Vu Lan, which takes place during the same time. It is believed that lost spirits leave hell on this day to wander the earth. Paper money is burnt to placate these tortured souls.

Le Van Duyet Temple Festival *(late Aug–early Sep)*, Le Van Duyet Temple *(see p64)*, Ho Chi Minh City. The festival takes place on the anniversary of the death of Le Van Duyet. People flock to his mausoleum to pray for a good harvest, safety, and happiness. Traditional opera and dance recitals are staged.

8TH LUNAR MONTH

National Day *(Sep 2)*. Marks Ho Chi Minh's 1945 proclamation of the Declaration of Independence. In Hanoi, the day is celebrated with lively parades in Ba Dinh Square.

Do Son Buffalo Fighting Festival *(early Sep)*, Do Son, Haiphong Province. A procession of six specially trained buffalos are ceremoniously led into the arena, and paired off to fight each other. A winner is declared when one of the buffalos runs away. It is a short respite, as at the end of the day, the animals are slaughtered and eaten.

Trung Thu or mid-Autumn Festival *(mid-Sep)*. Also known as the Children's Moon Festival, Trung Thu is a colorful affair, with much revelry and excitement all around. Children are given new toys and festive masks, and are treated to freshly baked moon cakes. Lantern processions, games, and martial arts demonstrations are all part of the festivities.

Decorated sweet moon cakes for the Trung Thu Festival

Whale Festival *(Sep)*. The worship of whales is an ancient practice likely rooted in the Khmer and Cham cultures. Large processions gather at the temples to make offerings. In Phan Thiet *(see p106)*, the festival also includes the Chinese

Locked horns at the Do Son Buffalo Fighting Festival, Haiphong

Cham dancers and musicians celebrating the Kate Festival

community, with elaborate parades throughout the city.
Kate Festival *(Sep–Oct)*, Po Klong Garai Towers, Phan Rang–Thap Cham *(see p107)*. This lengthy festival follows the Cham calendar, and is the most important celebration for the Cham minority. Droves of devotees in colorful processions, along with traditional musicians, make their way up to the towers to pay homage to the Cham deities, rulers, and revered national heroes.

9TH LUNAR MONTH

Keo Pagoda Festival *(mid-Oct)*, Vu Nhat Village, Thai Binh Province. The anniversary of the death of Buddhist monk Duong Khong Lo is remembered over three days. Events include a lavish procession and religious rituals, as well as cooking and duck-catching competitions, and a trumpet and drum contest.
Confucius' Birthday *(late Oct/ early Nov)*. Confucianism, as a system of state administration, may have disappeared under the communist regime, but Confucius is still venerated. The date has been declared Teacher's Day, and the sage is offered incense and prayers in many temples.

WINTER (NOV–JAN)

By now it is cold and rainy in the north, the traditional Viet homeland where most festivals originated, so there are fewer celebrations during this season.

10TH LUNAR MONTH

Oc Om Boc Festival and Ngo Boat Races *(mid-Nov)*, Soc Trang *(see p96)*. This Khmer festival is dedicated to the moon. Villagers deposit trays of rice, bananas, and coconuts in temples in the hope of abundant crops and plentiful fish. The main event has a series of *ngo* or canoe races, with competitors from Vietnam and Cambodia. Each boat is carved from a single tree.
Nguyen Trung Truc Temple Festival *(late Nov)*, Long Kien Village, Cho Moi District, An Giang Province. This temple is dedicated to the deified national hero, Nguyen Trung Truc (1837–68), renowned for leading the anti-French movement in southern Vietnam. Boat racing competitions and chess matches are enjoyable components of the revelries, along with the re-enactment of the sinking of the French ship, *Esperance*, at the hands of Nguyen Trung Truc and his partisans.

Festive array of incense sticks, candles, and spirit money

11TH LUNAR MONTH

Dalat Flower Festival *(Dec)*, Dalat *(see pp114–16)*. Held by the shores of Xuan Huong Lake, this festival showcases the many beautiful species of flowers that thrive in the cool uplands around Dalat. Along with the array of flowers, there is music and dancing, as well as displays of colored lanterns.
Trung Do Festival *(late Dec)*. This festival honors the Viet patriot Ly Bon who led a successful revolt against the Chinese in AD 542, later proclaiming himself as the Emperor Li Nam De. Traditional ball games known as *phet* are played during the boisterous celebrations.
Christmas *(Dec 25)*. Although predominantly a Buddhist country, Vietnam has a large Christian community as well. As such, Christmas is celebrated with enthusiasm, especially in the big cities where streets and stores are decorated with lights, fake snow, shiny baubles, and ornaments.

12TH LUNAR MONTH

New Year's Day *(Jan 1)*. No special events are associated with this recent addition from the Western calendar, but this day is officially recognized as a public holiday, and its status is gaining recognition. Still, it is nowhere close to attaining Tet's status.

PUBLIC AND OTHER HOLIDAYS

New Year's Day Jan 1
Tet Nguyen Dan Jan 23–26 (2012)
Founding Day of the Communist Party of Vietnam Feb 3
Hung Kings Day Mar 31 (2012)
Liberation Day Apr 30
Labor Day May 1
Ho Chi Minh's Birthday May 19
National Day Sep 2

The Climate of Vietnam

Though Vietnam has a tropical climate, there is considerable diversity from north to south and from coast to highlands. In general, the seasonal monsoons bring heavy rains between May and October, while it remains relatively dry from November to February. The hot season between February and April can be uncomfortable, with temperatures reaching up to 35°C (95°F), and humidity rising to a sticky 80 to 100 percent.

Regionally, the south is consistently warm and humid, with frequent downpours during the rainy season. The central coast suffers typhoons between July and November, but winters are often rainy and cool. The north experiences cold and wet winters between November and March, with occasional snowfall on Mount Fansipan. Summers in the north are warm and humid.

KEY

- Hot wet summer, cold dry winter with occasional frost
- Mild wet summer, cold rainy winter, with snow on higher belts
- Cool rainy summer, chilly dry winter with some rain
- Warm wet summer, cool winter with occasional rain
- Hot dry summer, cool rainy winter
- Moderate dry climate all year, with a brief winter monsoon
- Warm summer with heavy rainfall, cool dry winter
- Hot wet summer, warm dry winter with some rain
- Hot summer with heavy rainfall, warm wet winter

0 kilometers 200

0 miles 200

LAO CAI

°C/F				
	30/86	33/91	28/82	
	23/73	25/77	20/68	21/70
				13/55
☀	5.2 hrs	4 hrs	4.5 hrs	4.7 hrs
☂	52 mm	38 mm	81 mm	20 mm
Month	Apr	Jul	Oct	Jan

SON LA

°C/F				
		21/70	23/73	19/66	19/66
		13/55	18/64	13/55	
					5/41
☀	5.8 hrs	3.8 hrs	5.0 hrs	4.3 hrs
☂	279 mm	209 mm	38 mm	12 mm
Month	Apr	Jul	Oct	Jan

CHAU DOC

°C/F				
	35/95	32/90	30/86	31/88
	24/75	23/73	24/75	21/70
☀	5 hrs	4 hrs	7 hrs	8 hrs
☂	70 mm	190 mm	230 mm	10 mm
Month	Apr	Jul	Oct	Jan

Cai Rang Floating Market in the early morning, Can Tho

Ha Giang
Lao Cai
Sapa
Yen Bai
Son La
Dien Bien Phu
Thanh Hoa
Tuong Duong
Vinh
Chau Doc
Cao Lan
Ha Tien
Can Tho
Minh Hai
Ca Mau

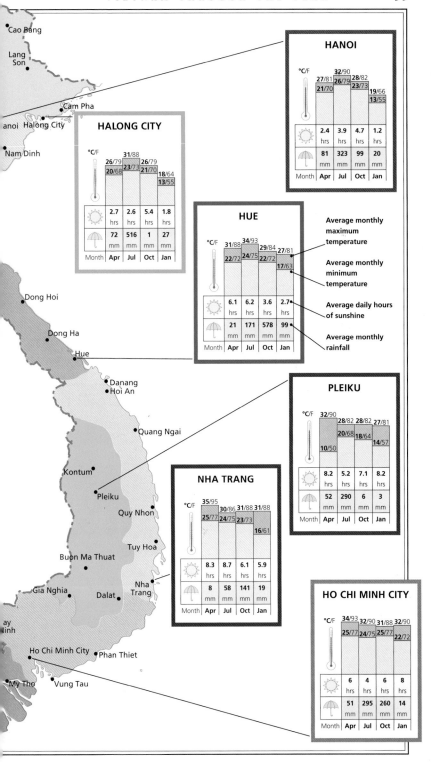

Cao Bang

Lang Son

Cam Pha

anoi Halong City

Nam Dinh

Dong Hoi

Dong Ha

Hue

Danang
Hoi An

Quang Ngai

Kontum

Pleiku

Quy Nhon

Tuy Hoa

Buon Ma Thuat

Gia Nghia   Dalat

Nha Trang

ay
inh

Ho Chi Minh City   Phan Thiet

My Tho   Vung Tau

HANOI

°C/F				
	27/81 21/70	32/90 26/79	28/82 23/73	19/66 13/55
☀	2.4 hrs	3.9 hrs	4.7 hrs	1.2 hrs
☂	81 mm	323 mm	99 mm	20 mm
Month	Apr	Jul	Oct	Jan

HALONG CITY

°C/F				
	26/79 20/68	31/88 23/73	26/79 21/70	18/64 13/55
☀	2.7 hrs	2.6 hrs	5.4 hrs	1.8 hrs
☂	72 mm	516 mm	1 mm	27 mm
Month	Apr	Jul	Oct	Jan

HUE

°C/F				
	31/88 22/72	34/93 24/75	29/84 22/72	27/81 17/63
☀	6.1 hrs	6.2 hrs	3.6 hrs	2.7 hrs
☂	21 mm	171 mm	578 mm	99 mm
Month	Apr	Jul	Oct	Jan

Average monthly
maximum
temperature

Average monthly
minimum
temperature

Average daily hours
of sunshine

Average monthly
rainfall

PLEIKU

°C/F				
	32/90 10/50	28/82 20/68	28/82 18/64	27/81 14/57
☀	8.2 hrs	5.2 hrs	7.1 hrs	8.2 hrs
☂	52 mm	290 mm	6 mm	3 mm
Month	Apr	Jul	Oct	Jan

NHA TRANG

°C/F				
	35/95 25/77	30/86 24/75	31/88 23/73	31/88 16/61
☀	8.3 hrs	8.7 hrs	6.1 hrs	5.9 hrs
☂	8 mm	58 mm	141 mm	19 mm
Month	Apr	Jul	Oct	Jan

HO CHI MINH CITY

°C/F				
	34/93 25/77	32/90 24/75	31/88 25/77	32/90 22/72
☀	6 hrs	4 hrs	6 hrs	8 hrs
☂	51 mm	295 mm	260 mm	14 mm
Month	Apr	Jul	Oct	Jan

THE HISTORY OF VIETNAM

The early history of Vietnam is obscured in the mists of time and legend, but tracing its journey through the centuries of recorded history tells the story of a nation constantly besieged by foreign invasions and civil wars. This historical narrative – from the reassertion of independence in AD 979, after 1,000 years of Chinese occupation to Reunification in 1975 – also reveals the unflinching Viet determination for autonomy and freedom.

Dong Son bronze drum

It is believed that more than 5,000 years ago, the Viet people learned to cultivate rice, and settled in the fertile lands around present-day Guangxi and Guangdong in China. Their neighbors to the north, the Han Chinese, forced them to flee southwards, where the Viet leader proclaimed himself Viem De, the "Red Emperor of the South," and established a kingdom called Xich Qui in the Red River Delta. This period represents the earliest mythical Viet state as well as the first recorded separation from China.

Legend has it that King De Minh of Xich Qui married a mythical mountain fairy, and their son, Kinh Duong, married the daughter of the Dragon Lord of the Sea. This union gave birth to Lac Long Quan, considered to be the first Vietnamese king. To maintain peace with the Chinese, he married Princess Au Co, a beautiful Chinese immortal, who bore him 100 sons. Lac Long Quan then sent his wife with 50 of their sons to the mountains and remained by the sea with the other 50. Thus, the Viet race came into being, with half of them living in the highlands,

and the other half in the Red River Delta. Lac Long Quan raised his eldest son to be king of the Kinh or Viets, and gave him the regal name Hung Vuong. He became the first of a line of legendary Hung Kings, whose dynasty, Van Lang, was based at Phu Tho on the left bank of the Red River, about 50 miles (80 km) northwest of present-day Hanoi. It is widely believed that the ancient bronze drums, excavated in Northern Vietnam and southern China, and attributed to the Dong Son civilization, were associated with this important dynasty.

THE ERA OF THE HUNG KINGS

According to folklore, the 18 Hung kings' combined rule lasted for 150 years. By the 3rd century BC, Van Lang was in decline. In 258 BC, Thuc Phan, ruler of Au Viet, a rival kingdom to the north, overthrew the Hung and founded a new state called Au Lac, with its capital at Co Loa near Hanoi. Scholars regard this as the first Viet state, which flourished under Thuc Phan, who ruled as An Duong Vuong.

TIMELINE

9000–6500 BC Neolithic period	**1000 BC** Van Lang prospers under Hung kings; development of wet rice cultivation and bronze casting	**400–100 BC** Dong Son civilization	**258–208 BC** Capital of Au Lac established at Co Loa
		551–479 BC Life of Confucius in China	
9000 BC	**5000 BC**	**1000 BC**	**500**
6500 BC Early agriculture		**2361 BC** Supposed first Chinese contact with Van Lang	**258 BC** Kingdom of Auc Lac established
2879 BC Semi-mythical Kingdom of Van Lang founded		*Bronze warrior from Dong Son civilization*	

Stone Age relic

◁ **The French use captive balloons for reconnaissance purposes at the capture of Hong Hoa in Indochina, 1884**

THE CHINESE CONNECTION

Through the ages, Vietnam's development has been marked by its proximity to China. In 207 BC, a renegade Chinese general, Trieu Da, conquered Au Lac and unified it with his own territories in southern China. Nam Viet, the kingdom he founded, had its capital at Fanyu in what is today Guangdong province in China. Trieu Da's rule marked the beginning of almost 1,000 years of Chinese occupation that made Vietnam a unique outpost of Chinese civilization in Southeast Asia.

Statue of a Han warrior

Nam Viet was probably as much Viet as it was Chinese. Although the ruling Western Han Dynasty (206 BC–AD 9) regarded the area south of the Yangtze River as on the fringes of Han civilization, Chinese ways and cultural values were increasingly imposed on Nam Viet. The kingdom became a tributary state of the Western Han in 111 BC when Trieu Da's successors acknowledged the suzerainty of Emperor Wudi (r.141–87 BC). With the establishment of Han authority, the Viet territories became the Chinese province of Giao Chi.

During the first centuries of Chinese rule, many attempts were made to Sinicize the Viets, but with limited success. While the Viets embraced many facets of Chinese culture, from education to Confucianism, Taoism, and Buddhism, they resolutely refused to become a part of China, and resistance and rebellions continued throughout the long years of Chinese rule.

In AD 40, two Viet noblewomen, the Trung Sisters (see p163), led the first and most famous bid for freedom. They proclaimed themselves queens of an independent kingdom, with their capital at Me Linh. However, just three years later, the Han re-established Chinese control over the region.

Despite repeated revolts, Chinese rule remained secure for the next nine centuries. By AD 679, Vietnam had become an appendage of the Tang Dynasty (AD 618–907) under the name An Nam or Pacified South, with its capital at Tong Binh on the banks of the Red River near present-day Hanoi.

THE CREATION OF DAI VIET

The millennium of foreign occupation ended in AD 938 when one of Vietnam's most celebrated national heroes, Ngo Quyen, ingeniously destroyed a Chinese fleet attempting to sail up the Bach Dang River near Haiphong by planting a barrier of iron-tipped stakes in the bed of the river. Following this triumph, he proclaimed himself King Ngo Vuong of Dai Viet, and transferred his capital from Dai La, the Tong Binh fortress, back to Co Loa, capital of the first free Viet Kingdom, Au Lac.

Painting depicting the Trung Sisters battle against the Chinese

TIMELINE

Cham sculpture

208 BC Capital moved to Fanyu in Guangdong

AD 1 Han overlords impose Chinese culture in Vietnam

40 Trung Sisters Uprising

100s Cham Kingdom established

200 BC	100 BC	0	100 AD	200	300

111 Nam Viet conquered by Han Emperor Wudi

43 Chinese reconquest

AD 1 Kingdom of Funan is established

300s Cham capital at Singhapura

Funan jewelry

Architectural ruins at My Son *(see pp130–32)*, the Cham religious capital between the 4th and 13th centuries

FUNAN AND CHAMPA

Even as the Chinese-influenced Viet culture evolved in the heart of the Red River Delta, the south saw the emergence of two Indic kingdoms – Funan and Champa. A precursor to the great Khmer Empire, Funan is believed to have been established in the Mekong Delta in the 1st century AD. At the height of its power, its influence extended across much of Cambodia and along the east coast of Thailand. It was probably founded by a merchant from India who, legend says, wed the daughter of a *naga* (serpent) deity and established the dynasty.

Between the 2nd and 6th centuries, Funan's rulers increased their wealth largely through commerce. There is evidence that they traded with China, India, and even the Roman Empire. But by the end of the 6th century, Funan was supplanted by a new Khmer power, the kingdom of Chen La. Located farther inland, it was less subject to Javanese attacks and disastrous floods. Today, little of

Statue from the Oc Eo era

Funan remains beyond the ruins of the port-city of Oc Eo near Rach Gia, and some artifacts in museums at Hanoi, Ho Chi Minh City, and Long Xuyen.

The earliest records of the Kingdom of Champa date from AD 192, when settlements of the Cham, believed to have originated in Java, began to appear along the central coast of Vietnam. At the peak of their power, they controlled the lands stretching from Vinh to the Mekong Delta, and excelled at maritime trade, their main exports being slaves and sandalwood. By about AD 800, Champa found itself increasingly threatened by the newly powerful Khmer kingdom of Angkor and the Viet expansion toward the south. The situation worsened over the centuries, and in 1471, the Cham suffered a terrible defeat at the hands of the Viet. Champa was reduced to a small piece of territory from Nha Trang south to Phan Thiet, which survived until 1720, when the king and many of his subjects fled to Cambodia rather than submit to the Vietnamese.

400	500	600	700	800	900

600s Tong Binh fortified by major Chinese citadel named Dai La

618–907 Tang Dynasty administration; capital moved to Tong Binh; Vietnam called An Nam or Pacified South by Chinese.

700s Cham capital at Indrapuram

907 Fall of Tang Dynasty

938 Independence under King Ngo Vuong of Dai Viet

544 Ly Bon Uprising

500s Kingdom of Funan supplanted by the Khmers

Empress Wu Zetian, Tang Dynasty

700s Red River dyke system strengthened and extended by Chinese

945 King Ngo Vuong dies

979 Viet advance to south begins

Temple of Literature, Hanoi, a center of learning

Buddhism became the state religion, while Confucianism was adopted for state administration during Ly Thai To's rule. Under this dynasty, Vietnam began to evolve as a powerful autonomous state, though it remained very much in China's cultural orbit. It followed a system of strong centralized government, with a national tax system, a codified legal structure, and a professional army. At the head stood the king who was absolute monarch and mediator between Heaven and Earth.

THE CONSOLIDATION OF DAI VIET

In AD 945, Ngo Vuong died, and Viet independence was threatened once again as control was divided between competing fiefdoms. Fortunately, in 968, Dinh Bo Linh, the most powerful lord, reunified the country, calling it Dai Co Viet. He took the name Tien Hoang De and founded the short-lived Dinh Dynasty (968–980). He also re-established a tributary relationship with China to stave off further invasions. Then, in 979, the throne was seized by Le Dai Hanh, who founded the Early Le Dynasty (980–1009) and continued the conquest of Champa.

THE LY DYNASTY

Held to be the first completely independent Vietnamese dynasty, the Ly Dynasty (1009–1225) was established by the learned and brave Ly Thai To. In 1010, he moved the capital back to Dai La in Tong Binh, giving it the auspicious name, Thang Long (see p160) or Ascending Dragon. Thang Long would remain Vietnam's capital for the next 800 years.

Nguyen Trai, advisor to Tran Hung Dao

THE TRAN DYNASTY

The Tran Dynasty (1225–1400) introduced land reforms and defended Vietnam from Mongol attacks. In 1288, the national hero Tran Hung Dao defeated a major Mongol invasion at the second Battle of the Bach Dang River by using Ngo Quyen's tactics of planting metal stakes in the bed of the river. At the same time, Vietnam continued its southward advance, absorbing Cham territory as far as Hue.

THE LATER LE DYNASTY

In 1407, the Ming invaded Vietnam but were ousted in 1428 by the nationalist leader Le Loi during the turbulent Lam Son Uprising. The Chinese were forced to recognize Dai Viet's autonomy after this victory, and Le Loi founded the Later Le Dynasty (1428–1788). His successor, Le Than Ton, inflicted a crushing defeat on Champa in 1471, pushing the frontier south of Qui Nhon. By this time Vietnam had become a major power on the Southeast Asian mainland.

TIMELINE

Statue of the Amitabha Buddha, Ly Dynasty

1009–1225 Ly Dynasty

1225–1400 Tran Dynasty

Mongol ruler, Kublai Khan

1000	1100	1200	1300

1010 Ly Thai To establishes capital at Thang Long

1070 Temple of Literature established

Metal-tipped stakes used to impale ships in the Battle of Bach Dang

1288 Tran Hung Dao defeats Mongols in the Battle of Bach Dang

A NATION DIVIDED

As the Le Dynasty extended its domain, it incurred the wrath of local fiefdoms. In 1527, Mac Dang Dung, an opportunist in the Le court, seized the throne. However, from 1539 onward, real power was divided between two warlord families, the Trinh and the Nguyen Lords. For more than two centuries, the nation would remain divided, with the Nguyen developing their capital at Hue to rival the Trinh capital at Thang Long. Under the Nguyen, the Viet conquest of lower Cambodia and the Mekong Delta began with the absorption of the Khmer settlement of Prey Nokor, later renamed Saigon.

A shrine to Quang Trung, leader of the Tay Son Rebellion

EARLY EUROPEAN INFLUENCES

In 1545, the Portuguese established the first European factories in Vietnam. At first, they helped the Nguyen Lords develop a foundry and weapons, but later, also aided the Trinh so they could benefit from the spice trade. The Dutch, followed by the French, replaced the Portuguese as leading traders in the 17th century. Christian missionaries also made inroads, the most important figure being Alexandre de Rhodes (1591–1660), a French Jesuit who converted thousands of locals to Christianity, leading to his expulsion. However, this led to the beginning of a French interest in the area for its wealth.

TAY SON REBELLION

In response to the years of civil war and harsh government under the Trinh and Nguyen Lords, the Tay Son Rebellion broke out in 1771. Supported by merchants and peasants, it was led by three brothers who overthrew the Nguyen in 1783. The last lord, Nguyen Anh, fled abroad and sought French assistance. In 1786, the Tay Son overthrew the Trinh, provoking a Chinese invasion. The greatest of the Tay Son brothers crushed the Chinese and proclaimed himself Emperor Quang Trung. He died in 1792, leaving behind a much weakened Tay Son.

TRIUMPH OF THE NGUYEN DYNASTY

In 1788, Nguyen Anh returned home and seized control of Saigon with the help of French missionary, Pigneau de Behaine (1741–99). Following Quang Trung's death, Nguyen Anh easily defeated the Tay Son in the north. In 1802, he declared Hue the new national capital and himself the first ruler of the Nguyen Dynasty.

Ngo Mon Gate, Hue Citadel, was built by Nguyen Emperor Gia Long

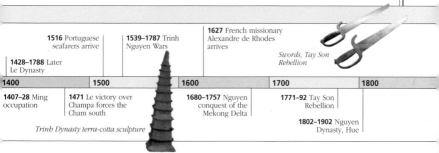

1516 Portuguese seafarers arrive

1428–1788 Later Le Dynasty

1539–1787 Trinh Nguyen Wars

1627 French missionary Alexandre de Rhodes arrives

Swords, Tay Son Rebellion

1400	1500	1600	1700	1800

1407–28 Ming occupation

1471 Le victory over Champa forces the Cham south

1680–1757 Nguyen conquest of the Mekong Delta

1771–92 Tay Son Rebellion

1802–1902 Nguyen Dynasty, Hue

Trinh Dynasty terra-cotta sculpture

French troops arriving in the Bay of Haiphong, 1884

ESTABLISHMENT OF FRENCH CONTROL

Nguyen Anh gave himself the title of Gia Long, deriving it from Gia Dinh and Thang Long, the old names of Ho Chi Minh City and Hanoi, and thus representing the unification of Vietnam. A strong ruler, he died in 1820.

Minh Mang (r.1820–41), the son of Gia Long, inherited the throne as well as a legacy of French involvement in Vietnamese affairs. Unlike his father, he felt no gratitude to the French. On the contrary, he was hostile to them and issued decrees prohibiting the spread of Catholicism. His son, Thieu Tri (r.1841–47) pursued similar policies, as did Tu Duc (r.1847–83) who denounced converts as "fools seduced by priests."

These anti-French measures instigated the imperialist faction in France to implement a "civilizing mission," which led to the loss of national independence for almost 100 years. In 1858–59, ostensibly responding to the execution of missionaries, France briefly occupied Danang. Two years

Paul Doumer, Governor of French Indochina

later, it seized Saigon and, in 1865, forced Tu Duc to form Cochinchina, a French colony. By 1883, France controlled the whole country, making Annam (the north) and Tonkin (the center) into protectorates. Tu Duc died the same year and his successors were reduced to being puppets of the French. Meanwhile, France occupied Cambodia and Laos, and in 1887, created the Indochinese Union, with its capital at Hanoi.

THE COLONIAL PERIOD

Paul Doumer, the French Governor of Indochina (1897–1902), invoked the An Nam or Pacified South of the 7th century, saying "when France arrived in Indochina, the Annamites were ripe for servitude." He would eventually be proved wrong, but for many decades, Vietnam suffered under the French imposition of heavy taxation, state monopolies on salt, alcohol, and opium, and enforced labor known as *corvée*. The French also profited from coffee and rubber plantations as well as Vietnam's extensive mineral resources. All this changed in 1940, when Nazi Germany occupied France and established the puppet Vichy regime. In Indochina, the Vichy authorities collaborated with Germany's Axis partner, Japan, and Vietnam fell under a new, brutal colonial yoke.

THE RISE OF SOCIALIST RESISTANCE

From the early 20th century, several nationalist movements began to emerge across Vietnam. The 1911 Revolution in China inspired the Viets, and the Viet Nam National Party (VNQDD) was formed in emu-

TIMELINE

1820–41 Emperor Minh Mang issues anti-French edicts

1858–59 France seizes Danang

1887 France creates Indochinese Union of Vietnam, Laos, and Cambodia

1865 Cochinchina declared a French colony

1820	1835	1850	1865	1880

1832 Last principalities of Champa extinguished

Emperor Minh Mang

1883 France establishes protectorate over Annam and Tonkin

1890 Birth of Ho Chi Minh near Kim Lien

lation of the Chinese nationalist Kuomintang. In 1930, the French sent Nguyen Thai Hoc, the VNQDD chairman, to the guillotine along with 12 of his colleagues. In 1941, Ho Chi Minh *(see p169)*, the architect of Vietnam's independence, returned to Vietnam after many years. He formed the Vietnamese Independence League or Viet Minh, and began organizing a nationalist movement against the

Ho Chi Minh *(left)* with military planners at Dien Bien Phu, 1953

French and Japanese. In March 1945, faced with imminent defeat in the Pacific War, Japan took over direct administration from the Vichy regime. However, Ho Chi Minh and his Viet Minh forces had already liberated parts of the far north and were fast advancing on Hanoi. The Japanese surrendered on August 15, 1945, and on September 2, Ho Chi Minh declared national independence at Hanoi's Ba Dinh Square.

THE FIRST INDOCHINA WAR

Following France's liberation from Germany, General Charles De Gaulle and senior military officials were determined to restore their hold on Indochina, and reinstated French troops in Vietnam. This led to an uprising in Hanoi in 1946 and the outbreak of the First Indochina War. From their stronghold in Viet Bac, the Viet Minh forces, directed by General Vo Nguyen Giap, fought back, taking over broad swathes of the country. The French retained control of Hanoi, Saigon, and most large towns, but could not win.

As Ho Chi Minh warned the French in 1946, "you can kill ten of my men for every one I kill of yours. But even at those odds, you will lose and I will win." By 1954, the Viet Minh inflicted their final defeat on the French at the Battle of Dien Bien Phu *(see p195)*. However, the United States, frantic to curb communism, had already been funding as much as 80 percent of the French war effort, and the stage was set for the Vietnam War.

PRELUDE TO THE VIETNAM WAR

The Geneva Conference was held in 1954, where France, Britain, the US, and the USSR decided to partition Vietnam at the 17th parallel, pending general elections in 1956. These elections were never held, and the partition became permanent. The North became the Communist Democratic Republic of Vietnam, with its capital at Hanoi under Ho Chi Minh, and the South became the anti-communist Republic of Vietnam, with its capital at Saigon under the US-allied and fervently Catholic Ngo Dinh Diem.

Viet Minh soldiers attack French military base, Dien Bien Phu

---

Bao Dai (right) with General Navarre

1911 Ho Chi Minh travels to Paris. Joins French Communist Party in 1920

1924 Ho Chi Minh becomes an agent of Comintern

1940 France occupied by Nazi Germany; Vichy regime

1945 Nguyen Emperor Bao Dai abdicates; Ho Chi Minh declares independence

1930 Ho Chi Minh forms Indochinese Communist Party in Hong Kong

1945 March 9, Japanese coup against the French; August 15, Japan capitulates

1954 France suffers crushing defeat at Dien Bien Phu

1946 First Indochina War begins as French seek to reimpose their rule

| 95 | 1910 | 1925 | 1940 | 1955 |

French Indochinese postcard

The Vietnam War

Tet Offensive campaign pin

From 1954, South Vietnam, under the leadership of President Diem, was propped up politically and financially by the US. Under Diem, communists and Buddhists were persecuted, whereas the North was hostile to Catholics, many of whom fled to the South. The entire nation was reeling with unrest and strife, and the time was ripe for an intervention by the US. In the meantime, the North allied with China and the USSR, and in 1960, the National Liberation Front (NLF) or Vietcong was formed with the mission of unifying the country. In 1960, US military advisors arrived in the South, thus initiating the 15-year war known to the Vietnamese as the "American War" and to the Americans as the "Vietnam War."

Guerrilla Warfare
Both the NLF and the allied North Vietnamese Army (NVA) were adept at preparing simple but deadly booby traps.

US SOLDIERS IN PADDY FIELDS, MEKONG DELTA

By 1967, there were half a million American soldiers in Vietnam, many of them one-year conscripts. Most were inexperienced and unmotivated, and had to fight in unfamiliar and difficult terrain, wading through rice paddies and swamps in search of their elusive opponents. More professional, specialist American forces mounted LRRPS or Long Range Reconnaissance Patrols, staying in deep jungle or marshland on dangerous five-day missions.

Gulf of Tonkin Incident (1964)
The US accused NLF torpedo boats of launching unprovoked attacks on the USS Maddox. *Lyndon Johnson used this incident as his reason for bombing the North and for sending American troops to Vietnam.*

Death from the Air
The US Air Force (USAF) and its South Vietnamese allies used a wide range of chemical warfare, including white phosphorus, on enemy positions. Here, a US aircraft is bombing Danang, 1966.

Ho Chi Minh Trail
With its narrow paths and frail bridges, the Ho Chi Minh Trail (see p151) was used by communist troops to travel from North Vietnam to Saigon.

TIMELINE

South Vietnam's President Ngo Dinh Diem, 1958

1954 Treaty signed at Geneva Convention, sanctioning Vietnam's partition

1960 Communists form the National Liberation Front in South Vietnam

1965 First US combat troops arrive; USAF bombing of North Vietnam begins

1955	1960	1965

Buddhist monk self immolates in protest against Diem's government, 1963

1963 Diem is assassinated, allegedly by South Vietnam generals

1964 North Vietnamese torpedo boats allegedly attack US destroyers in Gulf of Tonkin

The Tet Offensive (1968)
The longest and bloodiest battle was the January Tet Offensive, when communist forces seized the old imperial capital of Hue and held it against massive counterattacks for 25 days. Both sides suffered heavy losses.

Hamburger Hill (1969)
On May 10, the US 101st Airborne battalion attacked forces holding Ap Bia Mountain, near Laos. In ten days, 46 US soldiers were dead and 400 wounded, earning the peak the notorious epithet, "Hamburger Hill."

Napalm Bombings
A vicious but effective compound of jellied petroleum, napalm killed many thousands of people. When this infamous picture of young victims was beamed across the world in June 1972, US public opinion turned against the war.

Anti-War Protests
In the late 1960s and 70s, the anti-war movement grew in strength everywhere, including the US. These demonstrators are outside the American Embassy in London's Grosvenor Square.

Paris Peace Accords (1973)
Henry Kissinger and Le Duc Tho signed the treaty on January 23. US forces withdrew from Vietnam and the North released almost 500 US POWs.

April 29, 1975
The last remaining American personnel in Saigon were evacuated by helicopters to US Naval vessels in the South China Sea, even as the city was falling to victorious communist forces.

My Lai Massacre memorial

1968 Tet Offensive is launched in Jan–Feb; in March, the My Lai Massacre (see p119) shocks the world

1973 Ceasefire agreement is signed; US troops leave Vietnam

Anti-war badges worn during the 1970s

1970

1975

1969 Ho Chi Minh dies; Nixon proposes peace talks

1972 Americans bomb Haiphong Harbor

1975 South surrenders to North; provisional government installed

1971 *New York Times* prints extracts from Pentagon Papers exposing US involvement in Vietnam War

1971, Anti-war protestor atop a statue near Capitol Hill waves a Vietcong flag

REUNIFICATION AND ISOLATION

Following the overwhelming victory of the North in 1975, Le Duan, the general secretary of the Communist Party after Ho Chi Minh's death, came into power. It was his doctrinaire government's policies that shaped the next decade. In July 1976, Vietnam was officially reunified and the Socialist Republic of Vietnam proclaimed. Six months later, at the Fourth Party Congress, a decision was taken to press ahead with forced collectivization of industry, commerce, and agriculture in the south. Officials of the former southern regime were severely persecuted, many being sent for long periods of re-education in undeveloped border areas, a policy which denied Vietnam the services of thousands of skilled and educated citizens. To compound matters, Saigon was renamed Ho Chi Minh City – a designation never fully accepted in the South. In Cholon *(see pp68–9)* and

Vietnamese troops leaving Cambodia in 1989

across the south, persecution of the merchant class rapidly stopped businesses, a move that angered China as most commerce was controlled by the ethnic Chinese or Hoa. By 1977, great numbers of refugees, known as "boat people," had started to flee abroad, further depleting human resources. Also, a harsh trade embargo imposed by the US after 1975 added to Vietnam's economic disintegration.

Matters deteriorated on the regional front as well. In 1976, Pol Pot's Democratic Kampuchea (Khmer Rouge of Cambodia), supported by China, launched cross-border attacks on Vietnam. Vietnam responded by signing a security pact with the Soviet Union in 1978, and overthrowing Pol Pot later in the same year. Early in 1979, China retaliated by invading the north and destroying several provincial capitals before withdrawing unilaterally. Hanoi, execrated by China and most of the West, was forced into a closer alliance with the USSR. By the early 1980s, impoverished and isolated, Vietnam was well on the way to starvation and economic collapse.

RENOVATION

The death of Le Duan in 1986 brought about change. Nguyen Van Linh, a southerner, became party leader, and

Refugees, or boat people, sailing to Manila, 1978

TIMELINE

1975 Reunification of North and South under a communist government

1976 Socialist Republic of Vietnam established

1978 Vietnam invades Cambodia and overthrows Khmer Rouge

1979 China invades Northern Vietnam

Pol Pot – the Cambodian dictator

1986 Death of Le Duan; introduction of *doi moi*

1989 Vietnamese troops withdraw from Cambodia

Le Duan

1994 US embargo lifted

1995 Vietnam joins ASEAN; diplomatic relations with USA instated

| 1976 | 1980 | 1984 | 1988 | 1992 | 1996 |

a policy of *doi moi*, or economic reforms, was adopted at the Sixth Party Congress, opening the way to gradual economic and social reform under the Communist Party. The liberalization policy was accelerated by the collapse of the USSR and the end of the Cold War in 1991. Vietnam lost its ally and financial patron, and was forced to mend fences with China, establish closer links with its Southeast Asian neighbors, and open increasingly to the West.

As a result, in 1994, the US lifted its trade embargo, and in 1995, restored full diplomatic relations with Hanoi. In the same year, Vietnam became a full member of the Association of Southeast Asian Nations (ASEAN). In 1997, the policy of continuing economic reform was confirmed with the election of the forward-looking Tran Duc Luong as president and Phan Van Khai as prime minister.

Tran Duc Luong with US president Bill Clinton, 2000

REBIRTH

Since the turn of the 20th century Vietnam has seen a remarkable turnaround. In 2000, US President Bill Clinton's visit was indicative of fast improving relations between the two former enemies. In 2001, this was followed by the normalization of trade relations between Washington and Hanoi, and the election of Nong Duc Manh as Secretary General of the Communist Party – the most powerful position in Vietnam followed by the prime minister and president. Widely regarded as a modernizer, Nong Duc Manh promised on his election that he would focus on economic development and fight corruption and

unnecessary red tape. In 2006, Nguyen Tan Dung, the country's youngest prime minister, was confirmed by the National Assembly. The first leader of post-war Vietnam with no experience of the independence struggle, he has vowed to strive for development and to "pull the nation out of backwardness." All evidence points toward the achievability of this goal.

For several years Vietnam has been one of the fastest-growing economies in Asia. The year 2010 saw an influx of foreign brands and construction of many modern skyscrapers in Saigon. Although still autocratic, the government has abandoned the failed economics of state socialism and is embracing free market capitalism. However, the disparity in wealth between urban and rural Vietnam is wide, and many Human Rights groups accuse Hanoi of suppressing political dissent and religious freedom. Yet today, most Vietnamese enjoy more freedom than their forefathers did at any time in their country's long history.

High-rises in HCMC epitomize modern Vietnam

2000	2004	2008	2012	2016	2020

2001 Nong Duc Manh becomes Secretary General of the Communist party

2005 Prime Minister Phan Van Khai visits the US

2008 Massive inflation causes economic uncertainty

2010 Over multiple visits to Vietnam, US Secretary of State Hillary Clinton expresses support for Vietnam's side of territorial disputes with China

2000 President Clinton visits; Vietnam's stock exchange opens

2003 First US warship to visit HCMC

2006 Nguyen Tan Dung and Nguyen Minh Triet elected prime minister and president

Discussions between George Bush and Phan Van Khai on Vietnam joining the World Trade Organization, June 2005; Vietnam became a member in 2006

VIETNAM
AREA BY AREA

Vietnam at a Glance

A long and narrow country with amazingly diverse terrains, Vietnam encompasses the magnificent and remote valleys of the northwest, the high peaks and plateaus of its mountainous spine, and the pristine beaches and warm tropical waters of the southern coasts. The mighty Red River in the north and Mekong River in the south give rise to two immensely fertile deltas, lush forests, meandering canals, and vast paddy fields. Apart from its scenic wealth, Vietnam is a treasure trove of art and culture, evident in the museums and exquisite French architecture of Hanoi, the royal palaces of ancient Hue, and the elegant restaurants and vibrant nightlife of Ho Chi Minh City. This guide divides Vietnam into six regions; each area is color-coded as shown here.

NORTHERN VIETNAM
(see pp178–201)

HANOI
(see pp152–177)

Sapa (see pp196–7), *located in a remote part of Northern Vietnam, is known for its breathtaking beauty. Its landscape is marked by rice fields that rise in steep terraces along the flanks of the Hoang Lien Mountains, and has been farmed for centuries by the region's ethnic minorities.*

| 0 kilometers | 200 |
| 0 miles | 200 |

The Old Quarter (see pp156–7) *is Hanoi's unique commercial district. Originally known as 36 Streets, this center used to cater to the needs of the palace in the 13th century. Today, this colorful, bustling market is a treasure house of silk, freshly ground coffee, lanterns, and more.*

Tra Vinh (see p89) *is a fertile delta town, featuring several narrow canals winding through dense foliage, coconut palm trees, and fruit orchards. Known for its religious diversity, Tra Vinh is home to a large number of Khmer Buddhists and Christians.*

MEKONG DELTA AND SOUTHERN VIETNAM
(see pp84–101)

◁ Colorful wooden boats at Mui Ne Beach with red sand dunes behind

Hien Lam Pavilion in the Hue Citadel (see pp140–43) *is also known as the Pavilion of Splendor. This exquisite triple-roofed temple is situated within the Yellow Enclosure of the Imperial City and presides over the massive Nine Dynastic Urns.*

The Po Nagar Cham Towers (see p109) *were built in the 8th century and are among the most important Cham sites in Vietnam. Located in Nha Trang, these magnificent ruins provide an excellent insight into the architectural styles of the once mighty Cham Empire.*

ENTRAL VIETNAM
(see pp120–151)

SOUTH CENTRAL VIETNAM
(see pp102–119)

Mui Ne Beach (see p106) *stretches for 12 miles (20 km) and is one of the best beaches south of Nha Trang. Its windy weather between October and February is ideal for surfing. Mui Ne Village comes to life in the morning when the fish merchants are in action.*

HO CHI MINH CITY
(see pp52–83)

The Rooftop Garden of the Rex Hotel (see p60) *is one of Ho Chi Minh City's most popular restaurants, offering spectacular views across the bustling and atmospheric streets of the city's downtown district.*

HO CHI MINH CITY

The largest city in Vietnam is also its commercial capital and is fast becoming the nation's window to the world. Buzzing with frenetic activity, cosmopolitan Ho Chi Minh City looks outward, listens to pop music, and drinks French wine. Existing alongside the high-rise hotels, shopping malls, and chic restaurants are ancient pagodas and colonial buildings, recalling a checkered but vibrant past.

Originally established as a Khmer trading post, centuries ago, Ho Chi Minh City was destined for greater things. By the 18th century, the city, then named Saigon, had become the provincial capital of the Nguyen Dynasty. However, in the second half of the 19th century, control over the city passed to the French, and Saigon became the capital of French Cochinchina. This was a period of much infrastructural and architectural development, during which Saigon earned the epithet "Paris of the Orient." Many buildings of this era are in good condition even today. In 1954, the city was proclaimed the capital of South Vietnam *(see p43)*. The ensuing war between the US and the Communist North lasted until 1975, when North Vietnam took over Saigon and renamed it Ho Chi Minh City.

Today, under growing economic and cultural liberalization, the city has entered a period of modernization and is constantly evolving and reinventing itself. Populated by an estimated seven million people, the city is rapidly becoming the hub of manufacturing, entertainment, and cuisine in Vietnam.

Upscale restaurants and cafés offering a range of international delicacies are opening every day, while bars, clubs, and discos are at the center of a thriving nightlife. The best place to catch the action is Dong Khoi *(see pp56–7)* and the rest of District 1. Attracting many tourists, the area is home to historical buildings and museums, sophisticated shops, and roadside cafés, as well as people of all ages zipping around noisily on motorbikes and causing gridlock.

Large portrait of Ho Chi Minh presiding over the hallway of the General Post Office

◁ **Monks in the Prayer Hall of the Great Divine Temple, Cao Dai** *(see pp74–5)*

Exploring Ho Chi Minh City

The most prominent area in the city is around Dong Khoi Street in District 1, boasting fashionable shops, museums, and fine dining. It also features examples of French-colonial structures, such as the Municipal Theater, Notre Dame Cathedral, and the General Post Office. To the north are sprawling residential areas and the historic Jade Emperor Pagoda, known for its exquisite architecture and ornate carvings. To the west lies Cholon, or Chinatown. Home to the ethnic Chinese, or Hoa, this is the best place to find herbs, traditional Chinese medicines, and other goods, as well as some of the city's most ancient pagodas.

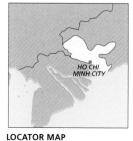

LOCATOR MAP
See Street Finder maps pp78–83

SIGHTS AT A GLANCE

Churches, Temples, and Pagodas
Cao Dai Holy See pp74–5 **30**
Giac Vien Pagoda **26**
Hoi Quan Nghia An Pagoda **21**
Jade Emperor Pagoda pp62–3 **11**
Le Van Duyet Temple **12**
Mariamman Hindu Temple **17**
Nghia An Hoi Quan Pagoda **21**
Notre Dame Cathedral **7**
One Pillar Pagoda of Thu Duc **27**
Phung Son Pagoda **25**
Quan Am Pagoda **23**
Thien Hau Pagoda **22**
Vinh Nghiem Pagoda **13**
Xa Loi Pagoda **16**

Historic Sights and Buildings
Cu Chi Tunnels **28**
General Post Office **8**
People's Committee Building **4**

Theaters
Municipal Theater **2**

Museums and Palaces
Fine Arts Museum **19**
Ho Chi Minh City Museum **5**
Museum of Vietnamese History **10**
Reunification Hall **9**
War Remnants Museum **15**
Women's Museum of Southern Vietnam **14**

Beaches, Springs, Nature Reserves, and Mountains
Binh Chau Hot Springs **34**
Cat Tien National Park **35**
Ho Coc Beach **33**
Nui Ba Den **29**

Towns and Markets
Ben Thanh Market **18**
Binh Tay Market **24**

Dan Sinh Market **20**
Long Hai **32**
Vung Tau **31**

Hotels
Caravelle Hotel **1**
Continental Hotel **3**
Rex Hotel **6**

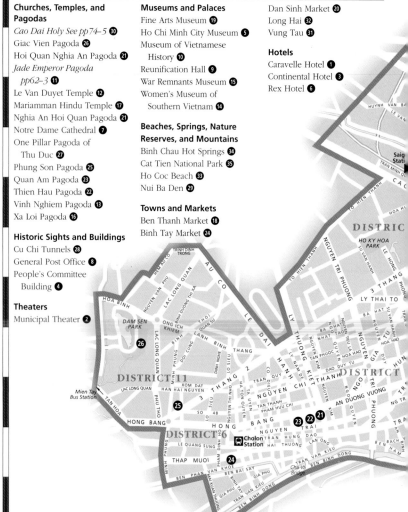

KEY

Street-by-Street area:
see pp56–7

✈ International airport

🚆 Train station

🚌 Long-distance bus station

⛴ Riverboat pier

═ National highway

▬ Major road

═ Minor road

— Railroad

-- International border

- - Provincial border

GETTING AROUND

The districts of Dong Khoi and Cholon are small enough to be explored comfortably on foot. However, the most popular mode of transport is the Honda *om*, or motorbike taxi. A ride to anywhere in town should cost no more than a few dollars. Radio-dispatched, metered taxis are also common now. Most travel agencies will arrange trips to the outlying areas of the city.

0 meters   800
0 yards   800

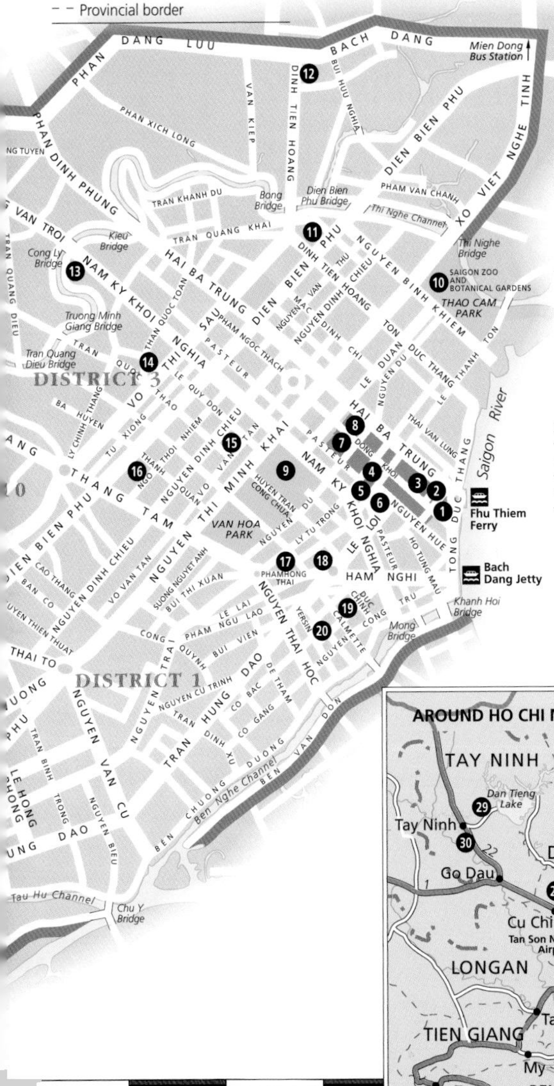

SEE ALSO

• *Where to Stay* pp232–4
• *Where to Eat* pp250–52

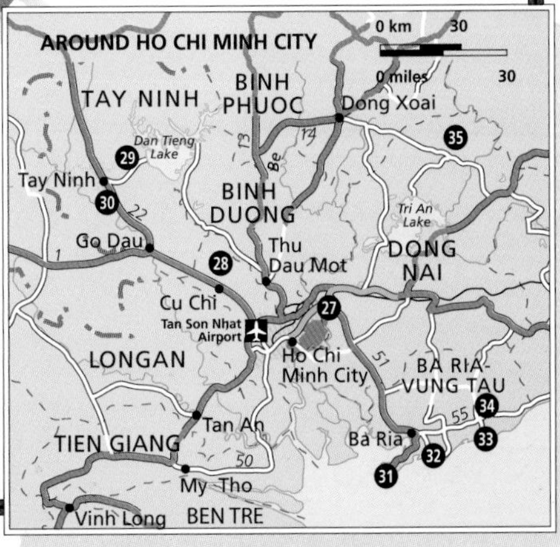

Mien Dong Bus Station

Thi Nghe Channel
Thi Nghe Bridge
Dien Bien Phu Bridge

Kieu Bridge
Cong Ly Bridge
Truong Minh Giang Bridge
Tran Quang Dieu Bridge

DISTRICT 3

Bong Bridge

Saigon Zoo and Botanical Gardens
THAO CAM PARK

⑫ ⑪ ⑩

Saigon River

VAN HOA PARK

⑬ ⑭ ⑮ ⑯ ⑰ ⑱ ⑲ ⑳ ⑨ ⑧ ⑦ ⑥ ⑤ ④ ③ ② ①

Phu Thiem Ferry

Bach Dang Jetty

Khanh Hoi Bridge
Mong Bridge

DISTRICT 1

Ben Nghe Channel

Tau Hu Channel
Chu Y Bridge

AROUND HO CHI MINH CITY

0 km   30
0 miles   30

TAY NINH   BINH PHUOC   Dong Xoai

Dan Tieng Lake
Tay Ninh ㉙
㉚ Go Dau

BINH DUONG
Thu Dau Mot

Tri An Lake
DONG NAI ㉟

㉘
Cu Chi
Tan Son Nhat Airport ✈
Ho Chi Minh City ㉗

LONG AN

BA RIA-VUNG TAU ㉞
㉝
㉜

Tan An

Ba Ria ㉛

TIEN GIANG

My Tho

Vinh Long   BEN TRE

Street-by-Street: Dong Khoi

Arguably the liveliest part of the city, the area around
Dong Khoi Street is the very nerve center of Ho Chi
Minh City. Dong Khoi Street itself became famous during
the French era, and was then known as the Rue Catinat.
Home to stately hotels, elegant boutiques, and cozy
cafés that coexisted with bars and brothels, it was at the
center of most of the action in Graham Greene's novel,
The Quiet American. The subsequent communist regime
shut down most of these establishments, but Vietnam's
economic liberalization in 1986 gave the area a new
lease on life as smart hotels, restaurants, and shops
slowly made a reappearance. Today, Dong Khoi's
vibrance is unparalleled in the country, and it does
justice to the city's old nickname "Paris of the Orient."

**View of Dong Khoi from
Diamond Plaza** *(see p263)*

★ **General Post Office**
*One of the most handsome
French-colonial buildings in
the city, the cavernous interior
of this massive structure, with
its comfortable benches,
provides a cool respite
from the heat outside* ❽

**The Metropolitan
Building** is home
to HSBC's head-
quarters and is a
popular café spot.

★ **Notre Dame Cathedral**
*This tall, late 19th-century
cathedral is built of locally
quarried stone and covered
with red ceramic tiles shipped
in from France. The statue of
the Virgin Mary was added
to the lawns in front of the
building in the 1950s* ❼

People's Committee Building
*The erstwhile Hôtel de Ville now houses
the office of the People's Committee
of Ho Chi Minh City.
It is one of the most
magnificent and
photogenic colonial
buildings in the
entire city* ❹

STAR SIGHTS

★ General Post Office

★ Notre Dame Cathedral

★ Municipal Theater

Lower Dong Khoi
This area has become one of Saigon's most fashionable spots for boutique shopping. Local brands such as Khai Silk can be found here, along-side well-known international brands such as Louis Vuitton (left).

Continental Hotel
Constructed in classic French-colonial style, this elegant hotel is a serene haven amid the bustle of the city. The central atrium is popular for afternoon tea and the patio offers al fresco dining in summer ❸

KEY

– – – Suggested route

0 meters _____ 150
0 yards _____ 150

The Vincom Shopping Center (Vincom Towers) is one of the largest modern shopping centers in Vietnam, selling a variety of imported brands.

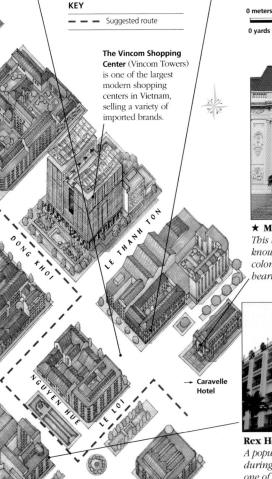

DONG KHOI

LE THANH TON

NGUYEN HUE

LE LOI

→ Caravelle Hotel

★ **Municipal Theater**
This lovely Neoclassical building, known as the Opera House in colonial times, was once the heart of French high society ❷

Rex Hotel
A popular base for several journalists during the Vietnam War, the Rex is one of the best known landmarks in the city. The hotel's rooftop bar offers superb views of the street below ❻

Caravelle Hotel ❶

19 Lam Son Sq, District 1. **Map** 2 F3.
Tel (08) 3823 4999. ⏰ daily. 🍴 🖵
🖥 www.caravellehotel.com

When it opened on Christmas
Eve in 1959, the Caravelle
Hotel, at ten stories, was the
tallest building in the city. At
its gala launch, the hotel was
praised by the local press for
its central air-conditioning
system and bulletproof glass.
Its designers were considered
almost prescient as the hotel
became a central headquarter
for diplomats and journalists
during the Vietnam War *(see
pp44–5)*. Both
Australia and
New Zealand
maintained
embassies here,
while the
*Washington
Post, New
York Times,
Associated
Press*, and
many other
news agencies
established bureaus in the
hotel. Reporters would joke
that they could cover the
entire war without leaving
their seats at the rooftop bar.
The glamor faded after the
fall of Saigon in 1975, when
the hotel was taken over by
the government. In 1998,
however, it was reopened
after extensive renovations.
   Today, with its soaring, new
marble-lined tower, Caravelle
is one of the city's most luxurious hotels. While old-timers
may have trouble recognizing
it, the rooftop bar, with its

curved balconied corners, still
tops the old wing and there
are few better places for an
evening cocktail.

Municipal Theater ❷

7 Lam Son Sq, Intersection of Le Loi
and Dong Khoi Sts, District 1.
Map 2 F3. **Tel** (08) 3829 9976.
⏰ varies. 📷 🖵

A superb, French-colonial
style building, the Municipal
Theater or Nha Hat Thanh
Pho was built in 1899 as a
concert hall for the French.
Still referred to
as the Opera
House, the
hall temporarily
served as the
headquarters
of the South
Vietnam
National
Assembly
in 1956.
A graceful stair-
case leads up to
the entrance, which is flanked
by two huge columns shaped
like Greco-Roman goddesses.
Winged figures and exquisite
scrollworks grace the eaves
below the roof, and the
grounds are speckled with
lovely fountains and statues.
   While the interior is not as
ornate, it is a fine setting for
performances that include
everything from traditional
Vietnamese theater and
Western classical music to
rock concerts and gymnastics.
Program details are posted
on the box office billboards.

**Finely carved figures on the
rooftop of the Municipal Theater**

**Diners relaxing in the Continental
Hotel's courtyard garden**

Continental Hotel ❸

132–134 Dong Khoi St, District 1.
Map 2 F3. **Tel** (08) 3829 9201.
⏰ daily. 🍴 🖵
www.continentalhotel.com.vn

With its stately façade, the
Continental is the grande
dame of hotels built during
French rule. The hotel is set
around a courtyard, which is
well-shaded with frangipani
trees, while inside, the red-
carpeted staircases retain their
original tropical hardwood.
The structure, for the most
part, has been spared the
"modernization" visited upon
some other historic buildings
in the city, and the hotel wears
its patina of age well.
   The hotel has also earned
a place in the annals of history
for attracting illustrious visitors
since its completion in 1886.
During the Vietnam War, top-
flight journalists, including
Walter Cronkite (b.1916),
would stay here and spend
hours on the famous terrace
bar, which they dubbed
"The Continental Shelf."
   Writers André Malraux
(1901–76) and W. Somerset
Maugham (1874–1965) are
other guests of note, but it
is Graham Greene (1904–91)
who immortalized the Continental in his novel *The Quiet
American* (1955). It is no
surprise that he captured the
spirit of the time and place
so well, since he lived in the
hotel for several months.

The plush lobby of the Caravelle Hotel decorated with Christmas wreaths

For hotels and restaurants in this region see pp232–4 and pp250–52

People's Committee Building ➍

Intersection of Le Thanh Ton and Nguyen Hue Sts, District 1.
Map 2 E3. ⬤ *to the public.*

Designed by French architect P. Gardes and completed in 1908, the People's Committee Building, once known as the Hôtel de Ville, is probably the most photographed building in the city. It was outside this building in 1945, that thousands of people congregated to establish the Provisional Administrative Committee of South Vietnam. Still the house of the city government, it sits regally at the city's center. Contrary to popular belief, this striking building has never been a hostelry, nor is it open to the public.

Modeled on the City Hall in Paris, it comprises two stories, with two wings off a central hall and a clock tower. It is capped with a red-tile roof, and its fanciful yellow-and-cream-colored façade is most often described as "gingerbread." Despite its obviously Parisian appearance, the building fits in well with the cityscape, especially at night when it is gorgeously floodlit.

Unfortunately, there is no way for the general public to see the chandelier-bedecked interior today. However, the square in front of the hall, featuring a statue of Ho Chi Minh cradling a child, is a popular vantage point to admire the structure.

Picture taken during the fall of Saigon (1975) at Ho Chi Minh City Museum

Ho Chi Minh City Museum ➎

65 Ly Tu Trong St, District 1.
Map 2 E4. **Tel** *(08) 3829 9741.*
⬤ *8am–5pm daily.* 🖼 📷

Once the French governor general's residence, this, like many of the city's buildings, looks as if it were shipped in pieces from France and reassembled here. Light grey with white trim and a colonnade, it strikes a commanding presence. The spacious halls, with high ceilings and chandeliers, are a much sought-after venue for wedding photographs.

Spread over two rambling floors, the museum purports to represent 300 years of the city's history. However, its original name, Revolutionary Museum, is a more accurate indicator of what to expect. The first floor has somewhat scattered displays of pictures of Saigon during the French rule, old maps, and crumbling documents from the time the city was founded in the 17th century. Also here are relics from Vietnam's natural history and ethnic wedding costumes.

The second floor is devoted to Vietnam's struggle against imperialism. Weapons such as AK-47 rifles and improvised bombs are showcased here, along with photographs of soldiers, letters from the front, and political manifestos. Many obligatory engines of war, including a Huey helicopter, a jet fighter, and an American-built tank can be seen on display outside. The museum also has an extensive collection of Vietnamese currency.

The imposing façade of the French-colonial People's Committee Building

VIETNAM ON FILM

The setting for more Hollywood films than any country in the region, Vietnam features in more than just war-related movies. The first Hollywood movie set here was *Red Dust* (1932), a romantic drama starring Clark Gable, while both versions of Graham Greene's *The Quiet American*, in 1957 with Audie Murphy and in 2002 with Michael Caine, concentrate on politics and ethics. Of course, war movies do abound, with Francis Ford Coppola's allegorical *Apocalypse Now* (1979) and Oliver

Scene from Oliver Stone's *Platoon*

Stone's realistic *Platoon* (1986) being two of the best known.

Beyond Hollywood, Regis Wargnier's *Indochine* (1993) is a sensuous romp through the lives of the privileged in colonial Vietnam. French-Vietnamese director Tran Anh Hung's *Cyclo* (1996) – banned in Vietnam – is a grim look at the seedier side of modern life in Ho Chi Minh City. His *Scent of Green Papaya* (1993), however, is a feast for the eyes.

Aerial view of the Rooftop Garden bar at the Rex Hotel

Rex Hotel ❻

141 Nguyen Hue Blvd, District 1.
Map 2 E4. *Tel* (08) 3829 2185.
⬜ 24 hrs daily. 🍴 💻 📷
www.rexhotelvietnam.com

Located in the center of the city, the Rex Hotel has played an important part in Ho Chi Minh City's history ever since its construction in the 1950s. Originally built by French colonial developers, it quickly became a focus of the social and military activities of American soldiers during the Vietnam War. It was from here that US military officers gave the daily press briefings that became known as "The Five O'Clock Follies," recognized for their blatantly self-serving nature.

Today, with its very popular rooftop bar, the Rex still serves as an important gathering place. Corporate conclaves are held here, gamblers flock to its bingo parlor, and innumerable weddings are celebrated in the central court.

Notre Dame Cathedral ❼

1 Cong Xa Paris Sq, District 1.
Map 2 E3. ⬜ 8–10:30am, 3–4pm
Mon–Sat; services on Sun. ♿

The basilica-style Notre Dame Cathedral, or Nha Tho Duc Ba, is the largest church ever built in the French Empire. When it was completed in 1880, its 40-m (120-ft) spires made it the tallest structure in the city. At first glance it seems to be brick-built, but in fact, the façade is made of red tiles brought over from Marseilles and attached to granite walls. Stained-glass windows from Chartres were installed, but destroyed during WWII and later replaced with plain glass. The interior is relatively unadorned, but the ambient lighting creates a calm atmosphere.

In front of the cathedral is a statue of the Virgin Mary. Made in Rome, it was brought to Vietnam in 1959 and named Holy Mary Queen of Peace, in the hope that she would bring peace to the war-torn country.

While the city's Roman Catholic community is no longer a political force, droves of worshippers still throng the church. The belfry, open on Sundays, affords lovely views.

Virgin Mary, Notre Dame Cathedral

General Post Office ❽

2 Cong Xa Paris Sq, District 1.
Map 2 E3. *Tel* (08) 3829 3274.
⬜ 7am–8pm daily. 📷

Designed by French architect Gustave Eiffel between 1886 and 1891, Buu Dien Trung Tam or the General Post Office is one of the most attractive buildings in the city. Its massive façade is coral colored with a cream trim and also features carvings of the faces of famous philosophers and scientists, below which are finely engraved inscriptions. In all, the building is no less than a temple to the art of communicating by mail. Strangely evocative of the inside of a railway station, the interior is vaulted and supported by wrought-iron pillars painted green, with gilded capitals. The floor tilework is intricate, especially in the foyer where huge antique maps illuminated by chandeliers depict the city and the region. A large portrait of Ho Chi Minh gazes over the daily bustle. Wooden writing benches are available for patrons' use, as is a kiosk selling souvenirs and stamps. As Vietnamese stamps are not adhesive, glue pots are placed near the door. The entire hall is cooled by overhead fans.

The cavernous, elongated interior of the General Post Office

For hotels and restaurants in this region see pp232–4 and pp250–52

The stern and imposing façade of Reunification Hall, a unique example of 1960s Vietnamese architecture

Reunification Hall ❾

135 Nam Ky Khoi Nghia St, District 1. **Map** 2 D3. **Tel** (08) 3822 3652. ⬚ 7:30–11am, 1–4pm daily, except during official functions. 🏛 📷

Set on well-maintained and spacious grounds, this historic building is a prominent symbol of the country's political history. During the 19th century, the Reunification Hall was the site of the Norodom Palace, former residence of the French governor general. It was later occupied by South Vietnam's President Ngo Dinh Diem (see p43), and named the Presidential Palace. In 1962, much of the structure was destroyed when Diem's own air force bombed it in a failed assassination attempt. The building was rebuilt soon after, but Diem was killed before he could move in.

It was in this former palace's International Reception Room that succeeding President Van Thieu received potentates and presidents, until he boarded a chopper from the rooftop helipad and fled before North Vietnamese troops took over Saigon. In 1975, the South surrendered to the North, and the palace gates were knocked down by a North Vietnamese Army tank. The photograph of this event has become emblematic of the reunification of Vietnam.

Today, the interior remains largely unchanged, with high and wide corridors that open onto cavernous lobbies and reception rooms. The living quarters, built around a sunny atrium, are lavishly furnished with glittering chandeliers and elaborate antiques. Also not to be missed are the elephants' feet in the "presidential gifts display" and the large lacquerwork piece depicting scenes from the Le Dynasty (see p40).

In the basement is a bunker and military operations center, with radio transmitters and maps. Oddly, the third floor also features a gambling room.

Adjoining the Reunification Hall is a park with trees that offers a place to relax.

Museum of Vietnamese History ❿

2 Nguyen Binh Khiem St, District 1. **Map** 2 F1. **Tel** (08) 3829 8146. ⬚ 8–11am, 1:30–4:30pm Tue–Sun. 🏛 ⚕ 🚻 **Saigon Zoo** 2 Nguyen Binh Khiem St. **Tel** (08) 3829 3728. ⬚ 7am–9pm daily. 🏛 ♿

Vase from the Le Dynasty

Built in a classic pagoda style, this very attractive museum, also known as Bao Tang Lich Su, contains a vast collection of artifacts, spanning almost the entire history of Vietnam. Relics from the beginning of the nation's cultural evolution can be seen in the form of prehistoric implements and tools. These are followed by bronze artifacts from the Hung Kings era (see p37). Stand-out exhibits include bronze drums belonging to the Dong Son civilization, and tokens from the Oc Eo culture, including a 2nd-century AD Roman coin.

Farther on are remnants belonging to the Nguyen Dynasty (see p41), with a rich collection of garments and jewelry. Also on display are numerous Cham and Khmer relics, such as a stone *lingam* and ceramics. A prominent exhibit is that of a mummy dating back to 1869. Somewhat out of place, although interesting, is the daily scheduled water puppet show (see p159). The museum is set on the expansive and scenic grounds of the **Saigon Zoo**, which provide an ideal setting for a relaxing meander.

Visitors interacting with elephants at the Saigon Zoo

Jade Emperor Pagoda ⑪

Statue in Women's Room

One of the city's most uniquely ornate pagodas, this small house of worship honors the King of all Heavens, Ngoc Huang or the Jade Emperor – chief deity of the Taoist pantheon. Built by the Cantonese community in 1909, its pink façade is almost simple, but the tile roof is an intricate work of art, as are the large wooden doors, richly carved with images of gods and men. Most remarkable, however, are the vibrantly colorful and gilded images of Buddhist divinities and Taoist deities inside the temple. Just about every surface is embellished with tiles and carvings, most of which are dense with religious imagery and symbols.

Carved panel depicting one of 1,000 torments in the Hall of Ten Hells

The King of Hell and his red, life-size horse head the Hall of Ten Hells, which is lined with wood reliefs depicting lurid scenes of damnation.

Women's Room

This fascinating enclosure is filled with two rows of six ceramic female figurines. Draped in colorful robes, each woman represents a lunar year, each juxtaposed with a vice or virtue. Kim Hoa, Goddess of Mothers, officiates over the colorful gathering.

The incinerator is used for burning votive paper offerings. The rising smoke is said to reach the ancestors in heaven.

Tortoise Shelter

This small sanctuary is home to several turtles, which are considered symbols of good luck and fortune in Vietnam. However, although images of turtles are common, such shelters are quite rare.

↗ To the main gate

STAR FEATURES

★ Main Sanctuary

★ Giant Demon Guards

★ Mother of Five Buddhas

Outer Courtyard
Shaded with flowering shrubs and an ancient banyan tree, the outer courtyard is a peaceful spot with park benches and a turtle pond.

For hotels and restaurants in this region see pp232–4 and pp250–52

VISITORS' CHECKLIST

73 Mai Thi Luu St, District 3.
Map 2 D1. 🚌 ⭘ *6am–6pm
daily. Since it can be hard to hail
a taxi from the temple, it is wise
to arrange for a pick up ahead
of time.*

Traditional Stacked Roof with Green Ceramic Tiles

*A pride of dragons, believed to represent a connection to the
divine, rise from the jungle of roof peaks, made of elaborate
woodwork and ceramic tiles.*

★ Main Sanctuary
*Attended by guardians and
resplendent in flowing robes,
the Jade Emperor presides
over the main sanctuary.*

Tortoise
Shelter

★ Giant Demon Guards
*Made from a resilient kind
of papier-mâché, the two
larger-than-life demon guards
are richly painted and robed
in finery. One holds an evil
dragon under his foot, and the
other a rampant tiger.*

★ Mother of Five Buddhas
*One of the most unusual altars
here is that of Phat Mau Chuan
De, Mother of Five Buddhas of
the Cardinal Directions. Her
Hindu-style effigy is flanked by
statues of her five sons.*

RELIGIOUS SIGNIFICANCE OF THE HEARTH

Ong Tao or the Kitchen God resides
in the family hearth and acts as the
Jade Emperor's snitch, as he knows
all that transpires in the home. He
is portrayed as a droll, fat fellow
whose trousers burned off as a
result of standing too close to the
fire. Most kitchens in Vietnam
contain an altar to him, and every
year, during Tet *(see pp28–9)*, Ong
Tao reports each family's conduct
to the Jade Emperor. If there is strife,
the family is punished, but if there is harmony, it
is rewarded. To get a good report, Ong Tao's altar is
never empty of offerings of food, drink, and incense.

**Offerings for Ong
Tao in a family altar**

Le Van Duyet Temple ⑫

1 Bis Phan Dang Luu St, Binh Thanh District. **Tel** (08) 3841 2517. ☐ sunrise–sunset daily. 🖼 Le Van Duyet Temple Festival (late Aug–early Sep).

Dedicated to General Le Van Duyet (1763–1831), this is perhaps the best example of a temple devoted to a national hero rather than to a deity or religion. Le Van Duyet helped suppress the Tay Son Rebellion (*see p41*), and was lauded by Emperor Gia Long. After Van Duyet's death, he was repudiated by Emperor Minh Mang (r.1820–41), but was restored to favor in the 1840s, and the temple was built to honor him.

The main sanctuary is bereft of any images other than a large portrait of Le Van Duyet, reminding devotees that they are worshiping a mortal. Also inside is a fascinating collection of the general's personal effects, such as crystalware, weapons, and a stuffed tiger. The patrons are mostly locals who come here to meditate, make offerings, or even seal a solemn oath in lieu of the services of a notary public. Over the years, the temple has grown into a complex of interconnected buildings, cloisters, patios, and courts. From the street, a gate leads into a large parkland, with tall trees shading the benches. The temple exterior is remarkable for its mosaic wall panels and reliefs. The outer sanctuary is unique for its lack of embellishment. All the pillars and altars are made of carved and polished wood, as are the giant cranes and the life-size horse seen here. In contrast, the inner sanctum adjoining it is a blaze of color, with red-and-gold dragon pillars.

Le Van Duyet's tomb is also located on the premises and an annual festival is held at the temple to commemorate the anniversary of his death.

Vinh Nghiem Pagoda ⑬

339 Nam Ky Khoi Nghia St, District 3. **Map** 1 B2. **Tel** (08) 3848 3153. ☐ sunrise–sunset daily. 🖼

Completed with aid from the Japan-Vietnam Friendship Association in 1971, this is, by some measures, the largest pagoda in the city. Certainly, its eight-story tower, located immediately to the left of a high gate, is the tallest. Each side of the tower is adorned with an image of the Buddha in high relief. To the right of the gate is a smaller, 16-ft (5-m) high tower, built of concrete blocks. The concrete is of

Vinh Nghiem Pagoda's eight-story tower soaring over its surroundings

such quality and color that the structure appears to be made of granite.

Across a 65-ft (20-m) courtyard is the large, squat main building. A steep staircase leads up to the sanctuary where five massive lacquer-ware doors lead into the vast first room. The walls here are lined with well-executed paintings of scriptural scenes and explanatory notes are posted alongside. Farther in is the main altar with a huge, seated Buddha, flanked by disciples.

Behind the sanctuary lies a solemn room, filled with photographs and memorials to the departed. A statue of the goddess Quan Am sits on the altar here.

On the second floor, a cloister leads into an art gallery where local artists show their works. Rock and topiary gardens flank the building.

Huge Buddha with swastika, Vinh Nghiem Pagoda

The spacious courtyard and richly embellished exterior of Le Van Duyet Temple

Women's Museum of Southern Vietnam ⓮

202 Vo Thi Sau St, District 3. **Map** 1 C3. **Tel** *(08) 3932 5696.* ⬛ *7:30–11:30am, 1:30–5pm daily.* ⬛⬛

To bring to light the cultural and military contributions made by South Vietnamese women over the ages, the Women's Museum of Southern Vietnam or Bao Tang Phu Nu Nam Bo was established in 1985. The ten rooms here span three stories and are filled with fascinating displays, ranging from military plaques and medals to a selection of beautiful ethnic costumes.

The tour usually begins from the third floor. The exhibits in this set of rooms are dedicated to women who were involved in the 20th-century communist struggle for independence and unification. Their photographs line the walls, and some of their personal effects are displayed in glass cases, providing a reminder that Vietnamese women were no strangers to combat. The second floor continues the theme, with the addition of statues and large paintings of historical events involving women. There is also a re-creation of the prison cell that once held a national heroine captive.

Cluster bomb, War Remnants Museum

However, the first floor, with its focus on traditional crafts and customs, is the most colorful. The anteroom, with a mock-up of a temple entrance bedecked with many artifacts, is dedicated to the ancient Vietnamese practice of goddess worship. In the next room, faux terraces feature mannequins dressed in exquisite regional costumes. In a large room to the left is a complex exhibit about the production of cotton cloth and rush mats. These products are woven by women in craft villages of the south.

The museum complex also boasts a movie theater, a small library, and a boutique.

Tank displayed on the grounds of the War Remnants Museum

War Remnants Museum ⓯

28 Vo Van Tan St, District 3. **Map** 2 D3. **Tel** *(08) 3930 2112.* ⬛ *7:30am–noon, 1:30–5pm daily.* ⬛⬛⬛

Located in the former US Information Service building, this exhibition was once known as the War Crimes Museum. The films, pictures, and other items on display here document atrocities committed by American, Chinese, and French soldiers in grim detail. Events are told from a Vietnamese perspective and are both moving and thought-provoking. Among the most disturbing exhibits are the formaldehyde-filled jars containing foetuses deformed as a result of the chemical defoliants used during the Vietnam War. Also displayed here are photographs showing the effects of torture, a video of a prisoner being thrown from a helicopter by Vietnam's aggressors, along with many American weapons, military vehicles, and even a French guillotine.

Xa Loi Pagoda ⓰

89 Ba Huyen Thanh St, District 3. **Map** 1 C4. **Tel** *(08) 3930 7438.* ⬛ *7–11am, 2–7pm daily.*

This was one of the most important pagodas during the communist revolution. Built in 1956, it was a center of resistance to Ngo Dinh Diem's *(see p43)* corrupt and anti-Buddhist regime in the early 1960s. Three of its monks immolated themselves publicly as a gesture of protest, and on one occasion, about 400 worshippers and clergy were arrested. These actions were crucial in galvanizing widespread opposition to the Diem regime, ultimately leading to the coup that resulted in his assassination in 1963.

Today, few traces of these tumultuous events remain as the pagoda's colorful seven-tiered tower rises above the temple complex. The roof soars to 49 ft (15 m), and large painted panels at the top of the walls depict scenes from the life of the Buddha. The monks' quarters are on the first floor of the two-storied main building, and the sanctuary, unusual for its spare decor, is above. The ample space is devoid of furnishings, pillars, censers, and displays so that the visitor is drawn to the massive bronze statue of the Buddha seated behind the solitary altar.

Colossal bronze Buddha inside Xa Loi Pagoda

Colorful images of goddesses on the façade of Mariamman Hindu Temple

Mariamman Hindu Temple **⑰**

45 Truong Dinh St, District 1.
Map 2 D4. **Tel** (08) 3823 2735.
◯ *sunrise–sunset daily.* ♿

Dedicated to Mariamman, an incarnation of Shakti, the Hindu Goddess of Strength, Mariamman Hindu Temple caters not only to the small community of Hindus in Ho Chi Minh City, but also to the many local Vietnamese Buddhists, who worship here either looking for good luck or driven by superstition.

Built in the late 19th century, the temple is quite small but beautiful, and superbly maintained by the government. The bright, coral-colored wall of the façade is surmounted by numerous images of deities, cows, and lions, all painted vividly in pink, green, and blue. Over the entrance, a stepped-pyramidal tower covered with more sculpted images, mostly female deities, rises from the rooftop.

Inside, an imposing statue of a red-robed lion guards the entrance, which opens into an uncovered portico that surrounds the main sanctuary. Three of the courtyard's walls are inset with altar nooks in which images of various gods and goddesses rest. Set in the center of the portico,

the sanctuary itself is slightly raised. Made of stone, it recalls the architectural style of Angkor Wat *(see pp212– 13)*, and forms the setting for the multi-armed represen-tation of Mariamman. The goddess is surrounded by many attending deities, including Ganesha, the Hindu Elephant God, as well as two female deities, who stand on either side of her. Two *lingam* (Hindu phallic symbols) also stand before her.

The altar is surrounded by numerous incense burners and brass figurine oil lamps. Worshippers hold incense sticks in both hands while praying. The rear of the sanctuary has a prayer wall against which the faithful press their heads in the hope that the goddess will be able to hear their prayers clearly.

Ben Thanh Market **⑱**

Intersection of Le Loi and Ham Nghi Blvds, District 1. **Map** 2 E4.
◯ *6am–5pm daily; later outside.*
♿ ▢ ⅋ ▯

One of the most recognizable landmarks in the city, this shopping center was built in 1914 by the French, who named it Les Halles Centrales or Central Market Halls. The main structure that houses the market is made of reinforced concrete and occupies an enormous area. Its most famous feature is the massive clock tower that dominates the neighborhood.

Home to several hundred shopkeepers, the market offers an amazingly extensive and varied selection of merchan-dise, ranging from food and leather goods to household items and clothing, as well as hardware and livestock. The atmosphere here is one of high energy and tremen-dous bustle as products arrive from around the country and, throughout the day, merchants sing out their wares, customers haggle, and tourists wander in search of great deals.

On entering through the main portal on Le Loi Boule-vard, general merchandise is on the left. To the right is clothing and textiles. Moving farther in, to the right are dry goods, such as tea, coffee, and spices, as well as packaged foods. Halfway in, fresh foods are on the right, and food stalls, where meals are available, to the left. The eateries here are famous for both quality and price. Since the signage is in English as well as Vietna-mese, patrons can point to the posted menu to order.

Well-stocked stall at Ben Thanh Market

For hotels and restaurants in this region see pp232–4 and pp250–52

Fine Arts Museum ⑲

97A Pho Duc Chinh St, District 1.
Map 2 E5. **Tel** *(08) 3829 4441.*
◯ *9am–4:30pm Tue–Sun.*

At first sight, this handsome building, painted a burnt yellow with white trim, appears typically French. Built on a large scale, the structure features columns and wrought-iron work on windows and balconies, all topped with a Chinese-style tiled roof.

Inside, the museum is home to three floors of Vietnamese art, which includes ceramics, lacquerware, sculptures, and oil paintings by Vietnamese and foreign artsist. The first floor contains a hodgepodge of modern, Belle Époque, traditional Chinese, and Soviet propaganda art. The second floor is given over largely to political art, almost all of it related to the Vietnam War. This floor also has a fine selection of ceramics, mostly of Chinese style or origin.

The museum's most interesting collection can be found on the third floor. Cham, Funan, Khmer, Chinese, and Indian works of art are well represented here. On display are many antiques, Oc Eo pottery and sculptures, Chinese objets d'art and wood carvings, and Cham statues. A main highlight is a set of wooden funeral statues from the Central Highlands dating from the early 20th century. Unfortunately, there is little in the way of English signage to help understand the exhibits.

Two galleries behind the museum also offer pieces of contemporary art for sale.

Stone bust, Fine Arts Museum

Dan Sinh Market ⑳

104 Yersin St, District 1. **Map** 2 E5.
◯ *sunrise–sunset daily.*

This vast, rambling warren of shops and stalls is known primarily for its wide range of war surplus products and memorabilia. Dan Sinh has everything needed for camp

War exhibit displaying helmets of unknown soldiers, Fine Arts Museum

and wilderness survival and that includes locally produced copies of uniforms, boots, field equipment, helmets, and anything else a soldier would need on the march.

Almost all of it is modeled on US Army issue gear. In addition to the practical, there are thousands of counterfeit "antique" Zippo cigarette lighters, said to be left behind by American troops during the war. Most are emblazoned with regimental insignia. Other military regalia, such as old dog tags, unit shoulder patches, Vietcong insignia, medals, belt buckles, and sun helmets are also available.

The market also has a vast selection of household goods and hardware. Every kitchen device imaginable is on sale, from woks to coffeemakers and cocktail shakers. Hand

and power tools, electrical appliances, and various types of compasses fill the shelves of this fascinating labyrinth of merchants' stalls.

Hoi Quan Nghia An Pagoda ㉑

678 Nguyen Trai St, Cholon.
Map 4 E4. **Tel** *(08) 3853 8775.*
◯ *sunrise–sunset daily.*

Renowned for its detailed woodwork and intricate carvings, this pagoda is one of the oldest in Ho Chi Minh City. Built in the 19th century, the temple is dedicated to Quan Cong, a deified Chinese general, and Nghia An, his horse's faithful groom.

On entering, to the left are two of the pagoda's most distinctive features – larger-than-life-size wooden statues of Quan Cong's red horse and Nghia An. Worshippers pray at these statues, touching them to collect blessings. Of the two, the horse is considered more sacred. Devotees ring the bell around its neck, and crawl under it to the other side, symbolically wiping up blessings along the way.

To the right is a glass encased altar to Ong Bon, Guardian of Happiness and Virtue. The main sanctuary, entered through wooden folding screen doors, features friezes of a tiger and dragon on either side of the hall. The glass cases behind the main altar have images of Quan Cong and his assistants – Quan Binh, his chief mandarin, on the right, and Chau Xuong, his chief general, on the left.

Chinese-style exterior of Hoi Quan Nghia An Pagoda

Cholon Walking Tour

Home to Chinese traders and merchants for more than three centuries, Cholon, which means big market, has long been one of Ho Chi Minh City's most vibrant commercial centers. Also known as District 5, its markets are always busy and brimming with a wide range of specialty shops selling everything from silks, spices, and medicinal herbs to hats, jade curios, and ceramics. With most of the city's vast ethnic Chinese or Hoa community concentrated here, Cholon is a religious hub and home to several Chinese-style pagodas and temples. These striking buildings are concentrated on and around Cholon's main street, Nguyen Trai, which runs through the heart of the area. The narrow streets of this bustling district are best traversed on foot.

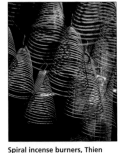

Spiral incense burners, Thien Hau Pagoda *(see p70)*

The electronics market is a one-stop destination for a range of products, such as TVs, toasters, air conditioners, and more.

Phuoc An Hoi Quan Pagoda ①
The Fujian community built this pagoda in 1902, dedicating it to Quan Cong. The ancient spears displayed before the main altar represent the cardinal virtues.

KEY

•••••••••• Suggested route

Quan Am Pagoda ②
The only temple complex in the city bisected by a street, this pagoda, also known as Ong Lang, has a colorful façade and an exquisitely detailed ceramic-tiled roof (see p70).

Thien Hau Pagoda ③
Perhaps the most outstanding feature of this pagoda is the finely carved frieze along its roof, depicting detailed scenes from Chinese legends (see p70).

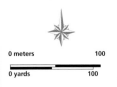

0 meters   100

0 yards   100

Trieu Quang Phuc Street
Pungent with the herbs from its numerous traditional Chinese medicine shops, Trieu Quang Phuc is one of Cholon's noisiest and busiest streets.

TIPS FOR THE TOUR

Tour length: *1 mile (1.6 km).*
Stopping-off points: *Xa Tay Market, next to Cholon Mosque, Trieu Quang Phuc Street, and the electronics market are great places to pick up a range of goods at affordable prices. The stretch on Tran Hung Dao has a number of decent, if expensive, eateries.*
Road safety: *Traffic can be heavy along Hung Vuong, so take care when walking here.*

Hoi Quan Nghia An Pagoda [4]
Lavishly decorated in red and gold, and embellished with elaborate woodwork, the main altar of Hoi Quan Nghia An is dedicated to Quan Cong, a revered Nguyen Lord (see p67).

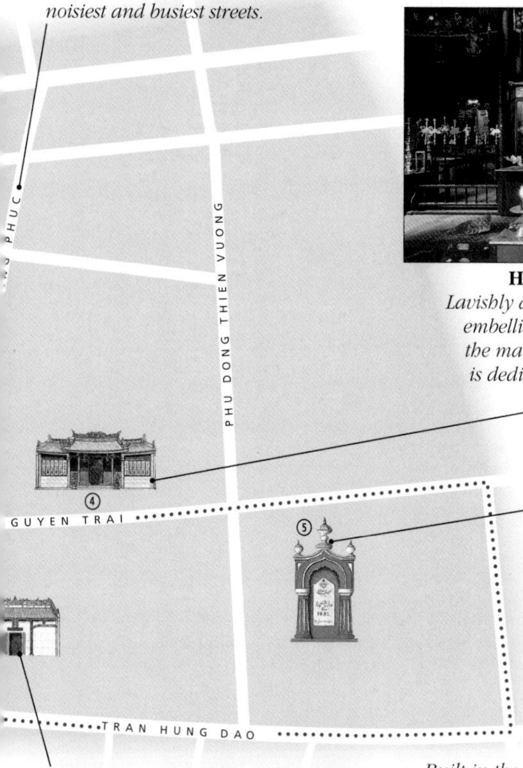

Cholon Mosque [5]
Built in the early 1930s, this unassuming little mosque has a serene charm. Its modest and simple architecture is in contrast to the ornate pagodas in the area.

Tam Son Hoi Quan Pagoda [6]
Dedicated to Me Sanh, the Goddess of Fertility, this 19th-century pagoda is colorfully decorated, with a number of shrines to various deities. Me Sanh's image graces a small altar at the back of the pagoda, and is worshipped by women hoping to conceive.

Thien Hau Pagoda ㉒

710 Nguyen Trai St, Cholon.
Map 4 E4. **Tel** (08) 3855 5322.
◯ sunrise–sunset daily.
🎏 Thien Hau Pagoda Festival (Apr).

Also named Hoi Quan Tue Thanh, but commonly known as Chua Ba, or Lady's Pagoda, this temple is dedicated to Thien Hau, Goddess of the Sea and Patroness of Sailors. Built in the early 1800s by the Cantonese congregation, this is one of the most popular and richly embellished temples in the city. The front courtyard is surrounded by high walls, topped by intricate friezes and carved tableaus. The entrance ceiling is more complex, with woodwork and gilt reaching halfway down to the floor.

Inside, the atrium, with its exquisite friezes and reliefs, features giant censers billowing fragrant smoke. The spacious central room has a display case of what seem to be brass clubs with Chinese inscriptions. In fact, these are the nozzles of the fire hoses used to extinguish a fire that threatened the temple in 1898. The walls of this room are covered with prayer flags – red strips of paper on which devotees write their prayers. It is believed that as the breeze rustles the paper, the prayers waft to Thien Hau.

Banks of hanging incense coils grace the main sanctuary ceiling, while three statues of Thien Hau, each flanked by two attendants, preside at the altar. Also hanging from the

Quan Am, resplendent in white, Quan Am Pagoda

ceiling is a carved wooden boat that recalls Thien Hau's connection to the sea. To the right is an image of Long Mau, Goddess of Mothers and Newborns.

Quan Am Pagoda ㉓

12 Lao Tu St, Cholon. **Map** 4 D4.
Tel (08) 3855 3543.
◯ sunrise–sunset daily.

This pagoda, also known as Ong Lang, was built by Chinese merchants in 1816 and honors Quan Am (or Kwan Yin), the Chinese Goddess of Mercy. The unusual pagoda is set in two parts, separated by a street. On the south side is a small plaza that adjoins a grotto set in a fish

Incense pot in
Thien Hau Pagoda

and turtle pond, while the north side houses the main temple complex.

The eye-catching roof and entryway are richly adorned with paintings of saints, gilded scroll-work, and carved wooden panels depicting dragons, houses, people, and scenes from traditional Chinese life and stories. Inside, the first altar is dedicated to the Buddha, and leads into the main sanctuary, featuring two rotating lotus-shaped prayer wheels inset with scores of Buddha images. Devotees make a donation to the temple and can then affix a label with their name onto one of the images. With each turn of the column their prayer is heard.

Next to the main altar is a representation of Quan Am, surrounded by the images of several other deities, including Amida, or the Happy Buddha, who represents the future; A Di Da, the Buddha of the Past; and Thich Ca, the Historical Buddha, Siddhartha. On either side of the altar are small incinerators. Paper money is burnt here for the benefit of departed souls. The pagoda maintains a large and unusual collection of live turtles for good luck. In a courtyard behind the sanctuary are more altars and images of gods and goddesses.

The entire complex is filled with oil lamps and votive candles. The latter are small oil-filled glasses with wicks that are regularly refilled and imbue the air with the fragrance of incense.

The elaborately carved sculptures and ceramic friezes along the roof of Thien Hau Pagoda

For hotels and restaurants in this region see pp232–4 and pp250–52

Binh Tay Market **24**

Thap Muoi St, Cholon. **Map** 3 C5.
Tel *(08) 3855 6130.* ◯ *8am–5pm daily.* 🍴 ♿

The literal translation of *cho lon* is "big market", and Binh Tay Market justifies the name. This grand marketplace is a pagoda-style tribute to trade. Originally a small collection of open-air stalls, a Chinese merchant took the initiative to build a permanent structure in 1826. Over time, it evolved into the huge emporium it is today.

This yellow building has four wings joined as a square, with a courtyard and a fountain in the middle. A tall clock tower looms in the center of the complex. Stacked pagoda-like roofs cover the bustle of commerce. Primarily a wholesale market, it is less touristy than Ben Thanh Market *(see p66).* A wide range of items and services are available here, from medicinal herbs and imported Chinese toys, to tailors and mechanics, and even caged birds.

Tempting sweets in rows of glass jars, Binh Tay Market

Phung Son Pagoda **25**

1408 3 Thang 2 St, District 11.
Map 3 B4. **Tel** *(08) 3969 3584.*
◯ *sunrise–sunset daily.*

Also known as Go Pagoda, the present complex was built between 1802 and 1820 on the remains of an ancient site. Local lore and, more recently, archaeological findings

Woman praying before a statue at the entrance of Phung Son Pagoda

suggest that this was once the site of a complex belonging to the Funan Empire *(see p39).* According to legend, at one time the temple was to be moved to a new site. But, as valuables were loaded upon a white elephant, the animal stumbled. This was taken as an omen for the pagoda to remain at its present location.

The complex has the monks' living quarters, while the main sanctuary is situated to the left and contains statues of various Buddhas. Connected to it is an atrium with images of Quan Am, Goddess of Mercy, and the Buddha, as well as a ceremonial drum and bronze bell.

The inner sanctum hosts a statue of Boddhidharma, who brought Buddhism to Vietnam from India. Strangely, this idol bears a startling resemblance to a traditional statue of Jesus.

Giac Vien Pagoda **26**

161/35/20 Lac Long Quan St, District 11. **Map** 3 A4. ◯ *sunrise–sunset daily.* **Dam Sen Water Park** 3 Hoa Binh St, District 11. **Tel** *(08) 3858 8418.* ◯ *9am–6pm daily.* 📷 ♿ 🍴

Established by the monk Hai Tinh Giac Vien in 1744, this temple is located on the

Swastika on portico, Giac Vien Pagoda

outskirts of the city, and is one of the most peaceful places around. Well known for its collection of more than 150 wooden statues, the pagoda seems to serve mainly as a dedication to the departed. Several large, beautifully carved tombs lie to the right of the entrance, as do some photographs of the dead. A columbarium houses funerary urns. Although the interior is dark, strategically placed apertures in the roof allow the sunlight to pierce the gloom with an almost cinematic effect.

The sanctuary's altar is a riot of several Buddha statues in varying sizes, some gilded, others plain wood or ceramic. A large A Di Da Buddha sits at the back and two small Bodhisattvas are perched in front; more than a dozen sit between. A stepped conical structure with a multitude of small Buddhas on every level fronts the altar, and is lit by fairy lights. On either side of the sanctuary are cloisters filled with bonsai trees and grottos. Close by is the **Dam Sen Water Park**, a welcome diversion, especially enjoyed by children. Water slides, an artificial river and lake, and shady rest spots all make for a fun-filled afternoon.

A large gilded Buddha sits at an altar in the Giac Vien Pagoda

Reconstruction of a kitchen unit inside the Cu Chi Tunnels

One Pillar Pagoda of Thu Duc ㉗

100 Dang Van Bi St, Thu Duc District. 🚐 *Tel* (08) 3897 2143. ◯ *sunrise–sunset daily.*

This little pagoda, based on the earlier Lien Phai Pagoda in Hanoi *(see p163)*, was built by monks who fled from there after the country was partitioned in 1954. During the Vietnam War *(see pp44–5)*, the temple was used by the Vietcong as an undercover camp. Despite President Diem's efforts to destroy the pagoda, local support provided by the monks kept the structure safe and intact.

Like its Hanoi counterpart, the building can be seen rising from the middle of a lotus pond. A narrow staircase leads from the pond's edge to the porch-like entrance. The façade has many windows, providing an almost unbroken 360-degree view. The interior is simple, with a low altar.

One Pillar Pagoda emerging from the waters of a lotus pond

Cu Chi Tunnels ㉘

25 miles (40 km) NW of HCMC. 🚐 to Cu Chi town, then by taxi. *Tel* (08) 3794 8820. ◯ 7:30am–5pm daily. 🖼 ✓

The small town of Cu Chi is famous for its elaborate network of tunnels, located at a distance of around 9 miles (15 km) from the town itself.

There are two different tunnel systems here. The one at Ben Dinh village was used by the Vietcong during the Vietnam War. The guided tour begins in a briefing room, where maps and charts display the extent of the network. Following an audio-visual presentation on tunnel history, visitors are led to an area set with faux booby traps and mannequins of Vietcong fighters. Close by are trapdoors that lead down into narrow tunnels. Although these have been widened to accommodate Western visitors, many still find them claustrophobic. Deep down in the depths, the chambers have been restored to the way they might have been at the time of war, with beds, stoves, and caches of ammunition.

The second set of tunnels is at Ben Duoc. Created mainly for tourism purposes, the tunnels here are better equipped than the actual ones used by the Vietcong.

Cu Chi town is known for its shooting galleries, but there is also a memorial pagoda, which features murals and a striking sculpture in the shape of a tear. The rather plain war cemeteries all over the area can be seen from the road.

Nui Ba Den ㉙

66 miles (106 kms) NW of HCMC on Hwy 22; 10 miles (15 km) NE of Tay Ninh town. 🚐 to Tay Ninh town, then by taxi. *Tel* (066) 382 6763. 🖼 ▣ 🖼 *Nui Ba Den Festival (Jun).*

There are two major attractions in Tay Ninh province, namely Cao Dai Holy See *(see pp74–5)* and Nui Ba Den or the Black Lady Mountain. Despite the proximity of these sights, few visitors visit Nui Ba Den, as it is off the beaten track and cannot be reached directly by public transport. However, those who do make the trip will find it's worth the effort.

Despite the amusement park atmosphere at the base, the real attraction here is the lovely forest-clad mountain itself. Set amid shimmering lakes and a vibrant green landscape, Nui Ba Den rises above the surrounding plains at a steep 3,235 ft (986 m). The summit boasts stunning views, as well a shrine to Black Lady, a pious woman named Huong, who died while defending her honor. Those who want the exercise can hike up the mountain to visit the temple, but there is also a chair lift for those who prefer a more relaxed mode of transport.

Once a Vietcong camp, the mountain was bombed and sprayed with deadly chemicals during the Vietnam War. Today, its caves, used as Buddhist sanctuaries, have regained their beauty. Each year, a festival honors the spirit of Nui Ba Den, with offerings, singing, and dancing.

A large, rotund statue holding a cigarette at the base of Nui Ba Den

Tunnel Complexes

Elaborate tunnel complexes, such as those at Cu Chi and Vinh Moc *(see p150)*, have been used by the Vietnamese for centuries. The tunnels were a key part of guerilla warfare during the Vietnam War *(see pp44–5)*, and played a major role in defeating American soldiers. Extending perhaps more than 125 miles (201 km), the tunnels were dug by local people using shovels.

A tear-gas canister used by US soldiers

Built at many levels, the tunnels had living spaces, kitchens, and clinics. Here, the Vietnamese could escape bombings, hide from the enemy, and mount surprise attacks. The American soldiers knew of the tunnels, and used infrared imaging and sniffer dogs in their search for them. They never quite succeeded in finding them since the tunnels were rerouted and enlarged to avoid detection.

ANATOMY OF THE TUNNEL SYSTEM

While most tunnels were fairly small and simple, the major ones had three levels, and could be up to 33 ft (10 m) deep. Everything needed to maintain human life was available here. At least one even had a small cinema.

Tunnel entrances *were so small and well camouflaged with leaves and branches that they were often invisible to enemy eyes. One method applied by the Americans for finding them was using stethoscopes to listen for subterranean activity.*

A cooking area used highly creative ways to keep smoke from rising to the surface.

"Tunnel rats" *was the nickname given to the special teams of US soldiers deployed for entering and disabling the tunnels. They wore masks as protection when releasing gases in the tunnels to drive out the Vietnamese.*

Well-hidden firing posts helped the Vietnamese shoot at the enemy and then disappear.

Bunker for strategy and planning

Underwater entrance

The infirmary was not only a place to treat the wounded; many babies were also born here.

Ammunition dump

Air-raid shelters, located at the lowest level of the tunnels, protected the Vietnamese from intense bombing.

Cramped and narrow passageways *were made as tight and constricted as possible so that the larger American soldiers would find it difficult to pass through the tunnels.*

Ingenious booby traps, *using everything from bamboo and iron staves to explosives, made the tunnels potential death traps for the unwary.*

Cao Dai Holy See ㉚

Symbols of Cao Daism

As the center of Cao Dai religion, which was founded in 1926 *(see p23)*, this vast complex draws nearly three million worshippers.

The main attraction here is the Great Divine Temple – a massive structure that reflects an unusual mix of Asian and European architectural elements. Amid the vibrant pinks, greens, and yellows of the decor are carvings of writhing serpents and dragons, and a multitude of Divine Eyes gazing from all directions. The prayer services, attended by hundreds of clergy in colorful robes, are held everyday and are a spectacular sight.

Colorful dragon motifs adorn the temple's columns

Maitreya Buddha
Dominating the central tower of the temple's front façade is a statue of the Buddha, reflecting the Cao Dai reverance for Buddhism.

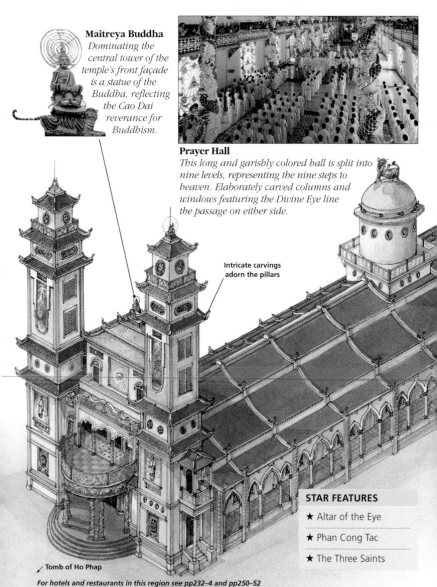

Prayer Hall
This long and garishly colored hall is split into nine levels, representing the nine steps to heaven. Elaborately carved columns and windows featuring the Divine Eye line the passage on either side.

Intricate carvings adorn the pillars

STAR FEATURES

★ Altar of the Eye

★ Phan Cong Tac

★ The Three Saints

Tomb of Ho Phap

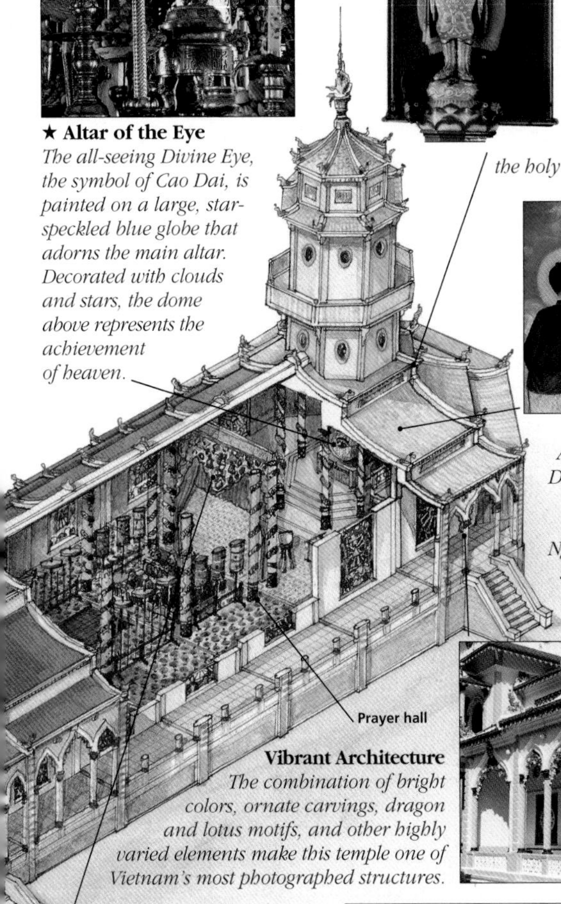

VISITORS' CHECKLIST

Long Hoa Village, 2.5 miles (4 km) E of Tay Ninh; 59 miles (96 km) NW of HCMC. 🚌 ℹ *Tay Ninh Tourist, 210B 30 Thang 4 St, Tay Ninh, (066) 382 2376.* 🕒 *daily.* **Services** *6am, noon, 6pm, midnight.*

★ Phan Cong Tac
One of the founders of Cao Daism, Phan Cong Tac was the chief medium, with the ability to communicate with the holy spirits during seances.

★ Altar of the Eye
The all-seeing Divine Eye, the symbol of Cao Dai, is painted on a large, star-speckled blue globe that adorns the main altar. Decorated with clouds and stars, the dome above represents the achievement of heaven.

★ The Three Saints
A mural depicts the three Cao Dai saints, Chinese leader Sun Yat Sen, French poet Victor Hugo, and Vietnamese poet Nguyen Binh Khiem as earthly signatories to "Third Alliance Between God and Man."

Prayer hall

Vibrant Architecture
The combination of bright colors, ornate carvings, dragon and lotus motifs, and other highly varied elements make this temple one of Vietnam's most photographed structures.

Statues of the Cao Dai pantheon, including Jesus, the Buddha, and Confucius, dominate the area above the altar.

GREAT DIVINE TEMPLE

The spiritual centerpiece of the Cao Dai complex, this temple was built between 1933 and 1955. Its vividly decorated three-tiered roof, stained-glass windows, and kaleidoscope of colors make for an unusual, striking building. The presence of the all-seeing Divine Eye represents supreme knowledge and wisdom.

PLAN OF CAO DAI HOLY SEE

KEY

Area illustrated

KEY LIST OF SITES

1. Great Divine Temple
2. Holy Mother's Temple
3. Tomb of Ho Phap
4. Amphitheater
5. Meditation Room
6. Public Works
7. Weaving House
8. Information Hall
9. Pope's Office
10. Lady Cardinal's Office

Fishing boats at Vung Tau harbor, against a scenic mountain backdrop

Vung Tau ③①

81 miles (130 km) E of HCMC
on Hwy 51. 🚍 250,000.
✈ *helicopter from HCMC.* 🚌
🚤 *hydrofoil from HCMC.* 🚏
ℹ *Ba Ria-Vung Tau Tourist, 33
Tran Hung Dao St, (064) 385 6445.*
www.*bariavungtautourism.com*
Bach Dinh Museum 4 Tran Phu St.
Tel (064) 385 2605. ◯ *7–11:30am,
1:30–5pm daily.* 📷

The peninsula town of Vung
Tau was once a pristine
beach resort, known by the
French as Cap St Jacques. It
is still a very popular seaside
getaway, but now that it is
developed and home to
an offshore oil industry, the
quality of the water and
beaches has been somewhat
affected. On weekends
it is crowded, noisy, and
expensive. During the week,
however, it is quieter, and
its proximity to Ho Chi Minh
City makes it a convenient
beach destination.
The two main beaches here
are **Bai Truoc** (Front Beach)
on the west and the long
and wide **Bai Sau** (Back
Beach) on the east side of
the South China Sea
peninsula. Bai Truoc
has the greater
concentration of
hotels, bars, and
restaurants, while
Bai Sau is less
developed,
and therefore
cheaper and
a much quieter place to stay.
In the vicinity of Vung Tau,
two promontories, **Nui Lon**
(Big Mountain) and **Nui Nho**
(Little Mountain), are both

Distinctive fishing
boat, Long Hai

worth visiting for splendid
views. Nui Nho features a
giant statue of Jesus; visitors
can climb up to the top in
order to take in the scenery.
A better stop is the **Vung
Tau Lighthouse**. Located
about a mile from the ferry
landing, it offers a superb
vantage point.
The local museum, **Bach
Dinh**, or White Villa, was the
residence of Emperor Thanh
Thai while he was under
house arrest by the French.
Inside are many interesting
exhibits from the Chinese
Qing Dynasty. The relics on
display were salvaged from
a 17th-century shipwreck.

Long Hai ③②

81 miles (130 km) E of HCMC
on Hwy 19; 30 miles (40 km)
NE of Vung Tau. 🚍 *from HCMC.*
ℹ *Long Hai Tourism, Hai Son
Group, (064) 386 8401.*
🎏 *Fisherman's Festival (Feb/Mar).*

Until recently, the stretch of
coastline between Vung Tau
and Phan Thiet was virtually
deserted but a number of
large resorts have now taken
up residence. Home to the
small town of
Long Hai, this
area is now
rather exagge-
ratedly referred
to as Vietnam's
Riviera. Nonetheless,
the beaches are rela-
tively unspoiled, prices
are low, seafood is
fresh, and the
atmosphere is
very relaxed.

A point of interest near Long
Hai is the **Mo Co Temple**,
where hundreds of boats from
all over the region converge
during the Fisherman's Festival.
Farther east is one of Bao Dai's
villas, now the posh Anoasis
Resort (*see p234*). The beach
is private, but a small fee
allows full use of its facilities
for the day. Although there is
no direct public transport or
hydrofoil from Vung Tau, the
drive to Long Hai offers many
worthwhile sights. A predominantly Catholic area, several
charming churches line the
highway, as do a number of
interesting temples.

Ho Coc Beach ③③

118 miles (190 km) E of HCMC; 22
miles (36 km) NE of Long Hai. 🍴 🏖

Ho Coc Beach's relative
seclusion is its best feature.
While popular with the
Vietnamese as a weekend
destination, there is little
public transport, only a few
accommodation options, and
a handful of simple cafés and
restaurants. The beach is
superb, with miles of clean,
white sand, studded here and
there with massive boulders.

Environs
Ho Coc lies adjacent to the
**Binh Chau - Phuoc Buu Nature
Reserve**. The trees come right
up to the beach, and several
trails leading into the wooded
area start from the sand itself.
The preserve was once home
to many large animals, but
most have now been relocated

Rustic, one-pillared beach house on
the sands of Ho Coc Beach

Choppy South China Sea washing over large boulders, Ho Coc Beach

for conservation and safety purposes. Nevertheless, the preserve is still inhabited by several species of monkeys and birds. The greenery and tranquil surroundings are extremely soothing. Guides may be hired for walking tours for a small fee.

Binh Chau Hot Springs ㉞

93 miles (150 km) SE of HCMC; 31 miles (50 km) NE of Long Hai. 🚗
ℹ️ Binh Chau Hot Springs Resort, (064) 387 0103. 📷 🍴 🖥️

With more than a hundred natural hot springs reputed to be imbued with therapeutic properties, Binh Chau is not frequented merely by the rheumatic and arthritic. Although the mineral-rich mud and hot springs are obviously the main attractions here, the place is an amusement center as well.

The Binh Chau Hot Springs Resort here is now a popular holiday destination, boasting a karaoke bar, tennis courts, and snooker tables. Public and private facilities for hot spring baths are on offer as well. The private baths are enclosed by wooden screens for dressing and overhead coverings for shade. These can accommodate two to ten people, and incur a higher charge than the public facilities. The public baths have a swimming pool. The water averages 40 degrees C (86 degrees F) though some pools can reach a boiling 87 degrees C (189 degrees F). As entertainment, baskets of eggs are available for dunking

into the pools to cook. People can boil eggs in the hot springs as well. Large statues of chickens indicate the spots where such a venture is possible. For a relaxing spa experience, therapeutic mud baths are also on offer here.

Amid the springs are verdant marshlands. There are also some well-marked walking trails in the area where visitors can take a stroll.

People boiling baskets of eggs, Binh Chau Hot Springs

Cat Tien National Park ㉟

155 miles (250 km) SE of HCMC.
🚌 🚗 from HCMC. Tel (061) 379 1228. 📷 🗺️ 🍴 🖥️
www.cattiennationalpark.org

Cat Tien is easily one of the most abundant, biologically diverse reserves of its kind. This is remarkable in light of the fact that it was subjected to sustained bombardment by defoliants during the Vietnam War. Even further back in time, it was a place of pilgrimage, as evidenced by the discovery of ancient religious artifacts traced to both the Funan and Champa Empires (see p39).

Today, this 277 sq miles (718 sq km) park is home to a wide range of flora and fauna. There are more than 1,600 varieties of plants, but new ones continue to be discovered. The park is perhaps best known for the almost-extinct Javan rhinoceros, but the reserve is also home to many other animals, including deer, elephants, and over 360 species of birds that attract bird-watchers from all over the world. Colonies of monkeys, including rare douc langurs, populate the trees, while 440 species of butterfly flutter amid wildflowers. Not surprisingly, Cat Tien is one of the most popular adventure destinations in Vietnam. Accommodations in the park are minimal but adequate, and are reached by crossing the Dong Nai River.

JAVAN RHINOCEROS

Of the huge number of species of fauna in Cat Tien National Park, there are few that have garnered as much concern in recent years as the endangered Javan rhinoceros (*Rhinoceros sondaicus*). Though these magnificent beasts once roamed the forests in large numbers, they were nearly hunted out of existence in colonial times. Outside Java, the only known examples of this creature are the estimated eight animals living in Cat Tien. Smaller in size than most rhinos, its skin is very pale, as a result of living under the thick tropical canopy. Males have an approximately 10-inch (25-cm) long horn, while females have a smaller or no horn.

The rare Javan rhinoceros

HO CHI MINH CITY STREET FINDER

Finding your way around the narrow streets and winding alleys of Ho Chi Minh City can be a challenging experience. The city is divided into 19 *quan*, or urban districts, and five suburban districts. Vietnamese addresses *(see p287)* are usually straightforward but they are more complicated in Ho Chi Minh City because the same street begins new numbering upon entering a new district. On the Street Finder, some words that are common in street names have been abbreviated, such as Nguyen, which appears as Ng. Note that in the south *duong*, meaning street, is usually added to the road name. *Pho* is added to the street name in the north.

A visitor exploring Ho Chi Minh City

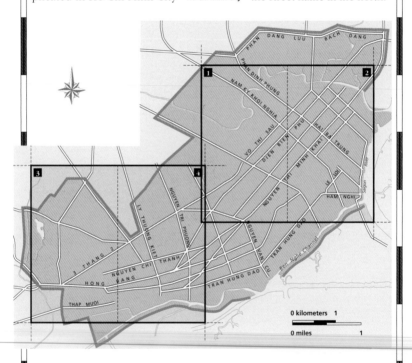

| 0 kilometers | 1 |
| 0 miles | 1 |

KEY TO STREET FINDER

- Major sight
- Other sight
- Other building
- 🚆 Train station
- 🚌 Long-distance bus station
- 🛥 Riverboat pier
- ℹ Tourist information
- ✚ Hospital
- ⊠ Post office
- Pagoda/temple
- ✝ Church
- ☾ Mosque

SCALE OF MAPS 1–2, 3–4

| 0 meters | 500 |
| 0 yards | 500 |

Street Finder Index

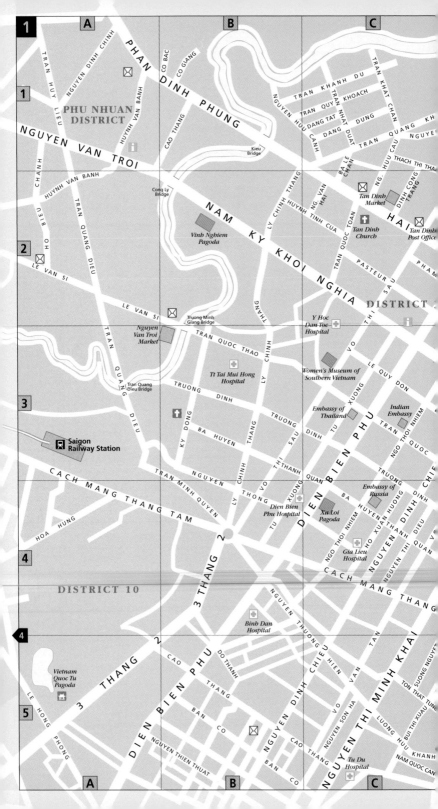

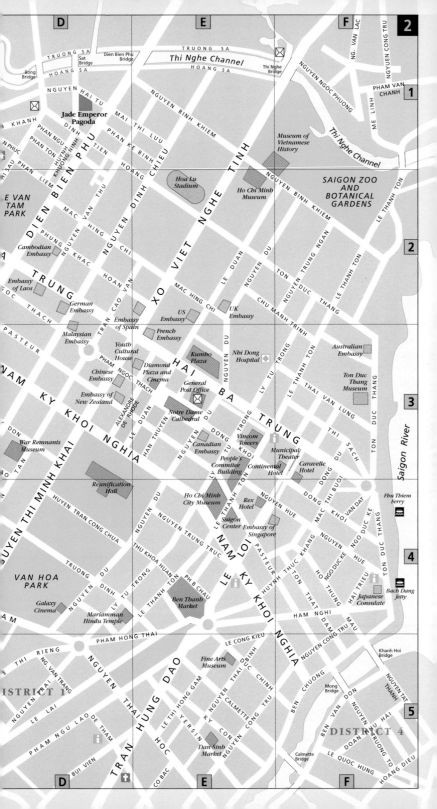

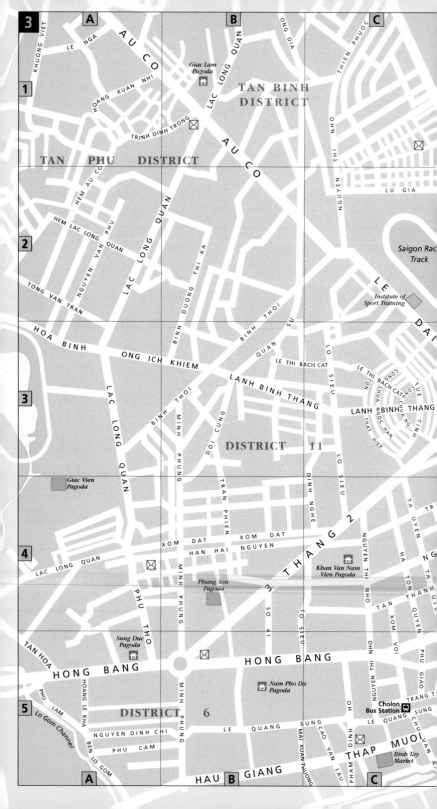

MEKONG DELTA AND SOUTHERN VIETNAM

*L*ife on the delta revolves around the Mekong River, with its green expanses of paddy fields, thick orchards, and intricate patchwork of canals. Floating houses, markets, and fishing boats bob on the rivers, while the islands boast dense forests and beautiful white-sand beaches. Amid the bells, drums, and chanting of the delta's many pagodas, an ancient way of life continues well into the 21st century.

With its origins on the high plateau of Tibet, the mighty Mekong River meanders along for 2,800 miles (4,500 km), gathering silt from China, Myanmar, Thailand, Laos, and Cambodia, before splitting into the distributaries that give the region the name Song Cuu Long or the River of Nine Dragons. These tentacled waterways bestow Vietnam's southern plain with rich alluvial soil that has made it a "rice basket," as well as a "fruit basket" filled with coconut, longan, and mango trees.

The delta has long been laid claim to by Cambodia, and in 1978, the Khmer Rouge orchestrated a savage massacre at numerous villages. Nevertheless, the delta and its people are extremely resilient, having survived the ravages of frequent floods, French and Cambodian occupation, many bombings, and the devastating effects of the chemical defoliant, Agent Orange. Despite this legacy of conflict and upheaval, life on the delta ebbs and flows to an age-old rhythm. Through necessity and tradition, the physical boundaries between land and water are transcended by farmers who row across canals that crisscross their emerald fields. In contrast, commercial towns such as Can Tho and Rach Gia are hurtling towards modernization. Everywhere, however, are attractive Khmer, Vietnamese, and Chinese-style pagodas that reflect the delta's ethnic diversity.

Nature is a major part of the delta's draw. Ha Tien's beaches feature white sand and towering limestone karsts, while the marshland around Bac Lieu is home to a variety of migratory birds. Off Vietnam's southern shore lie Phu Quoc and Con Dao Islands, which boast national parks and are both fast becoming popular as ecotourism destinations.

Boatman in a lone sampan surrounded by thick palm groves

◁ Bustling Cai Rang Floating Market in the early morning, Can Tho (see p94)

Exploring Mekong Delta and Southern Vietnam

The Mekong Delta is a unique region where life
on the water has remained unchanged for centuries.
Closest to Ho Chi Minh City, My Tho is known as a
launching pad for boat tours, as is Vinh Long, which
lies to its south. Can Tho, the delta's largest city has
several lively floating markets in its vicinity. To see
some floating architecture, head to Chau Doc, where
most people live and work on the water. Khmer
culture is prominent in Soc Trang and Tra Vinh, while
nature lovers will delight in Con Dao National Park.
The shores of Phu Quoc Island boast beautiful coral
reefs, and Ha Tien offers secluded beaches.

Well-stocked fruit stall at a local
market, Ben Tre *(see p89)*

SIGHTS AT A GLANCE

Towns and Cities

Bac Lieu ❾
Ben Tre ❸
Can Tho ❼
Cao Lanh ❻
Chau Doc ⓬
Ha Tien ⓭
My Tho ❶
Rach Gia ⑪
Soc Trang ❽
Tra Vinh ❹
Vinh Long ❺

Islands

Con Dao Islands ❿
Phoenix Island ❷
Phu Quoc Island ⑭

SEE ALSO

• **Where to Stay** pp235–6

• **Where to Eat** pp252–3

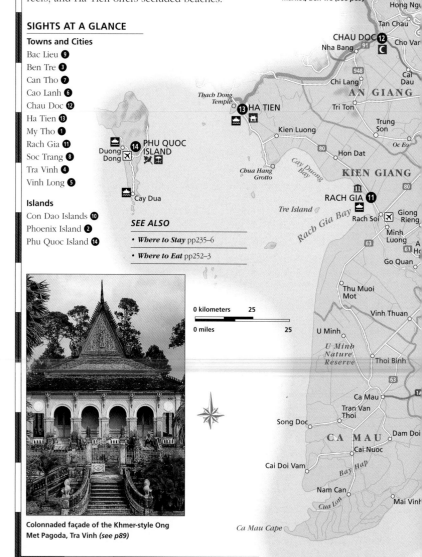

Colonnaded façade of the Khmer-style Ong
Met Pagoda, Tra Vinh *(see p89)*

For additional map symbols *see back flap*

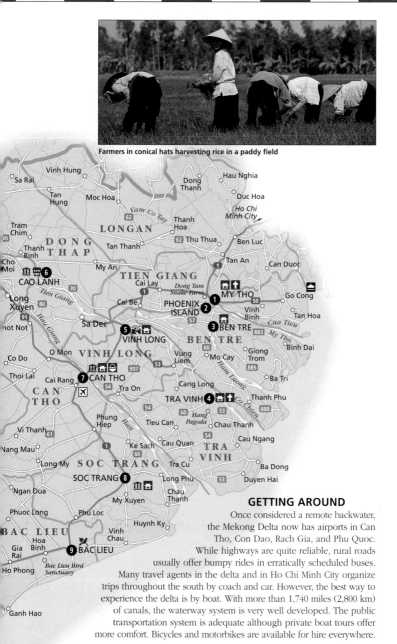

Farmers in conical hats harvesting rice in a paddy field

GETTING AROUND

Once considered a remote backwater, the Mekong Delta now has airports in Can Tho, Con Dao, Rach Gia, and Phu Quoc. While highways are quite reliable, rural roads usually offer bumpy rides in erratically scheduled buses. Many travel agents in the delta and in Ho Chi Minh City organize trips throughout the south by coach and car. However, the best way to experience the delta is by boat. With more than 1,740 miles (2,800 km) of canals, the waterway system is very well developed. The public transportation system is adequate although private boat tours offer more comfort. Bicycles and motorbikes are available for hire everywhere.

KEY

— Major road

= Minor road

▬ International border

— Provincial border

CON DAO ISLANDS

My Tho ❶

Road Map B6. 45 miles (72 km) SW of HCMC on Hwy 1. *170,000. from HCMC. Tien Giang Tourist, 63 Trung Trac St, (073) 387 2105.*

Because of its proximity to Ho Chi Minh City, My Tho, on the northernmost tributary of the Mekong River, is the most popular day-trip destination in the delta. It is an ideal base from which to hire a boat and cruise along the canals, stopping along the way to explore the surrounding islands.

A stroll through My Tho's wide tree-lined boulevards and waterfront market is almost a walk back in time. Wooden boats and barges crowd the shore, as vendors sell an impressive array of goods, from food to hardware and domestic items such as the giant earthenware urns used for bathing. The pungent aroma of dried fish and the fragrance of pineapple and jackfruit fill the air.

In addition to commerce, My Tho is also a religious center, with **Vinh Trang Pagoda** being one of its most noteworthy edifices. The temple's façade is embellished with mosaics made from broken pottery, a custom followed throughout Southeast Asia. Lily ponds and stone tombs surround the beautiful complex, and an image of the Buddhist goddess Quan Am is set into the heart of a banyan tree.

Serving the city's large population of Christians, **My Tho Church** functions both as

COCONUT MONK

Blackened funerary urn resting on a tortoise sculpture, Phoenix Island

The given name of the Coconut Monk was Nguyen Thanh Nam (1909–90). Although he went abroad to study chemistry in France, he eventually discarded the trappings of comfort and dedicated himself to a life of meditation and abstinence. Subsisting on a diet of coconuts and water, he even started a religion, Tinh Do Cu Si, a whimsical blend of Buddhism and Christianity. With hopes of restoring peace to Vietnam, he challenged the authorities on how to reunify the nation after its partition in 1954, and often ended up in jail because of his views. His bizarre headquarters on Phoenix Island remain his most enduring legacy.

a diocese and a Catholic school. Originally established in the 19th century, the current massive yellow building, with a high-vaulted ceiling and a red-tile roof, sits on sprawling grounds that are covered with trees and shrubs.

A short distance northwest of My Tho is the small but historically significant hamlet of **Ap Bac**. This was the site of the battle which resulted in the first major victory of the Vietcong against the US-backed South Vietnamese army in 1963.

Vinh Trang Pagoda
60 Nguyen Trung Truc St.
Tel (073) 387 3427. *9–11:30am, 1:30–5pm daily.*

My Tho Church
32 Hung Vuong St. **Tel** (073) 387 2290. *7am–6pm daily.*

Phoenix Island ❷

Road Map B6. 2 miles (3 km) from My Tho. **Sanctuary** *8:30–11am, 1:30–6pm daily.*

Midway between My Tho and Ben Tre are numerous small islands, the best known among them being Con Phung or Phoenix Island. This was the lonely bastion of the Coconut Monk. On this small spot of dry land, he built his odd little temple complex. On a circular base, about 75 ft (25 m) in diameter, are several free-standing blue-and-gold dragon columns, supporting nothing but the air above them. Nearby is a lattice-work structure that rather resembles a roller coaster. This is flanked by minarets and the monk's impression of a moon rocket. On the upriver

The handsome mosaic-embellished façade of Vinh Trang Pagoda, My Tho

For hotels and restaurants in this region see pp235–6 and pp252–3

Blue-and-gold dragon columns on the Coconut Monk's Phoenix Island

side, a huge funerary urn lies on the back of a giant tortoise sculpture. A small coconut candy factory operates on the perimeter of the island.

Neighboring Phoenix Island are several little islands, which make good venues for picnics. These include Con Tan Long or Dragon Island, home to bee-keepers and boatwrights (see p90); Thoi Son or Unicorn Island, full of narrow canals that irrigate lush longan orchards; and Con Qui or Tortoise Island, known for its coconut candy and potent banana liquor. Pineapples, jack-fruit, mangos are also grown here in abundance. Each of these little islands are served by a scheduled ferry.

Carved pillar, Phoenix Island

Ben Tre ❸

Road Map B6. 53 miles (86 km) SW of HCMC; 9 miles (14 km) S of My Tho. 🚹 112,000. 🚌 from HCMC. 🚤 from My Tho. 🚏 Ben Tre Tourist, 65 Dong Khoi St, (075) 382 9618.

Being off the tourist trail, Ben Tre does not get as many visitors as other delta cities, thus providing a rare glimpse into an ancient river town still living by its traditional ways.

The capital of Ben Tre Province, this town is famous in Vietnam for its coconut candy, and is lush with vast plantations yielding huge amounts of coconuts. To make the candy, the fruit's milk and flesh are boiled down to a sticky mass that is allowed to harden, then cut into small pieces and wrapped in edible rice paper. The process is fascinating to watch and the results delicious to taste.

A "country" market in every sense of the word, the central market offers little finery, with preference given to hardware, lengths of cloth, and food. However, the most interesting stalls belong to the fishmongers, who sell a variety of fresh and dried fish.

A notable religious site in Ben Tre is **Vien Minh Pagoda**. Established around 1900, it is now the head office of the provincial Buddhist association. The sparce interior is enlivened by colorful wall hangings and images sporting neon halos.

🏛 **Vien Minh Pagoda**
156 Nguyen Dinh Chieu St.
Tel (075) 381 3931.
🔓 sunrise–sunset daily.

Tra Vinh ❹

Road Map B6. 62 miles (100 km) W of Can Tho. 🚹 75,000. 🚌 from Vinh Long and Can Tho. 🚏 Tra Vinh Tourist Office, 64–66 Le Loi St, (074) 385 8556.

With its large Khmer, Christian, and Chinese population, Tra Vinh is distinguished by the diversity of its places of worship. Of the many Khmer-style religious buildings, **Ong Met Pagoda** is distinctive for its portico posts surmounted by four-faced images of the Buddha. The 10-ft (3-m) tall gilded *stupas*, mound-shaped reliquary monuments, are dedicated to deceased monks.

One of the most vibrant Chinese pagodas in town is **Ong Pagoda**, which was consecrated in 1556 and dedicated to the deified Chinese general Quan Cong of the 3rd century. The pagoda is known for its wildly colorful rear courtyard, one wall of which is engraved with red dragons disporting themselves between a range of blue mountains and a green sea. An interesting highlight is a fish pond where richly painted sculpted carp are shown in mid-leap as they break through the surface. These are all the works of Le Van Chot, who has a sculpture studio on the grounds.

However, it is the **Tra Vinh Church** that captures the spirit of the town's religious eclecticism best. Although the exterior of the building has a colonial-style design, a close examination of the eaves reveals "dragon flames," typically seen on Khmer-style temples.

Detail of statue, Ong Met Pagoda

Environs
About 3 miles (6 km) south of town, **Hang Pagoda** is a simple structure. Its main attraction are the hundreds of storks that nest here.

The **Khmer Minority People's Museum** has some interesting exhibits but there is no English signage. While household items, costumes, and jewelry are self-explanatory, religious items might need a guide. On the way to the museum, the tree-ringed **Ba Om Pond**, about 4 miles (7 km) southwest of Tra Vinh, is ideal for picnics. The **Ang Pagoda** also lies close by. The age of the present building is uncertain, but it has been a religious site since the 11th century. A pride of sculpted lions guard the entry, flanked by murals depicting the Buddha's life.

🏛 **Khmer Minority People's Museum**
4 miles (7 km) SW of town on 3 SEB Luong Hoa St.
Tel (074) 384 2188. 🔓 7:30–11:30am, 1:30–4:30pm daily.

Vendors in sampans at the early morning Cai Be Floating Market

Vinh Long ❺

Road Map B6. 84 miles (136 km) SW of HCMC; 46 miles (74 km) SW of My Tho. 🗺 126,000. 🚌 🚐 🛈 *Cuu Long Tourist, 1 Thang 5 St, (070) 382 3616.*

A small town on the bank of the Co Chien River, Vinh Long is mostly used by tourists as a base for exploring the islets dotting the waters around it. However, the town itself is also worth visiting. Vinh Long's large, French-colonial Catholic church draws attention to the fact that the area was once an important target for Christian missionaries. On the outskirts of town, **Van Thanh Mieu Temple** is a simple yet elegant structure, which was dedicated to Confucius in 1866. In 1930, a new building was added to it in honor of Phan Thanh Gian, who led a rebellion against the French.

Boat tours are a popular way to take in the dramatic sweep of the river and the charm of the offshore islands, most of which boast lovely flower gardens. **An Binh** and **Binh Hoa Phuoc** are popular amongst visitors as idyllic picnic spots. Just north of the ferry landing at An Binh, is the outwardly unassuming **Tien Chau Pagoda**. Inside, however, are startlingly lurid murals depicting the horrors of Buddhist Hell. In this scary vision, perdition for the lapsed includes being trampled by horses, devoured by serpents, and decomposing eternally.

Surrounded by orchards, sampans, and monkey bridges, the boatwrights, candymakers, beekeepers, and artisans ply their trades. The rhythm of life on the delta is fascinating, and Vinh Long is an ideal place to experience it. Homestays *(see p229)*, where visitors can eat, sleep, and work with a local family, are highly recommended.

Environs

Floating markets are common throughout the delta. **Cai Be Floating Market**, about an hour from Vinh Long by boat, is the easiest to reach. Open in the early morning, it is both a wholesale and a retail market, with large boats selling to merchants and small boats serving householders. Traders maneuver their boats agilely, loading fruit, coffee, and even hot noodles from one boat to another.

🏛 **Van Thanh Mieu Temple**
2 miles (3 km) S of town on Tran Phu Rd. **Tel** *(070) 383 0174.*
⏰ *8am–sunset daily.*

Cao Lanh ❻

Road Map B6. 100 miles (162 km) from HCMC. 🗺 140,000. 🚐 🛈 *Dong Thap Tourist, 2 Doc Binh Kieu St, (067) 385 5637.*

Although the town itself is not remarkable, the drive to Chau Doc *(see p100)* via Cao Lanh is pleasant. The **Dong Thap Museum**, which displays many of the traditional implements used by delta farmers and fishermen, including a large model of a boat and fish traps *(see p99)*, is a worthwhile stop.

The Soviet-style **War Memorial** is a big clam-shell structure, festooned with hammers, sickles, and flags. The cemetery at the memorial is filled with the graves of Vietcong soldiers. A mile southwest of town is **Nguyen Sinh Sac Tomb**, a memorial to Ho Chi Minh's father, surrounded by plaques stating his revolutionary credentials.

Statue in Dong Thap Museum

Environs

Stretching to the north of Cao Lanh, the rich swamplands of Dong Thap Muoi, or Plain of Reeds, are home to many birds. The **Tam Nong Bird Sanctuary**, 28 miles (45 km) northwest of town, once drew legions of bird-watchers who braved the long boat ride to see the red-headed cranes here. **Vuon Co Thap Muoi**, about 27 miles (44 km) northeast of Cao Lanh, is home to many white storks. Note that bird sanctuaries may close with no warning due to the periodic threat of bird flu *(see p283)*.

Southeast of Cao Lanh, the Rung Tram Forest once housed a hidden Vietcong base of resistance, **Xeo Quyt**. This restricted site can be reached by a 30-minute boat ride after seeking permission from the tourist office.

🏛 **Dong Thap Museum**
162 Nguyen Thai Hoc St.
Tel *(067) 385 1342.*
⏰ *7–11am, 1–4pm daily.*

🏴 **War Memorial**
Off Hwy 30 at the eastern edge of town. ⏰ *daily.*

BOATWRIGHTS OF THE MEKONG DELTA

The boatwright's craft is perhaps the oldest in the delta. Without it, there could be no transport, trade, and indeed, no homes for many. This skill is mastered by learning from family members who pass on age-old instructions, a few rules of thumb, and a few specialized tools. Often, when prized boats become decrepit, boatwrights dismantle them piece by piece to create exact replicas. Thus, any boat seen on the delta could be the descendant of one that looked identical nearly 500 years ago.

Boats awaiting completion at a dock

Vinh Long Boat Tour

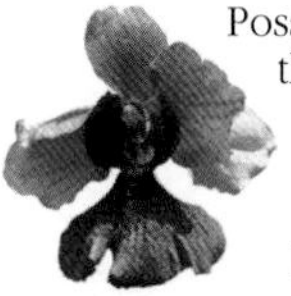

An orchid in bloom, Vinh Long

Possibly the best way of experiencing the timeless, bucolic character of the Mekong Delta is by taking a boat ride along the dense network of narrow canals around Vinh Long. Making its way through the small islands of An Binh and Binh Hoa Phuoc, the tour offers a close look at life on the river. Thatched houses sit amid luxuriant orchards and gardens interlaced with the sights and sounds of a colorful and bustling floating market.

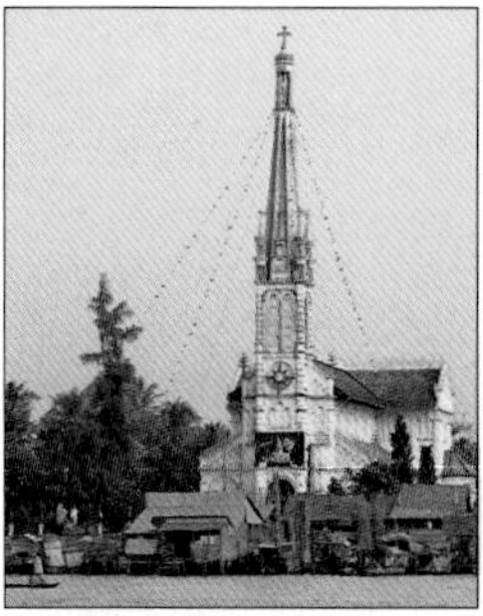

Church looming over the shore near Cai Be Floating Market

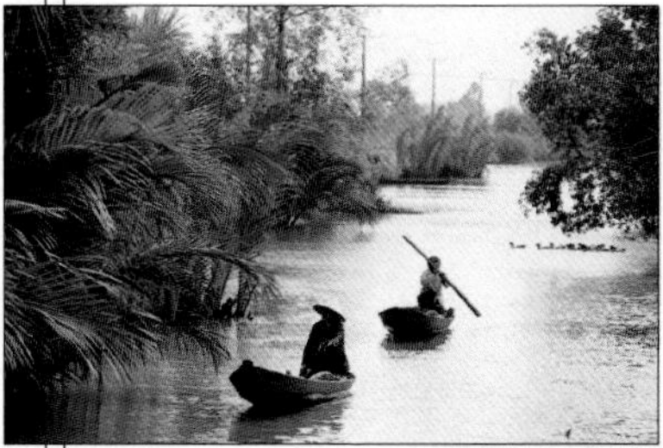

Vinh Long ①
Surrounded by a complex patchwork of canals and several islets, Vinh Long is almost an island itself. Situated on the banks of the Co Chien River, it is an ideal base for exploring the region.

Cai Be Floating Market ②
This lively market is packed with vendors selling a range of goods on boats. The best time to visit is in the early morning as the market disappears by noon. A small church on the nearby shore forms a scenic backdrop.

Dong Phu ③
A tiny village of farmers, orchardists, and boatmen, Dong Phu has barely change over the centuries.

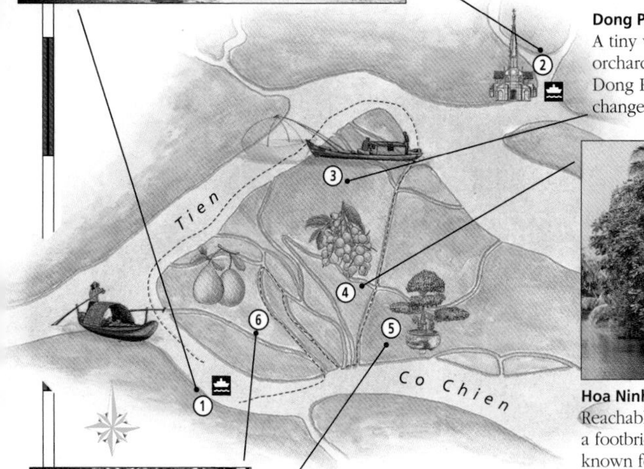
Tien
Co Chien
0 kilometers 3
0 miles 3

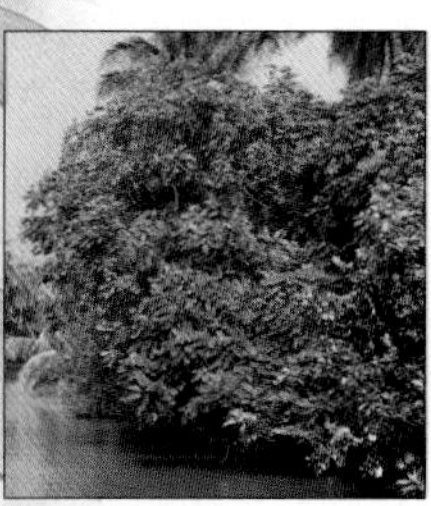

Hoa Ninh ④
Reachable only by boat and a footbridge, Hoa Ninh is known for its flower gardens filled with jasmine plants, as well as apricot, mango, and longan trees.

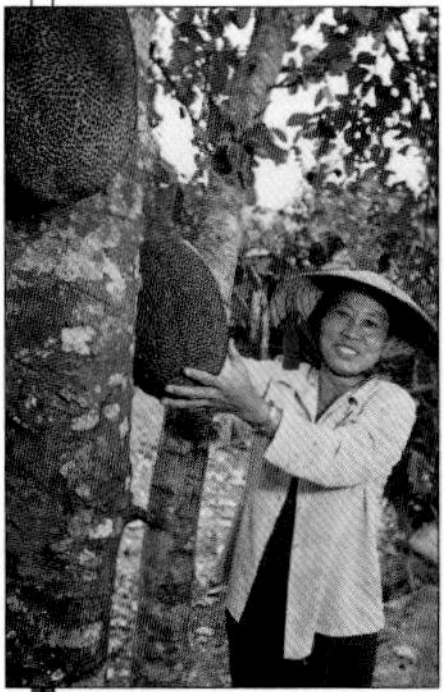

Binh Hoa Phuoc Village ⑤
Located on an island by the same name, this small village is known for its bonsai orchards, and offers cozy homestay facilities as well.

Fruit Orchards at An Binh ⑥
The thriving orchards on this island nurture an impressive variety of fruits, including longan, jackfruit, rose apple, and uglifruit, a citrus that tastes far better than it looks.

TIPS FOR TOURISTS

Length: *5 to 6 hours.*
Boat rentals: *Visitors can easily hire boats via Cuu Long Tourist, who have a monopoly on rentals. Private boats may be hired at the risk of incurring a fine.*
Stopping-off points: *Binh Hoa Phuoc Village is an ideal place to stop for a quick and tasty meal.*

Early morning fishing on the still waters of the Mekong Delta ▷

Can Tho ⑦

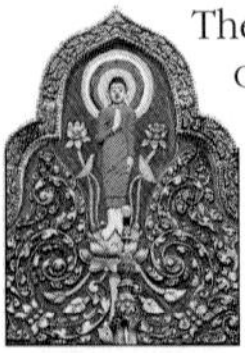

Munirangsyram Pagoda carving

The largest city on the delta, Can Tho is one of the most delightful destinations in the south. Bordering six provinces, it serves as a transportation hub for the region, as well as a major agricultural center, with rice milling as its main industry. The city is also an ideal base for day trips, especially to the floating markets – the highlight of a visit here. Within Can Tho, the Central Market, known for its fresh produce and river fish; the Can Tho Museum; and the Khmer Munirangsyaram Temple are all worth seeing.

⛩ Ong Pagoda

32 Hai Ba Trung St.
Tel *(0710) 382 3862.*

Devotees come to this small pagoda to pray before Than Tai, God of Fortune, and Quan Am, Goddess of Mercy. To ensure their prayers are heard, they often pay the temple calligrapher to pen their prayers onto scrolls and hang them on the wall. Several richly decorated urns burn constantly.

🏛 Can Tho Museum

6 Phan Dinh Phung St. ***Tel*** *(0710) 382 0955.* ◯ *8am–5pm daily.*

This excellent museum illustrates life in Vietnam. Exhibits include a traditional teahouse, a life-like tableau of a herbalist tending to a patient, and various artifacts.

⛩ Munirangsyaram Temple

36 Hoa Binh St. ***Tel*** *(0710) 381 6022.*
◯ *8am–5pm daily.*

An Angkor-like tower rises over this Khmer Theravada Buddhist temple. Inside, Doric columns blend beautifully with Asian features, such as seated Buddhas and ceramic lotuses.

Floating Markets

Can Tho is central to at least three floating markets, all providing a glimpse into a unique commercial culture. Traders paddle from boat to boat, selling a variety of goods amid a traffic jam of sampans.

The morning market of **Cai Rang** is the closest and largest, located just 4 miles (7 km) southwest of the city. A bridge nearby offers great views, but nothing compares to exploring the market by boat. A farther 9 miles (14 km) west, **Phong Dien** market possesses an endearing simplicity. Sampans can be rented for both these markets from the riverfront off Hai Ba Trung Street or from local tour operators. With its brightly-painted boats, **Phung Hiep** is the smallest market and is located about 20 miles (32 km) south of town. It is best to go there by road and rent a boat upon arrival.

VISITORS' CHECKLIST

Road Map B6. 105 miles (169 km) SW of HCMC. 👥 *335,000.* ✈ *10 km S.* 🚌 ⛴ ℹ *Can Tho Tourist, 20 Hai Ba Trung St, (0710) 382 1852.* 🏦 🎉 *Binh Thuy Temple Festival (Jan, May).*

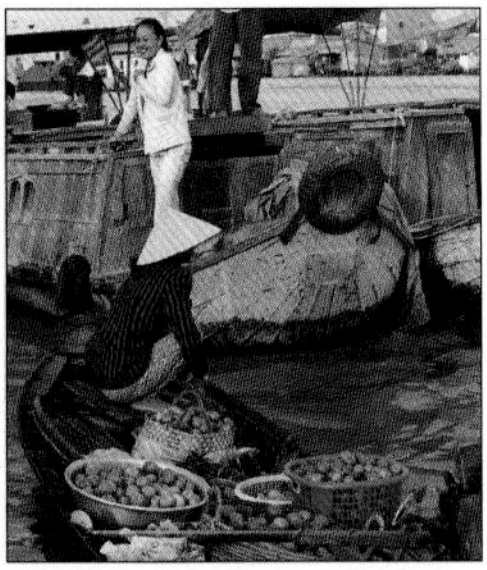

Fresh vegetables for sale at the Cai Rang morning market

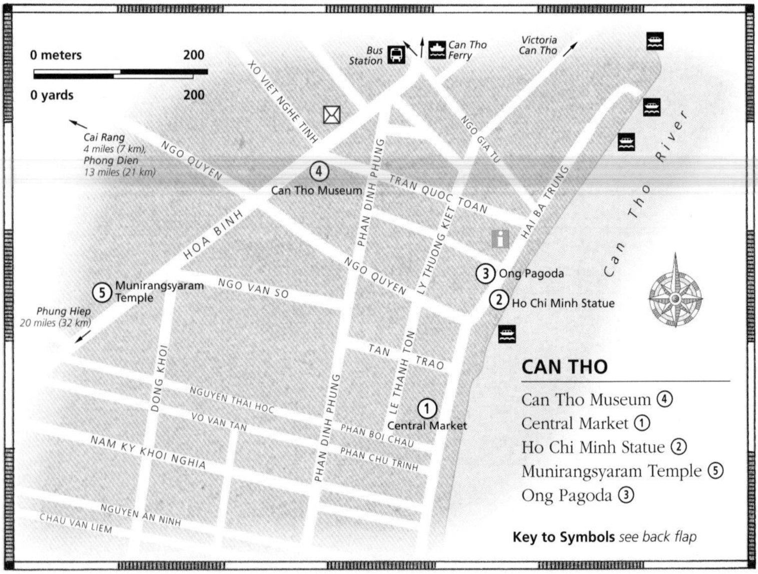
0 meters 200
0 yards 200
Bus Station
Can Tho Ferry
Victoria Can Tho
Cai Rang 4 miles (7 km), Phong Dien 13 miles (21 km)
Phung Hiep 20 miles (32 km)
XO VIET NGHE TINH
NGO QUYEN
NGO GIA TU
PHAN DINH PHUNG
TRAN QUOC TOAN
HAI BA TRUNG
Can Tho River
HOA BINH
LY THUONG KIET
NGO VAN SO
TAN TRAO
LE THANH TON
DONG KHOI
NGUYEN THAI HOC
VO VAN TAN
PHAN BOI CHAU
PHAN CHU TRINH
NAM KY KHOI NGHIA
NGUYEN AN NINH
CHAU VAN LIEM
④ Can Tho Museum
⑤ Munirangsyaram Temple
③ Ong Pagoda
② Ho Chi Minh Statue
① Central Market
CAN THO
Can Tho Museum ④
Central Market ①
Ho Chi Minh Statue ②
Munirangsyaram Temple ⑤
Ong Pagoda ③
Key to Symbols see back flap

Rice Cultivation

Rice is Vietnam's primary food staple and the country's most vital cash crop. The rice industry employs almost 80 percent of the country's population in one way or another. The majority of rice production in Vietnam takes place in the Mekong Delta, the fertile soil of which has contributed significantly to making Vietnam the world's third-largest exporter of rice. A significant portion of this enormous productivity is the result of hard manual and animal labor. Fields are usually ploughed not by tractors but by water buffaloes, and irrigation is managed not by pumps, but by teams of people wielding two-handed buckets or watertight woven baskets.

Rice farmer with harvest grain

Paddy farming is always a cooperative enterprise, facilitated by several members of the family.

Irrigation canals are also used to mark property lines.

Rich delta soil is critical to the abundance of the harvest.

TRANSPLANTATION

The seeds for paddy rice are germinated and allowed to shoot outside the fields, often in trays or pots. When the shoots are a few inches high, they are brought to the paddy field for final planting.

Baskets carry seedlings for transplantation.

Seedlings ready to be transplanted.

Harvesting *is done by stoop labor, usually by men and women using hand sickles.*

After threshing, winnowing, *and separating the grain from the sheaves and chaff, the rice is laid out on mats to dry in the sun.*

Although some rice is transported *by ox-cart and truck, water remains the most traditional as well as the most efficient means in the Mekong of getting the rice to market.*

Woman preparing rice paper at a factory

Mixture of water and rice powder

Cloth stretched over a boiler

Rice paper drying on bamboo mats

THE RICE WRAPPER FACTORY

Rice wrappers *(banh trang)* are ubiquitous in Vietnamese cuisine. Almost any food can be wrapped in one and eaten like a sandwich or burrito. The wrappers are prepared in various kitchens and factories throughout the country. A thin batter of rice flour and water is poured over a cloth stretched over a pot of simmering water. The rising steam cooks the mixture in a matter of seconds; the wrapper is then laid on a woven bamboo mat or tray to dry, giving *banh trang* its distinctive crisscross pattern.

Wildly colorful collection of painted clay animals at Chua Dat Set, Soc Trang

Soc Trang ❽

Road Map B6. 39 miles (63 km) SE of Can Tho. 🏠 *112,000.* ⓐ ℹ️ *Soc Trang Tourist, 131 Nguyen Chi Thanh St, (079) 382 1489.* 🎭 *Oc Om Boc Festival (mid-Nov).*

This lively town is famous for its festivals and religious sites. Once part of the Angkor Empire, the entire province is home to 90 Khmer, 47 Chinese, and 30 Vietnamese pagodas, many of which are in Soc Trang itself. Of the ten annual festivals held here, the largest is the carnivalesque Khmer festival, Oc Om Boc *(see p33)*, with its famous boat racing. Set in beautiful grounds, **Khleang Pagoda** is the best-known Khmer temple in town. The mandarin-orange building is topped by a peaked roof with gables, and festooned with colorful gar-goyels. The sanctuary is lit by lotus-motif chandeliers, and a gilt Buddha dominates the altar.

Altar statue, Khleang Pagoda

About 356 ft (200m) east of the Khleang Pagoda, is **Chua Dat Set**, or Clay Pagoda, populated by fantastic clay figures sculpted by Ngo Kim Tong, also known as the Clay Monk, between 1930 and 1970. Standing guard at the door is an almost life-size statue of an elephant, while a golden lion, giant phoenix, and numerous other beasts contribute to the menagerie of imagery inside the pagoda.

The **Khmer Museum** doubles as a cultural center at times, hosting traditional dance and music recitals. The exhibits at the museum include ethnic clothing, crockery, statues, and even a couple of boats. The building itself is a peculiar blend of Khmer and French-colonial architecture.

Environs

Earning its nickname from the legions of fruit bats living in its dense groves, **Chua Doi** or Bat Pagoda is 2 miles (4 km) west of town on Le Hong Phong Street. At sunset, the bats take flight, filling the sky like a great screeching cloud. The pagoda's other highlights are its friendly monks, their five-toed pigs, and the vibrant murals inside showing scenes from the Buddha's life. Farther west, 9 miles (14 km) from town, **Xa Lon Pagoda** began about 200 years ago as a thatched Khmer structure, though it was almost destroyed in 1968 by the intense combat of that year *(see pp44–5)*. Today a stout building, with exquisite exterior tilework, it serves as a pagoda as well as a Sanskrit school. Also worth a stop is the handsome, Khmer-style **Im Som Rong Pagoda**, located about one mile (1.6 km) east of Soc Trang.

🏛 **Khmer Museum**
23 Nguyen Chi Thanh St.
Tel (078) 382 2983. ⏰ 7:30–11am, 1:30–5pm Wed–Tue. 🔒 Thu.

Bac Lieu ❾

Road Map B6. 174 miles (280 km) from HCMC; 31 miles (50 km) SW of Soc Trang. 🏠 *131,000.* ⓐ ℹ️ *Bac Lieu Tourist, 2 Hoang Van Thu St, (781) 382 4273.*

This small town is primarily an agricultural center, with a major part of its revenue coming from the shrimp and salt farms located along the coast. Most visitors use the place as a base to explore the region, including the nearby sanctuary. However, there are some interesting pagodas worth visiting as well. The town also features some fine French-colonial buildings, such as the impressive **Cong Tu Bac Lieu**, once the palace of the prince of Bac Lieu Province. Now a hotel, the building has been restored to its 1930s splendor, taking visitors on a journey back in time.

Environs

The **Bac Lieu Bird Sanctuary** is about 3 miles (5 km) south of town. Its mangrove forests are home to a splendid variety of species. More than 50 types of birds either reside here or use it as a way station in their annual migrations. There are large flocks of white herons, which are the main attraction for most visitors. Unfortunately, other than some primitive toilets, the sanctuary lacks facilities. This has not deterred bird-watchers in the past, but the periodic threat of bird flu, resulting in fewer visitors in recent years.

Entrance to the French-provincial style Cong Tu Bac Lieu

Flora, Fauna, and Birds of the Mekong Delta

The rich soil and lush green habitat of the Mekong Delta is home to a wide variety of plant and animal species, with new ones still being discovered. Dense mangrove swamps and tropical forests cover a large portion of the delta, while a range of fruits, such as mangos, papayas, and bananas, grow in abundance. Several types of orchids, both wild

Banana flower, often used in salads

and cultivated, are common as well. The region is also part of the East Asia Flyover and lies along the path of many migratory birds, including species of storks and cranes, especially the rare red-headed crane, also known as the Sarus crane. The delta's fauna includes wild boar, monkeys, and deer, as well as numerous snake and other reptile species.

COCONUT TREES LINING DELTA WATERS

Among the most common and bountiful trees in the delta, coconut palms are an integral part of the region's economy. The fruit and its oil is used extensively in Vietnamese food, while the trees' long and strong leaves and branches are ideal for making roofs that often last for years.

Several colorful orchids *are abundant in the delta. So many species exist that new ones are always being found. Botanists struggle to catalog them all.*

Coconuts are eaten both green and ripe. The flesh is soft when green, and crunchy when ripe.

Delta waters carry rich alluvia from as far as Tibet, and support a diverse aquatic life.

Green Bee-eaters, *brightly colored birds with black beaks, nest in tunnels that they dig in the soft soil of the riverbank. They eat mostly bees and remove the sting by hitting the insect on hard ground.*

The painted stork, *a graceful and slender bird, is one of several rare varieties of stork that find safe refuge in the Mekong Delta's many bird sanctuaries.*

Many species of snake *reside in the Mekong Delta, but the best known are the king cobra and giant python. They are sometimes raised on farms but often taken from the wild for consumption.*

The crab-eating macaque, *or Macaca fascicularis, eats fruits and plants in addition to crabs and insects. These monkeys have black fur at birth, which eventually changes to grey or reddish brown.*

Crocodiles *can be seen in the wild but, like snakes, they are farmed abundantly. This practice saves them from being hunted to extinction.*

Con Dao Islands

Road Map B6. 62 miles (100 km) off the southern tip of Vietnam.
🏃 5,000. ✈ from HCMC, helicopter from Vung Tao. ⛴ from Vung Tao. ℹ Con Dao Transport, 430 Truong Cong Dinh St, (064) 385 9089.

A cluster of 16 islands, Con Dao may be remote but, with its remarkable forests, wildlife, and beaches, it is one of the most astounding destinations in Vietnam.

Declared a nature preserve in 1993, **Con Dao National Park** covers a massive portion of the archipelago, stretching across 154 sq miles (400 sq km). About two-thirds of it is on land, while the rest, including the beautiful coral reefs, is water. These seas are home to more than 1,300 aquatic species, such as sea turtles, dolphins, and dugongs, a manatee-like mammal (see p190). Visits to the nesting sites of the endangered green turtle can also be arranged. On land are 135 species of fauna and 882 types of flora, including orchids unique to the island. The only home of the pied imperial pigeon, this park is a bird-watcher's dream.

The largest and only permanently inhabited island in the group is **Con Son**, often referred to as "Bear Island" because of its shape. About 6 miles (10 km) in length, and with well-marked trails, the entire island can be walked in a day.

A freshwater turtle

These idyllic surroundings, however, hold the remnants of a sad past. Con Son became a devil's island of sorts after the French built the **Phu Hai Prison** here in 1862. Political dissidents and revolutionaries were imprisoned under cruel conditions, often kept shackled to the floor. A re-creation of this is displayed in one of the cell blocks. In 1954, Phu Hai was handed over to the South Vietnamese, who carried on the tradition. The most inhumane cells were "tiger cages." These were tiny holes in the ground with steel bars for roofs. Vietcong operatives were routinely brought here.

Children playing on a beach at sunset, Con Dao Islands

The **Revolutionary Museum** offers a tour of the complex, and also has displays on the treatment of political prisoners by the French and the South Vietnamese government.

For more cheerful outings, the islands boast many spectacular beaches. Diving is also possible offshore. **Dat Doc** on Con Son is the most popular beach, and dugong sightings have been reported here in recent years. Also on Con Dao is the isolated **Nho Beach**. To see the brown booby, a rare bird, visit **Hon Trung**, an hour's boat ride from Con Son. The beach on **Tre Nho Island** is a great picnic spot. The best time to visit Con Dao is between March and June; diving season runs June–September.

🏛 **Revolutionary Museum**
Near Saigon Con Dao Hotel, 18 Ton Duc Thang St, Con Son.
🕐 7–11am, 1:30–5pm Mon–Fri.

Rach Gia ⑪

Road Map B6. 72 miles (116 km) from Can Tho. 🏃 175,000.
✈ from HCMC. ℹ Kien Giang Tourist, 5 Le Loi St, (077) 386 2081.

A prosperous port town, Rach Gia boasts many religious buildings such as the charming **Pho Minh Pagoda**, which houses an order of mendicant nuns. Its Twin Buddhas, one in Thai style and the other

Vietnamese, sit companionably in the sanctuary. The sprawling 200-year-old **Phat Lon Pagoda** has a unique sanctuary, surrounded by many small altars. The main altar holds images of the Buddha in Khmer regalia. The pagoda has its own crematoria for the disposal of its monks' bodies, and tombs for those chosen for veneration.

The colorful **Nguyen Trung Truc Temple** is dedicated to a revered national hero who sacrificed his life in the struggle against the French in the mid-19th century. He was executed in Rach Gia's market square on October 27, 1868.

In addition to the pagodas, the town also hosts the **Rach Gia Museum**, featuring an interesting collection of Oc Eo artifacts and pottery.

Environs

The ancient city of **Oc Eo** was a major trading center of the Indianized Funan Empire (see p39), which once extended from southern Vietnam to as far as Malaysia. Artifacts recovered from an archaeological site located 6 miles (10 km) outside Rach Gia indicate that Funan's traders had contact with many nations of the region from the 1st to the 5th century AD. A Roman coin has also been unearthed in this area. Although there is not much to see at the excavation site, prior permission is required to visit it.

🏛 **Rach Gia Museum**
27 Nguyen Van Troi St.
Tel (077) 386 3727.
🕐 7–11am, 1:30–5pm Sat–Wed.

Houses in the Mekong Delta

Home to thousands of people who live not only beside the river, but on it, the Mekong Delta is known for two of Vietnam's most distinct forms of houses – stilt and floating. While stilt houses line the steep banks, villages of floating homes occupy the river, completely independent of land. Resting on tall

One of the grander stilt homes

bamboo poles, the stilt houses are firmly anchored to the ground. Floating houses, in contrast, sail adrift on pontoons or empty oil drums. Both types of houses are often connected to the shore by a monkey bridge – a crossing made of wooden poles tightly tied together, with the barest of footholds.

STILT HOUSES

Built to accommodate the annual Mekong River floods, stilt houses were traditionally made of wood, but are now increasingly built of corrugated iron. They usually comprise one or two spacious rooms, and open out onto a deck. At low tide, the house is accessed via a ladder from the floor to the bank, while at high tide, boats sail right up to the door.

Monkey bridges, *arched wooden structures, rarely feature any kind of safety railing. They are rickety, but delta people have used them for centuries.*

Bamboo stilts can be up to 20 ft (6 m) tall. Remarkably sturdy and flexible, they can withstand the swiftest currents.

Family sampan tied beside a stilt home.

Thatched roofs *were the norm in the delta, but corrugated metal is preferred now. In addition to being cooling, it lasts much longer.*

Floating villages, *complete with homes, shops, and even industrial buildings, can cover several acres of the Mekong's waters. Without permanent anchors, it is easy to move house when opportunities are better downstream.*

FISH TRAPS

Feeding fish in fish trap

A unique feature in many floating houses is the fish trap – a covered hole in the floor, under which is suspended a large net made of woven strips of bamboo or steel mesh. People of the delta have used this method to trap fish for generations, and today, utilizing scientific techniques, have begun using these traps as incubators for fertilized fish eggs. Fish caught in traps are kept until they are full grown and ready to eat.

Daily activities on the floating houses *include everything from fishing and shopping to growing herbs and raising hens. Residents live their entire lives on the water, rarely setting foot on land.*

Chau Doc ⓬

Road Map B6. 152 miles (245 km) SW of HCMC; 74 miles (119 km) NW of Can Tho. 🏙 110,000. 🚌 from HCMC, Can Tho, and Ha Tien. 🚤 from Ha Tien and Phnom Penh, Cambodia. 🚤 🚗

Life and commerce in Chau Doc, a bustling border town, centers on the water. Many people live not only by the river in stilt houses, but on it in floating houses *(see p99)*. The town's exceptionally busy market is also located along the riverfront. During a period of several centuries, control over Chau Doc has passed between the Funanese, Cham, Khmer, and Vietnamese. It is no surprise that this is one of the most ethnically and religiously diverse towns in the region. It is also home to the Hoa Hao sect, an indigenous Buddhist order founded in the 1930s, and based on the rejection of religious practice and the intercession of priests. The small community of Cham Muslims residing in Chau Doc worship at the green **Mubarak Mosque** across the Hau Giang River and the larger **Chau Giang Mosque**. Neither has a proper address, but boatmen know how to reach them.

In the town center, the **Bo De Dao Trang Plaza** is dominated by a statue of Quan Am, Goddess of Mercy, standing in a gazebo. Behind the deity, a statue of the Buddha sits under a tree facing a small pagoda.

Close by, **Chau Phu Temple** is dedicated to a Nguyen Lord, and also serves as a tribute to the dead, with many memorial tablets amid colorful artworks.

Environs
A sacred site for hundreds of years, **Sam Mountain** lies 4 miles (6 km) southwest of town. Its slopes are covered with shrines, grottos, pagodas, and ancient tombs. At the northern base, lies the **Phat Thay Tay An Temple**, packed with statues of elephants and monsters – all painted in lurid colors. Many women sell birds for release at the entrance. A statue of a monk guards the inner sanctum. Close by is **Chua Xu**, dedicated to a Vietnamese heroine, Lady Xu. Her statue is bathed and clad in finery every May. The view from the summit is most stunning, with the rice fields of Vietnam to the east and the plains of Cambodia on its west side.

Bronze statue, Phat Thay Tay An Pagoda, Chau Doc

Ha Tien ⓭

Road Map B6. 190 miles (306 km) W of HCMC; 57 miles (92 km) NW of Rach Gia. 🏙 95,000. 🚌 from HCMC and Chau Doc. 🚤 from Chau Doc and Phu Quoc Island. 🚗 ℹ *Kien Giang Tourist, 14 Phuong Thanh St, (077) 385 1929.*

Situated close to the idyllic shores of the Gulf of Thailand, and surrounded by limestone promontories, Ha Tien is one of the more attractive towns in the delta. Its charming focus is the US-army built

Statue of Quan Am at the entrance of Thach Dong Temple, Ha Tien

pontoon bridge, which is used by pedestrians and cyclists, and divides the town between the Dong Ho (East Lake) and the To Chau River. Ha Tien's tranquility belies its history. It became part of Vietnam after a battle with the Thai in 1708. The hero of the war, Mac Cuu, was laid to rest with his family in the **Mac Tombs**, which are located on a hillside, Nui Lang, just west of town. On the northern side of Nui Lang, the **Phu Dung Pagoda** contains elegant 18th-century tombs. Its sanctuary features exquisite high-relief panels.

Environs
Sitting snugly in a system of caves, halfway up a karst formation *(see p182)* about 2 miles (4 km) west of town, **Thach Dong Temple** goes all the way through the limestone. There are altars everywhere, but the religious focus is on the stone pagoda in the largest cave. A statue of Quan Am stands near its entrance, and at a short distance is the **Stele of Hatred**. This monument is dedicated to the 130 people killed here by the Khmer Rouge in 1978.

About 18 miles (30 km) to the southeast of Ha Tien lies the secluded beach resort of **Hon Chong**. At the southern end of the beach is the Hang Pagoda, a grotto with stalactites that resonate like organ pipes when struck. Offshore, Nghe Island has many caves and shrines. About an hour by boat, it is ideal for a day trip.

Floating houses lining the riverfront in Chau Doc

For hotels and restaurants in this region see pp235–6 and pp252–3

Phu Quoc Island ⑭

Road Map A6. 28 miles (45 km)
W of Ha Tien. 🏠 *84,000.* ✈
from HCMC. 🚢 *from Rach Gia
and Ha Tien.*

Claimed by Cambodia, this
kite-shaped island played a
key role in Vietnam's history
as the base for French missionary Pigneau de Behaine, who
sheltered the future emperor,
Gia Long, during the Tay Son
Rebellion *(see p41)*. Around
31 miles (50 km) long and just
12 miles (20 km) wide, Phu
Quoc Island is still relatively
undeveloped, with most tourist facilities in its main town,
Duong Dong. More like a big
village, it features a lighthouse,
central market, and fish factory,
which also offers tours.

Almost 70 percent of the
main island is occupied by
the **Phu Quoc National Park**.
Established in 2001, it is covered with tropical forest. At
present, there are few hiking
trails, but the pools at the
park's southern end are scenic
and good for swimming.

Halfway between Duong
Dong town and the park is the
Khu Tuong black pepper plantation. The Vietnamese staple,
nuoc mam (fish sauce) is also
produced here, and connoisseurs can attest to its quality.

Phu Quoc is also blessed
with many unspoiled beaches,
known in Vietnamese as *bai*.

Bai Truong, along
the southwest
shore, is the best
known. Lined by
many hotels, it offers
wonderful sunset views.
To its north is the rugged
Bai Ong Lang, with tiny
resorts nestled in its coves.
Just offshore is **Hon Doi Moi**
with a coral reef teeming with
marine life. It is also great for
snorkeling and diving. The
An Thoi island group at the
southern tip also has a coral
reef. The southeastern shore
hosts the barely developed but
stunning white-sand stretches
of **Bai Sao** and **Bai Dam**. Scuba
gear, island trips, and fishing
equipment can be arranged
in Duong Dong. Phu Quoc is
also home to a fascinating cultured pearl farm and gallery
on its southwest coast.

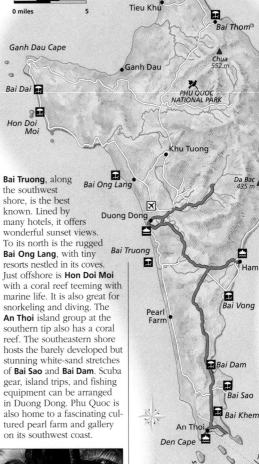

The beautiful Truong Beach, with its swaying palms and wooden boats

Key to Symbols *see back flap*

KEY

▬▬	Main road
═══	Minor road
-----	Ferry route

SOUTH CENTRAL VIETNAM

Covering much of the ancient Kingdom of Champa, South Central Vietnam possesses a densely populated coast scattered with fishing towns and quiet beaches, as well as a substantial hinterland inhabited by indigenous minorities. The resort towns of Nha Trang and Phan Thiet and the honeymoon hill station of Dalat are firmly on the tourist itinerary, but much of this region is relatively unexplored.

Under the steady influence of seaborne trade, Champa emerged during the 4th century AD as a powerful kingdom. At its peak, Champa extended from the Ngang Pass in the north to present-day Ho Chi Minh City and the Mekong River Delta in the south. From AD 1000, its power dwindled and one principality after another was annexed by the Vietnamese. By the late 18th century, only tiny Panduranga, extending from Phan Rang to Phan Thiet, held out, but it too fell in 1832. Today, Champa's remains, in the form of towers and temple complexes, cluster in the hills of the South Central region. People of the Cham minority still live in the old region of Panduranga, where the Kate Festival is celebrated with great ceremony in early fall.

The beaches of lower South Central Vietnam are some of the finest in the country. At Phan Thiet, an 11-mile (18-km) white-sand beach extends to the small fishing village of Mui Ne, Vietnam's fastest-growing resort. Up the coast, the seaside city of Nha Trang is justly celebrated for its seafood and its archipelago of offshore islands, which offer all manner of watersports. More beaches are a day-trip away and for those heading unhurriedly up the coast, tiny fishing towns and lovely, often deserted, stretches of sand beckon.

Inland, the main resort town is Dalat, a French-built hill station and a cool delight to visit. Deeper into the highlands, the towns of Buon Ma Thuot and Kontum are surrounded by villages populated by the Bahnar, Ede, and Jarai minorities. Some of these hamlets still feature traditional architecture, such as the extraordinary longhouses of the Bahnar, *nha rong*.

The region was badly scarred by the Vietnam War, and at Son My a moving memorial stands in remembrance of one of the worst atrocities of the time, the My Lai Massacre *(see p119)*.

Stepped vegetable fields on the fertile slopes around Dalat

◁ Delivering supplies to the distinctive red and blue fishing fleet of Nha Trang *(see pp108–10)*

Exploring South Central Vietnam

With its numerous beaches and easy accessibility, the long coastal strip of South Central Vietnam sees many more visitors than the interior, and the resorts of Mui Ne and Nha Trang make good bases from which to explore much of the southern coast. Travelers tend to hurry past the fishing towns in the north of the region on their way to Central Vietnam, although attractive beaches and ancient Cham temples make them worthwhile stopovers.

Dalat is the most pleasant place to stay in the Central Highlands. Up on the plateau, Buon Ma Thuot makes a decent base for visiting the country's largest wildlife preserve, Yok Don National Park, as well as outlying minority communities. Heading north, toward friendly Kontum, roads are less traveled, and access, due to unrest among some minority groups, is still limited.

Dambri Falls, the region's most beautiful waterfall

The notably well-preserved Cham temple-towers of Po Klong Garai, Phan Rang–Thap Cham

SIGHTS AT A GLANCE

Towns and Cities

Buon Ma Thuot **8**
Dalat **6**
Kontum **10**
Nha Trang **5**
Phan Rang–Thap Cham **4**
Phan Thiet **2**
Quang Ngai **13**
Quy Nhon **11**
Sa Huynh **12**

Beaches

Mui Ne Beach **3**

Areas of Natural Beauty

Lak Lake **7**
Ta Cu Mountain **1**

National Parks

Yok Don National Park **9**

GETTING AROUND

Traveling through the region along coastal Highway 1 or via the Ho Chi Minh City–Hanoi rail link is straightforward. Bus services ply the coast, as do a plethora of minibuses organized by hotels and travel agents. Dalat is also easy to access, and Route 27 from the coast is spectacular. Exploring the Central Highlands takes more effort, and although minibuses do exist, a car and driver (or motorcycle) might serve better. Route 14 from Ho Chi Minh City has seen upgrades, although north of Buon Ma Thuot the road is winding and steep.

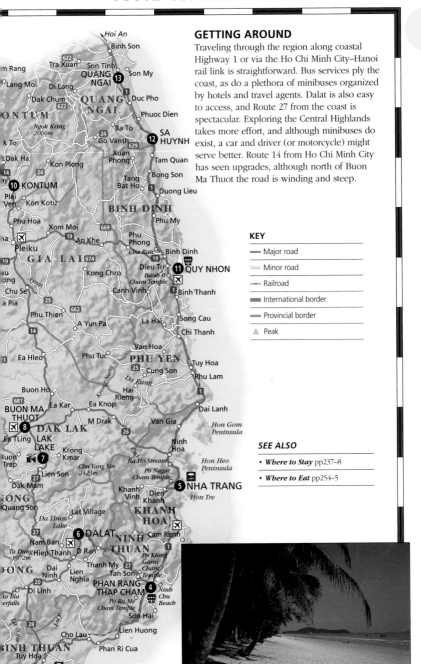

KEY

── Major road

═══ Minor road

┄┄ Railroad

▬▬ International border

▭▭ Provincial border

△ Peak

SEE ALSO

• **Where to Stay** pp237–8

• **Where to Eat** pp254–5

Coracle on the white-sand beach of Doc Let, north of Nha Trang on the Hon Heo Peninsula

The serene Reclining Buddha near the peak of Ta Cu Mountain

Ta Cu Mountain ❶

Road Map C6. 18 miles (30 km) S
of Phan Thiet. 🚌 **Pagodas & park**
ℹ️ (062) 386 7484. 🎫 🍴 📷 🚻

The scenery around Ta Cu
is flat and arid, and the
mountain, although only
2,100 ft (650 m), affords spectacular views of the coast on
clear days. **Linh Son Truong
Tho Pagoda** and **Linh Son
Long Doan Pagoda**, both
established in the mid-19th
century, are important sites
for the many Buddhist
pilgrims who come to this
holy mountain. However,
the main attraction for most
visitors – nearly all of whom
are Vietnamese – is a white
Reclining Buddha, 160-ft
(49-m) long and claimed
by the Ta Cu custodians to
be the largest in Vietnam.
It was sculpted in 1962.

A cable car, located near
Highway 1, is available to
carry visitors up the mountain
to the Reclining Buddha.
Alternatively, it takes two hours
to reach the site on foot.

Phan Thiet ❷

Road Map C6. 125 miles
(200 km) E of Ho Chi Minh City.
🚶 175,000. 🚌 🚐 🚆 ℹ️ Fish
Egg Tree Tours, (090) 443 4895.
🎭 Nghinh Ong Festival (Aug–Sep),
once every two years.

This pleasant seaside town
features an active fishing fleet
and a port extending along
both banks of the Ca Ty river.
For visitors staying at nearby
Mui Ne Beach, the town is
convenient for both shopping
and exploration.

Phan Thiet was once at
the heart of Panduranga, the
last semi-independent Cham
principality, which was finally
absorbed by the Nguyen
Emperor Minh Mang in 1832.
The town's Cham name is
Malithit, and there is still an
appreciable Cham element
among the local population.
Locally, it is chiefly celebrated
for its *nuoc mam* (fish sauce),
and aficionados dispute
whether the best sauce in
the country comes from
here or Phu Quoc Island
(see p101).

Environs
Just 4 miles (7 km) from the
center of Phan Thiet, on a hill
overlooking the town, stands
Thap Poshanu, the southernmost collection of Cham
religious buildings within the
former Kingdom of Champa.
The group consists of three
kalan, or sanctuary towers,
with supplementary structures
dating back as far as the
8th century AD, making them
some of the oldest Cham
archaeological remnants
in the country.

Mui Ne Beach ❸

Road Map C6. E of Phan Thiet.
🚌 🚐 ℹ️ (062) 374 8155.
www.muinebeach.net

A 12-mile (20-km) strip of
palm-shaded white sand,
Mui Ne Beach (Ham Tien)
curves from just east of Phan
Thiet to the small fishing
village of Mui Ne. The coast
is backed by two excellent
roads that run parallel to the
beach along its entire length.

By the end of the 1990s,
the beach had developed a
reputation among budget
travelers as a relaxed hideaway
within easy reach of Ho Chi
Minh City, but, as one of the
best beaches south of Nha
Trang, its growing reputation
has inevitably led to constant
and ever-increasing development. Almost the entire length
of beach is now overrun with
resorts and upmarket bars
and restaurants; the first high-
rise hotel was erected in 2009.
Today the area has become
an enclave for Russian
tourism. A number of resorts,
bars, and restaurants are

Mui Ne Beach's gargantuan rolling sand dunes

Russian-owned and street signs appear in Vietnamese, Russian, and English. Above the beach, at Sealinks, is a golf course and there are plans to construct several other courses here.

Activities at Mui Ne include swimming, sunbathing, and, between November and March, kite-boarding and windsurfing. The sea here is not suitable for diving, and there are no stunning offshore coral reefs.

About halfway along the road to Mui Ne Village, **Suoi Tien** or Fairy Stream flows through the sand dunes to the sea. Still farther east, where the road leaves the beach and curves inland, a track to the north leads to Mui Ne's celebrated sand dunes, where children rent out tray-like bobsleighs for "sand sledding."

At **Mui Ne Village**, maturing vats of quality *nuoc mam* (fish sauce) fill backyards and gardens. The fishing fleet land their catch in the early mornings, and it is fascinating to wander along the beach by the village, watching the fish merchants from Phan Thiet and farther afield park their pickups on the sand and bargain with the fishermen for the freshly landed catch. Unsurprisingly, the whole area has great seafood.

Phan Rang–Thap Cham ❹

Road Map C5. 65 miles (105 km) S of Nha Trang. ✈ *150,000.* 🚌 🚆
ℹ *45 Bac Ai St, (068) 388 8116.*
🎎 *Kate Festival (Sep or Oct).*

A twin city located on an arid coastal strip known for its grape and Cham textile production, Phan Rang–Thap Cham is an important road junction linking the coastal provinces with Dalat and the Central Highlands. Thap Cham means Cham Towers, and three of the country's best-preserved Cham religious complexes are situated here.

Well-preserved tower at Po Klong Garai temple complex

Mukha lingam, Po Klong Garai

Po Klong Garai is a group of three brick temple-towers in remarkably good preservation. Located on a hilltop, the temple was built in the 13th century by King Jaya Simhavarman III, and inscriptions in Cham script are clearly engraved on the entranceway. The temple has a *mukha lingam* with the face of King Jaya Simhavarman III in the main *kalan* or sanctuary. A statue of the bull Nandi, Shiva's mount, receives regular offerings. During the Kate Festival each autumn, traditional Cham musical ensembles play here, and folk dancers perform in the temple precincts.

Po Ro Me was built in the 17th century when the Cham principality of Panduranga was in decline. It too sits on a hilltop, but is more difficult to access than Po Klong Garai and a motorbike is recommended to reach the temple. The tower is dedicated to King Po Ro Me, and there is an image of him on a *mukha lingam* inside.

A third temple complex, Hoa Lai, is located a few miles north of Phan Rang.

Pleasant **Ninh Chu Beach**, shaded by casuarina trees, is located 4 miles (6 km) east of Phan Rang. During his regime (1967–75), it was reserved for President Nguyen Van Thieu and his cronies.

🛕 **Po Klong Garai**
Route 27, 4 miles (6 km) W of Thap Cham. **Tel** *(068) 388 8116.*
⏰ *sunrise–sunset daily.* 🎟

🛕 **Po Ro Me**
9 miles (14 km) S of Thap Cham.
⏰ *sunrise–sunset daily.*

Ancient Cham inscriptions on the entrance pillars at Po Klong Garai

Nha Trang

A bustling city and major fishing port, Nha Trang is also Vietnam's primary beach resort, with numerous comfortable hotels and a wide range of restaurants specializing in seafood. An elegant promenade by the seafront overlooks the Municipal Beach, which is usually packed with travelers sunbathing and vendors selling their wares. The busy Central Market, Cho Dam, is at the city's heart, while most tourist facilities, and many hotels and bars, are farther south. Outside town are the hot springs of Thap Ba and Ba Ho. Catch a ferry from Cau Da to one of the islands in the bay, where the waters are ideal for snorkeling.

Shiva, Po Nagar Cham Towers

Coracles pulled up on Nha Trang's Municipal Beach

🏠 Long Son Pagoda

No 18, 23 Thang 10 St. **Tel** *(058) 381 6919.* ◯ *7:30am–8pm daily.*
The most revered pagoda in Nha Trang, Long Son is located on the summit of Trai Thuy Hill to the south of the city. It was destroyed by a typhoon at the beginning of the 20th century and restored several times, most recently in 1940. It is now dedicated to the memory of the numerous Buddhist monks who were killed during or died protesting against the repressive regime of South Vietnam's President Ngo Dinh Diem (1955–63). Today, it remains a functioning pagoda, with monks in residence.

The pagoda is distinctly Sino-Vietnamese in style and is decorated with elaborate dragons and ceramic tiles. The main sanctuary building is dominated by a giant white sculpture of the Buddha, dating from the 1960s and a full 46 ft (14 m) tall. Seated behind the temple at the top of the hill, the sculpture is reached via 120 steep steps. From here, there are panoramic views over Nha Trang and the neighboring countryside. Another large white Buddha, this time reclining, is located halfway up the steps on the right. It was sculpted by an artisan from Thailand in 2003.

Giant Buddha, Long Son Pagoda

🏛 Nha Trang Cathedral

31 Thai Nguyen St. **Tel** *(058) 382 3335. Services held daily.*
The seat of the Catholic Diocese of Nha Trang, this church was constructed in provincial French Gothic style in the 1930s. The building is dominated by a tall, square clock tower surmounted by a large crucifix. Stained-glass windows look onto colonnaded cloisters running the length of each side of the building. The three cathedral bells, cast in France in 1786, are still in fine working order. The former cemetery of the cathedral has been leveled and the land used to extend the city's train station.

🏖 Municipal Beach

Nha Trang has a fine beach, almost 4 miles (7 km) long and sheltered by headlands to its north and south. Tran Phu Street follows the beach for its entire length, providing a fine promenade with great views across the bay. The entire esplanade area is undergoing rapid development, with new hotels and restaurants on the inland side, and numerous cafés and small food stalls between the road and the sea.

🏛 Alexandre Yersin Museum

10D Tran Phu St. **Tel** *(058) 382 2355.* ◯ *8–11am, 2–4:30pm daily.* 🎟
The Swiss physician Alexandre Yersin (1863–1943) moved to Vietnam in 1891 after studying in Paris under the renowned microbiologist Louis Pasteur. He quickly became fluent in Vietnamese and was involved in the founding of Dalat as a hill station in 1893. Yersin introduced cinchona trees to Vietnam for the production of the anti-malarial drug quinine. His most significant

The cement-brick belfry of Nha Trang Cathedral

For hotels and restaurants in this region see pp237–8 and pp254–5

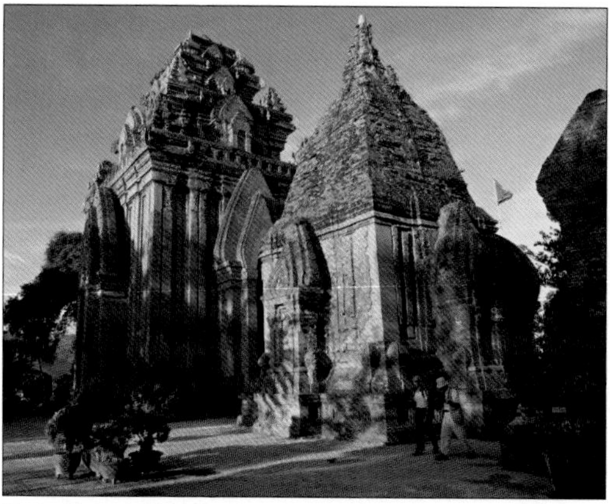

The North Tower (Thap Chinh) and Central Tower (Thap Nam), Po Nagar

achievement came in 1894, when he identified the microbe that causes bubonic plague.

The museum, located in Yersin's personal office within the Pasteur Institute, displays his lab equipment, desk, and books. Still operational, the institute produces vaccines and conducts medical research.

Cai River Estuary

Nha Trang's fishing fleet moors on the Cai River just north of downtown. A stroll over the bridge allows a vantage point for watching the blue boats at anchor, their red and yellow flags flapping in the breeze. The harbor is alive with activity and fishermen propel themselves from boat to boat in rotund, pitch-sealed coracles.

⛩ Po Nagar Cham Towers

North bank of Cai River. ***Tel*** *(058) 383 1569.* 🚗 🕒 *6am–6pm daily.* 📷

Dedicated to the goddess Po Yan Inu Nagar and one of the most important Cham sites in Vietnam, Po Nagar dates back to the 8th century, when it was constructed by the kings of the Cham principality Kauthara. Although a Cham goddess, Yang Ino Po Nagar is now very much a patron goddess of Nha Trang, venerated by ethnic Viet and Chinese Buddhists, as well as by local Cham Hindus.

Of the original eight towers, four remain standing. Built in 817, Thap Chinh, the North Tower, is the most impressive and houses an image of the Hindu goddess Uma in her incarnation as Po Nagar. At the entrance, her consort, the Hindu god Shiva, dances on the back of his holy mount, the sacred bull Nandi. The columns of a ruined *mandapa* or meditation hall also still stand. A small museum displays Cham artifacts.

VISITORS' CHECKLIST

Road Map C5. 280 miles (450 km) N of Ho Chi Minh City. 👥 *300,000.* ✈ *21 miles (34 km) S at Cam Ranh.* 🚆 🚌 ℹ *Khanh Hoa Tourist Company, 1 Tran Hung Dao St, (058) 352 6753.* 🎉 *Po Nagar Festival (mid-Apr).*

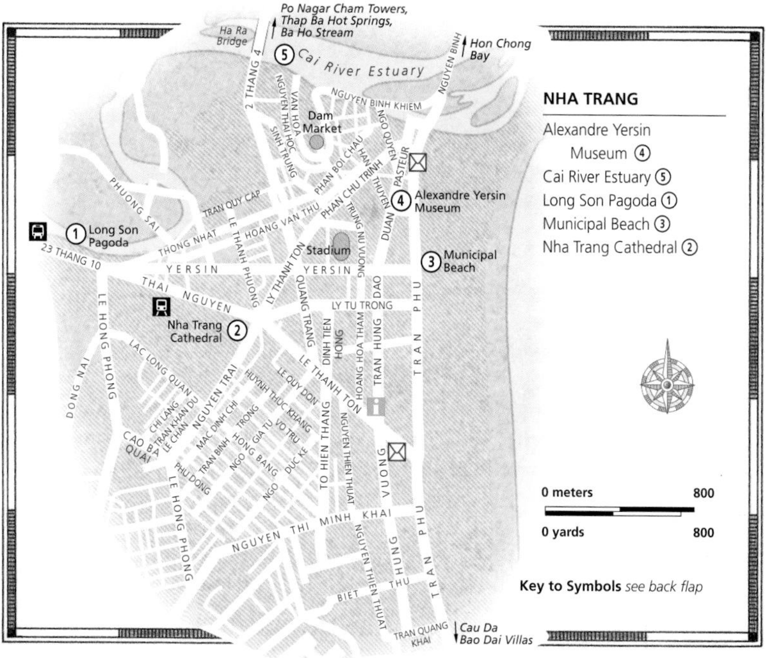

Po Nagar Cham Towers, Thap Ba Hot Springs, Ba Ho Stream
Ha Ra Bridge
Hon Chong Bay
5 Cai River Estuary
Dam Market
1 Long Son Pagoda
4 Alexandre Yersin Museum
Stadium
3 Municipal Beach
2 Nha Trang Cathedral
NGUYEN BINH KHIEM
2 THANG 4
PHUONG SAI
TRAN QUY CAP
THONG NHAT
HOANG VAN THU
23 THANG 10
YERSIN
THAI NGUYEN
LY TU TRONG
LE THANH TON
TRAN PHU
NGUYEN THI MINH KHAI
LE HONG PHONG
BIET THU
TRAN QUANG KHAI
Cau Da Bao Dai Villas
NHA TRANG
Alexandre Yersin Museum 4
Cai River Estuary 5
Long Son Pagoda 1
Municipal Beach 3
Nha Trang Cathedral 2
0 meters 800
0 yards 800
Key to Symbols see back flap

Pleasure boats for trips to the islands around Nha Trang at Cau Da

🚤 Hon Chong

2.5 miles (4 km) N of Nha Trang.
Tel (058) 383 2189. 🚗
🕐 6.30am–6.30pm daily. 🌐

Just north of Nha Trang, a stack of boulders named Hon Chong thrusts into the sea, creating a headland that shelters the beach. One of the rocks bears five indentations, said to be the handprint of a giant. The bay is picturesque but unsuitable for swimming because of several fishing villages in the area. However, it is a great place for reasonably priced seafood. There are views of Nha Trang Bay to the south, while Nui Co Tien, or Heavenly Woman Mountain, said to resemble the female physiognomy, is visible to the west.

Thap Ba Hot Springs

6 miles (10 km) NW of Nha Trang.
Tel (058) 383 0090. 🚗 🕐 7am–7:30pm daily. 🌐

Locals and visitors alike gather to wallow in the hot, muddy waters of Thap Ba. The mud is full of sodium silicate chloride and is thought to be beneficial in the treatment of arthritis and

Bathers soaking in tubs of warm mud at Thap Ba Hot Springs

rheumatism. It is also said to promote general relaxation. Bathers make a point of rubbing the curative mud all over their bodies, and sit in the sun until it dries and cracks. They then wash the mud off with clean, hot mineral water. Various types of water massage are also on offer, and a cool swimming pool is available for an invigorating post-mudbath dunk.

Ba Ho Stream plunging over boulders into a pool

🏞 Ba Ho Stream

15 miles (25 km) N of Nha Trang. 🚗

A terrific spot for a picnic, Ba Ho Stream or Suoi Ba Ho rises on the flanks of Hon Long Mountain (4,400 ft/1,342 m) and then runs east to the South China Sea. The river widens into three adjoining pools, which make for excellent but cold swimming, and each pool is linked to the next by a tumbling cascade of water. There are very few facilities, so take along food and drink. On weekends, the lakeside setting can be overrun as it is very popular with locals.

Cau Da

2 miles (3 km) S of downtown Nha Trang. 🚗 **Oceanographic Institute**
Tel (058) 359 0036. 🕐 6am–6pm daily. 🌐 **Bao Dai Villas Tel** (058) 359 0147. 🌐 for non-residents.

Sheltered in the lee of Chut Mountain or Nui Chut, Cau Da is a suburb of Nha Trang and the main pier for ferries and boat trips to the islands.

The **Oceanographic Institute**, housed in a colonial mansion near the pier, displays marine specimens in glass bottles and cases. Live creatures are kept in a series of tanks, as well as three outside ponds.

North of the docks, **Bao Dai Villas** command fine views across the South China Sea. During the 1920s, the last Nguyen emperor, Bao Dai, ordered five houses to be built in a hybrid Franco-Vietnamese style with Art Nouveau influences. After his abdication in 1945, the villas became the holiday residence of senior officials of the South Vietnamese government and, from 1975, they were used by high-ranking Communist officials. Today, the villas function as a hotel, which is sadly rather run-down despite having been restored and furnished with pieces reminiscent of Bao Dai's time and taste.

Regular ferries link Cau Da with the fishing village of Tri Nguyen on **Hon Mieu**, the closest of the islands in the archipelago. The local aquarium is more of a fish farm, with a café serving seafood overlooking the concrete pools. A gravel beach is nearby at Bai Soi.

Beaches Around Nha Trang

The numerous beaches scattered along the sandy shoreline to the north of Nha Trang, together with the small archipelago of pretty islands that lies just out to sea, add significantly to this seaside resort's appeal. Several tour companies organize day tours and usually offer a seafood lunch and plenty of iced beer. At the quieter and less developed northern destinations such as Dai Lanh and Hon Lao – the latter populated by monkeys – activities include swimming, snorkeling, and sunbathing. More organized, and often raucous, entertainment, such as waterskiing, parasailing, and drinking at a floating bar, is to be expected at the islands of the archipelago.

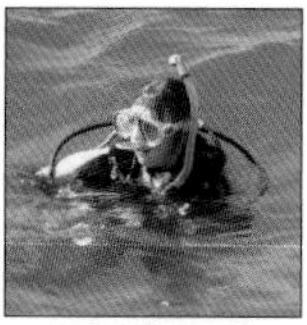

Scuba diver off Hon Ong

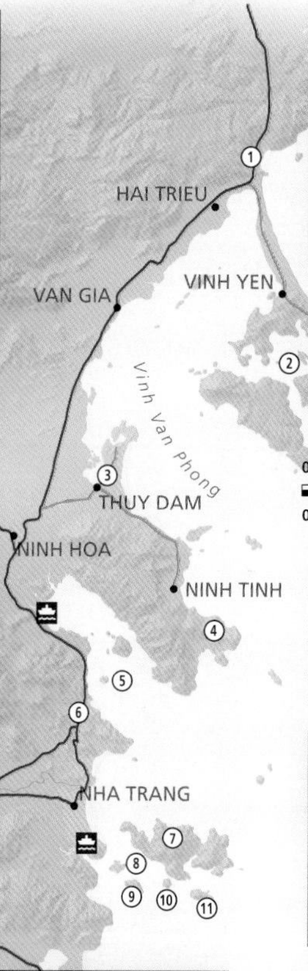

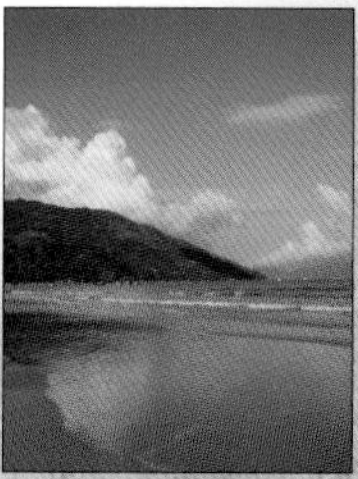

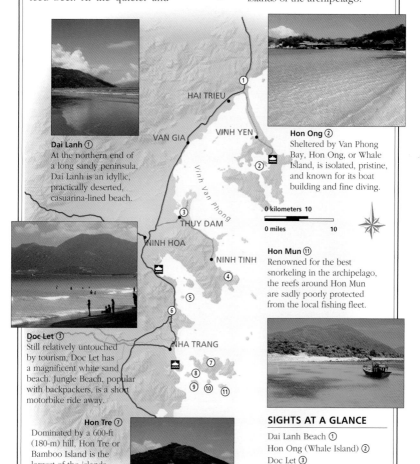

Dai Lanh ①
At the northern end of a long sandy peninsula, Dai Lanh is an idyllic, practically deserted, casuarina-lined beach.

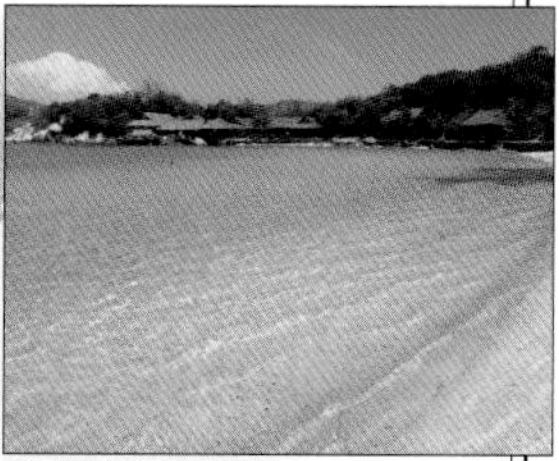

Hon Ong ②
Sheltered by Van Phong Bay, Hon Ong, or Whale Island, is isolated, pristine, and known for its boat building and fine diving.

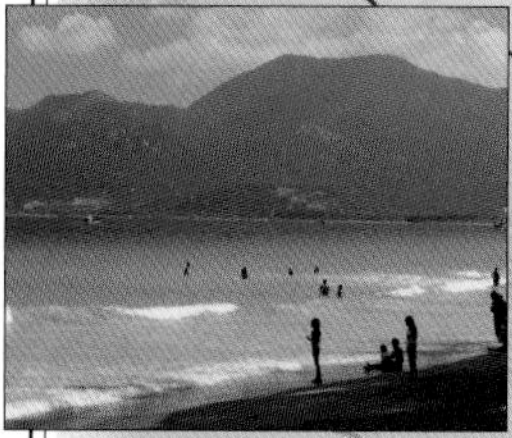

Doc Let ③
Still relatively untouched by tourism, Doc Let has a magnificent white sand beach. Jungle Beach, popular with backpackers, is a short motorbike ride away.

Hon Mun ⑪
Renowned for the best snorkeling in the archipelago, the reefs around Hon Mun are sadly poorly protected from the local fishing fleet.

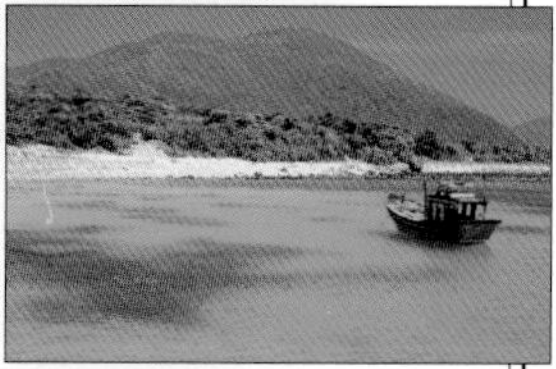

Hon Tre ⑦
Dominated by a 600-ft (180-m) hill, Hon Tre or Bamboo Island is the largest of the islands near Nha Trang. On the northeast coast, the white sands of Bai Tru Beach are home to the luxurious Vinpearl Resort *(see p238)*.

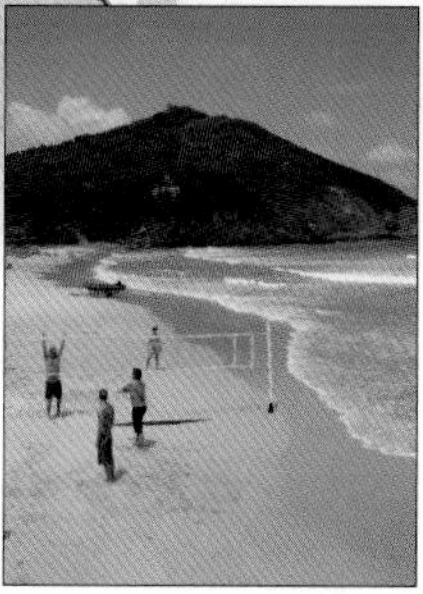

Key to Symbols *see back flap*

SIGHTS AT A GLANCE

Dai Lanh Beach ①
Hon Ong (Whale Island) ②
Doc Let ③
Jungle Beach ④
Hon Lao (Monkey Island) ⑤
Hon Chong *(see p110)* ⑥
Hon Tre (Bamboo Island) ⑦
Hon Mieu *(see p110)* ⑧
Hon Tam ⑨
Hon Mot ⑩
Hon Mun (Ebony Island) ⑪

Surf breaking on the palm-fringed shores of Nha Trang Beach ▷

Dalat ⑥

Pink flower, common in Dalat

In the mid-1890s, the physician Alexandre Yersin *(see p108)* visited Dalat and recommended it as a suitable location for a hill station and sanatorium. By 1910, the town had become a popular summer retreat for French colonists seeking a cool escape from the heat of the plains. Today, Dalat draws tens of thousands of Vietnamese honeymooners and holidaymakers, many of whom come to see the Valley of Love and Lake of Sighs, although such kitsch sights are of little interest to foreign visitors. Besides the fresh air and beautiful scenery, Dalat appeals to many for its fresh produce, wine, great food, and ethnic crafts. A short drive from Dalat are the Dambri, Elephant, Tiger, Datanla, and Pongour falls.

Swan-shaped pedal-boats on Xuan Huong Lake

♣ Xuan Huong Lake

This crescent-shaped lake located right in the center of town was created by a dam in 1919 and rapidly became the central promenade for the Dalat bourgeoisie. Once called Le Grand Lac by the French, it was later renamed in honor of Ho Xuan Huong *(see p15)*, the celebrated 17th-century Vietnamese female poet whose name means Essence of Spring. Paddling around the waters in a swan-shaped pedal-boat or a more traditional kayak is the most popular activity on the lake. A pleasant walk or cycle along the 4-mile (7-km) shore passes the town's **Flower Gardens** on the north shore.

⛪ Dalat Cathedral

Tran Phu and Le Dai Hanh Sts. **Tel** *(063) 382 1421.* ○ *daily.* *Mass at least twice a day.*
Dedicated to St. Nicholas and adding yet another French touch to this Gallic-inspired hill station, Dalat's Catholic cathedral was established to meet the spiritual needs of the colonists and the many local converts. Construction began in 1931 and was not complete until the Japanese invasion of the 1940s, an event which signalled the beginning of the end of French Indochina. The church boasts a 155-ft (47-m) spire and vivid stained-glass windows that were manufactured in 1930s France.

The dusty pink exterior of Dalat Cathedral

The exterior of Nga's Crazy House, built to resemble gnarled treetrunks

⚅ Hang Nga (Nga's Crazy House)

3 Huynh Thuc Khang St. **Tel** *(063) 382 2070.* ○ *7am–6pm daily.* 🎟
The "Crazy House," as this guesthouse is called by locals, epitomizes everything visitors to Dalat either love or hate. This flight of fancy is constructed of wood and wire, then covered with concrete to form a treehouse. With giant toadstools, oversized cobwebs, tunnels, and ladders, it is a monstrosity to some and a charming miniature Disneyland to others, particularly kids. For a small fee, visitors can poke around unoccupied rooms, including one in the belly of a concrete giraffe.

Dr Dang Viet Nga, the owner and architect, is the daughter of the former senior Communist Party hardliner Truong Chinh, who was also briefly the General Secretary of the party in 1986.

卐 Lam Ty Ni Pagoda

2 Thien My St. **Tel** *(063) 382 1775.* ○ *8:30am–6:30pm daily.*
This pagoda is very much suited to the atmosphere of eccentricity and questionable taste that surrounds many of Dalat's attractions. The building itself is unremarkable in the traditional sense, but has been extended and transformed by the pagoda's solitary inhabitant, the charming Buddhist monk Vien Thuc. He has lived here since 1964, long accompanied by a pack of amiable dogs who bark loudly at new arrivals. When not reading or

writing Zen poetry, he casts concrete busts, usually of himself. This industrious monk is also a prolific painter and creates dream-like landscapes and strange interpretations of the Buddhist religion and the cosmos. It is said that he makes a healthy profit from the sale of his work.

🏯 Bao Dai's Summer Palace

1 Trieu Viet Vuong St.
Tel *(063) 382 6858.*
⏰ *7:30–11am, 1:30–4pm daily.*
The last Nguyen Emperor, Bao Dai *(see p43)*, regarded as a powerless puppet of the French, lived in Dalat from 1938 until 1945 with his wife, Empress Nam Phuong, and various members of his family and immediate entourage. He spent much of his time hunting and womanizing.

The Summer Palace was constructed in 1933–8 in a curious, semi-nautical Art Nouveau style, and, with just 25 rooms, it is far from palatial. Although little sense of grandeur is in evidence here, the palace remains popular with tourists who browse the memorabilia on display, which include Bao Dai's desk and an etched-glass map of Vietnam.

🚉 Dalat Train Station

1 Quang Trung St, off Nguyen Trai St. **Tel** *(063) 383 4409. Departures 8am, 9:30am, 11am, 2pm, 3:30pm daily.* 📷
Built in 1932 in imitation of the station at Deauville in France, the Dalat Train Station retains its original Art Deco design. Bombing during the Vietnam War *(see pp44–5)* closed the line to Phan Rang, but a Russian engine travels a picturesque 10-mile (17-km) route to the village of Trai Mat.

🏛 Lam Dong Museum

4 Hung Vuong St. **Tel** *(063) 382 2339.* ⏰ *7:30–11:30am, 1:30–4:30pm Tue–Sat.* 📷
The wide range of artifacts on display traces the rich history of Dalat and its surroundings. Exhibits include pottery from the Funcn and Champa kingdoms, musical instruments, costumes of local ethnic minorities, and photographs. The museum is located in front of an elegant French-style villa, which was built for

Bronze Buddha, Thien Vuong Pagoda

VISITORS' CHECKLIST

Road Map C5.191 miles (308 km) N of Ho Chi Minh City. 🏯 *140,000.* ✈ 🚌 🚌 ℹ *Dalat Travel Service, 7, 3 Thang 2 St, (063) 382 2125.*

Bao Dai's father-in-law, Nguyen Huu Hao, in 1935, and later became the home of Bao Dai's wife, Empress Nam Phuong.

🏯 Thien Vuong Pagoda

2.5 miles (4 km) from the center of Dalat on Khe Sanh St.
A more orthodox pagoda than Lam Ty Ni, Thien Vuong was built by the local Chinese community in 1958. This hilltop pagoda, which has monks in residence, comprises three low, wooden buildings set attractively amid pine trees. In the main sanctuary stand three big sandalwood statues, with Thich Ca, the Historical Buddha, forming the centerpiece. Stalls selling local jams, dried fruits, and artichoke tea line the path leading up to the pagoda.

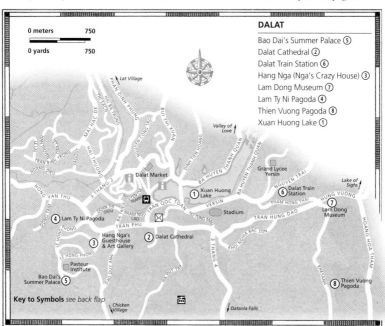

DALAT

0 meters 750
0 yards 750

Lat Village

Valley of Love

Dalat Market

Grand Lycee Yersin

Xuan Huong Lake ①

Dalat Train Station ⑥

Lake of Sighs

Lam Dong Museum ⑦

Stadium

④ Lam Ty Ni Pagoda

Hang Nga's Guesthouse & Art Gallery ③

② Dalat Cathedral

Pasteur Institute

Bao Dai's Summer Palace ⑤

⑧ Thien Vuong Pagoda

Key to Symbols *see back flap*

Chicken Village

Datanla Falls

🔺 Dalat Central Market
Town center. ⬜ daily. 🔲 🔳 🍴 🛒

Nestled in the lee of a tall hillside and surrounded by rows of cafés, Dalat Central Market is among the largest in the country. The stairs and ramps leading to the market are flanked with food vendors selling grilled corn, meat on skewers, sweet potatoes, hot soy milk, and sweet waffles stuffed with pork and cheese. The second floor of the central building is also devoted to food stalls.

The enormous concrete cockerel that gave Chicken Village its name

🏠 Chicken Village
11 miles (18 km) S of Dalat just off Hwy 20. 🚗 🛒

Renowned for the large and rather bizarre statue of a cockerel that stands at its center, Chicken Village, known locally as Lang Ga, draws a large number of sightseers.

It is inhabited by the K'ho people, who eke out a living growing fruit and coffee, and making textiles. The village lies just off the highway between Dalat and the coast, and tour buses stop regularly to allow visitors to watch the K'ho women weave and to buy their wares. As a result of their regular dealings with foreign tourists, the women of the village speak remarkably good English.

🏠 Lat Village
6 miles (10 km) N of Dalat. 🚗

Made up of a number of small hamlets, Lat Village is inhabited mainly by members of the Lat ethnic minority, part of the K'ho tribe, but also by other local minority peoples, including the Ma and Chill. The villagers, once impoverished, are now better off as a result of tourism. The attraction here is the local weaving and embroidery. Visitors are offered cups of hot green tea to drink while they watch the village women at work on their looms. There are some fine bargains and the people are friendly, but be prepared to haggle.

🚠 Dalat Cable Car and Thien Vien Truc Lam
2 miles (3 km) S of Dalat, off 3 Thang 4 St/Hwy 20. 🚗 ⬜ 7:30–11:30am Mon, 7:30–11:30am, 1:30–5pm Tue–Fri. 🖼

The Dalat Cable Car hangs across 1.5 miles (2.4 km) of picturesque villages, farmland, and mountain forests all the way to Thien Vien

The Dalat Cable Car, overlooking the Langbiang Plateau

Truc Lam, or Bamboo Forest Meditation Center. This Zen monastery was built in 1993 and houses about 180 monks and nuns. The temple overlooks Paradise Lake, which offers an abundance of free picnic tables and chairs.

🏞 Datanla Falls
3 miles (5 km) S of Dalat, Hwy 20. **Tel** (063) 383 2238. 🚗 ⬜ daily. 🖼

Set in the pine-forested hills to the southwest of Dalat, Datanla Falls are only a short distance from town, and a pleasant 15-minute walk from Highway 20. The falls, which tumble down a ravine in two cascades, are a popular destination for Vietnamese tourists, especially on weekends. It is not worth making the visit during the dry season.

🏞 Dambri and Bo Bla Falls
Dambri: 52 miles (85 km) SW of Dalat, off Hwy 20; Bo Bla: 50 miles (80 km) SW of Dalat on Hwy 28. 🚗 ⬜ 7am–5pm daily. 🖼

The most spectacular and easily accessible falls in South Central Vietnam are at Dambri, where the water cascades down a 295-ft (90-m) drop. It is a steep climb to the top but there is a cable car to carry the less energetic up in a few minutes. Above the falls, there is a small lake where boat rides are available.

A visit to Dambri Falls can easily be combined with a stop en route at Bo Bla Falls, another beauty spot, which lies just south of Di Linh.

A typical house in one of the hamlets at Lat Village

Lak Lake ❼

Road Map C5. 20 miles (32 km)
S of Buon Ma Thuot on Hwy 27.
Tel *(0500) 358 6184.* 🚌 🍴 💻

Lying in the center of the picturesque Dak Lak Plateau, this large, serene freshwater lake was once a favorite retreat of former Emperor Bao Dai, who built one of his hunting lodges on its banks. Although the surrounding hills have been largely stripped of forest, there are still spectacular views across the lake. The area is an excellent place to stop for refreshments when traveling on the mountain highway between Buon Ma Thuot and Dalat, and an increasing number of visitors, mostly on "Easy Rider" motorbike tours, come here. The people living around Lak Lake are mainly from the Central Highland's Mnong minority.

Buon Ma Thuot ❽

Road Map C5. 118 miles (194 km)
NE of Nha Trang. 🏠 190,000. ✈
ℹ *Dak Lak Tourist, 3 Phan Chu Trinh, (0500) 384 2115.*

The capital of the Central Highlands province of Dak Lak, Buon Ma Thuot makes a great base for exploring the remote lakes, rainforests, waterfalls, and hilltribe villages of the surrounding areas.

The government claims that ethnic Vietnamese, or Kinh, now make up the majority of the local population, but the indigenous minority peoples, the Ede and Mnong, still live in villages throughout the province. The Ede call the capital Buon Ma Thuot and the Mnong call it Ban Me Thuot; both names translate as "Village of the Father of Thuot."

The town is Vietnam's coffee capital, and its high production levels boost the country's position as a coffee exporter, ranking it second only to Brazil. The coffee plantations here are interesting to visit. Buon Ma Thuot is also significant for being the site of the last major battle of the Vietnam War on March 10, 1975. The **Victory Monument**

Farmers working in the fields beside picturesque Lak Lake

in the center of town features a replica of the first North Vietnamese Army tank to enter the city during the invasion. It is perched high on a plinth to commemorate the town's liberation.

In addition, there are two museums, the **Revolutionary Museum** on Le Duan Street, which explores the role Buon Ma Thuot played in the North's final push into Saigon in 1975, and the more interesting **Museum of Ethnography** on Nguyen Du. While in the process of an enormous renovation and expansion, the latter is a good place to gain an insight into the culture, traditions, and handicrafts of the local Ede and Mnong peoples and the various other hill tribes that live in the region.

🏛 **Revolutionary Museum**
1 Le Duan St. ◻ *8–11am, 2–5pm daily.* 📷

🏛 **Museum of Ethnography**
4 Nguyen Du St. ***Tel*** *(0500) 381 2770.* ◻ *7–11am, 2–5pm daily.* 📷

Environs
Tur, a small village lying 9 miles (14 km) southwest of Buon Ma Thuot, is inhabited by members of the Ede minority. Their society is matrilineal so property is always owned by the women. After marriage, men move into their wives' homes and the houses are extended. The longhouses are built on stilts, providing a space beneath the

living quarters to store firewood and house a variety of domesticated animals, such as goats, pigs, and fowl. Because of its proximity to Buon Ma Thuot and Highway 14, Tur is easily accessible and is a good place to see Ede longhouses. The village is located near the mighty Dak Krong, or Serepok River, which flows into Cambodia. A visit to Tur can easily be combined with a trip to the impressive Trinh Nu rapids nearby. Farther upstream, Dray Nur, Dray Sap, and Gia Long falls lead the visitor into wilder territory.

Buon Tuo Village, situated 8.5 miles (13 km) to the northwest of Buon Ma Thuot, has a number of impressive Ede longhouses.

A thriving coffee plantation at Buon Ma Thuot

Steep-roofed *nha rong* or communal house in Kontum

Yok Don National Park ❾

Road Map C5. 26 miles (40 km) NW of Buon Ma Thuot. **Tel** *(0500) 378 3049.* 🚌 minibus from Buon Ma Thuot. 🚌 🛏 ✎ 🍴 🛍 🚻

The largest of Vietnam's national parks, Yok Don covers almost 470 sq miles (1,200 sq km), extending along the Cambodian frontier and cut through by the mighty Dak Krong or Serepok River. The park is home to leopards, tigers, and wild elephants, but of the 67 species of mammal, no fewer than 38 are endangered, and the chances of seeing any of the larger mammals are slight. The once large herds of wild elephants have diminished to between 150 and 170 animals, but they remain visible.

Half-day treks include a visit to a Mnong village, which is the main attraction for most visitors to the park. Several shops selling handicrafts and sealed pots of a local rice liquor known as *ruou can*, complete with bamboo drinking straws, are clustered around the park's entrance. Accommodation is also available here.

Just beyond the northern limits of the park, and difficult to access without a private vehicle and government guide, **Thap Yang Prong** is the most remote of all Vietnam's Cham towers, and an indication of where the outposts and settlements of the former Kingdom of Champa during the 13th and 14th centuries were.

Kontum ❿

Road Map C4. 125 miles (200 km) NE of Quy Nhon. 🚶 *95,000.* 🚌 🚕 ℹ️ *Kontum Travel Service, 2 Phan Dinh Phung St, (060) 386 1626.*

This remote, laid-back town receives relatively few visitors, having been only recently opened to tourism by the authorities. Despite being heavily bombed during the Vietnam War, Kontum has retained a couple of beautiful French-colonial wooden churches and a few French-style shopfronts. As the town has few attractions of its own, most visitors come here to explore the surrounding countryside and the many minority villages, remarkable for their trademark *nha rong* or communal houses. At the east side of town, the **Seminary Museum**, within an old French Catholic seminary, displays minority handicrafts and clothing.

Ethnic groups, including Jarai, Sedang, Rongao, and Bahnar (*see p20*), inhabit villages in the region, many of which can be easily accessed from Kontum. Within walking distance, the Bahnar village of **Kon Kotu** is about 3 miles (5 km) east of town. This community's *nha rong* is made entirely of bamboo and wood, and boasts an immensely tall thatched roof typical of Bahnar design. **Kon Hongo** is 2.5 miles (4 km) to the west of Kontum and is peopled by the Rongao minority. Both journeys take visitors through pleasant countryside of sugar and cassava fields.

🏛 **Seminary Museum**
56 Tran Hung Dao St. ⏰ 7:30–10:30am, 2–4pm Mon–Fri. 📷

Quy Nhon ⓫

Road Map C5. 137 miles (220 km) N of Nha Trang. 🚶 *275,000.* ✈️ 🚌 🚕 🚗 ℹ️ *Binh Dinh Tourist, 4 Phan Chu Chinh St, (056) 389 2524.*

A substantial fishing port with reasonable beaches, Quy Nhon sees few visitors barring those who overnight here to break the trip between Nha Trang and Hoi An. **Long Khan Pagoda**, Quy Nhon's most revered Buddhist temple, is located right in the center of town on Tran Cao Van Street. Dating back to the early 18th century, it is dedicated to Thich Ca, the Historical Buddha. The temple receives much less interest than the many ancient Cham temples surrounding Quy Nhon. There is a busy beach in town, but

Grand Thap Doi Cham surrounded by a manicured garden, Quy Nhon

Buddha statues and offerings, Long Khan Pagoda, Quy Nhon

better stretches of sand are located about 3 miles (5 km) to the south, including **Quy Hoa Beach**, at the leper hospital of the same name. The **Thap Doi Cham** or Double Cham Towers, thought to date from the second half of the 12th century, are just 1 mile (1.6 km) west of the town center.

Environs
One of the major surviving works of Cham architecture and in a remarkably good state, **Banh It**, or Silver Tower, stands on a hilltop near Highway 1, about 12 miles (20 km) north of Quy Nhon. Farther north along Highway 1 are the few remains of **Cha Ban**, once called Vijaya and capital of the Cham principality of the same name. Founded in AD 1000, the city was razed to the ground in 1470 by the Dai Viets, signalling the end of Champa as a kingdom. Only the walls of the citadel and the Can Tien Cham Towers still stand.

Sa Huynh ⑫

Road Map C4. 37 miles (60 km) S of Quang Ngai. 🏠 50,000. 🚌 🚐 🚹 (055) 386 0454. 🎏 *Seafood Catching Festival (early May).*

Known for its palm-fringed beach and salt pans, this attractive little fishing port is most celebrated as the site of the pre-Champa culture of Sa Huynh, which flourished

around 2,000 years ago. In 1909, 200 burial jars were unearthed, the first of many more finds in the area. Unfortunately, no artifacts of this bronze-age society are accessible to the public here, but the remains can be viewed in the National Museum of Vietnamese History in Hanoi *(see pp162–3),* and at the Museum of Sa Huynh Culture in Hoi An *(see p125).* The town's laid-back atmosphere is what really attracts visitors. The beach is relatively deserted, and the waves are sufficiently powerful for surfing. Sa Huynh is also a great place for seafood.

Roof detail, Long Khan Pagoda, Quy Nhon

Quang Ngai ⑬

Road Map C4. 110 miles (177 km) N of Quy Nhon. 🏠 112,000. 🚌 🚐 🚹 *Quang Ngai Tourist, 310 Quang Trung St, (055) 382 2836.*

A sleepy provincial capital, Quang Ngai is a hidden gem with ancient archaeological finds within short driving distance.

Environs
Son My was the site of the appalling My Lai Massacre of 1968 and a chilling **Memorial Park** has been set up in the sub-hamlet of Tu Cung. A dark, granite museum documents the events in horrific detail. On display are the photographs of the atrocity that shocked the world and contributed substantially to American disillusionment with the war. Motorbike taxis in Quang Ngai make the 9-mile (15-km) trip east to Son My.

Five miles (8 km) northeast of Quang Ngai, the 1,200-year-old **Chau Sa** citadel is evidence that the Cham once controlled the area. Closer to the western mountains, a mysterious ancient wall stretches some 70 miles (113 km). It was apparently built by the Vietnamese to regulate trade betwen the local H're minority and the Viets.

MY LAI MASSACRE
During the Vietnam War, the area around Quang Ngai was considered sympathetic to the Vietcong. On March 16, 1968, a strong force of US infantry moved into the area seeking revenge for the deaths of several colleagues in the district. Over the next 4 hours, in the worst documented US war crime of the Vietnam War, about 500 Vietnamese civilians were systematically murdered, half of them women and children, as the US soldiers ran out of control.

Lieutenant William Calley, who organized the massacre, was convicted of murder but was released a few years later pending appeal on the orders of President Nixon. No others were ever convicted.

The moving My Lai Massacre Memorial at Son My near Quang Ngai

CENTRAL VIETNAM

ound by the forested peaks of the Truong Son Range to the west, with the white shores of the South China Sea to its east, Central Vietnam is a study in contrasts. It offers several fine beaches as well as a rare assortment of historical treasures, including four of Vietnam's UNESCO World Heritage Sites, namely the awe-inspiring Phong Nha Cave, My Son, Hue Citadel, and the Old Quarter of Hoi An.

Flecked with rice paddies and home to a burgeoning fishing industry, the inhabited regions of Central Vietnam are largely limited to its narrow coastal strip. The unspoilt hinterland gives way to the dramatic peaks of the Truong Son Range, which divide Vietnam from Laos. The region is home to hill people, as well as to the Hai Van Pass, one of the most scenic vantage points in the country. In the foothills near Dong Hoi is the mysterious Phong Nha Cave.

Some of the country's most outstanding architectural legacies are located in Central Vietnam. Among them, Hoi An still houses exquisite structures built by Chinese, Japanese, and French traders, dating as far back as the 16th century, while Hue, with its grand Citadel and Royal Tombs, stands as an abiding memory of the

Nguyen Dynasty (1802–1945). In ruins, but just as evocative, is the Cham temple complex at My Son, which was constructed between the 4th and 12th centuries AD. Most of these sites still bear traces of the damage they suffered during the Vietnam War.

Of more current historical interest are the villages – and now national shrines – of Hoang Tru and Kim Lien where Ho Chi Minh spent part of his childhood, as well as the former Demilitarized Zone (DMZ). Not far north of Hue, the DMZ witnessed some of the bloodiest battles of the Vietnam War and stands as a grim reminder of the vicious struggle of that era. Battle sites such as Khe Sanh and Vinh Moc have become poignant places of pilgrimage and mourning for both the Vietnamese and Americans.

Four of the Nine Dynastic Urns, each of which commemorates an emperor, Hue Citadel

◁ Shop-lined street in Hoi An, a historic port dating back to the 16th century *(see pp124–9)*

Exploring Central Vietnam

Home to some of the most spellbinding historic sites in the country, Central Vietnam's natural beauty is no less compelling. On the drive between Hue and Danang, the Hai Van Pass, surrounded by rolling hills and green valleys, offers the most spectacular views. As a base for exploring north of the pass, the old imperial city of Hue is elegant and the most convenient; nearby the small town of Lang Co has one of the best beaches in the region. North of Hue, the Demilitarized Zone evokes a tumultuous past, while the magnificent Phong Nha Cave stands among the most tranquil and scenic surroundings. South of the Hai Van Pass, both Hoi An and My Son are steeped in history and filled with centuries-old architectural marvels.

The ornate interior of the House of Phung Hung *(see p124)*, Hoi An

SIGHTS AT A GLANCE

Towns and Cities
Ba Na Hill Station ❹
Danang ❺
Dong Hoi ⓮
Hoi An pp124–9 ❶
Hue p138–45 ❿
Kim Lien ⓰

Historic and Military Sites
Demilitarized Zone (DMZ) ⓬
Khe Sanh Combat Base ⓫
My Son pp130–32 ❷

Beaches
China Beach ❸
Lang Co Beach ❽
Thuan An Beach ❾

Areas of Natural Beauty
Phong Nha Cave ⓯
Suoi Voi ❼

National Parks
Bach Ma National Park ❻

Tunnels
Vinh Moc Tunnels ⓭

KEY

— Major road
=== Minor road
▬▬ Railroad
▬▬ International border
— Provincial border
△ Peak

SEE ALSO

• *Where to Stay* pp238–40

• *Where to Eat* pp255–7

0 km   25
0 miles   25

Vibrantly colored dragon boats along the banks of the Perfume River *(see p148)*, Hue

GETTING AROUND

The best way to travel around Central Vietnam is to hire a car but if this is not feasible, the minibus services are the next best option. These ferry travelers from one destination to the other and are useful for day trips such as to the DMZ, out of Hue, or the Hai Van Pass on the way to Hue. Visitors can also get around by train, using the Reunification Express between Ho Chi Minh City and Hanoi. At Hoi An and Hue, visitors can explore by hiring a bike or walking. Even better is a breathtaking boat trip down the Perfume River from the wharf by Le Loi Street. Hotels and tour operators organize these tours.

Exhibit at the Museum of Cham Sculpture *(see p134)*, Danang

Hoi An ❶

Located on the north bank of the Thu Bon River, the historic town of Hoi An was an important trading port from the 16th to the 18th century. Attracting traders from China, Japan, and even Europe, the town acquired a rich cultural heritage, rivaled by few other cities in Vietnam. Designated a UNESCO World Heritage Site in 1999, Hoi An features long, narrow tube houses *(see p27)*, Chinese pagodas and ornate community halls, family shrines, and the Japanese Covered Bridge. There is also a recently restored small French-colonial quarter southeast of Hoi An.

Pottery, Museum of Sa Huynh

A shrine to the Tao god, Bac De, Japanese Covered Bridge

🏯 House of Phung Hung
4 Nguyen Thi Minh Khai St. **Tel** *(0510) 386 2235.* ☐ *8–11:30am, 1:30–5pm daily.* 🔲 🔲
Built in 1780, this house has been home to the same family for eight generations.

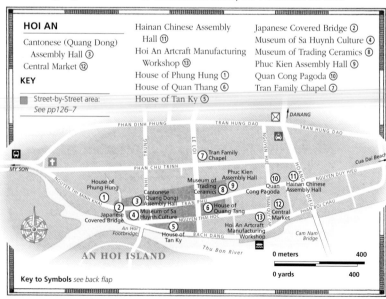
Colorful images of Chinese deities, House of Phung Hung

The clan made its fortune in perfumed woods and spices, and also sold porcelain and silk from the shop out front. Supported by 80 hardwood columns, the house shows a distinct Chinese influence in the galleries and window shutters. Japanese influence is evident in the glass skylights, while the general layout and design of the house is very much Vietnamese in style.

🏯 Japanese Covered Bridge
Intersection of Tran Phu and Nguyen Thi Minh Khai Sts. ☐ *sunrise–sunset daily.*
One of the town's most prominent landmarks, this rust-colored bridge *(see p126)* was constructed in 1593 by the

prosperous Japanese trading community, who were based on the west side of the town, in order to link it with the Chinese quarter farther to the east. However, in 1663, the Tokugawa Shogun Iemitsu issued edicts forbidding the Japanese from trading abroad, thus bringing the community to an abrupt end. In 1719, a Vietnamese temple was built into the northern section of the structure. Although a new name for the bridge, Lai Vien Kieu or Bridge from Afar, was carved over the temple door, locals continue to call it the Japanese Bridge. An effigy of Bac De, a reincarnation of the Taoist deity, the Jade Emperor, dominates the altar.

HOI AN

Cantonese (Quang Dong) Assembly Hall ③
Central Market ⑫

KEY

▢ Street-by-Street area: See pp126–7

Hainan Chinese Assembly Hall ⑪
Hoi An Artcraft Manufacturing Workshop ⑬
House of Phung Hung ①
House of Quan Thang ⑥
House of Tan Ky ⑤

Japanese Covered Bridge ②
Museum of Sa Huynh Culture ④
Museum of Trading Ceramics ⑧
Phuc Kien Assembly Hall ⑨
Quan Cong Pagoda ⑩
Tran Family Chapel ⑦

[Map of Hoi An with numbered landmarks, showing PHAN DINH PHUNG, TRAN HUNG DAO, Tran Family Chapel ⑦, Phuc Kien Assembly Hall ⑨, Museum of Trading Ceramics ⑧, Quan Cong Pagoda ⑩, Hainan Chinese Assembly Hall ⑪, Central Market ⑫, Cantonese (Quang Dong) Assembly Hall ③, House of Phung Hung ①, Japanese Covered Bridge ②, Museum of Sa Huynh Culture ④, House of Quang Tang, Hoi An Artcraft Manufacturing Workshop ⑬, House of Tan Ky ⑤, Thu Bon River, AN HOI ISLAND, Cua Dai Beach, Cam Nam Bridge, DANANG, MY SON]

0 meters 400
0 yards 400

Key to Symbols see back flap

The bridge, which is roofed in grey tiles, combines grace and strength in its short span across a tiny tributary of the Thu Bon River. It is a convenient pedestrian link between the art galleries of Tran Phu Street to those in the western part of town. Despite undergoing many renovations, the bridge's Japanese characteristics are intact.

🏛 Cantonese (Quang Dong) Assembly Hall

176 Tran Phu St. ◯ 7:30am–5pm daily. 🖼

Quang Dong is the Vietnamese name for the Chinese province of Guangdong, which was formerly known as Canton by Western countries. Built by seafaring merchants in 1786, this building is enlivened by bas-reliefs and colorful hangings. The main altar is dedicated to the great warrior Quan Cong (see p67), identifiable by his red face – emblematic of loyalty in Chinese society. Thien Hau, Goddess of the Sea, is also revered here.

Woodwork detail, Cantonese Assembly Hall

🏛 Museum of Sa Huynh Culture

149 Tran Phu St. **Tel** (0510) 386 1535. ◯ 8am–5pm daily. 🖼

The small port of Sa Huynh (see p119), some 99 miles (160 km) south of the historic town of Hoi An, was the site of an eponymous prehistoric culture (1000 BC–AD 200). In 1909, more than 200 burial jars, filled with bronze tools, ornaments, and the remains of the dead, were unearthed from here. These fascinating artifacts, characterized by a very distinctive style of bronze work can now be admired in the small museum, which is housed in a fine Franco-Vietnamese building.

🏠 House of Tan Ky

101 Nguyen Thai Hoc St. **Tel** (0510) 386 1474. ◯ 8am–noon, 2–4:30pm daily. 🖼

Perhaps the most celebrated of Hoi An's many traditional abodes, the House of Tan Ky is an excellent representation of an authentic 18th-century

Sino-Vietnamese shophouse style of construction. Built around a small courtyard, this structure, as is often the case in Hoi An, is an architectural hybrid. It carries fine Chinese crab-shell motifs on the ceiling, while its roof is supported by typically Japanese triple-beam joists. The floor is made with bricks imported from Bat Trang in the Red River Delta. Exquisite mother-of-pearl inlay Chinese poetry hangs from the columns that support the roof.

🏠 House of Quan Thang

77 Tran Phu St.
◯ 7:30am–5pm daily. 🖼

This one-story shophouse is a fine example of craftsmanship typical of Hoi An's traditional dwellings. Dating from the 18th century, this house was built by a seafaring trader from Fujian in China, whose family have lived and prospered here for the last six generations. The house has a dark teak façade, and is roofed in curved Chinese-style tiles. It can be accessed via the shop front, which leads into an interior courtyard. The walls of this enclosure are adorned with stucco bas-reliefs of flowers and trees. Beyond this beautiful courtyard is a narrow terrace used for cooking

VISITORS' CHECKLIST

Road Map C4. 493 miles (793 km) S of Hanoi. 🚐 80,000. 🚌 from Danang. 🚍 🚕 ⓘ Hoi An Tourist Office, 12 Phan Chu Trinh. 🎭 Lantern Festival (every month). **Ticketing System:** Admission tickets for sights in the Old Quarter can be bought at the Tourist Office. **www**.hoian-tourism.com

purposes. The wooden windows and shutters are finely carved.

🏛 Tran Family Chapel

21D Le Loi St. **Tel** (0510) 386 1723. ◯ 7:30am–5pm daily. 🖼

This ancestral shrine was established more than two centuries ago to honor the forefathers of the Tran family. These venerable ancestors moved to Vietnam from China in the early 18th century, and eventually settled in Hoi An. The current descendants claim that they are the 13th generation since the migration from China. Over time, members of the family intermarried with local Vietnamese natives, and the chapel is appropriately hybrid (see p129). Artifacts belonging to the ancestors and memorial tablets decorate the main altar. A forefather who achieved the rank of mandarin is honored in a portrait in the reception hall of the chapel.

Carved wooden brackets in a courtyard, House of Tan Ky

Street-by-Street: Hoi An Old Quarter

Possessing an impressive historical and cultural legacy, Hoi An is a mosaic of various cultures. Its Old Quarter is redolent of an ancient period, along with a sense of timelessness. Its historic buildings, attractive tube houses, and decorated Chinese community halls have earned it the status of a UNESCO World Heritage Site. In efforts to protect the Old Quarter's character, stringent conservation laws prohibit alterations to buildings, as well as the presence of cars on its streets.

In addition to its many monuments, the town has a wide array of delightful shops, offering almost everything Vietnam is famous for, as well as excellent roadside cafés. Combined with Hoi An's laid-back ambience, this creates an ideal setting where visitors can relax and unwind.

Sino-Japanese interiors of the ancient Tran Family Chapel

★ Cantonese Assembly Hall
Dating from 1885, this decorated community center is also known as the Quang Dong Assembly Hall (see p125). Traditional Chinese paintings, with images of divine storks and the Goddess of Mercy, are showcased here.

To Tran Family Chapel

★ Japanese Covered Bridge
Symbolic of Hoi An and its rich mercantile past, this covered bridge was built in 1593 by the Japanese trading community to link them with the Chinese quarter in the eastern section of the town.

TRAN PHU

KEY

− − − Suggested route

STAR SIGHTS

★ Cantonese Assembly Hall

★ Japanese Covered Bridge

★ House of Tan Ky

The Museum of Sa Huynh Culture is set in a French-colonial house, and displays funerary urns, jewelry, and ceramics belonging to a 2,000-year-old society that flourished around Hoi An.

Chinese Assembly Hall was built in 1740 to serve the local Chinese community.

Bach Dang Street overlooking Hoi An's Thu Bon River

Phuc Kien Assembly Hall

Tran Phu 48

Museum of Trading Ceramics
The ceramic ware displayed here dates from between the 16th and 18th centuries, including pieces from China, Japan, and Southeast Asia.

Tran Phu 77, a typical Hoi An tube house, has belonged to the same Fujian Chinese family for six generations.

To Central Market

0 metres   50

0 yards   50

★ **House of Tan Ky**
This unique 18th-century, two-story shophouse incorporates elements of Vietnamese, Chinese, and Japanese architectural design.

Roadside Cafés
The town's numerous cafés and restaurants offer visitors inviting places to relax and enjoy a selection of appetizing dishes and great drinks.

🏛 Museum of Trading Ceramics

80 Tran Phu St. **Tel** *(0510) 386 2944.*
⬜ *7:30am–5pm daily.* 🈺
Housed in a traditional timber shophouse, with balconies and wood paneling, this museum is dedicated to Hoi An's historic ceramic trade, which flourished from the 16th to 18th centuries. Many pieces on display were recovered from shipwrecks, some near Cham Island off the mouth of Thu Bon River.

The riotously colorful façade of Phuc Kien Assembly Hall

🏮 Phuc Kien Assembly Hall

46 Tran Phu St. **Tel** *(0510) 386 1252.*
⬜ *7:30am–5pm daily.* 🈺
A flamboyant building, this assembly hall was founded by merchants who had fled from the Chinese province of Fujian after the downfall of the Ming Dynasty in 1644. The temple complex is dedicated to Thien Hau, Goddess of the Sea, who is regarded as the savior of sailors. She presides over the main altar in the first chamber, and is flanked by attendants who are said to alert her whenever there is a shipwreck. To the right of the altar is a detailed model of a sailing junk, while in a chamber at the back, an altar honors the founding fathers who are represented by six seated figures.

🏮 Quan Cong Pagoda

24 Tran Phu St. **Tel** *(0510) 386 2945.*
⬜ *7am–6pm daily.* 🈺
Also known as Chua Ong, this pagoda was founded in 1653, and is dedicated to the 3rd-century Chinese general, Quan Cong, a member of the

Taoist pantheon. An impressive gilded statue of him presides over the main altar, accompanied by two fierce-looking guardians, and a white horse, Quan Cong's traditional mount.

🏮 Hainan Chinese Assembly Hall

10 Tran Phu St. **Tel** *(0510) 394 0529.*
⬜ *8am–5pm daily.*
This assembly hall was built in 1875 by Hoi An's immigrant community from Hainan Island in China. It is dedicated to the memory of 108 Hainanese seafarers killed by a renegade Vietnamese pirate-general in 1851. A lacquered board in the entry hall recounts their story in Chinese characters.

🏪 Central Market

Between Tran Phu and Bach Dang Sts. ⬜ *sunrise–sunset daily.*
Best visited in the morning, when the pace is not frantic, this lively market occupies two narrow streets that run south from Tran Phu to the banks of the Thu Bon River. There are stalls selling all kinds of fresh produce, kitchen utensils, and other equipment. To the east of the wharf is the market specializing in fresh seafood and meat. The main draws, though, are Hoi An's popular fabric and clothing stores (*see p264*), which specialize in exquisite and inexpensive silks. Custom-made outfits can be ordered in less than a day.

🏛 Hoi An Artcraft Manufacturing Workshop

9 Nguyen Thai Hoc St. **Tel** *(0510) 391 0216.* ⬜ *7am–6pm daily.* 🈺
Tue–Sun. **www**.hoianhandicraft.com
This handicrafts workshop specializes in the production of

Making lanterns at the Hoi An Artcraft Manufacturing Workshop

elegant lanterns, a specialty of Hoi An. These lanterns are handmade, using silk mounted on bamboo frames. Visitors can watch artisans at work, or make their own lanterns under expert supervision.

Traditional recitals featuring the *dan bau* (*see p24*), a Vietnamese stringed musical instrument, are also staged in the workshop (10:15am and 3:15pm daily), and refreshments are available for visitors in the courtyard.

🏖 Cua Dai Beach

2.5 miles (4 km) E of Hoi An.
Cua Dai Beach is most easily reached by cycling down Cua Dai Road. The white sands look out onto the islands of the Cham archipelago making it a popular destination. Some of Vietnam's most attractive hotels such as the Victoria Hoi An Beach Resort and Spa (*see p240*), Hoi An Riverside Resort (*see p239*), and Ancient House (*see p239*) line the route and front the beach.

One of the finest beaches of Vietnam, Cua Dai Beach

For hotels and restaurants in this region see pp238–40 and pp255–7

Architectural Styles of Hoi An

Hoi An developed most of its uniquely eclectic townscape between the 16th and 19th centuries. During most of this time, it was a major port open to several foreign influences. The Japanese established a community west of the Covered Bridge during the 16th century, while the Chinese founded many communities in the center and east of town in the 18th century. Japanese and Chinese influence can be seen on the town's buildings. Later, the French left a distinct colonial stamp on the southeastern part of town. Over the years, many elements of these diverse architectural styles blended harmoniously with indigenous Vietnamese features. Hoi An was relatively untouched by the Vietnam War, and so the old world charm is still in place.

Yin-Yang, a potent symbol of Taoism

European-style balcony   Chinese roof

Vietnamese eyes, also known as *mat cua* or watchful eyes, are intended to protect the building and its inhabitants from malevolent influences.

French louvered shutters

French-colonial architecture *is reflected in the town's colonnaded houses. Most are painted warm yellow, with blue or green woodwork, and have verandas, balconies, and wooden shutters.*

CULTURAL AND ARCHITECTURAL MIX

Hoi An's is a unique architectural amalgamation, not seen elsewhere in the country. In particular, Japanese, Chinese, and French influences are evident in Vietnamese tube houses, which feature Chinese tiled roofs, Japanese support joists, and French louvered shutters and lampposts. The town is a mosaic of cultures and yet a synthesis of all the influences, thus holding an inimitable position in the country.

Vietnamese tube houses *have two courtyards, an outer one to separate business from private quarters, and an inner one for the household's women. Most of them are elaborately decorated with carved wood, stucco, or ceramic designs.*

The Chinese dragon *is a mythical creature most closely associated with Sino-Vietnamese tradition, signifying continuity, power, stability, and prosperity. It is ubiquitous in Hoi An's buildings.*

The Tran Family Chapel, *which dates back more than two centuries, exhibits various Chinese and Vietnamese architectural elements, but is chiefly distinguished by its Japanese-style, triple-beam roof joists.*

My Son ②

Bas-relief of elephants on the 10th-century B5 tower

A religious center between the 4th and 13th centuries, the Cham site of My Son became known to the world when French archaeologists rediscovered it in the late 1890s. Traces of around 70 temples may still be found at My Son, though only about 20 are still in good condition. The monuments are divided into 11 groups, the most important of which are Groups B, C, and D *(see p132)*. Group A was almost completely destroyed by US bombing during the Vietnam War. The most striking edifices are the famous Cham towers, which are divided into three parts: the base represents the earth, the center is the spiritual world, and the top is the realm between earth and heaven.

C1 Tower
This kalan or sanctuary was dedicated to Shiva, depicted as a standing sculpture in human form. The image is displayed at the Museum of Cham Art (see p134).

The low walls separating Groups B and C are of fine brickwork secured with limestone.

Ruins at B4
Built in the architectural style of structures at Dong Duong, another Cham city, the ruins here feature religious images carved on stone pilasters and elaborately embellished false doors.

★ **Shiva Lingam in B1**
A phallic symbol associated with Shiva, the lingam is shown within or above the yoni, a symbol of the goddess. Water was poured over the lingam and flowed through a spout on the yoni to symbolize creation.

Finely carved stone pillars belonging to the 8th century distinguish the ruins of B5.

★ **B5 Tower**
This 10th-century tower at B5 was used as a repository for temple treasures. It shows traces of the architectural marvel it was, with a boat-shaped roof, carved pilasters, and fine reliefs of Gajalakshmi, Goddess of Prosperity.

STAR FEATURES

- ★ Shiva Lingam in B1
- ★ B5 Tower
- ★ Deities on C1
- ★ Gallery at D2

★ Deities on C1
The 8th-century celestial figures on C1 show distinct Javanese influence. The low wide belts worn by the figures are thought to be of Indian origin, and it is believed that the style came to Cham via Indonesia.

VISITORS' CHECKLIST

Road Map C4. 25 miles (40 km) SW of Hoi An. 🚌 🚲 *from Hoi An and Danang.* **Tel** *(0510) 373 1757.* 🕐 *6:30am–4:30pm daily.* 📷 *Carry a hat, sunscreen, and bottled water. Stay on well-trodden areas; this area was once mined.*

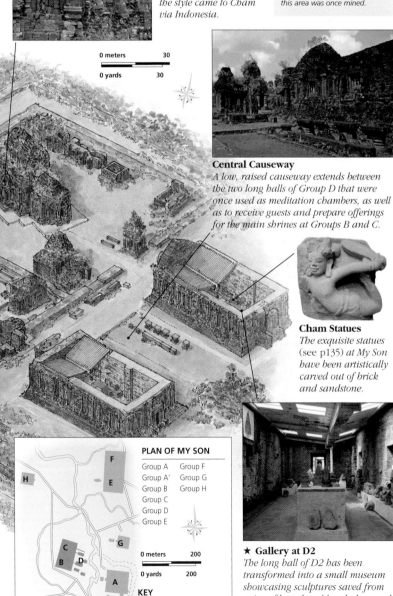

0 meters 30
0 yards 30

Central Causeway
A low, raised causeway extends between the two long halls of Group D that were once used as meditation chambers, as well as to receive guests and prepare offerings for the main shrines at Groups B and C.

Cham Statues
The exquisite statues (see p135) at My Son have been artistically carved out of brick and sandstone.

PLAN OF MY SON

Group A	Group F
Group A'	Group G
Group B	Group H
Group C	
Group D	
Group E	

0 meters 200
0 yards 200

KEY

▨ Area illustrated

★ Gallery at D2
The long hall of D2 has been transformed into a small museum showcasing sculptures saved from ruins of looted and bomb-damaged shrines. It is sheltered by the addition of a modern roof.

Exploring My Son

Designated a UNESCO World Heritage Site, the temple complex of My Son is set in a dense, vegetated valley beneath Hon Quap or Cat's Tooth Mountain. Although centuries of pillage and more recent bombings have taken their toll, the ruins provide a glimpse into a fascinating Indianized culture. Evocative as the complex is, the groups of monuments are rather unimaginatively named after letters of the alphabet. The most important edifices at Group B are reached first, while Group C is less well preserved. To the east, the halls of Group D house displays of Cham sculpture, while Groups E, F, G, and H require some imagination to truly appreciate.

Sculpture of an *apsara* in D2 gallery

Group C in a state of ruin at My Son

Groups A and A1

Said to be among My Son's most impressive edifices, Groups A and A1 were almost completely destroyed by USAF bombing in 1969. Little remains beyond rubble, but there are plans for restoration.

Records show that Group A once featured a striking tower, A1, said to have been the most important *kalan* (sanctuary) here. Unlike most Cham temples that only face east, A1 also had a door to the west, usually associated with death. This may have served as a link with Cham kings said to be interred in Groups B, C, and D. Also noteworthy is A9, with its winding patterns.

Groups B, C, and D

Situated at the center of the complex, Group B is remarkable for exhibiting elements of both Indian and Javanese art. The main sanctuary, built in the 11th century, was dedicated to King Bhadravarman, who built the first temple at My Son in the 4th century,

and to Shiva. One of the most unique structures in this group of monuments is B6, whose roof is decorated with an image of the Hindu god Vishnu being sheltered by a 13-headed *naga*. Group C forms a contiguous complex with Group B, separated only by a brick wall. Its central tower, C1, combines many elements from the older structures, including the tympanum and lintel. Built in the late 8th century, C7 is a squat tower with a stone altar, and is an architectural link between the styles of the Cham cities of Hoa Lai and Dong Duong. Toward the east of Groups B and C, the *mandapa* or meditation halls of Group D are now galleries for sculpture. Shiva *lingam*, as well

as statues of Shiva and Nandi are housed in D1, while D2 contains a stone Garuda, a Dancing Shiva, and *apsaras*.

Groups E, F, G, and H

Although the monuments in the northernmost reaches of the complex are the most damaged, they still offer fragments of beautiful craftsmanship. Built between the 8th and 11th centuries, Group E differs from the usual design of Cham temples. The main *kalan* has no vestibule, and only one temple faces eastwards. Adjoining it, Group F is badly damaged, but a finely carved *lingam* survives in the altar.

The 11th-century Group G is also in dire condition. Its tower's base features bas-reliefs of Kala, God of Time. Group H is also badly damaged, and a carved stone tympanum of a Dancing Shiva that once adorned the temple is now in the Museum of Cham Sculpture *(see p134).*

Detail of *gopuram* or temple tower

Façade carvings made of brick

Carving of deity on the entrance

Stone pillars

Reconstruction of the once-spectacular Group A1 temple

Holiday resort set against the misted mountain tops of the Truong Son Range, Ba Na Hill Station

China Beach ❸

Road Map C4. 3 miles (2 km) SE of Danang. 🚗 🍴 🛍 📷

The long stretch of beaches between the Marble Mountain and the South China Sea is known to the Vietnamese as the My Khe, My An, and Non Nuoc beaches. However, these white sandy shores were known to US servicemen as China Beach and were later highlighted by an eponymous popular TV series. Though banned by the government, a number of developers have taken to using the designation China Beach in an attempt to encourage foreign visitors.

During the Vietnam War, the Americans – for whom Danang was among the most important and secure bases in South Vietnam – developed My Khe and My An beaches as a rest-and-recreation center for US forces taking a few days leave from the war.

Today, nothing remains of the former R&R facilities, although several souvenir stalls and seafood restaurants have sprung up here. A number of upscale resorts are also being developed, particularly in My Khe. The beach is fast becoming a popular destination for surfing and swimming (see p272). Summer months are the safest as the sea can be quite choppy.

Ba Na Hill Station ❹

Road Map C4. 25 miles (40 km) W of Danang. 🚗 🚡 🍴 🛍

A conveniently close getaway from Danang, this old French hill station is set at an altitude of 4,593 ft (1,400 m), and is often shrouded in clouds or mist. In its French heyday, during the early 20th century, it is said to have been home to more than 200 villas, as well as restaurants and clubs. Sadly, Ba Na's glory days did not last long. Effectively abandoned during the Indochina Wars, it soon fell into disrepair.

In recent years, however, the hill station has witnessed a resurgence of interest from the tourism authorities, and is being redeveloped into a vacation destination. Attractions include crumbling old French villas, karaoke bars, a cable-car ride, hikes to cascading waterfalls, views over Danang and the South China Sea, and the Chua Linh Ong pagoda.

SAVING MY SON

Some of the greatest non-human casualties of the Vietnam War were the archaeological sites at My Son and Dong Duong. The situation in the area was particularly grave during and after the Tet Offensive in 1968 (see p45), when massive bombing raids by

Warning sign at My Son

the US resulted in widespread destruction. Previously, French archaeologists had listed around 70 structures at My Son. Only 20 escaped irreparable damage. Following this devastation, Philippe Stern, a leading authority on Cham history and art, complained bitterly to the US authorities, including President Richard Nixon. His attempts eventually bore fruit. In January 1971, the US ambassador was instructed by the US State Department to take all possible measures to preserve the historic site at My Son.

Today, with aid from UNESCO, archaeologists are still struggling to piece together what remains of My Son. Fortunately, the French left detailed architectural drawings, but the task remains all but impossible, and much of My Son has disappeared forever.

Street vendor selling snacks to visitors on China Beach

Altar to Quan Am, Goddess of Mercy, Pho Da Pagoda

Danang ❺

Road Map C4. 67 miles (108 km) S of Hue; 599 miles (964 km) N of HCMC. 🏙 *750,000.* ✈ ⊠ *from Hanoi, HCMC, and Nha Trang.* 🚆 *Reunification Express from Hanoi and HCMC.* 🚌 *from Hanoi, Hue, HCMC, and Nha Trang.* ℹ *Danang Tourism, 118 Le Loi St, (0511) 382 3160.* **www**.*danang.gov.vn*

Situated almost halfway along the country's coastline, on the western bank of the Han River, Danang is one of the most prominent ports in Vietnam. It is also the country's third largest city. Though not a major destination in its own right, Danang is an excellent hub for exploring several nearby attractions, and is very well connected, with an organized air, road, and rail infrastructure linking it to points north and south. Three of Vietnam's world heritage sites – Hoi An (*see pp124–9*), My Son (*see pp130–32*), and Hue Citadel (*see pp140–43*) – as well as scenic beaches are main points of interest here.

The city became prominent during the 19th century. After being captured by the French in 1859, it rapidly developed, replacing Hoi An as the main port for Central Vietnam. Further expansion took place during the Vietnam War (*see pp44–5*), when Danang became an important military

base for the Americans. Vestiges of all three eras can still be seen in and around the city.

The **Museum of Cham Sculpture**, or Bao Tang Dieu Khac Champa, is one of the city's highlights. Founded in 1915 by École Française d'Extrême Orient, the museum showcases the world's best collection of Cham sculpture, including altars, sandstone pieces, busts of Hindu gods such as Vishnu, Shiva, and Brahma, and carvings of scenes from the epic *Ramayana.* All the sculptures were recovered from nearby Cham sites, including Tra Kieu, the first Champa capital, My Son, and Dong Duong among others, and date from the 7th to the 13th century.

The pink-colored **Danang Cathedral** was constructed in 1923 and has five tiers rising to a steeple crowned with a cockerel. Another interesting sight is the **Cao Dai Temple**, the largest after its main counterpart, Cao Dai Holy See (*see pp74–5*) in Tay Ninh. Also worth visiting are **Phap Lam Pagoda**, honoring the Thich Ca Buddha, and **Pho Do Pagoda**, which is pale cream, with orange tiles and green trimming. The central temple building, which houses the main altar, is flanked by two triple-roofed towers with flaring eaves. This lovely pagoda is also used as a Buddhist college for training monks and nuns.

Stained-glass window, Danang Cathedral

The noteworthy **Ho Chi Minh Museum** boasts four galleries detailing the late president's life and revolutionary achievements, as well as an amazing reproduction of his famous ethnic minority-inspired stilt house (*see p168*) located in Hanoi.

Environs

Some of Vietnam's most breathtaking vistas can be seen at **Hai Van Pass** on Truong Son Range, about 18 miles (30 km) north of Danang. The summit of the pass offers splendid views of mountains covered in thick clouds, with the blue waters of Danang Bay below. A short distance southeast of the city are the **Marble Mountains**. As the name suggests, these rocky formations are made of marble, and comprise several caverns that have long sheltered a series of shrines dedicated to the Buddha or to Confucius. Just northeast of Danang is **Monkey Mountain** or Nui Son Tra, named after its primate population. To the west of this are the **Tombs of Spanish and French Soldiers**, killed in the 1858 French attack on Danang.

🏛 **Museum of Cham Sculpture**
Corner of Bach Dang and Trung Nu Vuong Sts. **Tel** *(0511) 382 1951.* ☐ *8am–5pm daily.* 🎫 🗎 🖿

🎎 **Cao Dai Temple**
63 Hai Phong St. **Tel** *(0511) 382 9463.* ☐ *6am–6pm daily.*

🎎 **Pho Da Pagoda**
340 Phan Chu Trinh St. **Tel** *(0511) 382 6094.* ☐ *5am–9pm daily.*

Limestone promontories, Marble Mountains, Danang

Cham Art and Sculpture

The Cham Empire existed in Vietnam for around 1,600 years, from the 2nd century AD to its downfall in 1832. Today, a thriving Cham community survives, but all that remains of their ancient kingdom is its artistic legacy, which reached its zenith in the 8th and 10th centuries. Part of this heritage is architectural, visible in the red brick temples found scattered across Central Vietnam. Other elements

Goddess Uma, the consort of Shiva

are sculptural, carved chiefly in sandstone and marble or, more rarely, cast in bronze, and discovered at sites such as Tra Kieu, My Son, and Dong Duong. Religious in inspiration, Cham art derives from the Indic tradition and represents Hindu deities with their celestial mounts, dancing girls, and demons. This tradition is expressive and exudes a unique sensuality.

The makara *is a mythical sea creature from the Hindu pantheon. Cham art was inspired by Hinduism and many such Hindu sculptures decorate their temples.*

DANCING GIRL OF TRA KIEU

The early 10th-century dancing *apsara*, or celestial nymph, from an altar pediment at Tra Kieu, outside Danang, is celebrated for her sensuality and grace. Close attention was paid to hairstyle, costume, and jewelry in Cham art.

The headgear of the dancer is an elongated and elaborately decorated hair retainer.

Exquisite ornaments on the *apsara's* dress, both emphasize and conceal her femininity.

This altar pediment *is embellished with a circular arrangement of sculpted breasts. The breast is a common motif in Cham art. It is thought to represent the Hindu mother goddess, Uma.*

Garuda *is the eagle mount of the Hindu god, Vishnu. Cham sculptors used stone or terra-cotta to carve various Hindu mythical gods and animals.*

This altar frieze, *dating back to the late 12th century, depicts a rider on horseback drawing a chariot. The fine detailing is clearly visible despite the sandstone's weathering.*

Recovered from an altar in My Son, *this well-preserved example of 7th- to 8th-century Cham art shows a flautist playing within an elaborate marble niche.*

Five Lake Cascade Trail, Bach Ma National Park

Bach Ma National Park ❻

Road Map C4. 28 miles (45 km) SE of Hue. **Tel** (054) 387 1330.
🚌 from Hue and Danang to Cau Hai. 🚐 from Danang, Hue, Hoi An, and Cau Hai. ◯ daily. 🎟️🖼️📷 🍽️
💻📷 www.bachma.vnn.vn

Located in the Hue-Danang provincial frontier, at an elevation of 4,757 ft (1,450 m), Bach Ma National Park was originally established as a hill station in the 1930s by the French. The Viet Minh did not take kindly to this imperialist occupation, and the area was subjected to many attacks during the First Indochina War *(see p43)*. By the time the war came to its close, most of the French had abandoned their beautiful villas. Later, in the 1960s, the Americans fortified Bach Ma and there were many bitter confrontations with the members of the Vietcong in the hilly forests. After the communist victory in 1975, however, the hill station lay forgotten for many years.

Fortunately for Bach Ma, in the early 1990s it underwent a revival. In 1991, the authorities granted national park status to this vast 85 sq miles (220 sq km) of forested land. Although sprayed with defoliants during the Vietnam War, the forest is showing encouraging signs of recovery due to dedicated conservation efforts.

Edward's pheasant,
Bach Ma National Park

The park is home to a wide variety of flora and fauna, which includes more than 2,140 plant species. Many of these are said to have medicinal properties. Almost 130 species of mammals have been identified in the park area. Among them are the rare *saola*, the giant muntjac, as well as the recently discovered Truong Son muntjac *(see p201)*. Primates living here include langurs, lorises, macaques, and the white-cheeked gibbon. It is likely that leopards and tigers inhabit remote corners of the park, but this has not been confirmed. Bach Ma National Park is also a bird-watcher's paradise, with an astounding 358 species listed by the park authorities, among them the endangered Edward's pheasant. While

little remains of the former French hill station, a few ruins can be seen amid the foliage, lending the jungle an eerie atmosphere. A narrow path leads to an observation post at the park's highest point which, weather permitting, affords glorious views across the rugged Truong Son Range.

Bach Ma National Park can only be reached by private transport. Those who enjoy walking may disembark at the small town of **Cau Hai** on Highway 1, and walk along the surfaced road leading to the park's headquarters. Only the fit should attempt the 11 mile (18 km) walk. The park also offers hiking trails *(see p273)*. Check that the park is open before visiting as road repairs can affect accessibility.

Suoi Voi ❼

Road Map C3. 40 miles (65 km) S of Hue; 9 miles (15 km) N of Lang Co on Hwy 1. **Tel** (054) 389 1804.
🚌 from Hue. ◯ 6:30am–9:30pm daily. 🎟️ 📷

A popular weekend destination for the inhabitants of Hue or Danang, Suoi Voi, also known as Elephant Springs, is named after a huge rock that resembles the animal. This is a wonderful bathing spot, not usually frequented by visitors.

On the way from Hue, in order not to miss its tucked away location, look out for a large sign that indicates a track leading off to the right toward the springs. About 1.5 miles (2.5 km) from here, passing the old Thua Lau Church on the way, is the entrance gate and car park for Suoi Voi. From here, the walk to the main springs is about a mile (1.6 km). Once there, the effects of the long, dusty walk can be washed away in its refreshing waters. Several large boulders surround the tree-filled area. All this is set scenically against the thickly jungled peaks of the Truong

Macaque monkey, Bach Ma National Park

Visitors enjoying a relaxed lunch at a seaside restaurant, Lang Co Beach

Son Range. Excellent for a break on the way to or from Hue, Suoi Voi is a perfect picnic spot. Facilities are minimal but there are usually food stands near the springs.

Lang Co Beach ❽

Road Map C3. 47 miles (75 km) S of Hue; 22 miles (35 km) N of Danang on Hwy 1. 🚉 *from Hue and Danang.* 🚌 *from Hue or Danang.* 🍴 🖥 📱

To appreciate the full beauty of the Lang Co Peninsula, it is best to first catch a glimpse of it from the summit of the Hai Van Pass or from the wonderful, atmospheric train ride between Hue and Danang. Looking north from here, an idyllic picture in shimmering blue, white, and green appears. A narrow spit of pristine white sand runs south from the Loc Vinh commune, dividing a gleaming saltwater lagoon

to its west from the choppy South China Sea to its east. It is an idyllic location, with miles of palm-fringed, soft white sand contrasting beautifully with the aquamarine waters of the lagoon and the changing shades of the wave-flecked sea.

The beach is ideal for a leisurely swim, especially in the summer months before July, after which the area can get rather wet and dreary. Fortunately, an excellent seafood lunch can be enjoyed here in any season. There are also several resorts in the area for those wishing to make a longer stay. The sleepy Lang Co village provides a glimpse into Vietnam's simple coastal way of living.

Just south of Lang Co, a new bridge vaults across the lagoon, leading to the new road tunnel that carries Highway 1 beneath the Hai Van Pass. This sheltered area around the bridge provides a convenient harbor for local fishermen. A stroll along this inland part of the spit reveals brightly-painted fishing boats as well as coracles, which are tiny circular boats that look a little like wicker baskets.

Thuan An Beach ❾

Road Map C3. 9 miles (15 km) NE of Hue on Hwy 49. 🚌 🍴 🖥 📱

One of the best beaches in the Hue region, Thuan An is located at the northern end of a long, slender island that

runs all the way south from the mouth of the Perfume River *(see p148)*, almost up to the little town of Phu Loc.

The beach is in many ways comparable to the one at Lang Co, some 56 miles (90 km) farther south. Like it, Thuan An features a pleasing strip of white sand flanked by tall, swaying coconut palms. It is washed by the calm blue waters of the Thanh Lam Lagoon to the southwest, while the rather stormy waves of the South China Sea lap its northeast shores.

Still relatively undeveloped, the village of Thuan An is sparsely settled by fishermen, whose boats are pulled up along the sandy shores. The manufacture of *nuoc mam* or fish sauce is an important industry here. Its pungent – some may say putrid – odor permeates the air in certain areas. The vats used for fermenting the liquid are obvious not only from the smell but also because of their vast size.

Thuan An is a convenient and enjoyable destination for a cycling day trip from Hue. Getting to the beach is half the fun, as it entails a ride through numerous tranquil villages and rural scenery, dotted with several quaint pagodas along the way. The island and beach can be accessed via a small bridge over the Thanh Lam Lagoon. A narrow road runs along the length of the island, hugging the lagoon side, as far as Thanh Duyen Pagoda on its southernmost tip.

Lagoon near Lang Co Beach, with a clear view of the summit of the Hai Van Pass

Hue ⑩

One of the most significant cultural and historic centers of Vietnam, the former imperial city of Hue is celebrated for its tradition of intellectual thought, Buddhist piety, and the sophistication of its cuisine. Despite the damage it suffered during the Indochina Wars, it remains a place of great beauty, with the Perfume River *(see p148)* flowing through it. To the north is the Citadel *(see pp140–3)*, containing the Forbidden City and the royal palaces, while to the south are many ancient pagodas and tombs, and the town's French Quarter. Excellent hotels and restaurants along with its palpably French atmosphere add to the city's many attractions.

Sculpture in Dieu De Pagoda

Business as usual in the constantly busy Dong Ba Market

🏛 Imperial City
See pp140–43.

🏛 Royal Antiquities Museum
150 Nguyen Hue St.
Tel (054) 352 4429. ◯ 7am–5pm daily. 📷 🚫
This museum is located in the former private residence of Emperor Khai Dinh and his adopted son Bao Dai. Both were passionate about French fashion and lifestyle, but Khai Dinh took his obsession to an extreme, living like a spoiled French playboy rather than a responsible monarch. The villa is more French than Vietnamese in style. Like Khai Dinh's tomb *(see p145)*, it departs from typical Nguyen architecture, reflecting instead this occupant's flamboyant personality.
   The exhibits, which were officially opened in 2010 after an extensive restoration project, include silver crafts, fine porcelain, antique furniture, and items from the royal wardrobe.

🏛 Dieu De Pagoda
29 Le Quy Don St. **Tel** (054) 381 5161. ◯ sunrise–sunset daily.
Built during the reign of Thieu Tri (r.1841–7), the third Nguyen Emperor, Dieu De fell into disrepair over the years, but was restored in 1889 by Emperor Than Tha. Renovated many times since, it dates from 1953 in its present form.
   The pagoda is distinguished by drum and bell towers, and a sanctuary dedicated to the Thich Ca Buddha, or the Historical Buddha. As with other Buddhist pagodas in Hue, it is closely associated with the politics of nationalism and opposition to the oppressive Diem regime (1955–63). In May 1963, Buddhist monk Nun Nu Thanh Quang immolated himself here in protest.

🏛 Dong Ba Market
Northeast of Tran Hung Dao St. ◯ daily.
Hue's bustling Dong Ba Market is located to the north of the Perfume River, near the southeast corner of the Citadel. A popular local shopping center, it attracts huge crowds daily. Stalls here overflow with an astonishing variety of goods, from fresh produce and fish to clothing, toys, shoes, and cosmetics. The market is at its busiest and most fascinating in the early hours of the morning, even though it is open throughout the day.

🏛 Notre Dame Cathedral
80 Nguyen Hue St. **Tel** (054) 382 8690. ◯ during mass.
Built between 1958 and 1962 in a hybrid Franco-Vietnamese style, this large and somewhat unappealing church serves around 1,500 local believers. Two masses are held daily at 5am and 5pm, with a third mass at 7am on Sunday. At other times, the main gates are generally locked.

🏛 Bao Quoc Pagoda
Bao Quoc St. **Tel** (054) 383 6400. ◯ sunrise–sunset daily.
Giac Phong, a Buddhist monk from China, founded this historic pagoda on Ham Long Hill in 1670. It was later granted royal status by the Nguyen Lord, Phuc Khoat (r.1738–65). In the late 18th century, the powerful Tay Son *(see p41)* rebel, Quang Trung, used this house of worship for storing armaments. The temple was also given royal support by Emperor Minh Mang (r.1820–41). In 1940, it became a school for training Buddhist monks, a function it

The colonnaded entryway of Bao Quoc Pagoda

fulfills to this day. Though it was renovated in the mid-20th century, the pagoda retains its charm and aura of antiquity even today.

🏛 Tu Dam Pagoda

1 Duong Lieu Quan St.
Tel (054) 383 6118.
◯ *sunrise–sunset daily.*
Founded in the 17th century, this temple's chief importance is as a center for supporting Buddhism, a cause that has been at the heart of Central Vietnam's political culture for a long time. The Vietnamese Buddhist Association established its headquarters here in 1951, and the temple was a major hub of activity during the Buddhist agitation against President Diem's unpopular Catholic regime during the mid-20th century. As was the disturbing trend at the time, in 1963 a monk burned himself to death in

An exquisite urn in the courtyard of Tu Dam Pagoda

the pagoda's courtyard in protest against the oppressive administration.

The central altar is presided over by the Thich Ca Buddha, and a tree in the temple grounds is said to have been grown from a cutting of the original *bodhi* tree in India.

VISITORS' CHECKLIST

Road Map C3. Capital of Thue Thien Hue Province, 62 miles (110 km) N of Danang.
🏙 *300,000.* ✈ *from Hanoi and Ho Chi Minh City.* 🚉 *Reunification Express Hanoi and Ho Chi Minh City.* 🚌 *from Hanoi, Vinh, Danang, Nha Trang, and Ho Chi Minh City.* 🚏 🛈 *Hue Tourist, Chu Van An St, (054) 381 6263.* **www.**huetouristvietnam.com

---

🌉 Thanh Toan Covered Bridge

Thanh Thuy Chan Village, 4 miles (7 km) E of Hue.
The little known but delightful covered bridge at Thanh Toan is architecturally similar to the famous Japanese Covered Bridge *(see p124)* at Hoi An, as well as the covered bridge across the canal at Phat Diem. Getting to it is half the fun, and provides a great trip through scenic villages.

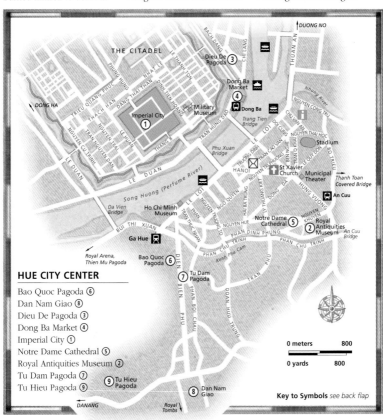

HUE CITY CENTER

0 meters   800
0 yards   800

Key to Symbols *see back flap*

Hue Citadel: Imperial City

Finely detailed mosaics, Royal Library

Designated a World Heritage Site in 1993, the Citadel was established by Emperor Gia Long (r.1802–20) in 1805. The huge fortress comprises three concentric enclosures – the Civic, Imperial, and Forbidden Purple Cities. The Citadel was designed using the rules of Chinese geomancy, along with the military principles favored by French architect Sebastien de Vauban. The result is an unusual yet elegant complex, where beautiful palaces and temples coexist with massive ramparts, bastions, and moats. Despite the horrific damage caused by the Indochina Wars, recent restoration work has re-imagined some of the Citadel's lost architectural grandeur.

Richly decorated gilt and lacquer altar to a Nguyen king, The Mieu

Hung Mieu

Dedicated to the veneration of Emperor Gia Long's mother and father, this 19th-century temple is known for the glazed carvings on its tiled roof. Particularly noteworthy are the large gargoyle-like stone dragons keeping vigil over the spacious paved courtyard.

The Mieu honors ten Nguyen Emperors, and has recently been restored to its original splendor.

★ Nine Dynastic Urns

Cast between 1835 and 1837, these massive bronze funerary urns stand in the courtyard facing The Mieu. They represent the might of nine Nguyen Emperors, and are richly embellished with bas-reliefs of a host of powerful symbols.

STAR FEATURES

★ Nine Dynastic Urns

★ Thai Hoa Palace

★ Ngo Mon Gate

Hien Lam Pavilion

Built by Emperor Minh Mang in 1824, Hien Lam Pavilion is a three-storied galleried portico, with a wooden façade, decorated with engraved wooden beams and panels in floral designs.

For hotels and restaurants in this region see p240 and pp256–7

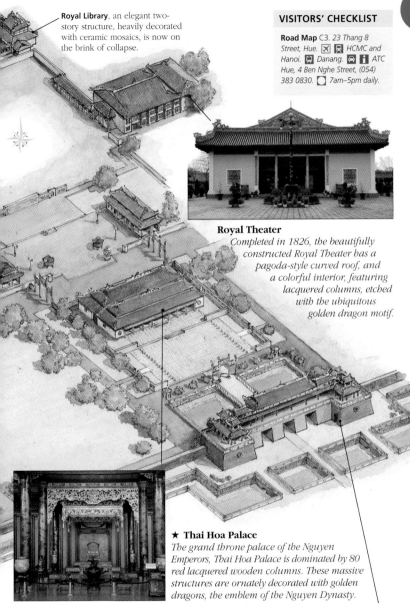

Royal Library, an elegant two-story structure, heavily decorated with ceramic mosaics, is now on the brink of collapse.

VISITORS' CHECKLIST

Road Map C3. 23 Thang 8 Street, Hue. ☒ 🚌 HCMC and Hanoi. 🚌 Danang. 🚌 🚶 ATC Hue, 4 Ben Nghe Street, (054) 383 0830. ◯ 7am–5pm daily.

Royal Theater
Completed in 1826, the beautifully constructed Royal Theater has a pagoda-style curved roof, and a colorful interior, featuring lacquered columns, etched with the ubiquitous golden dragon motif.

★ Thai Hoa Palace
The grand throne palace of the Nguyen Emperors, Thai Hoa Palace is dominated by 80 red lacquered wooden columns. These massive structures are ornately decorated with golden dragons, the emblem of the Nguyen Dynasty.

★ Ngo Mon Gate
The majestic main entrance to the Citadel, Ngo Mon is a superb example of Nguyen architecture. Massive stone slabs form the foundation, upon which rests an elaborate watchtower, where the emperor sat enthroned on state occasions.

Exploring Hue Citadel: Imperial City

At the very heart of the vast Hue Citadel lies the Imperial City, also known as Dai Noi or the Great Enclosure. Over the past few years, this historic and unusually evocative part of the Citadel has undergone extensive restoration work, which has allowed more than just a glimmer of its former glory and grandeur to shine through. Entrance to this royal city is via the imposing Ngo Mon Gate, beyond which a bridge leads between lotus-filled ponds to the splendid Thai Hoa Palace. Behind this is an open courtyard that overlooks a stretch of land, once home to the Forbidden Purple City.

Figurine of a royal court musician

🏯 Cot Co or Flag Tower

Looming over the Citadel at a height of 120 ft (37 m), the Flag Tower or Cot Co has dominated Hue's skyline since 1809, when Emperor Gia Long (r.1802–20) erected it over a big 59-ft (18-m) brick redoubt.

On January 31, 1968, during the Tet Offensive (see p45), Cot Co achieved international recognition when the communist forces seized the Citadel, hoisting the National Liberation Front's yellow-starred banner on the Flag Tower's mast.

Nine Deities' Cannons

Cast by Emperor Gia Long in 1803 as symbolic protection for his new capital, these colossal cannons were made out of bronze. Each weapon is said to represent one of the four seasons and five elements – earth, metal, wood, water, and fire. The cannons can be seen flanking the Ngan and Quang Duc Gates on either side of Cot Co.

🏯 Five Phoenix Watchtower

Located above the huge stone slabs of the Ngo Mon Gate, this elaborate pavilion was where the emperor sat enthroned on state occasions. Viewed from above, it is said to resemble a group of five phoenixes. The middle section of the roof is covered with yellow glazed tiles, and decorated with dragons, banyan leaves, and bats, while the panels along the eaves are embellished with ceramic orchid, chrysanthemum, and bamboo mosaics. Above the pavilion, a concealed staircase leads up to a room from where women of the court could see through finely carved grills.

🏛 Thai Hoa Palace

🖼 in the throne room.

Originally built by Emperor Gia Long in 1805, Thai Hoa or Hall of Supreme Harmony housed the throne room of the Nguyen Emperors. The most impressive of Hue's remaining palaces, it has been beautifully restored. It is easy to envisage the hall as the venue for coronations, royal anniversaries, and the reception of ambassadors. On these occasions, the emperor would sit on the resplendent throne, wearing a crown with nine dragons, a gold robe, jade belt, and other attire. Only the most senior mandarins were allowed to stand in the hall, while others waited outside.

🏯 Halls of the Mandarins

On either side of a paved courtyard, just behind Thai Hoa, are the Halls of the Mandarins. One hall was for the military, and the other for civil mandarins. In keeping with their ranks, they would gather at their pavilions to dress in ceremonial robes for imperial functions. Some of these gorgeous vestments are now kept on display here.

Ancient bronze cauldron in the courtyard, Halls of the Mandarins

⛩ Forbidden Purple City

No man except the emperor was permitted to set foot in the 25-acre (10-ha) city-within-a-city known as Tu Cam Thanh or Forbidden Purple City – any male who crossed its threshold was condemned to death. Only the queen, nine separate ranks of concubines, female servants, and court eunuchs were allowed to enter.

Built during 1802 and 1833, the Forbidden City once comprised more than 60 buildings arranged around numerous courtyards, but unfortunately, it was damaged extensively by heavy bombing during the 1968 Tet Offensive.

🎭 Royal Theater

Rebuilt in 1825, the Duyet Thi Duong or the Royal Theater is once again a leading venue for traditional entertainment, offering performances of nha nhac (see p25) or court music. Declared a Masterpiece of the Oral and Intangible Heritage of Humanity by UNESCO, nha nhac features bamboo lutes, zithers, and fiddles, accompanied by drums.

Four of the Nine Deities' Cannons, one for each season and element

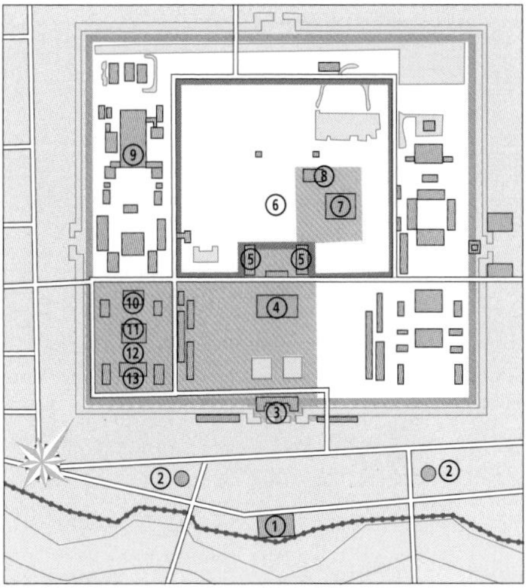

PLAN OF IMPERIAL CITY

Cot Co [1]
Dien Tho Palace [9]
Five Phoenix Watchtower [3]
Forbidden Purple City [6]
Halls of the Mandarins [5]
Hien Lam Pavilion [13]
Hung Mieu [10]
Nine Deities' Cannons [2]
Nine Dynastic Urns [12]
Royal Library [8]
Royal Theater [7]
Thai Hoa Palace [4]
The Mieu [11]

KEY

Imperial City

Forbidden Purple City

Area illustrated *(see pp140–41)*

Wall of The Citadel

Royal Library

In the northeastern quarter of the Forbidden City, the Royal Library was constructed by Emperor Minh Mang in 1821, as a retreat where he read in solitude. The decrepit building stands before an artificial pond, with a rock garden to its west. Small bridges, crossing other lakes and ponds, connect various galleries, creating a tranquil atmosphere. The library has been used to stage performances of Hue music, as well as various theatrical events.

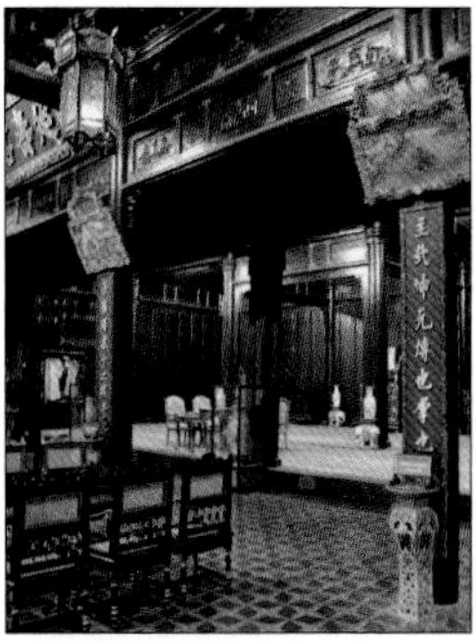

Antique furnishings and wood paneling, Dien Tho Palace

Dien Tho Palace

Once the exclusive preserve of the Queen Mothers, Cung Dien Tho or the Residence of Everlasting Longevity was built in 1803 during the reign of Emperor Gia Long. Open to the public, the elegant building is surrounded by a wall that is pierced on the south by Cua Tho Chi or the Gate of Everlasting Happiness. Inside the building, the crafted furniture is carefully inlaid with delicate mother-of-pearl, and carved lanterns hang from the ceiling, which is ornamented with fans made from feathers. To the east of the entrance to the palace is the Truong Du Pavilion, with a small artificial lake and a graceful rock garden.

Hung Mieu

Emperor Minh Mang built Hung Mieu in 1821 to honor his grandparents. The temple was seriously damaged by fire in 1947 at the beginning of the First Indochina War, but has now been restored. It is renowned for its refined design and fine roof carvings.

The Mieu

Located in the southwest area of Imperial City, The Mieu or the Temple of Generations is dedicated to the Nguyen Dynasty, and contains altars honoring emperors, from Gia Long to Khai Dinh. The building has a roof of yellow glazed tiles, the ridge of which is decorated in the shape of a wine gourd. The altars were once stacked high with gold ingots, but today these have been replaced with gilt and lacquer ornamentation.

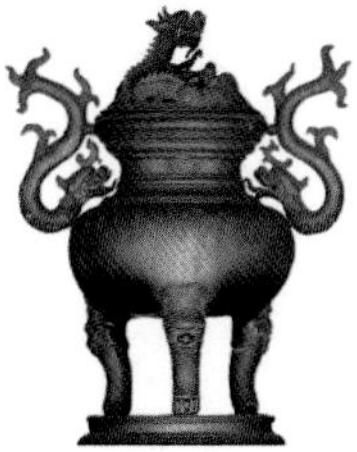

Miniature funerary urn, The Mieu

Nine Dynastic Urns

Cast on the orders of Emperor Minh Mang, Cuu Dinh or Dynastic Urns of the Nguyen Dynasty weigh up to 2.75 tons each. Decorated with traditional patterns, and rich in symbolic detail, they play a big role in the cult of imperial ancestor veneration.

Hien Lam Pavilion

Located in the center of the The Mieu court, Hien Lam was built in 1824 by Emperor Minh Mang to honor those who gave the great Nguyen Dynasty its formidable status. As a mark of respect, it was declared that no other building in the Citadel could rise higher than Hien Lam, which is distinguished by its pyramid shape, as well as its finely crafted wooden façade and brick paving.

⋔ Dan Nam Giao

2 miles (3 km) S of city center,
southern end of Dien Bien Phu St.
◯ 8am–5pm daily. 📷

Built by Emperor Gia Long in
1802, Dan Nam Giao or the
Altar of Heaven stands beyond
the former French Quarter on
the east side of the Perfume
River (see p148). For more
than a century, this was the
most important ceremonial
site in the country. Approximately every three years,
between 1806 and 1945, the
Nguyen Emperors reaffirmed
the legitimacy of their rule
through a series of elaborate
sacrifices to the Emperor
of Heaven. The ritual was
consciously modeled on
the rites practiced in Beijing
by the Chinese emperors at
the 15th-century Tian Tan
or Temple of Heaven.

Today, not much remains
of this ceremonial site other
than a series of three raised
terraces. The first two are
square-shaped and are said to
represent humanity and earth.
The circular terrace at the
top symbolizes the heavens.
Though there isn't much of
the building left, the site has
plenty of atmosphere. In this
setting, it is easy to conjure
up images of the emperors as
the rightful Sons of Heaven,
interceding with the gods on
behalf of their subjects.

⛩ Tu Hieu Pagoda

Thon Thuong 2, Thuy Xuan Village,
3 miles (5 km) SW of Hue. Tel (054)
383 6389. ◯ 6am–6pm daily.

Set amid the attractive pine
woods to the north of Tu
Duc's tomb, Tu Hieu Pagoda
is surrounded by a delightful

The crumbling but fairly intact remains of the Royal Arena

crescent-shaped lotus pond.
One of the most serene pagodas in the Hue region, it was
established in 1848 by imperial eunuchs. Since they could
not have children, the eunuchs
financially secured the temple,
thus guaranteeing that future
generations of monks would
always be on hand to perform
the necessary ceremonies for
their lives in the hereafter.
Indeed, several monks still
inhabit Tu Hieu and hold
prayer services daily.
The main shrine
is dedicated to
Sakyamuni
Buddha, also
known as the
Thich Ca Buddha.
Lesser altars
carry images and
tablets honoring
various deities and
some prominent
eunuchs of the past.

⛩ Thien Mu Pagoda

3 miles (5 km) SW of Hue Citadel.
◯ sunrise–sunset daily.

Rising on a bluff above the
northwest bank of the Perfume
River, Thien Mu or Heavenly
Lady Pagoda is an iconic
symbol of Hue. Founded in
1601 by Lord Nguyen Hoang,
the pagoda is dominated by a
seven-story octagonal tower,
Thap Phuoc Duyen, which
translates as Source of Happiness Tower. A pavilion close
by shelters a huge bronze bell
cast in 1710. Weighing more
than 4,409 lb (2,000 kg), it
can purportedly be heard at
least 6 miles (10 km) away.
A second pavilion houses a
stone stele erected in 1715,
which eulogises the history of

Buddhism in Hue. Inside, the
main shrine is presided over
by a laughing bronze Buddha
and statues of the ten kings
of hell and 18 arbat or holy
disciples of the Buddha. Close
by is a striking image of the
Thich Ca Buddha.

The monks' quarters and
gardens are at the back of the
temple. In an open garage to
the west is the car that drove
monk Thich Quang Duc (see
p44) to Saigon in June 1963,
where he immolated
himself in protest
against the Diem
regime. Images
of this horrific
event were
shown all over
the world,
provoking
widespread shock
and outrage.

Thich Quang Duc's blue
Austin, Thien Mu Pagoda

♖ Royal Arena

Phuong Duc Village, 3 miles (4 km)
SW of Hue. ◯ sunrise–sunset daily.

Built for the entertainment of
the Nguyen Emperors and the
mandarins, this amphitheater
is also known as Ho Quyen
or the Tiger Arena. It was used
to stage combats between
elephants, symbolizing
royalty, and tigers, signifying
the former Champa Kingdom.
As a result, these contests were
rigged so that the elephant
would win. To achieve this,
the tiger was declawed and
had its mouth sewn shut.

Fortunately, no fights have
been held since 1904, but the
place remains in fairly good
condition. The viewing platforms are intact, as are the
five doors opposite leading
to the tigers' cages.

Lotus pond in front of the small and
serene Tu Hieu Pagoda

Exploring the Royal Tombs

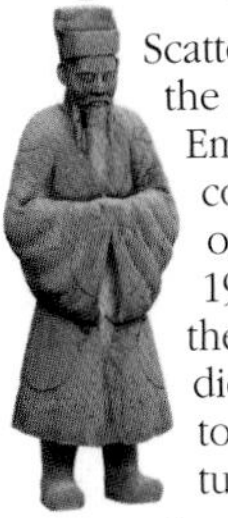

Statue at the Tomb of Tu Duc

Scattered across the scenic countryside to the south of Hue, the tombs of the Nguyen Emperors *(see p41)* are among the area's most compelling attractions. Although 13 rulers sat on the imperial throne between 1802 and 1945, only seven were given the honor of their own mausoleum, or *lang,* as the others died during exile or in disgrace. All seven tombs have features of outstanding architectural merit, and can be reached by bicycle, motorbike, taxi, and by boat. The tomb of Duc Duc is most modest of the lot.

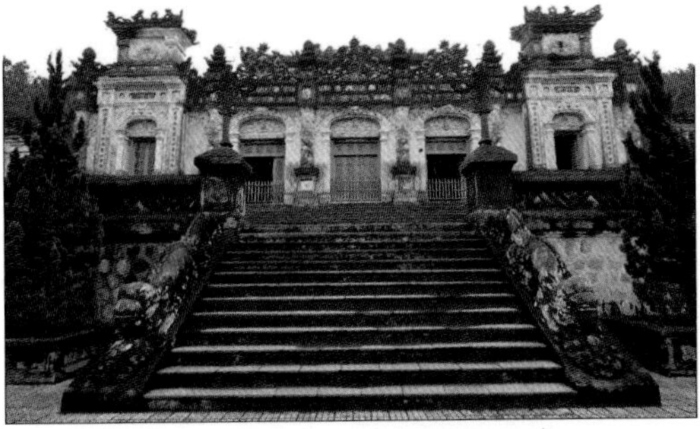

Concrete exterior of the least traditional royal tomb, Khai Dinh

🏛 Tomb of Tu Duc

4 miles (6 km) SW of Hue. ***Tel*** *(054) 383 6428.* 🕐 *7am–5pm daily.* ✋

Considered by many to be the most elegant tomb in Vietnam, the mausoleum of Tu Duc (r.1848–83) was designed by the king himself. Set on a pine-forested hill, it is flanked by beautiful lotus ponds and aromatic frangipani trees. Tu Duc was known to have preferred the quiet comforts of his future tomb to his own palace. It is said that when Tu Duc died, he was buried secretly along with a great treasure. All those involved in his burial were later executed to keep his final resting place safe from desecration.

🏛 Tomb of Dong Khanh

0.3 miles (0.5 km) SE of Lang Tu Duc. ***Tel*** *(054) 383 6427.* 🕐 *7am–6pm daily.* ✋

The smallest of all Nguyen tombs is the mausoleum of Dong Khanh (r.1885–88). The French influence is quite prominent in its interior, where images of Napoleon Bonaparte hang from the red-lacquered ironwood pillars. The tomb benefitted from a restoration project completed in 2009.

🏛 Tomb of Thieu Tri

1 mile (1.5 km) S of Lang Tu Duc. 🕐 *7am–5pm daily.* ✋

The small tomb of Thieu Tri (r.1841–47) features several artificial ponds, although it lacks the usual extensive walled gardens. The complex is divided into two parts. To the east, a delicate temple salutes the deceased, while to the west is the tomb itself.

🏛 Tomb of Khai Dinh

6 miles (10 km) S of Hue. ***Tel*** *(054) 386 5875.* 🕐 *6am–5.30pm daily.* ✋

Khai Dinh (r.1916–25), the penultimate Nguyen Emperor, was the last to be buried in a royal tomb at Hue. His tomb makes use of concrete, combining European and Vietnamese architectural styles in a unique but not entirely successful fusion. Built into the side of a hill, the tomb rises steeply through three levels. In the temple at the summit is a bronze bust of the emperor, cast at Marseilles in 1922.

🏛 Tomb of Minh Mang

7 miles (12 km) S of Hue. ***Tel*** *(054) 356 0277.* 🕐 *7:30am–5:30pm daily.* ✋

Located on the west side of the Perfume River, the mausoleum of Emperor Minh Mang, who died in 1841, is one of the most impressive royal tombs. The complex comprises picturesque lakes and gardens, as well as numerous buildings.

🏛 Tomb of Gia Long

10 miles (16 km) SE of Hue. ✋

The mausoleum of the first Nguyen Emperor, Gia Long, is best reached by boat, either from Hue or from the tiny village of Tuan, opposite Lang Minh Mang. The most remote of all, it suffered extensive damage during the Vietnam War and sadly is still in a state of disrepair.

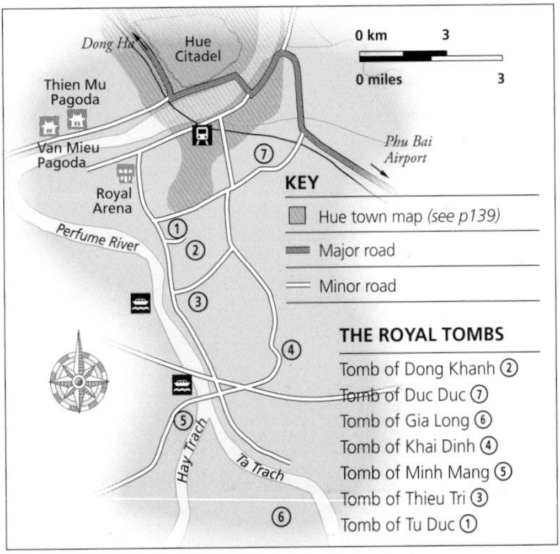
Dong Ha
Hue Citadel
Thien Mu Pagoda
Van Mieu Pagoda
Royal Arena
Perfume River
Phu Bai Airport
Hay Trach
Ta Trach
0 km 3
0 miles 3
KEY
Hue town map (see p139)
Major road
Minor road
THE ROYAL TOMBS
Tomb of Dong Khanh ②
Tomb of Duc Duc ⑦
Tomb of Gia Long ⑥
Tomb of Khai Dinh ④
Tomb of Minh Mang ⑤
Tomb of Thieu Tri ③
Tomb of Tu Duc ①

The impressive tomb of the Nguyen Emperor, Khai Dinh ▷

Perfume River Boat Tour

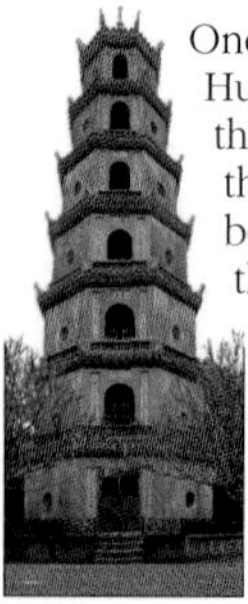

The multi-tiered Thien Mu Pagoda

One of the main highlights of a visit to Hue is a boat ride along Song Huong or the Perfume River. Though not very long, the slow-winding river is extraordinarily beautiful. The effect is enhanced by the reflection of the Citadel, pagodas, towers, and the scenic countryside. Added to this spectacular view is the picturesque river traffic – women sculling tiny, single-oared vessels, larger boats piled high with fish and fresh vegetables, and fishermen in narrow crafts, casting their nets or retrieving fish traps.

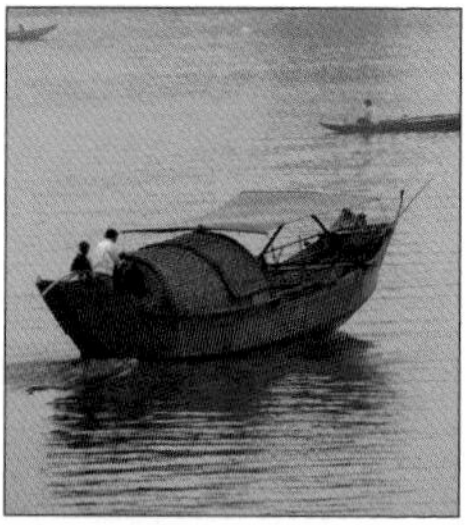

A fishing boat on the calm blue waters of Perfume River

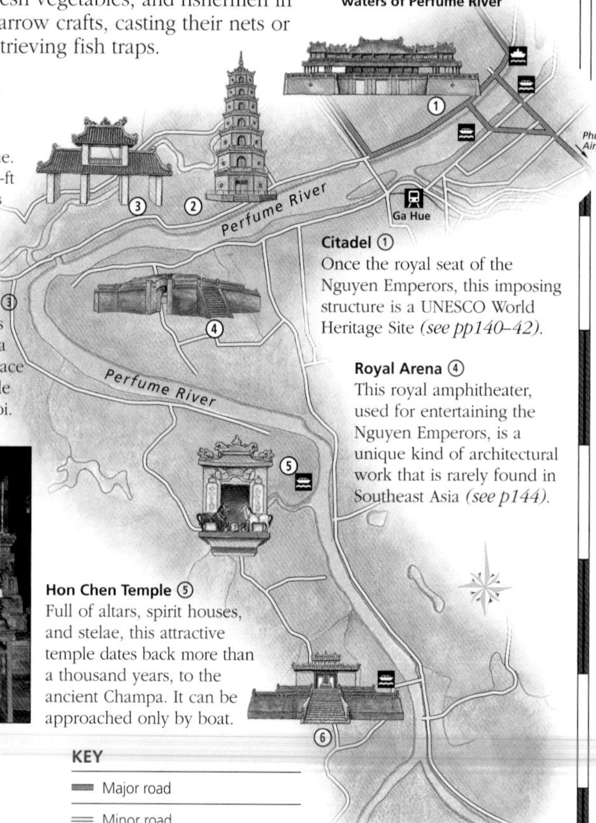
Perfume River
Perfume River
Ga Hue
Phu Bai Airport

Thien Mu Pagoda [2]
Set amidst verdant greenery, this is the oldest pagoda in Hue. Built in 1601, the 69-ft (21-m) high tower is an official symbol of the city of Hue *(see p144)*.

Temple of Literature [3]
This tiny temple was built by Emperor Gia Long in 1808 to replace the venerable Temple of Literature in Hanoi.

Citadel [1]
Once the royal seat of the Nguyen Emperors, this imposing structure is a UNESCO World Heritage Site *(see pp140–42)*.

Royal Arena [4]
This royal amphitheater, used for entertaining the Nguyen Emperors, is a unique kind of architectural work that is rarely found in Southeast Asia *(see p144)*.

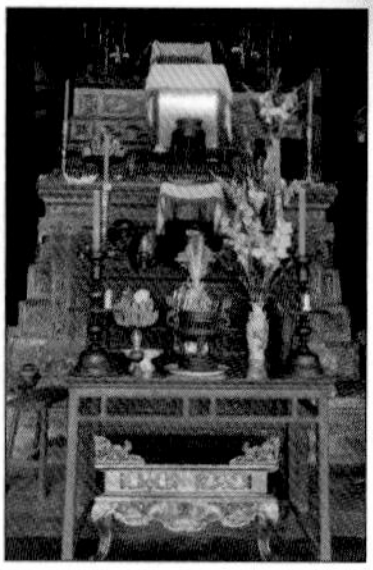

Hon Chen Temple [5]
Full of altars, spirit houses, and stelae, this attractive temple dates back more than a thousand years, to the ancient Champa. It can be approached only by boat.

0 kilometers 2

0 miles 1

KEY

Major road

Minor road

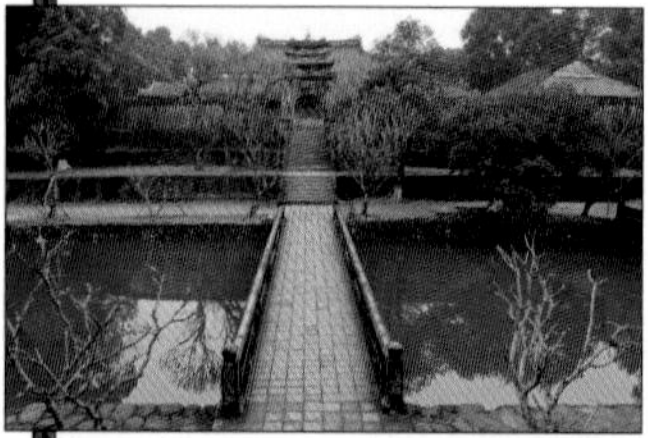

Tomb of Minh Mang [6]
This is possibly the best preserved royal tomb in Hue. Graceful statuary, ponds, and beautifully landscaped gardens add to the mausoleum's grandeur *(see p145)*.

TIPS FOR THE TRIP

Tour boats: *Hire boats from the wharf by Le Loi Street. Try to haggle the price quoted. Or take a well-organized tour.*
Time taken: *Half a day.*
Stopping-off points: *Snacks available at Thien Mu and Minh Mang. Most boatmen arrange a lunch on request.*

Khe Sanh Combat Base ⓫

Road Map B3. 90 miles (145 km) NW of Hue on Hwy 9. **Tel** (053) 388 0840. 🚌 minibus from Hue. 🚌 **Museum** 1 mile N of Khe Sanh town. ◯ 7am–5pm daily. 📷 💻

Situated close to the Laos border, the Khe Sanh Combat Base lies about 2 miles (3 km) away from Khe Sanh village, now known as Hoang Ho. It was initially developed as an airstrip by the Americans in 1962, and later enlarged and developed into a US Special Forces base charged with intercepting traffic on the Ho Chi Minh Trail (see p151).

However, Khe Sanh is best known as the site of one of the most ferocious battles of the Vietnam War, and as the beginning of the end for the Americans in Vietnam. In 1968, the famous US General William Westmoreland started a massive build up at the base with a view to forcing the North Vietnamese Army into direct confrontation. Vietnam's General Vo Nguyen Giap took the bait, but in a masterful double-play, used the siege, which lasted from January to April 1968, to distract attention from the Tet Offensive (see p45). Diversionary tactic or not, the heavy deployment of bombs and relentless gunfire resulted in a number of casualties. An estimated 207 American and 9,000 Vietnamese soldiers died, and several thousand civilians lost their lives.

Although this battle was not, as President Johnson feared, another Dien Bien Phu (see p195), the Americans, though undefeated, were forced to withdraw from Khe Sanh. They took great pains to bury,

The historic Hien Luong Bridge over the Ben Hai River, DMZ

remove, or destroy, rather than abandon their military equipment where it could be used as propagandist evidence of their "defeat."

Today, Khe Sanh is on the tourist map, with guided tours available. The drive along Highway 9, past statues and plaques, is part of the Central Vietnam experience. Though nothing had been left behind, American weaponry and vehicles were brought in from elsewhere in the south to fill the small **Museum** here.

Demilitarized Zone ⓬

Road Map B3. 53 miles (90 km) NE of Khe Sanh on Hwy 9. **Tel** (053) 385 2927. 🚌 minibus from Hue. 🚌 from Hue. ◯ 7am–5pm daily.

Though it lost all strategic and political importance after reunification in 1975, the Demilitarized Zone (DMZ)

has become a major tourist attraction and can be visited on a day trip from Hue or Dong Ha. Most tours start with the **Hien Luong Bridge** over the Ben Hai River, which once formed the frontier, and a visit to the well-constructed Vinh Moc Tunnels (see p150). The Truong Son National Cemetery, based to the west of Highway 1, honors the many thousands of North Vietnamese soldiers and Vietcong fighters killed in the area.

From here, it is convenient to head inland from Dong Ha along Highway 9, passing former US bases en route. Camp Carroll, Khe Sanh, and Hamburger Hill (see p45) have entered popular consciousness through Hollywood movies (see p59). While there is not very much in the way of "sights," the DMZ provides an often saddening tour. It is especially popular with military historians and American visitors.

Military memorabilia from the Vietnam War, DMZ

HISTORY OF THE DMZ

During the 1954 Geneva Conference, a decision was taken to establish the DMZ at the 17th Parallel as a "provisional demarcation line" between North and South Vietnam (see pp44–5). The boundary stretched 3 miles (2 km) on either side of Ben Hai River, continuing to the Lao border. From the beginning, however, the North Vietnamese Army (NVA) managed to penetrate the DMZ with their tunnels, trails, and guerilla tactics. In response, the Americans and South Vietnamese planted mines and built extensive electrified fences along Highway 9 in what became known as the McNamara Line after Robert McNamara, the then US Secretary of Defense. Ironically, the DMZ saw some of the heaviest fighting of the Vietnam War, particularly during the siege of Khe Sanh and the 1972 Easter Offensive, when the NVA seized the entire area, leading to a massive American retaliation.

Canon displayed at Khe Sanh near DMZ

The cavernous depths of a tunnel at the Vinh Moc complex

Vinh Moc Tunnels ⓭

Road Map C3. 8 miles (13 km) E of Ho Xa on Hwy 1; 12 miles (20 km) NE of the DMZ. **Tel** (053) 382 3184. 🚌 minibus from Hue and Dong Ha. 🚌 ⬜ 7:30am–5pm daily. 🗺 🖼

Some of the most resilient tunnels built in Vietnam were at Vinh Moc, a village along the South China Sea shore. Occupied by hundreds of people between 1968 and 1972, these tunnels were intended for long-term inhabitation. They are different from the better-known ones at Cu Chi (see p72), which was more of a frontline fighting base.

Vinh Moc's troubles began because of its location. After the nation's partition in 1954, villages along the north of the Demilitarized Zone (see p149), including Vinh Moc, found themselves under almost constant attack. Moreover, Vinh Moc faces Con Co Island, a North Vietnamese base used for transporting weapons and supplies to the south, making it a key target for strikes by the South Vietnamese Army. The United States Air Force (USAF) also contributed to the huge barrage of bombs, and Vinh Moc was nearly razed to the ground. While some inhabitants fled, others decided to stay, even if they had to go underground. The villagers, aided by the Vietcong, worked with nothing but spades, baskets, and their bare hands to excavate the complex tunnel network.

Created in about 18 months, the network stretches for 2 miles (3 km), with 13 entrance points. Family rooms, a hospital, and a meeting hall fill its three levels. The villagers and the North Vietnamese soldiers, lived here for more than four years – 17 children were born here. From these tunnels, almost 12,000 tons of military supplies and equipment were sent to Con Co.

Today, the marvel created by the villagers of Vinh Moc can be seen almost exactly as they were in 1972. Unlike Cu Chi, it is possible to negotiate these tunnels standing up straight, though taller visitors do have to stoop. The museum here makes for a fascinating browse. An added advantage are the sunny beaches nearby.

Bombed church in Dong Hoi

Dong Hoi ⓮

Road Map B3. 101 miles (162 km) N of Hue on Hwy 1. 🏯 100,000. 🚌 🚍 from Vinh, Dong Ha, and Hue. 🚍 ℹ Quang Binh Tourist, Huu Nghi St, (052) 382 2669. **www**.quangbinh.gov.vn

The capital of Quang Binh Province, Dong Hoi was once a charming little fishing village. However, mirroring Vietnam's changing economic policies, it has evolved into a leading transit town. Though there are no major sights here, it is remarkable to see how the town has recovered from the ravages of war. What was rubble a few decades ago has now changed to wide avenues and well-maintained buildings.

It is also interesting to note that for the best part of 150 years, Dong Hoi marked the de facto frontier between the Trinh and Nguyen Lords (see p41). Two major ramparts were constructed to keep the enemies separated, but all that remains of them is a crumbling gateway.

Though often only used as a stopover on the way to the Phong Nha Cave, there are some fine beaches nearby. Nhat Le, 2 miles (3 km) north of town, has one of the best.

Phong Nha Cave ⓯

Road Map B3. Son Trach Village, 34 miles (55 km) NW of Dong Hoi. **Tel** (052) 367 5323. 🚌 from Dong Hoi. 🚌 ⬜ from Son Trach. 🚌 ⬜ 6am–5pm. 🗺 🖼 🍴 🖼 🖼

By far the largest and most spectacular cave in Vietnam, Phong Nha dates back at least 20 million years and well deserves its designation as a UNESCO World Heritage Site. Its name translates somewhat alarmingly as Wind's Fangs, but this is only an allusion to its stalagmites. Packed with underground grottos, stalactites, stalagmites, and river systems, it extends back into the hills for many miles. The main cavern is some 5 miles (8 km) deep, with several smaller yet stunning caves clustered near it. Although speleologists have penetrated 22 miles (35 km) into the cave system, there are further mysteries of Phong Nha still to be revealed.

Not surprisingly, this is a very popular destination, and fleets of sampans wait at the visitors' center to ferry passengers upstream for about 3 miles (5 km), and then into the huge cavern. About a mile (1.6 km) into the cave is an area once held sacred by the Cham. The cave wall still bears an inscription carved by them many centuries ago.

Outside the cave, steep steps lead up 410 ft (125 m) to **Tien Son Cave**, another mighty cavern filled with fantastic stone formations. Water collected in its deep recesses is said to make men strong and women beautiful. Both caves are illuminated in places with bright, even garish, colors to enhance the effect for visitors.

A sampan dwarfed by the magnificence of Phong Nha Cave

Kim Lien ⑯

Road Map B2. 9 miles (14 km) NW of Vinh. 🚐 *minibus from Vinh.* 🚐

A pilgrimage site of sorts, Kim Lien is celebrated as the birthplace and childhood home of Ho Chi Minh *(see p169)*, who was born in nearby **Hoang Tru** village in 1890. He stayed there until he was five years old, and then moved to Hue with his father. In 1901, however, he returned and stayed here for another five years.

A man who always shunned the trappings of power, Ho Chi Minh vetoed the construction of a museum to his life at Kim Lien, arguing that the funds could be better used. Since his death in 1969, museums and shrines have proliferated here. About a mile (1.6 km) away at Hoang Tru, is a reconstruction of the house where he was born. A small museum nearby displays pictures and other personal memorabilia related to the leader's life. Also in this area is a reconstruction of the house where he lived from 1901 to 1906. In keeping with the great man's high principles, entry to all these sites is absolutely free of charge.

A bamboo loom in the model of Ho Chi Minh's childhood home, Kim Lien

HO CHI MINH TRAIL

A complex network of hidden tracks and paths, the Ho Chi Minh Trail, or Duong Truong Son, was used as a strategic connection between North and South Vietnam during the Vietnam War (1957–75). Built on simple tracks that had existed for centuries, the trail provided logistical support to communist forces in the south, supplying them with weapons, food, and legions of North Vietnamese troops (NVA).

Section of the trail running through bomb craters

It is assumed that the labrynthine trail started in the north near the port of Vinh. From there, it wound its way west through the Truong Suong Range, before snaking along the Vietnamese-Lao border and crossing into Laos and Cambodia. It finally entered South Vietnam at various obscure points. It is estimated that the total length of tracks and roads forming the trail was around 12,427 miles (20,000 km).

In 1972, South Vietnamese forces mounted a large scale incursion into Laos to cut the trail, but withdrew after sustaining heavy losses. Other failures followed despite massive bombing and defoliation by the South Vietnamese and Americans. In the meantime, NVA activity continued along the trail, playing a decisive role in the victory of the North.

HANOI

The oldest and one of the most attractive capital cities in Southeast Asia, Hanoi exudes a rare sense of gracious charm and timelessness. At its core exists a 600-year-old ancient quarter, augmented by a century-old colonial city. Today, the rich cultural heritage of both blends in perfect harmony with growing modernization, as Hanoi claims its position as the heart of Vietnam.

Hanoi, the "City within the River's Bend," was founded by Emperor Ly Thai To in AD 1010, near Co Loa, the ancient capital of the first Viet state dating back to the 3rd century BC. Ly Thai To structured this city, then known as Thang Long, around a massive citadel. To the east of this, a settlement of guilds was established to serve the needs of the royal court. By the 16th century, this area had developed into Hanoi's celebrated Old Quarter *(see pp156–7)*.

The arrival of the French in the 19th century marked a period of reconstruction, as they tore down parts of the citadel and some ancient temples to make way for the new European quarter. However, this cultural vandalism was compensated for, to a large extent, by the magnificent colonial architecture they bequeathed the city. During the First Indochina War *(see p43)*, the city's central districts escaped largely unharmed, and subsequently, in 1954, Hanoi was proclaimed the capital of independent Vietnam. Sadly, this was not the end of its violent history as it was then plunged into the conflict-ridden years against the US. Hanoi entered the 21st century a little run down yet structurally sound despite the years of warfare. The Opera House is still grand, as is the Sofitel Legend Metropole Hotel.

Today, Hanoi is emerging as an elegant, cultured, and affluent city, where museums and galleries coexist with chic shops and fashionable restaurants. One can wander, in a few minutes, from the narrow streets of the Old Quarter to the imposing mansions and buildings lining the leafy boulevards of the former French Quarter. Hanoi's past has also ensured a superb culinary legacy, where French and Chinese cuisines blend marvelously with Viet traditions. The same is true of Hanoi's lively arts scene, which is among the most sophisticated in Southeast Asia.

Well-maintained French-colonial building in the old French Quarter of Hanoi

◁ Aerial view of a street at night in the bustling Old Quarter *(see pp156–7)*

Exploring Hanoi

Hanoi's most significant sights and districts are marked on this map. Hoan Kiem Lake is popular for romantic strolls, morning exercise, and evening entertainment. The natural focus of the city center is to the north of the lovely lake. Known as the Old Quarter or 36 Streets, this area is packed with every imaginable merchandise, from shoes and silk to bamboo and lacquer products. To the south, which constitutes the downtown area, are the boulevards and architectural marvels of the former French Quarter. To the west is the tranquil Temple of Literature, and Ho Chi Minh Mausoleum, notable for its grandeur.

SIGHTS AT A GLANCE

Churches, Temples, and Pagodas
Ambassador's Pagoda **7**
Bach Ma Temple **2**
Hai Ba Trung Temple **11**
Hung Kings' Temples **26**
Kim Lien Pagoda **21**
Lien Phai Pagoda **12**
One Pillar Pagoda **17**
St. Joseph's Cathedral **5**
Tay Phuong Pagoda **25**
Temple of Literature pp166–7 **13**
Thay Pagoda **24**

Historic Buildings
Co Loa Citadel **22**
Ho Chi Minh's Stilt House **19**

Markets
Dong Xuan Market **1**

Museums and Theaters
Ho Chi Minh Mausoleum **18**
Ho Chi Minh Museum **16**

Hoa Lo Prison Museum **6**
Museum of Ethnology **23**
National Museum of Vietnamese History **10**
Opera House **9**
Thang Long Water Puppet Theater **3**
Vietnam Fine Arts Museum **14**
Vietnam Military History Museum **15**

Lakes
Ho Tay **20**
Hoan Kiem Lake **4**

Hotels
Sofitel Legend Metropole Hotel **8**

SEE ALSO

• *Where to Stay* pp240–3
• *Where to Eat* pp257–9

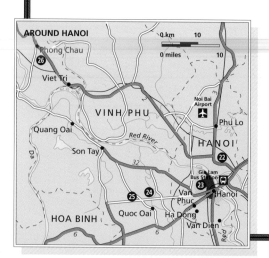

AROUND HANOI

Phong Chau **26**
Viet Tri
VINH PHU
Quang Oai
Son Tay
Noi Bai Airport
Phu Lo
HANOI
Gia Lam Bus Station
22
Van Phuc **23** Hanoi
25 **24**
Quoc Oai Ha Dong
Van Dien
HOA BINH
Red River
Da
32
6
6
Red

0 km   10
0 miles   10

KEY

Street-by-Street area: *see pp156–7*

✈ International airport

🚉 Train station

🚌 Long-distance bus station

⛴ Riverboat pier

▬ Major road

═ Minor road

— Railroad

– – Provincial border

GETTING AROUND

Hanoi's Old Quarter is small and fascinating enough
to explore on foot, as is the area around Hoan Kiem
Lake. Self-driven cars are not yet an option, though
the brave, or reckless, may rent a bicycle or motorbike.
Farther afield, it is better to take a taxi, since the city
bus service is still in its infancy. Most hotels and travel
agencies can arrange taxis or minibuses to visit
sights within the city as well as to the outskirts,
on full or half-day tours.

LOCATOR MAP
See Street Finder maps pp174– 7

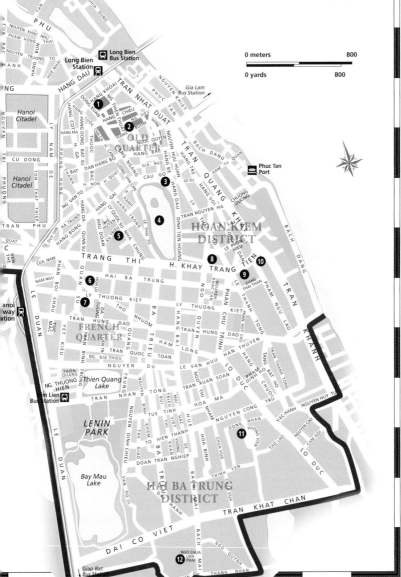

Street-by-Street: Old Quarter

Lacquered tray, Hang Gai Street

Buzzing with noise and activity, the Old Quarter is the oldest and most lively commercial district in Hanoi. During the 13th century, several artisans settled along the Red River to cater to the needs of the palace. Later, the crafts became concentrated in this area, with each street specializing in a particular product. Over the years, 36 distinct crafts guilds came into existence, and the area earned its nickname of 36 Streets. Today, with narrow alleys packed with hundreds of small shops, restaurants, and ancient tube houses (*see p27*), the Old Quarter retains its historic charm.

View of the centuries old, narrow, and long tube houses in the Old Quarter

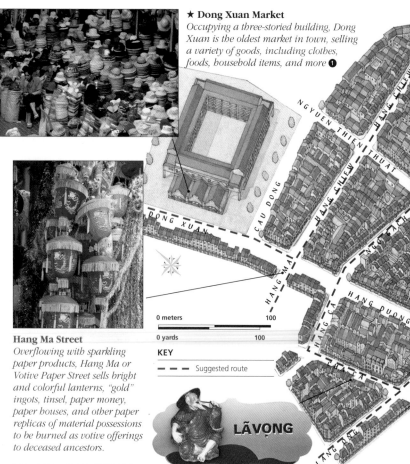

★ Dong Xuan Market
Occupying a three-storied building, Dong Xuan is the oldest market in town, selling a variety of goods, including clothes, foods, household items, and more ❶

Hang Ma Street
Overflowing with sparkling paper products, Hang Ma or Votive Paper Street sells bright and colorful lanterns, "gold" ingots, tinsel, paper money, paper houses, and other paper replicas of material possessions to be burned as votive offerings to deceased ancestors.

KEY

‒ ‒ ‒ Suggested route

0 meters 100
0 yards 100

Cha Ca La Vong
One of Hanoi's oldest eateries, Cha Ca La Vong has been serving a single dish – monkfish in a marinade of galangal, saffron, fermented rice, and fish sauce – for more than a century.

STAR SIGHTS

★ Dong Xuan Market

★ Bach Ma Temple

Hang Buom Street

Formerly the Sailmakers Street, Hang Buom now sells a remarkable selection of locally made sweetmeats and candies, many different varieties of fresh ground coffee, and imported alcohol, chiefly whiskies, brandies, and even wines.

Quan Chuong or the Gate of the Commander of the Regiment is the only remaining gateway to the Old Quarter out of the original 36.

Hang Mam Street or Pickled Fish Street is now lined with shops selling marble headstones, often engraved with an image of the deceased.

To Den Ngoc Son

★ Bach Ma Temple

The oldest religious building in the Old Quarter, this small temple is dedicated to the city's guardian spirit, represented by a magical white horse ❷

STREET NAMES IN OLD QUARTER

Most of the streets in the Old Quarter are named after the trade guilds that they once represented. The street names generally begin with the word *bang*, which means merchandise, while the second word describes the type of product. Streets here include Hang Gai (Silk Street), Hang Tre (Bamboo Street), Hang Bac (Silver Street), Hang Huong (Incense Street), and so on. Today, most of the streets in the Old Quarter offer products other than just what their name suggests. Even so, the survival of this system of guild streets is probably unique in East Asia.

Musical instruments, Hang Non Street

Memorial House Museum

Once the home of an affluent Chinese family, this beautifully restored tube house provides an excellent insight into the lives of merchants who lived in the Old Quarter centuries ago.

Memorial altar to General Ma Vien set amid flowers, Bach Ma Temple

Dong Xuan Market ❶

Intersection of Dong Xuan and Hang Chieu Sts, Old Quarter. **Map** 2 E2. **Tel** (04) 3829 5006. ☐ 6am–6pm daily. ☐ ☐

As the oldest and largest covered market in Hanoi, Cho Dong Xuan holds a dominant position in the city. Near the end of the 19th century, the French tore down the old East Bridge Market that stood at this site, and replaced it with a covered building with five large halls. Dong Xuan is named after a hamlet that once stood on this site and is now a commercial center. However, in 1994, the market suffered a major setback when a massive fire burnt down much of the building. Although it was rebuilt in 1996, all that remains of the original structure is the restored 1889 façade.

Today, this bustling three-story structure is packed with a wide range of clothing and household goods, fresh vegetables, meat and fish, and varieties of rice. Apart from local items, some low-cost, foreign goods are sold too.

Located nearby is the historic **Long Bien Bridge**. Its strategic importance as the only bridge across Hanoi's Red River made it a prime target of the US Air Force during the Vietnam War *(see pp44–5)*. It survived the heavy bombing and is now used by crowds of hawkers and pedestrians.

Bach Ma Temple ❷

76 Hang Buom St, Old Quarter. **Map** 2 E2. ☐ sunrise–sunset daily.

This small yet elegant temple is the oldest building in the Old Quarter *(see pp156–7)*, dating in its original form from the founding of the capital city of Thang Long *(see p160)*, which became known as Hanoi in the 11th century. According to legend, when King Ly Thai To established the capital in 1010, the city walls kept falling down until a magical white horse appeared and indicated where the new fortifications should be built. In an expression of his gratitude, Ly Thai To built the Bach Ma or White Horse Temple, and Bach Ma became the guardian spirit of the city.

The temple was restored in the 19th century, with contributions from the Hoa Chinese community settled on Hang Buom Street. Although a statue of the white horse still feature prominently, the Hoa also introduced the veneration of Ma Vien, the Chinese general who re-established Chinese control over Vietnam in AD 43. An antique, carved palanquin is also on display.

Thang Long Water Puppet Theater ❸

57 B Dinh Tien Hoang St, Hoan Kiem District. **Map** 2 E3. **Tel** (04) 3825 5450. ☐ performances at 4pm, 5:15pm, 6:30pm, and 8pm daily; also 9:30pm Sun. ☐ extra for still and video cameras. ☐ ☐ **www**.thanglongwaterpuppet.org

This is possibly the best place, not just in Hanoi, but in the entire country, to see performances of the traditional art of *roi nuoc* or water puppetry. The showmanship is excellent as master puppeteers make extensive use of dramatic music from the traditional orchestra and startling special effects, such as smoke, firecrackers, and water-spraying dragon puppets to create a lively performance. At the end of the show, the bamboo curtain behind the watery stage rises to show the puppeteers, standing waist deep in water. Seats closest to the stage provide superb opportunities for photography.

Exterior of the popular Thang Long Water Puppet Theater

Water Puppet Theater

Originating in the Red River Delta, and believed to date back almost a thousand years, *roi nuoc* or water puppetry is one of the most authentic expressions of Vietnamese culture. In times past, performances were held in villages, using rivers, lakes, or rice fields. Today, they are staged in large water-filled tanks at theaters. Hiding behind the stage, the puppeteers stand waist deep in water and maneuver their wooden charges to the music of a traditional orchestra. Special effects, including fire-breathing dragons, smoke, and fireworks add excitement to the show. The tales are told from the age-old perspective of a peasant culture and feature traditional protagonists and villains such as warrior heroes, corrupt landlords, and cruel rulers.

Water puppets for sale

Live singers and instrumentalists *greatly enhance the puppeteers' performance. The music rises to a crescendo at key moments in the story and accompanies the show at all times.*

Ty ba, *a popular plucking stringed instrument, used by musicians in many traditional orchestras. Made of light wood, it has four strings on its long neck.*

POPULAR THEMES

The themes of *roi nuoc* are usually traditional and pertain to rural life. Mythical beasts in Viet culture such as dragons, phoenixes, and unicorns, feature prominently, as do water buffalos and other domestic animals.

A wealthy mandarin, a typical villain, is carried in a palanquin by servants.

An elaborate parasol symbolizes rank and authority.

A fake palm tree adds a rural touch to the set.

Puppets *are carved from water-resistant wood, generally that of the fig tree or sung, and painted with bright colors.*

Village folk *surround a dragon, a much-loved and auspicious mythical creature that is one of the most prominent characters.*

Puppeteers *emerge from behind the curtain at the end of the show. Their skill is acknowledged by claps and rousing cheers.*

Scenic setting of The Huc or the Sunbeam Bridge, Hoan Kiem Lake

Hoan Kiem Lake ❹

Hoan Kiem District. **Map** 2 E3.
◯ *24 hours daily.* ⊞ ◻ ⬚
Den Ngoc Son Hoan Kiem Lake.
◯ *7am–7pm daily.*

Situated in the heart of Hanoi, this delightful body of water also lies close to the hearts of the Vietnamese people. Legend has it that in the early 15th century, during the Ming Chinese occupation *(see p40),* General Le Loi was presented with a magical sword by a divine, golden turtle, which lived in the lake's waters. With the help of this sword, Le Loi expelled the Chinese from Thang Long, present-day Hanoi, and established himself as Emperor Le Thai To. Some time later, when the emperor was sailing on the lake, the divine turtle once again rose to the surface and reclaimed the sword. Since

then, the lake has been known as Ho Hoan Kiem, or the Lake of the Restored Sword.

In the mid-19th century, a small pagoda called **Thap Rua** or Turtle Tower was built to commemorate this supernatural event. Located on an islet in the center of the lake, the structure has since become a prominent city icon.

On an island at the northern end of Hoan Kiem Lake stands **Den Ngoc Son** or Jade Mountain Temple, one of the most beautiful and revered religious buildings in the capital. The temple can be accessed by an attractive red-painted, arched wooden bridge. This is the celebrated **The Huc** or Sunbeam Bridge. Dating from the Nguyen Dynasty in the early 1800s, the temple's building

is exquisitely preserved. Decorated with upswept eaves and elaborate carved dragons, the predominant colors are red, gold, yellow, and black. The temple was established by a mandarin named Nguyen Van Sieu. A stylized stone ink slab rests atop the temple's gate, while nearby, a tapering stone pillar represents a traditional writing brush. The ideograms on the stele translate as "writing on a clear sky." In the antechamber, a giant turtle that died in the lake in 1968 is preserved. Den Ngoc Son is dedicated to the spirits of the soil, medicine, and literature, as well as to Tran Hung Dao, the general who defeated the Mongols in the 13th century *(see p40).*

To the east of the lake is the large, bronze **Statue of Ly Thai To**, honoring the great founder of Thang Long. The statue, which has already become quite popular with pious Vietnamese, is venerated with incense and flowers.

Today, Hoan Kiem Lake is one of the city's most popular venues, generally packed with couples taking a stroll, people practicing Tai Chi, and old men playing chess. The lake also plays a major role during the city's Tet celebrations *(see pp28–9),* with stages for live music and a huge fireworks display.

The brilliantly lit up Thap Rua reflected in Hoan Kiem Lake

THE FOUNDING OF THANG LONG

In AD 968, Tien Hoang De, the first ruler of the Dinh Dynasty, moved his capital from Dai La, situated in the immediate vicinity of modern-day Hanoi, to Hoa Lu, 50 miles (80 km) to the south in Ninh Binh Province. With this move, Tien Hoang intended

Puppets of golden dragons, an auspicious mythical creature

to relocate to a region that would be as far removed as possible from the Chinese frontier. However, this shift would not last for long. Just 42 years later, Ly Thai To, founder of the Ly Dynasty, grew dissatisfied with the physical isolation of Hoa Lu and determined to move the capital back to Dai La. In 1010, he returned to the former capital, defeated the Chinese in a violent battle, and established his kingdom here. According to legend, as he entered the city, a golden dragon took off from the top of the citadel and soared into the heavens. This event was taken by the emperor as an auspicious sign, and he renamed the city Thang Long or Ascending Dragon.

Neo-Gothic façade and imposing spires of St. Joseph's Cathedral

St. Joseph's Cathedral ❺

Nha Tho St, Hoan Kiem District.
Map 2 E3. **Tel** (04) 3828 5967.
⏰ 5am–7pm daily. **Chua Ba Da**
3 Nha Tho St, Hoan Kiem District.
⏰ sunrise–sunset daily.

Hanoi's most important church, St. Joseph's Cathedral, also known as Nha Tho Lon, was inaugurated in 1886, and provides a focal point for the city's Catholics. Built in the late neo-Gothic style, the building, with its majestic spires, is architecturally similar to a cathedral that might be found in any French provincial town. The interiors, which are more noteworthy, feature an ornate altar, French stained-glass windows, and a recent bas-relief painting of the Three Kings, complete with camels, on the cathedral's rear wall. St. Joseph's is usually packed to capacity on Sundays and on major holidays such as Easter and Christmas. However, on most days, its main doors are generally closed except during mass, but it is possible to gain entry via the side door.

Located on the south side of the cathedral is **Chua Ba Da** or Stone Lady's Pagoda. Dating back to the 15th century, the pagoda was once known as Linh Quang or Holy Light. However, according to legend, the discovery of a woman's stone statue when the pagoda was being constructed led to its more common local name.

Entered by a narrow way, Chua Ba Da is an oasis of tranquility in the heart of old Hanoi. The pagoda features several statues of the Thich Ca or Sakyamuni Buddha, and also contains two large, antique bronze bells.

Hoa Lo Prison Museum ❻

1 Hoa Lo St, Hoan Kiem District.
Map 2 D4. **Tel** (04) 3934 2253.
⏰ 8–11:30am, 1:30–4:30pm daily.

Located in downtown Hanoi, the infamous Hoa Lo Prison was built by the French administration in 1896. Originally intended to hold around 450 prisoners, by the 1930s the number of detainees had soared to almost 2,000, the majority of them being political prisoners. During the

Mural showcasing colonial torture, Hoa Lo Prison Museum

Vietnam War, Hoa Lo Prison achieved notoriety as a place of incarceration for downed US pilots, who ironically nicknamed it the Hanoi Hilton. Named Maison Centrale during the French rule – the original sign still hangs over the entrance – most of the prison complex was demolished in 1997 in order to make way for the Hanoi Central Tower building. However, the architects preserved enough of the old prison to create the Hoa Lo Prison Museum.

The majority of the exhibits here include a horrifying array of shackles, whips, and other instruments of torture, as well as tiny solitary confinement cells, which date from the French-colonial period. Also on display is part of the old, narrow sewer system through which more than 100 prisoners escaped in August 1945.

A small section of the museum is devoted to the American period, contriving to show how well US prisoners (including US senator John McCain) supposedly fared in contrast to the brutality shown to the Vietnamese by the French. At the back of the museum is a guillotine, a surprisingly simple yet terrifyingly efficient killing machine.

Ambassador's Pagoda ❼

73 Quan Su St, Hoan Kiem District.
Map 2 D4. **Tel** (04) 3942 4633.
⏰ 7:30–11:30am, 1:30–5:30pm daily.

Established as a stopping point for visiting Buddhist dignitaries, Chua Quan Su or Ambassador's Pagoda is named after a guesthouse that once stood here in the 15th century. The official center of Mahayana Buddhism in Hanoi, it is one of the most popular pagodas in the city, attracting hundreds of followers, especially during important Buddhist holidays.

The present-day pagoda dates from 1942 and houses images of the past, present, and future incarnations of the Buddha – the A Di Da or Amitabha, Thich Ca or Sakyamuni, and Di Lac or Maitreya Buddhas. Many nuns and monks are in attendance. A small shop by the entrance sells Buddhist paraphernalia and ritualistic items.

Ornate altar with multi-armed Buddha, Ambassador's Pagoda

Sofitel Legend Metropole Hotel ❽

15 Ngo Quyen St, Hoan Kiem District. **Map** 2 F4. **Tel** *(04) 3826 6919.* ☐ *24 hours daily.* ♿
🍴 ▯ ⌨ **www.sofitel.com**
Government Guest House 10 Ngo Quyen St, Hoan Kiem District. 📷 *to public.*

Hanoi's most prestigious and oldest hotel, the Metropole was built in French-colonial style, with plenty of wrought iron and Art Nouveau decorations. Originally opened in 1901, it was for many years the most favored accommodation in all of French Indochina. Notable guests, both past and present, include actors, writers, heads of state, and many other well-known public figures, such as W. Somerset Maugham (1874–1965), Charlie Chaplin (1889–1977), Graham Greene *(see p58)*, Noël Coward (1899–1973), Michael Caine, and Vladimir Putin.

Although the hotel became deplorably rundown during the austere years of state socialism between 1954 and 1986, it has since been magnificently restored to its former glory and luxurious grandeur.

The striking **Government Guest House**, just to the north of the Metropole, was built in 1919 as the palace of a French governor. Its colonial façade and multi-tiered portico in cast iron are attractive and well worth a second look.

Opera House ❾

1 Trang Tien St, Hoan Kiem District. **Map** 2 F4. **Tel** *(04) 3933 0132.* ☐ *during performances.* 📷 ♿ ⌨

Modeled on the Paris Opera designed by Charles Garnier, the Hanoi Opera House, also known as Nha Hat Lon or Big Song House, opened in 1911. It formed the centerpiece of French-colonial architecture, not just in Hanoi, but in all of French Indochina.

Before World War II, the Opera was at the center of the city's cultural life. At the end of the French rule, however, it gradually fell into disrepair. During the years prior to the

Courtyard garden and restaurant of the Sofitel Legend Metropole Hotel

nation's economic and cultural liberalization in the late 1980s, visiting Chinese or Russian artists would appear. Performances such as the militant ballet *Red Detachment of Women* or a musical recital by an ensemble from Kiev, now in the Ukraine, were held here. By the mid-1980s, even these limited cultural exchanges had ceased, and the Opera House was all but abandoned. Then, in 1994, the authorities decided to restore and reopen the Opera in a three-year project costing US$14 million. Today, the colonnaded building, with refurbished gilt mirrors and grand stairways, is a magnificent sight. The 600-seat theater, boasting state-of-the-art audio facilities, stages Vietnamese operetta, ballets, and piano recitals. Home to the Hanoi Symphony Orchestra, it also hosts shows by visiting companies such as the Philadelphia Symphony Orchestra.

National Museum of Vietnamese History ❿

1 Pham Ngu Lao St, Hoan Kiem District. **Map** 2 F4. **Tel** *(04) 824 1384.* ☐ *8–11:30am, 1:30–4pm Tue–Sun.* 📷 ⌨ *by prior arrangement.* 📷 **http://**baotanglichsu.vn

Originally known as the École Française d'Extrême-Orient, this museum was built in 1925. Designed by Ernest Hébrard, it heralded a new hybrid style of architecture – Indochinoise – incorporating several elements of French, Khmer, and Vietnamese styles. Anchored by an octagonal pagoda, the building is painted ochre-yellow, and offset by dark green shutters. And although it is ornamented with fanciful colonnades, brackets, and balustrades, the overall effect is Oriental.

Known in Vietnamese as Bao Tang Lich Su, the museum is one of the best in Vietnam. It is spread over two floors and features a fine collection of

Sculpture, Vietnamese History Museum

artifacts from the prehistoric Dong Son culture of the Red River Delta, as well as the ancient Sa Huynh and Oc Eo civilizations of southern Vietnam. The museum also has sculptures dating from the Champa Empire. Some of the exhibits include wooden stakes from the 13th-century Battle of Bach Dang *(see p40).* The park behind the

Grand colonnaded façade of the Opera House

For hotels and restaurants in this region see pp240–43 and pp257–9

Indochinoise architecture of the National Museum of Vietnamese History

Lien Phai Pagoda ⓲

Ngo Chua Lien Phai St, Hai Ba
Trung District. **Tel** (04) 3863 2562.
☐ 7–11am, 1:30–5:30pm daily.

Lien Phai Pagoda or the
Pagoda of the Lotus Sect, is
one of the few surviving relics
of the Trinh Lords *(see p41)*
in Hanoi. According to the
inscription on the central stele,
Lord Trinh Thap had a palace
in this area, and one day his
workers dug up a huge rock
shaped like a lotus root in the
palace gardens. Trinh Thap
took this as an indication
from the Buddha that he
should abandon his privileged
life and become a monk. He
ordered a temple to be built
at the palace where the stone
was discovered. The pagoda
was built in 1726, and Trinh
Thap spent the remainder of
his life here as a monk. When
he died, his ashes were interred in the pagoda, and some
of his calligraphy hangs by
the main altar. The most
impressive structure
here is the Dieu Quang
or Miraculous Light
Tower, which rises
through ten levels.
The Lotus Sect,
founded by Trinh
Thap, honors the A
Di Da or Amitabha
Buddha, and believes
that by chanting his
name and ridding
oneself of desire,
one can be reborn in
the Western Paradise
of Sukhavati or Pure
Land. This sect is very
popular in China
and Japan.

museum has a garden with
statues of Cham goddesses and
Khmer lions, and Vietnamese-
style dragons.

Hai Ba Trung Temple ⓫

Dong Nhan St, Hai Ba Trung District.
☐ only during festivals. 🎎 Hai Ba
Trung Festival (early Mar).

One of the most important
temple complexes in the
country, the Hai Ba Trung
Temple is dedicated to the
popular cult of deified heroes.
It honors the heroic Trung
Sisters, who were successful
in expelling the Chinese for a
brief period in the first century
AD. Founded by Emperor Ly
Anh Ton in 1142, the temple

enshrines the supposedly
petrified mortal remains of
the sisters.
    The temple stands on the
west bank of a small artificial
lake called Huong Vien, and
is entered through a broad
gateway flanked by tall white
columns bearing auspicious
Chinese symbols and
characters for longevity,
and surmounted by
stylized lotus flowers.
The temple is generally
not open to the public.
However, during the
annual festival *(see p30)*,
it attracts hundreds of
devotees. During this
grand event, both the
statues are bathed in
water from the nearby
Red River and dressed
in new red robes.

**Guardian, Hai Ba
Trung Temple**

TRUNG SISTERS

The first century AD was a period of resentment against
Chinese rule. In AD 40, Trung Trac and her sister, Trung
Nhi, set up an army with the aid of the Vietnamese lords.
Fighting fearlessly, they expelled the Chinese, and
established their own kingdom at Me Linh in the Red
River Delta. In AD 43, however, the Chinese quelled
the rebellion. To avoid capture, the sisters committed
suicide by jumping into the Hat River. Centuries later,
stone figures of two women washed up on a sandbank
in the Red River. Believed to be the earthly remains of
the Trung Sisters, petrified and turned into statues, they
were taken to Dong Nhan village, now Hai Ba Trung
District, and installed in a temple there. Today, the
sisters are honored as heroes of national independence.

Ornate altar venerating the Trung Sisters

Temple of Literature ⓭

See pp166–7.

A many-armed statue of the Buddha, Vietnam Fine Arts Museum

Vietnam Fine Arts Museum ⓮

66 Nguyen Thai Hoc St, Ba Dinh District. **Map** 1 C3. **Tel** (04) 3823 3084. ◯ 8:30am–5:30pm Tue–Sun. ▨ ▯ www.vnfineartsmuseum. org.vn

Housed in a fine old colonial building, Bao Tang My Thuat or Fine Arts Museum boasts a varied and interesting selection of Vietnam's architecture, artifacts, paintings, sculpture, and many other works of art. The exhibits are displayed chronologically, starting with a fine collection of Stone and Bronze Age relics on the first floor. Several wood, stone, and lacquer sculptures feature as well, illustrating the versatile nature of Vietnamese art. One of the highlights here is an extraordinary Bodhisattva or Enlightened Being that supposedly has 1,000 eyes and arms.

The exhibition rooms on the second floor contain some of the country's best lacquer

paintings, and the third floor hosts many watercolor and oil works by Vietnamese artists. Other exhibits include carvings from the Central Highlands, wood-block paintings from the Dong Ho culture, and ethnic clothing. Replicas of antique pieces are for sale in the museum shop.

Vietnam Military History Museum ⓯

28A Dien Bien Phu St, Ba Dinh District. **Map** 1 C3. **Tel** (04) 3823 4264. ◯ 8–11:30am, 1–4:30pm Tue–Thu & Sat–Sun. ▨ ▯

Located at the southern end of the historic Hanoi Citadel, the Vietnam Military History Museum is set in former French barracks, comprising a complex of 30 galleries. Tracing the development and history of Vietnam's armed forces over the centuries, it features a varied collection of displays relating to the country's early battles against the Chinese and the Mongols. Precedence is, however, given to the nation's more recent wars against France, Cambodia's Khmer Rouge, China, and the US. The exhibits include films, black-and-white photographs, and other archival footage. The diorama of the Battle of Dien Bien Phu *(see p195)* is definitely worth seeing.

The courtyard outside the museum is filled with several reminders of war, including wrecked French, Soviet, and American military equipment, weaponry, and fighter planes, as well as a carefully preserved Soviet MIG-21, a must-see.

Next to the museum is the hexagonal Flag Tower or **Cot Co**. This is one of the few vestiges of the citadel, and was rebuilt by Emperor Gia Long in 1803. Like the Turtle Tower on Hoan Kiem Lake *(see p160)*, the tower is an important symbol, not just of Hanoi, but of Vietnamese armed forces. Unlike most of the citadel, which is a closed military area, Cot Co is open to the public. The view from the top of the tower is one of the best in the city.

Stern, whitewashed façade of the Ho Chi Minh Museum

Ho Chi Minh Museum ⓰

19 Ngoc Ha St, Ba Dinh District. **Map** 1 B2. **Tel** (04) 3823 0899. ◯ 8–11:30am, 2–4pm Tue–Thu & Sat–Sun. ▨ ▯

Established in 1990 – one century after Ho Chi Minh's birth *(see p169)* – this museum chronicles and celebrates the revolutionary leader's life and achievements in an often bizarre series of displays. These include an eclectic mix of his personal memorabilia, as well as black-and-white photographs from his youth and the long period he spent abroad in Europe and China. Images and papers documenting the independence struggle, founding of the Communist Party, and the fight against French imperialism and US intervention are also featured. Unapologetically partisan, the museum is nevertheless informative, unusual, and well presented.

Tank of the National Liberation Front in the Vietnam Military History Museum

Steps leading up to the small and charming One Pillar Pagoda

Until Emperor Gia Long moved the capital to Hue in 1802, the Hanoi Citadel contained both the Royal City and the Forbidden City of a long line of rulers stretching back to Emperor Ly Thai To in AD 1010. Although closed to the public, the citadel is currently undergoing the most thorough and productive archaeological excavations ever undertaken in Vietnam. In 2004, some of the treasures – unicorn heads of carved marble and roof ornaments – recovered from the 11th–15th centuries, when Hanoi was at its cultural peak, were displayed. In 2010, Hanoi celebrated the millennium of its founding, and exhibited some of these finds.

Vietnamese flag above the citadel

One Pillar Pagoda ⓱

8 Chua Mot St, Ba Dinh District.
Map 1 B2. **Tel** (04) 3843 6299.
◻ daily.

Rivaling Cot Co as one of Hanoi's most prominent icons, the Chua Mot Cot or the One Pillar Pagoda was constructed by Emperor Ly Thai Tong in AD 1049. Situated within the tiny Dien Huu Pagoda, also dating from the 11th century, this wooden pagoda is built, as the name suggests, on a single stone pillar, standing in an elegant lotus pond. According to legend, the king, who had no son, had a dream in which he was visited by Quan Am, Goddess of Mercy. She was sitting on a lotus flower and presented him with a baby boy. Soon after, Ly Thai Tong married a new young queen who bore him a son. To show his gratitude, the emperor ordered the construction of a single-pillared pagoda representing a lotus flower. Over the centuries, One Pillar Pagoda has been damaged and reconstructed on numerous occasions. However, none of these acts of destruction is harder to fathom than its burning by the French in 1954.

Ho Chi Minh Mausoleum ⓲

Ba Dinh Sq, Ba Dinh District. **Map** 1 B2. ◻ 7:30–10:30am Tue–Thu & Sat–Sun. ◼ closed for about two months a year, usually in Oct & Nov, for embalming maintenance. ◼

On the west side of Ba Dinh Square, a heavy grey structure, built of stone quarried from Marble Mountain near Danang (see p134), is Ho Chi Minh's last resting place.

An unassuming man, who notably shunned the comforts and trappings of power, Ho Chi Minh had allegedly requested that he be cremated and his ashes scattered in Northern, Central, and Southern Vietnam, symbolizing the national unity to which he had devoted his life. In keeping with these beliefs, it is said that he also vetoed the construction of a small museum on his life at his home village near Kim Lien (see p151), arguing that the funds could be better employed in building a school. However, after Ho Chi Minh's death in 1969, the leading members of the Vietnamese politburo reportedly altered his final testament by deleting his request to be cremated. Instead, with the help of Soviet specialists, the leader was embalmed and installed at the Ho Chi Minh Mausoleum in 1975.

The building's exterior is considered by many as both ponderous and unappealing. Astonishingly, the architects supposedly intended the structure to represent a lotus flower, though it is difficult to understand how.

Inside, the mood is somber and decidedly respectful. Ho Chi Minh, dressed in simple clothing favored by Chinese nationalist leader Sun Yat Sen, lies in a chilled, dim room, his crossed hands resting on dark cloth covers.

The mausoleum is an important pilgrimage site for many Vietnamese, especially from the north, and should be approached with respect and reverence. Any kind of noisy behavior, loitering, and inappropriate clothing is strictly forbidden.

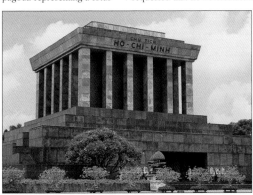

The somber exterior of Ho Chi Minh Mausoleum

Temple of Literature ⓭

The oldest and possibly the finest architectural complex in Hanoi, Van Mieu or the Temple of Literature, was established in 1070, during the Ly Dynasty (1009–1225). Founded in honor of the Chinese philosopher Confucius, it served as a center for higher learning, educating future mandarins for more than seven centuries. The temple was modeled on the original Temple of Confucius in the Chinese city of Qufu, and consists of five courtyards, the first two of which feature well-tended gardens. Each courtyard is separated by walls and ornamental gateways, and a central pathway through the complex divides it into two symmetrical halves.

Gateway guard of Bai Duong

Van Mieu Gate, the elegant entrance to the Temple of Literature

Human Chess
During Tet, the fourth courtyard is the venue for human chess. Dressed in colorful costumes, the participants, each representing a chess piece, move according to directions given by other players.

Well of Heavenly Clarity
A square pool known as Thien Quang Tinh or the Well of Heavenly Clarity dominates the third courtyard. On either side of the pond are covered buildings that house 82 stone stelae, the most prized relics of the temple.

★ Khue Van Cac
Also known as the Constellation of Literature, this ornate gate was built in 1805 to reflect the brilliance of Van Mieu's literary legacy. Its upper story features four radiating suns facing the cardinal points.

STAR FEATURES
★ Khue Van Cac
★ Temple of Confucius
★ Tortoise Stele
★ Altar of Confucius

Buddhist monks strolling through the gardens of the first courtyard

For hotels and restaurants in this region see pp240–43 and pp257–9

VISITORS' CHECKLIST

Quoc Tu Giam Street.
Map 1 B4. **Tel** (04) 3823 5601.
⬚ 7:30am–6pm Apr–Sep,
8am–5pm Oct–Mar.

The Music Room
A small orchestra of traditional musicians and singers stage regular performances next to the Altar of Confucius, using traditional Vietnamese stringed instruments (see pp24–5).

A magnificent bell tower was added to the fifth courtyard during recent restoration.

Great Drum
The counterpart of the bell tower to the west of Quoc Tu Giam is a giant drum standing to the east. These two towers appear together in traditional Sinitic architecture.

The former Quoc Tu Giam or National Academy now displays historic text books and learning tools, as well as images of three Ly Dynasty emperors.

★ Temple of Confucius
Located just behind Bai Duong, is the long, red-lacquered and gilt temple to Confucius. Inside are statues of the great philosopher and four of his main disciples, all dressed in rich robes of red and gold.

★ Tortoise Stele
Mounted on giant tortoise pedestals, these stone stelae are inscribed with the names and brief personal details of scholars who passed Van Mieu's examinations. Dating from the 15th to the 18th centuries, only 82 stelae out of the original 112 stelae survive today.

★ Altar of Confucius
Bai Duong or the House of Ceremonies hosts the elaborately decorated altar of Confucius, flanked by statues of cranes standing on top of tortoises – an auspicious symbol. The king and his mandarins would make offerings and sacrifices here.

Colorful swan-necked leisure boats docked on the shores of Ho Tay

Ho Chi Minh's Stilt House ⑲

1 Bach Thao St, Presidential Palace, Ba Dinh District. **Map** 1 B2.
⏰ 7:30–11:30am, 2–4pm Tue–Thu & Sat–Sun. 🌿 **Botanical Gardens** Hoang Hoa Tham St. ⏰ 7:30am–10pm daily. ♿ ▭

Believing that the Presidential Palace was too grand for him, Ho Chi Minh, on becoming president of the Democratic Republic of Vietnam in 1954, arranged for a modest wooden structure to be built in a corner of the palace's extensive grounds. Modeled on an ethnic minority stilt house, this unassuming two-story structure is known as Nha Bac Ho or Uncle Ho's House. Next to the stilts and surrounded by plants are the tables and chairs that were used by members of the politburo during meetings with Ho Chi Minh.

A female statue, Botanical Gardens

Wooden stairs at the back of the house lead to two simple rooms: a study and a bedroom, both kept just as they were when the great man was alive. The study has an antique typewriter and a bookcase packed with titles in many languages. The bedroom is even more spartan, with a bed, electric clock, an old-fashioned telephone, and radio as the only concessions to comfort. Surrounding the modest house are carefully tended gardens with weeping willows, mango trees, and fragrant frangipani and jasmine. Ho Chi Minh lived here from 1958 to 1969, watering his garden and feeding the carp in his fishpond.

Close to the presidential stilt house, the **Botanical Gardens** boast two lakes and abundant greenery, as well as a permanent sculpture exhibition.

Ho Tay ⑳

Map 1 A1. ♿ ❚❚ ▭ 🚻
Tran Quoc Pagoda Kim Ngu Island, Thanh Nien Causeway.
⏰ sunrise–sunset daily. **Quan Thanh Temple** Intersection of Thanh Nien Causeway and Quan Thanh Sts. ⏰ sunrise–sunset daily.

To the west of Hanoi are two beautiful lakes, separated from the Red River by the great dyke to the north. The larger of the two is Ho Tay or West Lake, which is home to Hanoi's sailing club. It is separated from Truc Bach or White Silk Lake to the east by an artificial causeway.

In times past, Ho Tay was associated with the Trinh Lords, who built palaces and pavilions along its shores, as well as many Buddhist temples. The palaces are gone, but many temples remain, including the city's oldest, **Tran Quoc Pagoda**. According to legend, it was established by the banks of the Red River during the reign of Trinh Lord, Ly Nam De (r.544–8), but was moved to its current location during the 17th century. Also worth a visit is **Quan Thanh Temple**, reputed to have been patronized by Emperor Ly Thai To, founder of the Ly Dynasty (see p40). Rebuilt in 1893, it is dedicated to Tran Vo or Guardian of the North. An image of this Taoist divinity dominates the altar.

Today, the area around Ho Tay is becoming increasingly upscale, with lots of luxury hotels along its shore. Farther north, along the raised dyke, are many places to eat, specializing in *thit cho*, or dog meat.

Kim Lien Pagoda ㉑

Ho Tay, Tu Liem District.
Tel (04) 3852 9962.
⏰ sunrise–sunset daily.

Situated on the northern shore of Ho Tay, the very attractive Kiem Lien Pagoda is somewhat out of the way, but well deserving of a visit. Legend has it that Princess Tu Hoa, daughter of 12th-century Emperor Ly Than Tong, brought her ladies-in-waiting to the area so they could cultivate silkworms for cloth. In 1771, a pagoda was built on the foundations of her palace and named Kim Lien, which means Golden Lotus, in memory of the princess.

Now entered through a triple-arched gate, it comprises three pavilions, that are laid out in three lines, supposedly representing the Chinese character *san* or three. They each have sweeping eaves and stacked roofs.

The brick-built exterior of Tran Quoc Pagoda

Ho Chi Minh

Acclaimed as the leader and primary force behind Vietnam's struggle for independence, Ho Chi Minh was born in 1890 at Hoang Tru village, near Kim Lien. After studying in Hue, Ho Chi Minh, then known as Nguyen Tat Thanh, left Vietnam in 1911 to travel the world. Influenced by socialist ideologies during his stay in Europe, he founded communist organizations in Paris, Moscow, and China. He returned

Communist symbol, Ho Chi Minh Museum

to Vietnam in 1941, where he took the name Ho Chi Minh (Bringer of Enlightenment) and formed the Vietnamese Independence League, or Viet Minh. In 1955, he became president of the Democratic Republic of Vietnam, leading long and bitter wars against France and the United States. Though he died six years before reunification, Vietnam's independence is considered his greatest achievement.

Nguyen Ai Quoc or Nguyen the Patriot is a pseudonym that Ho Chi Minh adopted during the 1920s. Greatly taken with socialist beliefs, he was a founding member of the French Communist Party in Paris, part of the Soviet Union Communist Party, and founder of the Indochinese Communist Party in China.

The prestigious Quoc Hoc School in Hue *is where Ho Chi Minh studied, along with future general Vo Nguyen Giap and Pham Van Dong, the future prime minister of Vietnam.*

A photograph dated 1945 shows Ho Chi Minh *preparing for a military campaign against the French. Full-scale war broke out in 1946, and the Viet Minh, led by Ho Chi Minh, waged a bloody battle that would last eight long years.*

Camped in secret tunnels and caverns, *Ho Chi Minh spent hours perfecting military strategies, which included employing underground resistance and guerilla tactics to expel the French forces, who were finally defeated in 1954.*

Personally a gentle and unassuming man, *Ho was much loved by children and adults alike. He could also speak several languages fluently, including Chinese, Russian, French, and English.*

Revered and loved as the father of modern Vietnam, *Ho Chi Minh is featured in the form of statues and portraits throughout the country, honoring his commitment to the unity of the nation. Kim Lien (see p151), his childhood village, is now a national shrine.*

Reconstruction of a Central Highland ethnic home, Museum of Ethnology

both tourism and a revival of traditional culture, the festivities include elaborate games of human chess, cockfighting, singing, and dancing. On the final day, An Duong is carried in state from the *dinh* back to his temple.

The Hanoi Architecture and Planning Department is currently working on restoring the vast area originally covered by the citadel.

Museum of Ethnology ㉓

60 Nguyen Van Huyen St, Cau Giay District. **Tel** (04) 3756 2193. 🚌 🎥 🕐 8:30am–5:30pm Tue–Sun. 🎥 🎫 🖥 📷 **www**.vme.org.vn

Located west of the city center, the Bao Tang Dan Toc Hoc or the Museum of Ethnology offers informative and well-documented displays on the country's many ethnic groups (*see pp20–21*). These range from the dominant Kinh to the smallest minorities in the highlands of the north and center.

Exhibits in the main building include elaborate and colorful hill-tribe costumes, weaving designs, musical instruments, fishing implements, work tools, and other functional objects. The displays continue on to the extensive grounds outside, with fascinating examples of minority housing from the Central Highlands, such as communal houses, steep pitched roofs, and elaborately carved tombs. A highlight here is the re-creation of a Black Thai house.

The museum also serves as a research center for Vietnam's 54 recognized ethnic groups.

Co Loa Citadel ㉒

10 miles (16 km) N of Hanoi, Dong Anh District. 🚌 🕐 8am–5pm daily. 🎥 🎫 🎭 Co Loa Festival (Feb).

The first known capital of an independent Vietnamese kingdom, this ancient fortress dates from a time when mythological history was slowly evolving into historical fact. The stories surrounding its creation and subsequent fall rest on oral tradition long since written down but impossible to verify.

Believed to have been built by King An Duong Vuong (*see p37*) in the 3rd century BC, the citadel was invaded soon after by the Chinese. According to legend, the son of the Chinese general tricked An Duong's daughter, My Chau, into giving him her father's magic crossbow, which was used by the Chinese to defeat the king. Fact or fiction, the remains of this great citadel and the huge quantity of bronze arrowheads found buried around the fortress indicate that fierce battles once took place here. At present, only vestiges of the citadel remain. In the center of the complex are temples dedicated to An Duong and My Chau. Both these structures are well preserved. However, it seems evident that they were built a few centuries after the citadel's destruction in 208 BC.

Stylized stone lions sitting guard outside distinguish the temple dedicated to King An Duong. A major festival takes place at the temple each year in honor of the legendary king, and a statue of him is carried in a palanquin from the temple to the local *dinh* or communal house. In efforts to promote

Mural depicting people from the Dong Son culture, Co Loa Citadel

Massive clay image of a warrior behind the altar at Thay Pagoda

Thay Pagoda ㉔

20 miles (32 km) W of Hanoi, Ha Tay Province. 🚌 ⭕ *sunrise–sunset daily.* 📷 🎭 *Thay Pagoda Festival (5–7 Apr).*

Dedicated to the Thich Ca or the Sakyamuni Buddha, Chua Thay or Master's Pagoda is named for Tu Dao Hanh – a 12th-century monk and master water puppeteer. The temple is mainly renowned for being home to more than 100 religious statues, including the two largest in Vietnam. Made of clay and papier-mâché, these giant weigh more than 2,200 lb (1,000 kg) each.

Inside, to the left of the main altar stands a statue of the master, and to the right is a statue of Emperor Ly Nhan Tong (r.1072–1127), believed to be a reincarnation of Tu Dao Hanh, and under whose reign this attractive house of worship was established. The pagoda also hosts a variety of water puppet shows *(see p159)* during its much-anticipated annual festival.

Tay Phuong Pagoda ㉕

24 miles (38 km) W of Hanoi, Ha Tay Province. 🚌 ⭕ *sunrise–sunset daily.* 📷

This small temple is perched on top of a hill said to resemble a buffalo, and lies a short distance west of Thay Pagoda,

hence its name, which means Western Pagoda. Originally dating from the 8th century, it is best known for its impressive collection of more than 70 finely carved, jackfruit-wood statues representing incarnations of the Buddha, Confucian disciples, and various *arhats* (Buddhist saints) in meditative poses. The Tay Phuong Pagoda is also distinguished by particularly fine wood carvings of flowers and mythical animals, such as the phoenix and dragons. Other striking features of the temple include a large bell cast in 1796, and the double-tiered roof, which has elegant, upward-sweeping eaves, beautifully decorated with symbols of the sun, moon, and stars.

Jackfruit-wood statue, Tay Phuong Pagoda

Hung Kings' Temples ㉖

62 miles (100 km) NW of Hanoi, Phong Chau District, Phu Tho Province. 🏛 **Museum Tel** *(021) 386 0026.* ⭕ *8–11:30am, 1–4pm daily.* 📷 *in museum.* 📖 🚻 🎭 *Hung Kings' Temple Festival (Apr).*

Believed by the Vietnamese to be the very earliest relics of their civilization, the temples of the Hung Kings are located on Mount Nghia Linh. Built by

rulers of the Vang Lang Kingdom, between the 7th and 3rd centuries BC, they are objects of great veneration. Frequently restored over the centuries, the temples are surprisingly well preserved and cared for. Flights of stone stairs climb sharply upwards through the trees to the lowest temple, **Den Ha**, the middle temple, **Den Hung**, and ultimately the superior temple near the top of the hill, **Den Thuong**.

The entire area is filled with a plethora of pagodas, lotus ponds, and small shrines. The most important of these is **Lang Hung** – a tiny shrine, with candle and incense holders, located a few meters lower down the slope from Den Thuong. This is, supposedly, the main tomb of the Hung Kings, though it is evident that it has undergone some extensive reconstructions.

The views from Mount Nghia Linh's summit sweep across the surrounding rural Phu Tho landscape, and are absolutely spectacular. At the foot of the mountain there is a small **Museum**. A varied selection of displays such as frog drums, pottery, arrowheads, and other historic relics are shown here.

One of the pleasing Hung Kings' Temples, set amid lush greenery

HANOI STREET FINDER

The stately city of Hanoi is divided into four principal districts. Named after the lovely lake at the center of town, Hoan Kiem District is filled with bustling alleys. To the north of the Hoan Kiem District is the fascinating Old Quarter *(see pp156–7)*, while to the south is the city's elegant former French Quarter. The other three districts are Hai Ba Trung, Ba Dinh, and Dong Da.

Cham musicians

Note that the street names can be preceded by the word *pho*, which is a central city street; *duong*, which is a more common road; or *dai lo*, which is a large avenue or boulevard. Some common words used in street names have been abbreviated on the Street Finder. For example, Nguyen is Ng and Hang is H. The symbols used for sights and other features on the Street Finder are listed in the key below.

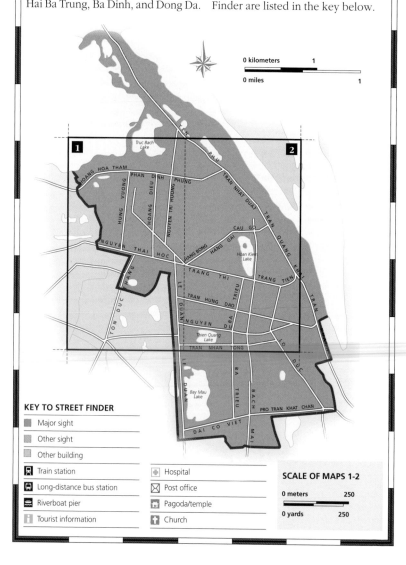

0 kilometers 1

0 miles 1

KEY TO STREET FINDER

	Major sight
	Other sight
	Other building
	Train station
	Long-distance bus station
	Riverboat pier
	Tourist information

	Hospital
	Post office
	Pagoda/temple
	Church

SCALE OF MAPS 1-2

0 meters 250

0 yards 250

Street Finder Index

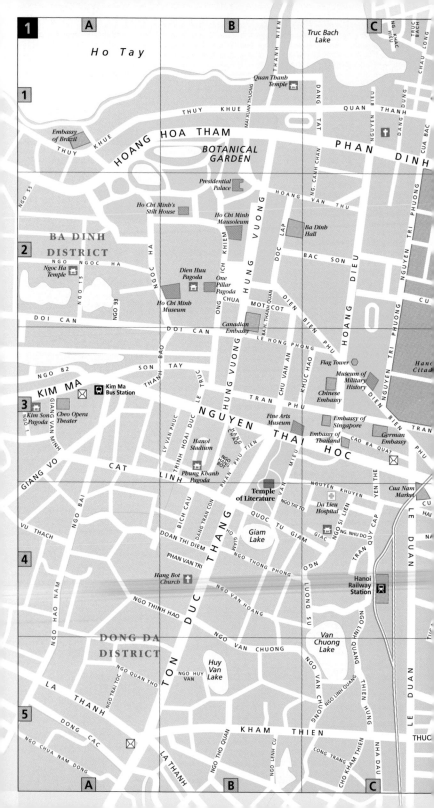

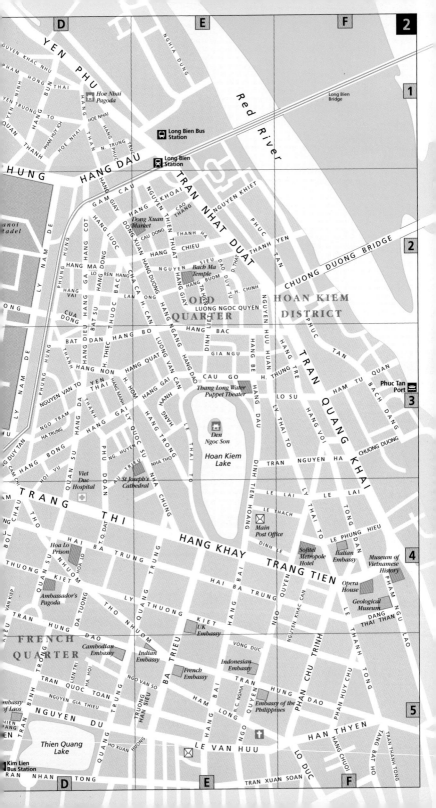

NORTHERN VIETNAM

*N*orthern Vietnam is a rich repository of history and tradition, with many of the country's oldest temples and fortresses. It is also blessed with great natural grandeur, ranging from the high mountains and craggy canyons of the west, to the magical karst islands rising from Halong Bay in the east. In addition, the northwest mountains are inhabited by several diverse and culturally unique ethnic minorities.

Crowned by the serrated peaks of the Hoang Lien Mountains, Northern Vietnam boasts a remarkably unspoiled topography, as well as a diverse cultural landscape. The pristine forests and plunging valleys in the mountainous reaches of the north and northwest are inhabited by dozens of minorities such as the Hmong, Thai, Dao, and Nung. Their villages in Son La, Lai Chau, Bac Ha, and Sapa are extremely picturesque, with wooden stilt houses punctuating jade-green terraced rice fields. Also in the far west, the valley of Dien Bien Phu is of great historical importance. It is famous as the site of the Viet Minh victory over the French in 1954 – a triumphant chapter in Vietnam's history.

The northeast, on the other hand, is known for the hundreds of enchanting karst outcrops that loom over the Gulf of Tonkin's Halong and Bai Tu Long Bays. Similar formations soar above the tropical forests of Cat Ba Island, also home to golden beaches and spectacular coral reefs. In sharp contrast, the nearby port city of Haiphong, in the northernmost province of the Red River Delta, bustles with commerce and industry. Just south of here are the region's fertile flatlands, home to the ethnic Viet or Kinh people, and marked by extensive paddy fields.

Northern Vietnam also has its share of national parks such as Ba Be and Cuc Phuong, celebrated for flora and fauna endemic to the region, as well as for their lakes, waterfalls, and prehistoric caves. The area is renowned for the festivals and events that enliven its religious sites, including especially the Perfume Pagoda, which is thronged by hundreds of Buddhist pilgrims for three months every year.

Rural hamlet set amid the lush terraced fields surrounding Sapa

◁ Colorfully attired Hmong women shopping at the weekly market in Bac Ha *(see p197)*

Exploring Northern Vietnam

The oldest settled part of the country, Northern Vietnam is unusually rich in culture and history. The fertile plains of the Red River Delta are full of ancient temples, clan houses, and pagodas, including the very scenic and highly venerated Perfume Pagoda. Farther north, neatly cultivated fields and urban settlements give way to the magnificent Hoang Lien Mountains. The most popular destination here is the hill resort of Sapa, from where it is easy to visit nearby Bac Ha, and explore the surrounding remote areas that are home to several minority peoples. In the east, Halong Bay is Vietnam's most celebrated natural beauty spot, while to the south are the dense green forests of Cuc Phuong National Park.

The crystal clear waters of Thac Bac or Silver Waterfalls near Sapa (see pp196–7)

SIGHTS AT A GLANCE

Towns and Cities

Bac Ha **16**

Cao Bang **18**

Dien Bien Phu **14**

Haiphong **5**

Halong City **2**

Hoa Binh **10**

Moc Chau **12**

Ninh Binh **7**

Sapa **15**

Son La **13**

Tam Dao **19**

Areas of Natural Beauty

Bai Tu Long Bay **4**

Halong Bay pp182–4 **1**

Mai Chau Valley **11**

National Parks

Ba Be National Park **17**

Cuc Phuong National Park **9**

Islands

Cat Ba Island **6**

Religious Sites

Perfume Pagoda pp192–3 **8**

Yen Tu Pilgrimage Sites **3**

Group of Flower Hmong girls dressed in traditional outfits, Bac Ha Market (see p197)

SEE ALSO

0 kilometers   50

0 miles   50

(Map labels:) Nam Cum · Lao Cai · **16 BAC HA** · **LAI CHAU** · Fansipan 3,143m · **15 SAPA** · Pho Rang · Qua · Lai Chau · Nam Ma · **LAO CAI** · Muong Lay · Hong · **DIEN BIEN** · Muong Muon · Tuan Giao · Lien Son · **YEN BAI** · Tran Phu · **DIEN BIEN PHU 14** · Thuan Chau · **SON LA** · Phu Yen · **13 SON LA** · Hat Lot · Ma · Yen Chau · **12 MOC CHAU** · Phu Hua 2,452 · Muong Xen · **NG** · Tuong Duong · Con Cuo · Phou Sam Sao · Hoang Lien Son

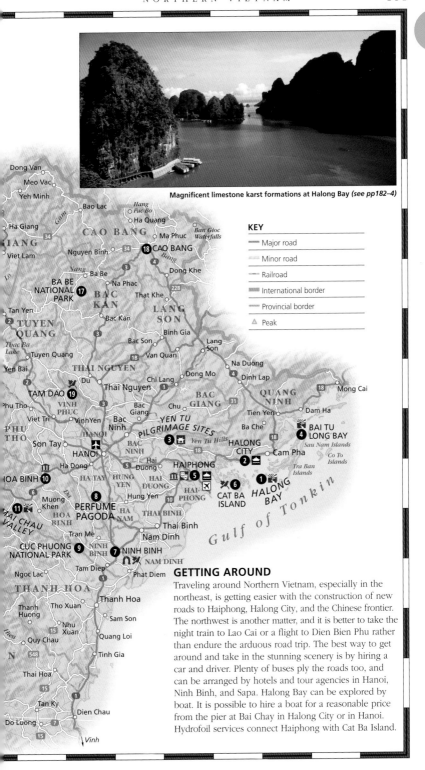

Magnificent limestone karst formations at Halong Bay (see pp182–4)

KEY

— Major road

= Minor road

— Railroad

▬ International border

— Provincial border

△ Peak

GETTING AROUND

Traveling around Northern Vietnam, especially in the northeast, is getting easier with the construction of new roads to Haiphong, Halong City, and the Chinese frontier. The northwest is another matter, and it is better to take the night train to Lao Cai or a flight to Dien Bien Phu rather than endure the arduous road trip. The best way to get around and take in the stunning scenery is by hiring a car and driver. Plenty of buses ply the roads too, and can be arranged by hotels and tour agencies in Hanoi, Ninh Binh, and Sapa. Halong Bay can be explored by boat. It is possible to hire a boat for a reasonable price from the pier at Bai Chay in Halong City or in Hanoi. Hydrofoil services connect Haiphong with Cat Ba Island.

Halong Bay ❶

Blue rock thrush, Halong Bay

Designated a UNESCO World Heritage Site, the magnificent Halong Bay is spread across a 580 sq mile (1,500 sq km) area, with more than 2,000 pinnacle-shaped limestone and dolomite outcrops scattered across it. According to legend, the bay was formed when a gigantic dragon – *ha long* means descending dragon – plunged into the Gulf of Tonkin, and created the myriad islets by lashing its tail. Geologists have explained that the karst topography is the product of selective erosion over the millennia. The result is a labyrinthine seascape of bizarrely shaped outcrops, isolated caves, and sandy coves *(see p184)*.

LOCATOR MAP

▨ Area illustrated

--- World Heritage Site area

Dragon Boats

These brightly painted boats represent the legendary beast that created Halong Bay. Dragons are also held to be symbols of royalty and good luck in Vietnam.

Hang Thien Cung or Celestial Palace Grotto features sparkling stalactites and stalagmites. Like Hang Dau Go, it is softly illuminated with colored lights.

Tuan Chau

Dao Tuan Chau, a large island to the southwest of Bai Chay, is the site of Ho Chi Minh's former residence. It is now a sprawling recreation complex.

★ Hang Dau Go

Named Grotte des Merveilles or Cave of Marvels by the French in the 19th century, Hang Dau Go is full of strangely formed stalactites and stalagmites, enchantingly lit with green and blue colored floodlights.

Bai Cha

Dau Go

CAT BA

FORMATION OF KARST

Across much of the Gulf of Tonkin, both offshore in Halong Bay and on land at Tam Coc, weathered limestone pinnacles rise almost vertically from the surrounding plain, creating truly breathtaking scenery. These karst outcrops are made of sediment that settled on the seafloor in prehistoric times, which subsequently rose to the surface through geological upheaval and erosion. On exposure to warm, acidic rainfall, these striking alkaline limestone formations are worn into strange, almost spectacular shapes providing a remarkable sight.

Limestone rock eroded due to acidic action

STAR FEATURES

★ Hang Dau Go

★ Hang Bo Nau

★ Hang Sung Sot

Floating Villages
Located near Hong Gai's harbor, these villages include not only houseboats, but also floating fuel stations, herb gardens, kennels, and even pigpens.

Sailing Junks
Along with tourist junks, some lovely, traditionally made junks still sail the bay. Rough cotton and hand-sewn, the fan-shaped sails are dipped in vegetable dye for protection, giving them their dark ochre color.

Ferries at Halong City constantly shuttle back and forth between Bai Chay in the west and Hong Gai in the east.

Dao Titop is home to a tiny, isolated beach. It is also possible to hike to the top of the islet.

Dong Tam Cung, which was discovered only in the mid-1990s, is one of the most impressive caves in the bay.

★ Hang Bo Nau
A favorite among photographers, Hang Bo Nau, also known as Pelican Cave, is famous for the framed views it offers of ships sailing in the bay.

Hang Trong or Drum Cave is filled with stalactites and stalagmites that produce a sound like distant drumming when wind blows through the cave.

0 kilometers   2

0 miles   2

★ Hang Sung Sot
Hang Sung Sot or Cave of Awe is best known for its phallus-shaped rock, a fertility symbol. The formations in the inner chamber are said to resemble a group of sentries conversing.

Exploring Halong Bay

Sailing past the evocatively shaped islets and dramatic caves of Halong Bay can be a magical experience. At least an entire day can be spent exploring the islands and grottos, many of which house religious shrines. Most of the best-known sites lie in the western part of the bay and these are often overcrowded. It generally makes for a more relaxing trip to charter a private boat, hire a knowledgeable guide, and sail around the less visited areas of the shimmering bay.

Hang Dau Go

One of the most famous caves in Halong Bay, Hang Dau Go or Hidden Timber Cave is on Dau Go Island, on the way to Cat Ba Island *(see p189)*. The cave's name dates from the 13th century when General Tran Hung Dao *(see p40)* used it to hide his lethally sharpened wooden stakes. The weapons were later planted in the shallow waters near the shore to destroy enemy Mongol fleets.

Hang Dau Go is filled with many bizarre-shaped stalactites and stalagmites.

Hang Thien Cung

Also on Dau Go Island, Hang Thien Cung or the Celestial Palace Grotto can be reached by a steep flight of steps. It was discovered only in the mid-1990s. Floodlights in pink, green, and blue illuminate the sparkling stalactites that hang from the high ceiling.

Hang Sung Sot

Aptly known as the Cave of Awe, Hang Sung Sot is located on Bo Hon Island, which the

Pink-lit, phallus-shaped rock, revered by locals, in Hang Sung Sot

French knew as the Isle de la Surprise. The first cavern in the three-chambered Sung Sot features a large, phallus-shaped rock, lit in lurid pink, and worshipped as a fertility symbol by the locals.

The formations in the inner chamber, named the Serene Castle, on the other hand, are fascinating, seeming to come alive when the reflections of the water outside play upon them. Nearby, **Hang Bo Nau** or Pelican Cave draws visitors for the fantastic views it offers across the bay.

Dong Tam Cung

A massive karst fissure, Dong Tam Cung or Three Palaces consists of three chambers, each of which is packed with stalactites and stalagmites. All three grottos are illuminated by strategically placed spotlights, which emphasize the strange, massed, carrot-shaped array of stalactites. Opinion is divided, but some consider Dong Tam Cung to be even more impressive than Hang Dau Go.

Hang Trong

A short distance southeast of Hang Bo Nau, the small Hang Trong or Drum Cave echoes faintly with an eerie percussive sound when a strong wind blows past its stalactites and stalagmites.

Dao Tuan Chau

A large island to the south of Bai Chay, Tuan Chau has been developed as a recreation complex, with a few restored French-colonial villas and a resort holding unimpressive whale, dolphin, and sea lion shows. Better reasons to visit are the seafood restaurants and small sandy beaches.

Dao Titop

The main attraction of this island is its isolated beach, which is very popular with swimmers. It is possible to hike to the top of the islet where there is the most spectacular view of Halong Bay. Visitors can enjoy the few watersports facilities available at the small beach, including swimming and parasailing.

The brightly painted houses of a floating village in Halong Bay

Ferries running between the towns of Bai Chay and Hon Gai, Halong City

Halong City ❷

Road Map C1. 102 miles (164 km)
E of Hanoi on Hwy 18; 37 miles
(60 km) NE of Haiphong on Hwy 10.
🏙 185,000. 🚌 from Haiphong
and Hanoi. ⛴ from Haiphong. 🚉
🛈 Quang Ninh Tourism Department,
(04) 3362 6127. 🎎 Long Tien
Pagoda Festival (late Apr).

Formed in 1994 with the
official amalgamation of the
towns of **Bai Chay** and **Hon
Gai**, Halong City is bisected
by the narrow Cua Luc straits.
Located to the west of the
straits, Bai Chay is becoming
an increasingly affluent tourist
town, home to a number of
tour operators, hotels, and
restaurants. It is also popular
with the Vietnamese for its
nightlife, which centers around
karaoke bars and massage
parlors of questionable repute.
However, for most visitors,
the attractions of Halong Bay
apart, there is little of appeal
in Bai Chay, which is simply a
convenient place to stay and
eat. Local authorities have tried
to improve the situation by
laying two artificial stretches
of beach on the seafront, but
not much has changed. The
waters remain muddy, and
the new sand is now polluted.
On the east side of Cua Luc,
the town of Hon Gai is the
older, more historic part of
Halong City. Although this
town has its share of hotels
and restaurants, it does not
revolve around tourism. In fact,
most of its wealth comes from
industry, particularly the huge
opencast coal mines that dominate the coast east of Cua Luc.

Beyond the coal dust of the
docks is **Nui Bai Tho** or Poem
Mountain, one of the few
attractions of Halong City.
The limestone mountain has
earned its name from the
weathered inscriptions on its
sides, written in praise of the
beauty of Halong Bay. The
earliest of these is said to have
been composed by King Le
Thanh Tong in 1468. On the
northern lee of the mountain
stands Long Tien Pagoda,
Halong City's most colorful
and interesting religious site.

Yen Tu Pilgrimage Sites ❸

Road Map B1. 81 miles (130 km)
NE of Hanoi; 9 miles (14 km) N of
Uong Bi. 🚌 from Hanoi, Halong
City, and Haiphong to Uong Bi.
🍴 🏢 🎎 Yen Tu Pagoda Fest
(mid-Feb–end Apr).

The holy mountain, Yen Tu,
at 3,477 ft (1,060 m)
is the highest peak in
the range of the same
name. It is named for
Yen Ky Sinh, a monk
who attained nirvana
at the peak, about
2,000 years ago. Yen
Tu became further
renowned during the
13th century, when
Emperor Tran Nhan
Tong (r.1278–93)
retired there to become
a monk. Some of the
800 religious structures
claimed to have been
built by the emperor
and his successors are
still present here.

For centuries, thousands of
pilgrims have made the arduous ascent to the summit of
Yen Tu by foot, although now
a cable car whisks sightseers
to Hoa Yen Pagoda, just over
halfway up the mountain.
From here, it is still necessary
to make the climb on foot to
the most important structure
at the summit, **Chua Dong** or
Bronze Pagoda. This is the
spiritual home of the Truc
Lam or Bamboo Forest sect of
Mahayana Buddhism, and was
built during the 15th century.
It was recently beautifully
refurbished, with 70 tons
of bronze used to form a
215 sq ft (20 sq m) temple
intended to symbolize a lotus.

Environs
Situated on the western slopes
of the Yen Tu range, about
3 miles (5 km) north of Sao
Dao on Highway 18, are two of
the country's most important
pilgrimage sites. **Chua Con Son**,
one of the attractive pagodas
in the north, is dedicated to
Nguyen Van Trai, the poet-
warrior who aided Emperor
Le Loi (see p40) in expelling
the Chinese from Vietnam in
the 15th century. The popular
pagoda is always active, with
monks and nuns chanting
prayers almost constantly.
Located nearby is the small
temple, **Den Kiep Bac**, which
is dedicated to Tran Hung
Dao, a general of the Tran
Dynasty (see p40) during the
late 13th century and a deified
national hero. An annual
festival is held in his honor
during the 8th lunar month.

Stairway to the revered Chua Con Son, Yen Tu

The limestone monolithic islands in Halong Bay (see pp182–3) ▷

Tiny floating village near the town of Cai Rong, Bai Tu Long Bay

Bai Tu Long Bay ❹

Road Map C1. 37 miles (60 km)
E of Halong City. 🚌 *from Halong City.* 🚤 *from Halong City and Cai Rong.*

An island-peppered stretch of shallow coastal waters, Bai Tu Long Bay may not be quite as celebrated as Halong Bay, but it is just as spectacular. With hundreds of karst out-crops, tiny islets, as well as a few large islands and lovely beaches, it is less crowded and more pristine than Halong Bay.

The largest, most developed island in the area is **Van Don**, accessible by both road and sea from the industrial port of Cua Ong. Gorgeous beaches and dense mangrove swamps line the southeast coast of the island, making it a popular destination. Most of the accommodation in the Bai Tu Long area is concentrated in Van Don's main town, the colorful fishing port-town of Cai Rong.

This makes it an excellent base for excursions to neighboring islands. Unfortunately, Bai Tu Long Bay offers few tourist facilities. This is partly due to its isolated location, lying beyond the grimy coastal coal belt that stretches from Hon Gai District in Halong City to the small town of Cam Pha. As a result, most visitors prefer to charter a boat from the Bai Chay pier in Halong City, and then return to stay overnight in Halong City after exploring the bay. Another option is to drive from Hon Gai to Bai Tu Long Bay, passing through Cam Pha and Cua Ong. The huge, open-cast coal mines on the way are quite a sight. From here, boats may be chartered to explore the outlying reaches of the bay.

Environs
The outermost of the three islands south of Van Don is **Quan Lan**. The main attraction on this destination is Bai Bien, a splendid white-sand beach. This is one of the few places beyond Cai Rong with facili-ties for an overnight stay.

Co To, well into the South China Sea, is the most distant island lying off Cai Rong. The ferry journey takes about five hours each way. With a small beach and simple accommoda-tion at Co To village, it makes for a quiet getaway.

About 12 miles (20 km) from Cai Rong is **Bai Tu Long National Park**. Spread over Ba Mun Island and its surrounds, this park, established in 2001, is slowly gaining popularity as an ecotourism destination.

Silhouette of karst formations near Van Don Island, Bai Tu Long Bay

Haiphong ❺

Road Map B1. 62 miles (100) km
E of Hanoi on Hwy 5. 🏛 *1,837,000.* ✈ *from HCMC and Danang.* 🚉 *from Hanoi.* 🚌 *from Hanoi and Halong City.* 🚤 *from Cat Ba Island.* ℹ *Vietnam Tourism, 55 Dien Bien Phu Street, (031) 374 7216.* **www**.haiphong.gov.vn

The third-largest city in the country after Ho Chi Minh City and Hanoi, Haiphong is the north's most important port. Its strategic location made it the target of foreign invaders over the years. It also faced heavy bombing during the First Indochina War *(see p43)*, and later, in the war against the US. Having survived its violent past, Haiphong today is a leading industrial metro-polis, specializing in cement manufacture, oil refining, and coal transportation.

Haiphong draws few tourists, even though the atmosphere is relaxed, and the food and accommodation good. The most attractive and noteworthy sights of this city are the beau-tiful French-colonial buildings. These include a 19th-century cathedral by Tam Bac River, the **Opera House** on Quang Trung Street, and the **Haiphong Museum**, the Gothic façade of which is more remarkable than the exhibits inside. Situated some distance away from the town center, the 17th-century **Du Hang Pagoda**, on Chua Hang Street, is known for its elaborate architecture, while **Dinh Hang Kenh**, on Nguyen Cong Tru Street, is a fine old communal house.

🏛 **Haiphong Museum**
11 Dien Tien Hoang St.
🕐 8–11:30am Tue & Thu,
7:30am–9:30pm Wed & Sun.

The colorful, embellished entrance to Du Hang Pagoda, Haiphong

Cat Ba Island ⑥

Road Map C1. 28 miles (45 km)
E of Haiphong; 14 miles
(22 km) S of Halong City.
🚶 22,000. 🚤 hydrofoil
*from Haiphong, charter
boats from Halong City
and Bai Chay.* **www.**
catbalangur.org

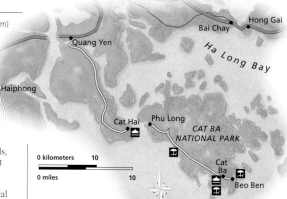

The largest island in
a scenic sprawling
archipelago of more
than 350 islets and islands,
Cat Ba is one of the most
delightful destinations in
Northern Vietnam.

The island's main appeal
has always been its relative
isolation and bucolic charm.
Waterfalls, freshwater lakes,
hills, mangrove swamps, and
coral reefs are just some of the
features of Cat Ba's amazingly
diverse ecosystems. Although
these characteristics are evident
in the island's forests, idyllic
beaches, and sparse sprinkling
of tiny villages, **Cat Ba Town**
is now becoming increasingly
polluted and crowded. Nevertheless most boats dock here
as it is the only settlement in
the area where it is possible
to stay overnight and eat in
some comfort. With its shabby
little karaoke bars, a few small
restaurants serving fresh seafood, some seedy massage
parlors, and a couple of noisy
discotheques, there is little
to recommend it except as
a gateway to the beautiful
Cat Ba National Park, the
main attraction of the island.

In 1986, to help safeguard
the island's varied habitats,
almost half of Cat Ba was
given the status of a national
park. Famous for its rugged
landscape, with craggy limestone outcrops, lakes, caves,
grottoes, and thick mangroves,
the park offers visitors much
to explore and experience.
The astonishing range of flora
found here is also impressive,
with more than 800 species
cataloged to date. The forests
also sustain a variety of fauna,
including wild boars, deer,
macaques, as well as a large
number of bird and reptile
species. The park is especially
renowned for its community
of endangered Cat Ba langurs,
found only here on Cat Ba

Island. Today, their number is
estimated at a dismal count
of 65 animals.

Apart from sightseeing, the
park also offers activities such
as trekking *(see p273)* and
camping for the adventurous.
However, facilities are very
limited, and currently visitors
need to bring along their own
equipment and supplies. The
shortest and most popular trek
climbs to the 656-ft (200-m)
summit of Ngu Lam peak,
where a watchtower offers
superb views across the park.
A longer hike, which can take
between four to six hours,
leads through the park's tree-
canopied interior, past the vast
Frog or Ech Lake, to the small
hamlet of Viet Hai. From here,
boats can be chartered back
to Cat Ba Town.

Boats may also be chartered
from Cat Ba to explore the
Halong Bay *(see pp182–4)*, a
short distance to its north, or

A bright Musella bloom in the
Cat Ba National Park

the smaller but picturesque
Lan Ha Bay, which is located
to its northeast, and has tiny
but exclusive beaches that
can be enjoyed for a small fee.

🏹 Cat Ba National Park
12 miles (20 km) NW of Cat Ba
Town. 🔆 *sunrise–sunset daily.*
🈺 🈺 *for a small fee.*

Small hotels and guesthouses overlooking the waterfront, Cat Ba Town

Coral Reefs and Sea Life in Vietnam

Set amid the warm waters of the tropics, Vietnam's 2,037-mile (3,260-km) long coastline, with its numerous offshore islands, is home to many resplendent coral reefs. These extend from the cool waters of Halong Bay in the north, through the warmer seas off Nha Trang and Phu Quoc, to the remote Con Dao Islands in the south. They also provide an immensely diverse habitat for a variety of sea life. The World Wild Fund for Nature (WWF) has identified nearly 280 species of coral living in Vietnamese waters – almost 20 percent of the world's coral species. Though most of the reefs here are endangered by dynamite fishing and cyanide poisoning, various organizations are working actively toward the preservation of Vietnam's magnificent coral heritage.

Poisonous scorpion fish inhabitant of the reef

Hard coral   Soft coral   Schools of colorful fish.

The rare green turtle *grows to 5 ft (1.5 m) in length and can weigh up to 440 lb (200 kg), making it the largest hard-shelled sea turtle.*

REEF ECOSYSTEM
Coral reefs are composed of the skeletons of millions of algae and coral polyps, accumulated over millennia. They flourish best in clear tropical waters, and form an immensely diverse habitat for a range of life forms, including mollusks, turtles, and a countless variety of brightly colored fish.

Moray eels *frequent coral reefs to a depth of 656 ft (200 m). On average 5-ft (1.5-m) long, they are voracious predators that hide in crevices in the coral.*

The cuttlefish, *a small relative of the squid, has an internal shell, eight arms, and two tentacles covered with suckers for catching prey.*

Stingrays *are armed with a razor-sharp tail that is covered with toxic venom. Propelled by their large pectoral fins, these fish appear to fly through the water.*

Dugongs *or sea cows are gentle mammals that grow up to 10 ft (3 m) in length, and inhabit the shallow reef waters where they graze on sea grass.*

MARINE MAMMALS OF VIETNAM

Vietnam's seas are home to many species of marine mammals, such as dolphins, porpoises, and even whales. The endangered Irrawaddy dolphin lives in coastal waters and estuaries, swimming as far as 932 miles (1,500 km) up the Mekong River. The agile bottlenose dolphin, the humpback, and the southern right whale are among some of the rare marine mammal species seen in the waters off Vietnam.

Humpback whale

Southern right whale

Bottlenose dolphins frolicking in water

Farmers at Kenh Ga using buckets to irrigate a field, a common practice

Ninh Binh ❼

Road Map B2. 59 miles (95 km) S
of Hanoi on Hwy 1. 🚂 55,000.
🚆 Reunification Express between
Hanoi and HCMC. 🚌 Hanoi. 🛈
Ninh Binh Tourist, Tran Hung Dao Rd,
Hoa Lu District, (030) 387 1263.

An ideal base from which to
explore the southern part of
the Red River Delta, Ninh Binh
is becoming a popular tourist
destination. While the town
itself is not remarkable, it does
feature several interesting
attractions in its vicinity.

The historic site of **Hoa Lu**,
7 miles (12 km) northwest of
Ninh Binh, was established as
a royal capital in AD 968 by
Emperor Tien Hoang De, the
founder of the Dinh Dynasty
(r.968–980). A massive palace
and citadel constructed by him,
though now mostly in ruins, is
still impressive. An imposing
temple, restored in the 17th
century and dedicated to the
emperor, stands intact. Inside
is a statue of Tien Hoang,
flanked by three of his sons.
The stone pedestal of the royal
throne is placed in front of the
temple. The hillside nearby is
home to Tien Hoang's tomb,
and offers great scenery.

A second royal temple in the
vicinity is dedicated to Le Dai
Hanh, founder of the Early Le
Dynasty (r.980–1009), which
succeeded the Dinh Dynasty.
They are credited with replac-
ing Chinese currency with
Vietnamese coinage.

Tam Coc or Three Caves at
6 miles (10 km) southwest of
Ninh Binh town is often promoted as Vietnam's "Halong
Bay on Land." It also features
karst outcrops, but while those
at Halong Bay thrust upwards
from the waves, at Tam Coc
they rise majestically from a
sea of green rice fields. It takes
about three hours to visit Tam
Coc, punted in metal boats
along the watery landscape
and through three long caves.
In places, these are so low that
it is necessary to duck, while
boatwomen propel the craft
by pushing on the cave roof
with their hands. Nearby, **Bich
Dong** or Jade Cavern is just
2 miles (3 km) north of Tam
Coc. This unique pagoda is cut
into the side of a karst outcrop.

Not far from here, the idyllic
fishing village of **Kenh Ga** is
worth a visit. Centered on a
small island and surrounded
by stark karst formations, it
largely comprises of gently
floating houseboats. Currently,
it is reachable only by boat.
The pier is at Tran Me, just
4 miles (7 km) south of Ninh
Binh. It takes three hours or
so to tour Kenh Ga, and it is
wonderfully relaxing to chug
slowly along to Van Trinh
Grotto observing tranquil rural
scenery en route. About a mile
(1.6 km) east of Tran Me are
the reed-filled marshes of **Van
Long Nature Reserve**, where a
small community of the rare
Delacour's langur live, secure
among the inaccessible limestone outcrops.

Around 19 miles (30 km)
southeast of Ninh Binh, Phat
Diem town is home to **Phat
Diem Cathedral**, one of the
most well-known churches
in Vietnam. Alexandre de
Rhodes, a French Jesuit priest
who developed the nation's
Romanized writing system,
preached here in 1627, but it
was Tran Luc, a Vietnamese
priest, who organized the
construction of this unique
cathedral. It was completed in
1898, and combines European
Gothic church architecture
with Sino-Vietnamese temple
tradition. The complex is
dominated by a huge bell
tower with curved Chinese
eaves, and a gateway that
could easily be mistaken for
an entrance to a temple if it
were not for the prominent
crucifixes and angels. Behind
the bell tower, the cathedral
extends back along a dark,
cool nave, the roof supported
by 52 ironwood tree trunks.

🦋 **Van Long Nature Reserve**
Gia Vien Dist, Ninh Binh Province.
Tel (030) 364 0246. 🔲 daily.
📷 🎫 by arrangement.

🛕 **Phat Diem Cathedral**
Tel (030) 386 2058. 🔲 daily. ♿

Boats approaching one of the many low, long cave passages found at Tam Coc

For hotels and restaurants in this region see pp243–4 and pp259–60

Perfume Pagoda ⑧

Statue, Thien Tru Pagoda

Nestled in forested limestone cliffs, and overlooking the Suoi Yen River, Perfume Pagoda is arguably one of Vietnam's most spectacular sights. Located on Nui Huong Tich or Fragrant Vestige Mountain, the pagoda is actually a complex of around 30 Buddhist shrines. The most fascinating of these is the Huong Tich Pagoda, which is set in a deep cavern in the mountainside, and is dedicated to Quan Am, the Goddess of Mercy. Each year, during the Perfume Pagoda Festival *(see p30),* thousands of Buddhists embark on a pilgrimage up the mountain, praying for absolution, good health, and, in the case of childless couples, a baby.

Thien Tru Pagoda nestled amid the lush green peaks of Nui Huong Tich

★ Huong Tich Pagoda
This revered grotto is filled with incense smoke and several gilded figurines of the Buddha and Quan Am. The phrase "Most Beautiful Cavern under the Southern Sky" is carved near its entrance, where 120 steps lead into the cave.

Tien Son Pagoda is set in a cave and is one of the holiest shrines here. It is dedicated to Quan Am and contains four ruby statues.

Cua Vong

Thanh Son

Huong D

Steps leading to Huong Tich
The steep walk up to Huong Tich takes at least an hour. During the Perfume Pagoda Festival, thousands of pilgrims throng the steps, greeting everyone with a pious nam mo A Di Da phat, or "praise to the Amitabha Buddha."

Giai Oan Pagoda or the Undoing Injustice Pagoda is popular with pilgrims seeking purification and justice.

★ Thien Tru Pagoda
Also known as the Heavenly Kitchen Pagoda, this 18th-century shrine rises through three levels on the mountainside. An elegant triple-roofed bell pavilion stands in front of the temple and a statue of Quan Am dominates the main altar inside.

★ Suoi Yen River
A fleet of boats, all rowed by women, ferries tourists up this breathtaking river on their way to the Perfume Pagoda. The hour-and-a-half journey is a tranquil glide through verdant paddies, the profound silence broken only by the slap of the oars.

Den Trinh Pagoda is the first stop on the mountain as all pilgrims are required to "register" or pray and ask for acceptance of their journey up to Huong Tich.

STAR FEATURES

★ Huong Tich Pagoda

★ Thien Tru Pagoda

★ Suoi Yen River

Trip to Perfume Pagoda
Rowboats made of metal await passengers for the trip to the magnificent Perfume Pagoda from the township of My Duc.

Rare *Cervus nippon* deer in Cuc Phuong National Park

Cuc Phuong National Park 9

Road Map B2. Nho Quan District, 28 miles (45 km) W of Ninh Binh; 87 miles (140 km) SW of Hanoi. *Tel* (030) 384 8006. 🚌 *minibus from Ninh Binh.* 🚗 ⬜ *8am–5:30pm daily.* 📷 🎫 *by arrangement with park authorities.* 🍴 🏪 🚻 **www**.cucphuongtourism.com

Established as Vietnam's first national park in 1962, Cuc Phuong covers 86 sq miles (223 sq km) of largely primary tropical forest, and is home to an impressive variety of fauna, including almost 100 species each of mammals and reptiles, and more than 300 types of birds. The park is also famous for its range of flora, which includes soaring 1,000-year-old trees and medicinal plants.

One of the main highlights at the park is the **Endangered Primate Rescue Center**. Set up in 1993, the sanctuary cares for animals rescued from hunters, promotes breeding and conservation programs, and also rehabilitates endangered primates for release into the wild. Home to many species of langur, gibbon, loris, and other primates, the center is a great place to see these animals at close range.

Cuc Phuong has excellent trekking opportunities (*see p273*) and many attractions such as waterfalls, prehistoric caves, and nearby Muong villages that offer overnight stays.

✈ **Endangered Primate Rescue Center**
Tel (030) 384 8002. ⬜ *daily.* **www**.primatecenter.org

Hoa Binh ❿

Road Map B3. 46 miles (74 km) SW of Hanoi. 🚶 *75,000*. 🚌 *Hanoi*. ℹ️ *Hoa Binh Tourist, 54 Phuong Lam, (018) 385 4327.* **www**.hoabinhtourism.com

A pleasant little town, Hoa Binh means "peace." Ironically, its strategic location next to the Song Da or Black River Valley made it the site of many battles during the First Indochina War *(see p43)*. Relics from these turbulent times are displayed in the **Hoa Binh Museum**. A French landing craft and a destroyed French tank can be seen on its grounds.

Traditionally home to the Muong community, the town has shaded avenues and some decent eateries, which makes it a convenient stop on a tour from Hanoi to neighboring places such as Moc Chau and around Mai Chau Valley.

A few miles northwest of Hoa Binh is **Song Da Reservoir**. As the largest hydroelectric power station in Vietnam, it plays a critical role in the country's economic development.

🏛 **Hoa Binh Museum**
6 An Duong Vuong St.
Tel *(018) 385 2177.* ⏰ *7–11am, 1:30–4:30pm daily.* 📷

French tank captured in the First Indochina War, Hoa Binh Museum

Mai Chau Valley ⓫

Road Map B2. 87 miles (140 km) SW of Hanoi; 43 miles (70 km) SE of Moc Chau on Hwy 6. 🚶 *45,000*. 🚌 *from Hanoi and Son La.*

Surrounded by the foothills of the Truong Son Range, this charming and fertile valley is dotted with green rice paddies and small, quaint stilt-house villages. Most of the inhabitants here are White Thai. Well

White Thai girls in traditional costume perform a folk dance, Mai Chau

known for their hospitality, families here offer homestay *(see p229)* facilities in stilt huts. As the standards of hygiene and cuisine are good, this is an authentic yet comfortable way of experiencing life on the hills. Some of the larger homestays even put on displays of traditional Thai music and dancing. At night, visitors can enjoy the local alcohol *ruou can*, which is drunk communally from large jars through long bamboo straws.

One of the main highlights here are the excellent trekking opportunities provided by the valley's delightful trails, fields, and villages.

Moc Chau ⓬

Road Map B1. 124 miles (200 km) SW of Hanoi; 75 miles (121 km) SE of Son La on Hwy 6. 🚶 *119,000*. 🚌 *from Hanoi and Son La.*

The semi-rural, market town of Moc Chau, surrounded by a plateau of the same name, is renowned for its tea plantations and its burgeoning dairy industry. The generous yield of fresh cow's milk, as well as the creamy yogurt and rich sweets made here are transported to Hanoi daily.

Since Moc Chau is not as convenient as Mai Chau for longer stays, most people stop here only for refreshments on the drive from Hanoi to Son La. Ethnic minorities such as the Hmong *(see pp198–9)* and Thai occupy the neighboring hamlets, which are definitely worth a visit.

Son La ⓭

Road Map A1. 199 miles (320 km) NW of Hanoi on Hwy 6; 93 miles (150 km) E of Dien Bien Phu on Hwy 6. 🚶 *60,000*. ✈️ *Hanoi*. 🚌 *from Hanoi and Dien Bien Phu.*

Bisected by the narrow Nam La River, the busy little town of Son La was once known as "Vietnam's Siberia." The infamous French-era prison, **Nha Tu Cu Cua Phap**, which earned it this label, stands menacingly on a wooded hill. Son La's isolation and cold weather were considered ideal conditions for the incarceration of Vietnamese nationalists and revolutionaries. Recalcitrant prisoners were shackled and confined in windowless cells, and the prison guillotine saw regular use. However, as is often the case, the prison also served as a revolutionary academy of sorts. Some of the political prisoners held here included luminaries such as

Black Thai women selling their wares in makeshift stalls, Son La

Truong Chinh and Le Duan, both of whom later became General Secretaries of the Vietnamese Communist Party. The prison complex also includes a museum displaying remnants of French brutality and torture such as cramped underground cells and leg irons. Somewhat incongruously, exhibits such as hill tribe artifacts and clothing are also displayed here.

A major attraction in town is the market on the east bank of the Nam La. Fresh fruit and vegetables, as well as handicrafts and cloth hand-woven by the White and Black Thai are on sale here. Chickens, ducks, and pot-bellied pigs are for sale, while most food stalls serve Son La's specialty, goat meat or *thit de*. The more adventurous can sample *tiet canh*, congealed goat's blood served with chopped peanuts and shallots.

Located 3 miles (5 km) south of town are the warm water springs known as Suoi Nuoc Nong. It is possible to bathe here for a small fee. The scenery around Son La is very attractive and the drive to Dien Bien Phu leads past picturesque fields, hills, and interesting minority villages.

Wooden stilt huts amid the verdant paddy fields around Son La

🏛 Nha Tu Cu Cua Phap
Dai Khao Ca. **Tel** (022) 385 2022.
◯ 7:30–11am, 1:30–4:30pm daily. 🈸

Dien Bien Phu ⓮

Road Map A1. 292 miles (470 km) NW of Hanoi; 93 miles (150 km) W of Son La. 🏘 100,000. ✈ Hanoi. 🚌 from Hanoi, Son La, and Lai Chau. **www**.dienbienphu.org

Situated in a fertile valley near the Lao border, this historic town's main claim to fame is the decisive battle of Dien Bien Phu *(see p43)*. In 1954, following French infiltration of the area, Viet Minh troops systematically broke down the French position. In the end, General de Castries, commander of the French army, and his troops were captured. Today, the town has moved past its violent history and is developing at a rapid pace.

Dien Bien Phu was once part of the Lai Chau Province, a section of which is due to be submerged by the waters of the rising Son La Dam. As a result, the new province of Dien Bien Phu was created, leading to a boom in construction work, both for administrative buildings and for resettlement purposes.

Rapidly being encroached on by new buildings, the main battlefield on the east bank of the Nam La River has a few old, rusty French tanks lying around even today. Nearby

Marble headstone of a hero, Dien Bien Phu Martyrs' Cemetery

stands a poignant memorial to the French dead. Chronicling the great battle, **Dien Bien Phu Museum** is full of weapons, pictures, maps, dioramas of the battlefield, and personal possessions of soldiers. Just opposite is the **Dien Bien Phu Martyrs' Cemetery**, where the Viet Minh fallen are buried. To the north is the famous **Hill A1**, named Eliane by the French, after one of General de Castries' mistresses. The most interesting relic here is the French general's subterranean bunker, covered with a rusting, corrugated iron roof and reinforced with concrete.

On the hilltop is a monument to martyred Vietnamese heroes, and a tunnel entrance used by the Viet Minh to reach a French camp, which they blew up with a mine. Farther north is the 120-ton victory monument in bronze, which commemorates the battle's 50th anniversary. This is the largest monument in the entire country.

🏛 Dien Bien Phu Museum
1 Muong Thanh. **Tel** (023) 383 1341. ◯ 7:30–11am, 1:30–4:30pm daily. 🈸

View of the spectacular Tram Ton Pass, north side of Mount Fansipan, Sapa

Sapa 🕒

Road Map A1. 236 miles (380 km)
NW of Hanoi. 🏘 30,000. 🚃 from
Hanoi to Lao Cai. 🚌 Lao Cai.
ℹ️ Sapa Tourism, Cau May St,
(020) 387 1975. 🛍 Sat & Sun.
www.sapa-tourism.com

With cascading rice terraces
and lush vegetation, Sapa is
perched on the eastern slopes
of the Hoang Lien Mountains,
also known as the Tonkinese
Alps. Jesuit priests first arrived
here in 1918 and sent word of
the idyllic views and pleasant
climate back to Hanoi. By
1922, Sapa was established as
a hill station where the French
built villas, hotels, and tennis
courts, transforming the place
into a summer retreat.

In this scenic setting, French
colonists or *colons* would flirt,
gossip, eat strawberries, and
drink lots of wine. These
idyllic conditions lasted until
World War II and the Japanese
invasion of 1941. Many villas
and hotels were destroyed or
abandoned in the next four
decades during wars with the
French and the US *(see pp43–
5)*. Still more destructive was
the Sino-Vietnamese War of
1979, when the town itself
was damaged.

Fortunately, following the
introduction of Vietnam's economic reforms or *doi moi* in
the 1990s and the subsequent
gradual opening of the country
to tourism, Sapa gained a
fresh lease on life. Revived
by local entrepreneurs and
rediscovered by foreign
visitors, the town slowly
regained the distinction it
enjoyed in colonial times.
Set on several levels joined
by small sloping streets and
steep flights of steps,
Sapa is home to
diverse hill peoples,
as well as ethnic Kinh
and a growing army of
visitors who come for
the stunning views
and fresh mountain
air. Trekking has
become a popular
activity, and walks
to nearby villages
are open to all.
Visitors mostly time
their stay to coincide
with the weekend
market, when many

hill people flock to Sapa from
nearby villages to trade food
and crafts. A major section of
hill people are the Black
Hmong, who generally wear
indigo, followed by the Red
Dao. Young women turn up
for this colorful bazaar wearing exquisitely embroidered
skirts and jackets, elaborate
headdresses, and heavy silver
jewelry. The small and simple
Sapa church, which was built
in 1930 and set in a square,
forms the center of town where
the locals collect on feast days.

Southeast of the town is
Ham Rong or Dragon Jaw's
Hill. A gentle climb leads up
through rockeries and grottos
to a summit. From here, there

Hotels with balcony views in Sapa

Black Dao woman in traditional
garb, and a child

are magnificent views of the tree-filled valleys below, dotted with the colorful villas. Dance performances by the ethnic minorities are staged at the top of the hill.

Environs

The "Gateway to Sapa," **Lao Cai** lies at a distance of about 25 miles (40 km) northeast of Sapa. A rather unappealing border town, it is not really a place to linger in. However, if crossing to China or passing through to visit Sapa and Bac Ha, it is comfortable enough, with adequate hotel facilities and some good restaurants.

About 5 miles (8 km) from Sapa, **Mount Fansipan** is the country's highest peak. Around 10,312-ft (3,143-m) tall, it is covered in lush subtropical vegetation to a height of about 656 ft (200 m), and then by temperate forest. Although the terrain can be difficult and the weather bad, the peak attracts trekkers *(see p273)*. Warm clothes, sturdy boots, camping gear, and a guide are essential for the five-day round trip. There is no sign of humanity for most of the climb, with only lush green forests and spectacular mountains for company. The silence is broken only by the sounds of birds, monkeys, and the gentle rustling of trees.

The lovely Black Hmong *(see p198)* village of **Cat Cat** is just 2 miles (3 km) south of Sapa. Visitors normally walk down the steep trail, but take a motorcycle taxi for the uphill ride back to town. The Hmong live in houses of mud, wattle, bamboo, and thatch, surrounded by vats of indigo-colored liquid, which is used to dye their clothing. Just 2.5 miles (4 km) beyond Cat Cat is the less commercialized Hmong village of **Sin Chai**, while the Red Dao *(see p21)* village of **Ta Phin** is only about 6 miles (10 km) from Sapa. The route to Ta Phin passes through a low-slung valley that is carved

Colorful embroidered accessories by the Red Dao

with curved rice terracing, which glints very brightly in the sun. Just before Ta Phin is an abandoned, semi-destroyed French seminary, which was built in 1942.

Just around 9 miles (15 km) northwest of Sapa, on the road to the Tram Ton Pass is the **Thac Bac** or Silver Waterfall. This powerful 328-ft (100-m) high cascade is a magnificent sight, attracting many visitors. Here, women – Kinh, Black Dao, and Red Hmong – set up stalls selling delicious fruit.

Bac Ha ⓰

Road Map A1. 205 miles (330 km) NW Hanoi, 43 miles (69 km) E of Lao Cai. 🚶 *7,000.* 🚌 *from Lao Cai and Sapa.* 🚐 *Sun.* 👤 *(020) 388 0264.* **www**.*bachatourist.com*

A small town at 2,953 ft (900 m) above sea level in the Chay River massif, Bac Ha has a deserted air for much of the week. However, on Sunday mornings, it attracts hill peoples, such as the Dao, Tay, Thai, Nung, and the colorful Flower Hmong among many others from all over the surrounding mountains. All of them head for Bac Ha's dusty town center and market, leading ponies stacked high with firewood, and carrying baskets loaded with merchandise. Goods sold and exchanged include bush meat, vegetables, fruits, spices, and exquisitely embroidered goods. Most hill

Brightly dressed Flower Hmong women gathered at Bac Ha market

people also use this occasion to stock up on necessities as well as luxuries that are not available in the hills. Toiletries, religious paraphernalia, and incense sticks, as well as needles, thread, and cloth for embroidery are just some of the products in demand here.

Environs

Many visitors to Bac Ha also head farther north in order to combine a visit to the Sunday market with a trip to the small settlement of **Can Cau**. Located about 12 miles (20 km) from Bac Ha town, this charming village hosts a Saturday market, which is very popular with locals and visitors alike, especially for being delightfully vibrant and extremely colorful.

Bac Ha district is also known for its potent maize alcohol, distilled most especially at the small village of **Ban Pho**, a Flower Hmong settlement just 2.5 miles (4 km) to the west of Bac Ha town.

Local hill people completing their weekly shopping, Bac Ha market

Hmong of Northern Vietnam

One of the largest ethnic minority groups in Vietnam, the Hmong or Meo were a nomadic group who emigrated from China to Vietnam in the early 19th century, and settled in the northern highlands. Known for their independent spirit – *hmong* means free in their language – the group has remained fiercely loyal to its indigenous customs, resisting assimilation with the Viet majority. Today, the Hmong have largely abandoned slash-and-burn agriculture, and lead a settled, often impoverished life, farming and raising livestock. These people are categorized under five main subgroups – Flower, Black, Green, Red, and White – based on the dress of the women.

Vietnamese is taught in schools to encourage assimilation

Hmong villages, *known as* giao, *are small communities featuring wooden huts with thatched roofs. Unlike other hill communities, their homes are not built on stilts. They are usually constructed according to ancient customs, stipulating that houses must be built on land blessed by ancestors.*

The ritualistic *sacrifice of buffalos is common during festivals. The Hmong are traditionally animists, who believe that the meat will appease the region's guardian spirits. A number of special musical instruments are used for such ceremonies, including large drums, water buffalo horns, and the* queej, *a kind of mouth harp.*

Bright strips of cloth, embroidered in vibrant patterns of flowers, birds, and geometric designs decorate the blouses of the women.

The Black Hmong *are distinguished by their black-dyed clothing. The men dress in baggy trousers, short tunics, and skullcaps, while women wear trousers or skirts and leggings, often piling their hair into an open hat. Most Black Hmong villages are found around Sapa.*

Dry rice cultivation, *which is based on traditional slash-and-burn agriculture, has been adopted by the Hmong on the uplands. Maize, corn, and rye are other staples, while hemp and cotton are grown for cloth. In some remote areas, poppies are illegally harvested for opium.*

Indigo *is used by the Black and Green Hmong to dye trousers, skirts, and sashes, which are hand-woven out of hemp. Batik is often utilized to further embellish these richly colored outfits.*

Hmong textile stalls *are a staple of the weekly markets of the northern highlands. The Hmong have been relatively successful in selling their handicrafts to visitors. Their appliqué work and embroidered fabrics are now very popular.*

Gui, or woven baskets, into which babies are tucked, are strapped to the backs of Hmong mothers, which helps keep their hands free for daily tasks.

Flower Hmong flock to Bac Ha *market once a week to sell fresh produce, honey, bamboo, and herbs. They also stock up on necessities such as matches, cloth, needles, and kitchenware.*

Appliqué bags and aprons are indicators of marital status and social position.

COLORFUL FLOWER HMONG

Admired for their extravagant and elaborate clothing, the Flower Hmong are the largest subdivision of the Hmong in the country. The vividly patterned costumes worn by the women include brightly colored head scarves, full pleated skirts, as well as flamboyant silver or tin jewelry. The women are also successful in business, and often sell clothes and accessories featuring their exquisite embroidery, batik, and appliqué work.

Red Hmong *women are known for their giant, bouffant hairdos. They painstakingly collect all the hair they shed naturally, and then weave it around a headpiece, along with their living tresses. Occasionally, the hair of dead relatives is also woven in.*

Heavy silver jewelry *is worn by Hmong women both as adornment and as a mark of status. The intricately crafted earrings, necklaces, and bracelets often feature the snake motif – a talisman against evil forces. Men and children also wear jewelry, as it is believed to bind the body and soul together.*

Dawn breaking above the shimmering expanse of Ba Be National Park's lake

Ba Be National Park ⑰

Road Map B1. 149 miles (240 km) N of Hanoi; 37 miles (60 km) N of Bac Kan Town. **Tel** (0281) 389 4026. 🚌 Hanoi. 📷 🎫 by arrangement with park authorities. 🍴

Located in a remote upland region, this lush park is centered around three linked lakes – Ba Be means Three Bays. Together they form the country's largest freshwater lake area. Covering about 39 sq miles (100 sq km), the park is dominated by dramatic limestone peaks, waterfalls, and grottos. The region's tropical forests are also home to an abundance of wildlife, including the François langur and the endangered Tonkin snub-nosed monkey.

Some of the main attractions in Ba Be National Park include the **Dau Dang Falls**, a spectacular series of cascades, found at the northwest end of the lake. Also worth seeing is the **Hang Puong**, a fascinating grotto that tunnels its way all through the mountains. Situated around 7 miles (12 km) up the Nang River, this narrow cave can be navigated in a small boat, though the trip takes the better part of a day. To the south of the lake lies **Pac Ngoi**, a charming village, which is inhabited by the Tay minority. The surrounding hills are home to other ethnic peoples.

Cao Bang ⑱

Road Map B1. 168 miles (270 km) N of Hanoi on Hwy 3. 🏘 45,000. 🚌 Hanoi and Lang Son.

Well off the beaten track in the high mountains along the Chinese frontier, the thickly forested area around the small town of Cao Bang is home to several ethnic minorities, including the Tay, Dao, and Nung. While the town itself is not particularly distinctive, its surroundings are spectacular, and many visitors are drawn to its abundant trekking opportunities. The Vietnamese regard it as a place of historical significance. The scions of the 16th-century Mac Dynasty ruled here, and years later, Ho Chi Minh (see p169) made it his first base on returning to Vietnam after nearly three decades.

Nung girl in rural Cao Bang

Environs

Around 37 miles (60 km) northwest of town, **Hang Pac Bo** or Water Wheel Cave is where Ho Chi Minh stayed on his return in 1941 from self-imposed exile. The cave has great historical importance as the birthplace of the Viet Minh struggle. A small museum here makes for an interesting stop.

About 56 miles (90 km) northeast of Cao Bang, **Thac Ban Gioc** is the largest waterfall in Vietnam. It straddles the Sino-Vietnamese border and it is necessary to get a pass at Cao Bang's police station to visit the area.

Tam Dao ⑲

Road Map B1. 53 miles (85 km) NW of Hanoi. 🚌 Hanoi.

Established as a hill station by the French in 1907, Tam Dao is a cool and scenic getaway, easily accessible from Hanoi. It derives its name from the Three Islands, which are in fact, a line of three peaks, all around 4,600 ft (1,400 m) high. On clearer days, they can be seen rising above the clouds like islands in a sea of mist. The steep road from Vinh Yen to Tam Dao offers picturesque views as it winds past pine forests and narrow valleys.

While the hills around Tam Dao are lovely, with terraces lined with gourds and tomato vines growing on cane frames, the town itself is somewhat rundown. The architecture is a mix of crumbling French-colonial houses and stern, box-like Soviet-style hotels. Fortunately, there are now signs of reconstruction and renovation everywhere.

At present, the primary attraction in the area is **Tam Dao National Park**. Frequented mostly by nature-lovers from Hanoi, it is home to a wide variety of birdlife, as well as over 60 species of mammals. Trekkers who want to explore the park can find information at any of the guesthouses in the town of Tam Dao.

🦋 Tam Dao National Park

Ho Son Commune, Tam Duong District. **Tel** (0211) 389 6710. ⏰ 7–11:30am, 1:30–4:30pm daily. 📷

The Three Islands, which give Tam Dao its name, rise above lesser hills

Flora, Fauna, and Birds of Northern Vietnam

Under a thick, rich canopy of evergreen forests, the rugged mountainous hinterland of Northern Vietnam protects an amazingly diverse biosphere. Thousands of types of flora flourish here, as do a plethora of bird, mammal, and reptile species. However, a vast number of animals, many endemic to Vietnam, are currently under threat. Critically endangered species include the

Young fern shoots in a forest

kouprey and the Tonkin snub-nosed monkey. The Asian elephant and the white-rumped black lemur are also facing serious threat. Fortunately, the authorities are beginning to take notice and have adopted a proactive stance against poaching. With sustained conservation and reforestation measures, it is hoped that the north will eventually reach an ecological balance.

FLORA

The mountains and valleys of Northern Vietnam are covered with thick forests, sheltering a wealth of tropical and sub-tropical flora, ranging from towering rainforests, dwarf bamboos, and tiny ferns to creeping vines, exquisite orchids, and colorful rhododendrons.

Karst mountains covered with forests dominate the landscape, especially around Tam Coc, Cao Bang, and Halong Bay.

The Annamese silver pheasant *lives on the slopes of the Truong Son and Hoang Lien Son Mountains. Its red legs, red face, and black crest set off its lovely silver plumage.*

A dazzling variety of orchids *bloom all over Vietnam. Of around 40 endemic species, 18 are found on Mount Fansipan (see p197).*

Millions of cave swiftlets, *tiny, fast-flying insect-catchers which live in the limestone caves of the north, leave their nests at dawn and return at dusk.*

FAUNA

The Truong Son Range has revealed more previously unknown large mammals than any other location during the late 20th century. These include the Vu Quang ox, the giant muntjac, and the Truong Son muntjac. Deer, wild boars, as well as many primate species inhabit the forests, especially in Cuc Phuong *(see p193)*.

The red-shanked Douc langur *has bright maroon hind legs and reddish patches around the eyes. Its long tail adds to its considerable agility.*

The Vu Quang ox, *or saola, is a rare forest-dwelling bovine, first discovered in 1992 at Vu Quang Nature Reserve. Weighing around 198 lb (90 kg), it has a brown coat with a black stripe along the back. Both sexes have large, curving horns.*

The Indochinese tiger *once roamed the forests of Northern Vietnam freely. Mainly due to the use of tiger parts in traditional medicine, only about 150 of these majestic beasts exist in Vietnam today.*

EXCURSION TO
ANGKOR

INTRODUCING ANGKOR

The ancient capital of the great Khmer Empire, Angkor is beyond doubt, one of the most magnificent wonders of the world and a site of immense archaeological significance. Located in dense jungle on the hot and torpid plains of western Cambodia, its awe-inspiring temples transport visitors into an enchanting and mysterious world of brooding grandeur and past glory.

Situated in southwestern Indochina, the flat, low-lying country of Cambodia covers an area of about 69,500 sq miles (180,000 sq km), bordering Laos to the north, Thailand to both the north and west, and Vietnam to the east. Although Cambodia's capital is now Phnom Penh, this title was once held by Angkor. For nearly six centuries, between AD 802 and 1432, it was the political and religious center of the great Khmer Empire, which once extended from the South China Sea almost to the Bay of Bengal.

Classical dancer, Cambodian Royal Ballet

The remains of the metropolis of Angkor now occupy 77 sq miles (200 sq km) of northwest Cambodia, and although its old wooden houses and palaces decayed centuries ago, the stunning array of stone temples erected by a succession of self-styled god-kings still stand. Set between two *baray* or reservoirs, Angkor today contains around 70 temples, tombs, and other ancient ruins. Among them is the stunning Angkor Wat, the world's single largest religious complex.

RELIGION

Ancient Cambodia was highly influenced by South Asia, and Hindu gods such as Vishnu and Shiva were revered. From the 10th century AD onward, Buddhism gradually began to spread throughout the Khmer Empire, receiving a significant boost during the reign of Angkor monarch Jayavarman VII (r.1181–1215). As the two religions flourished, Angkorian architecture incorporated elements from both Hinduism and Buddhism. Eventually, Theravada Buddhism or the Way of the Elders emerged as the predominant school, and replaced Hinduism as the national religion.

HISTORY

The Khmer Empire was founded in the beginning of the 9th century AD, when Jayavarman II (r.802–850) proclaimed himself *devaraja* or the divine king of the land. A follower of Shiva, he built a gigantic, pyramidal temple-mountain representing Mount Meru, the sacred mythical abode of the Hindu gods.

Meandering river near Siem Reap *(see p208)*, the gateway to the temples of Angkor

Buddhist monks walking past the grand Angkor Wat complex *(see pp212–13)*

This structure laid the foundation of Angkor's architecture *(see pp214–15)*. His successor, Indravarman I (r.877–89) expanded the empire, but it was Yasovarman I (r.889–910) who shifted the former capital at Roluos to Angkor. He established his new seat of power by constructing a magnificent temple on the hill of Phnom Bakheng and another one on the massive East Baray. Angkor's grandest structures, Angkor Wat was built by Suryavarman II (r.1113–50), and Angkor Thom by Jayavarman VII. Following Jayavarman VII's death, Angkor entered a long era of decline, lying forgotten as Thai invaders ravaged the land.

It was not until the 19th century that spellbound European explorers stumbled upon Angkor. Following their "discovery," the ancient city underwent a period of restoration until the mid-20th century, when it disappeared again behind a curtain of war. During the Vietnam War *(see pp44–5)*, Vietnamese communists used Cambodia as a staging post, and the US responded with large-scale bombings, killing thousands of Cambodians, and giving rise to Pol Pot's Khmer Rouge. This extreme Maoist party seized power in 1975, and by the time it was overthrown by the Vietnamese in 1979, it had killed an estimated two million Cambodians in one of the worst acts of genocide in history.

ANGKOR TODAY

Since the collapse of the Khmer Rouge in the early 1990s, Angkor has gradually reopened to the world. Miraculously, in a nation so devastated by war, the great temple complexes have survived remarkably unscathed. Today, after painstaking clearance of unexploded ordinance and dense vegetation, restoration and conservation are once again in full swing. One of the most important archaeological sites in the world, Angkor attracts millions of visitors each year, providing a substantial boost to Cambodia's economy.

KEY DATES IN HISTORY

AD 802 Khmer Empire established.

AD 900 Capital moved from Roluos to Angkor.

1113–1150 Suryavarman II builds Angkor Wat.

1181–1201 Jayavarman VII builds the Bayon and Angkor Thom.

1352–1431 Siam attacks Angkor on four separate occasions.

1863 Cambodia becomes a French protectorate.

1953 Cambodia gains full independence from France under King Sihanouk.

1970 US begins carpet bombing of northern and eastern Cambodia.

1975 Khmer Rouge seizes power.

1979 Vietnamese forces overthrow Khmer Rouge.

1998 Khmer Rouge leader Pol Pot dies.

2005 UN approves tribunal for trying surviving Khmer Rouge leaders.

Exploring Angkor

Set among dense green forests and neat rice paddies, the massive monuments at Angkor are arguably the most remarkable and striking architectural masterpieces in Southeast Asia. Located north of Siem Reap, in the heart of Angkor, the vast Angkor Wat complex, with its imposing towers, and the great city of Angkor Thom, with its impressive causeway and gigantic smiling faces of the Bayon, are breathtaking sights, especially during sunrise or sunset. Farther north are the smaller yet unique temples of Preah Khan and Preah Neak Pean. To the east of Angkor Thom is the magical Ta Prohm, with large trees growing through the temple walls. Farther out, the pink sandstone structure of Banteay Srei lies to the northeast, while to the southeast are the ruins of the Roluos Group, the oldest in Angkor.

Exquisite carvings of dancing *apsaras* at Bayon, Angkor Thom

SIGHTS AT A GLANCE

Historic Monuments

Angkor Thom pp216–19 4
Angkor Wat pp212–13 2
Banteay Srei 9
Phnom Bakheng 3
Prasat Kravan 8
Preah Khan 5
Preah Neak Pean 6
Roluos Group 10
Ta Prohm 7

City

Siem Reap 1

SEE ALSO

• ***Where to Stay*** pp244–5

• ***Where to Eat*** pp260–61

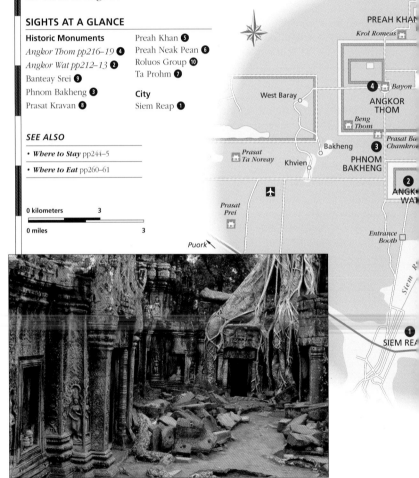

Thick tree roots covering the stone walls and ceilings of Ta Prohm

GETTING AROUND

The temples at Angkor require both time and motorized transport to visit. It is possible to visit the main sites by motorbike, but the most comfortable way to travel in this hot and dusty area is in an air-conditioned car with a driver. In colonial times, the French defined two circuits, both starting at Angkor Wat, which are still used today. The 11-mile (18-km) "small circuit" takes at least a day and covers the central temples of the complex, continuing to Ta Prohm, before returning to Angkor Wat by way of Banteay Kdei. The "great circuit," a 17-mile (27-km) route, takes in the small circuit as well as the outer temples, going past Preah Neak Pean to Ta Som before turning south to Pre Rup. It takes at least two full days.

LOCATOR MAP

KEY

☐	Urban areas
✈	International airport
🏛	Temple
══	Archaeological sites
━━	Major road
══	Minor road

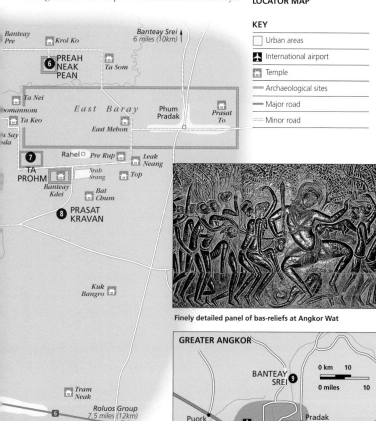

Banteay Pre
Krol Ko
Banteay Srei
6 miles (10km)
6 PREAH NEAK PEAN
Ta Som
Ta Nei
Romannom
Ta Keo
East Baray
Phum Pradak
Prasat To
East Mebon
u Say eda
Rahel
Pre Rup
Leak Neang
7 TA PROHM
Srah Srang
Top
Banteay Kdei
Bat Chum
8 PRASAT KRAVAN
Kuk Bangro
Tram Neak
Roluos Group
7.5 miles (12km)
Phnom Penh

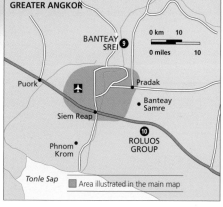

Finely detailed panel of bas-reliefs at Angkor Wat

GREATER ANGKOR
BANTEAY SREI **9**
0 km   10
0 miles   10
Puork
Pradak
Banteay Samre
Siem Reap
10 ROLUOS GROUP
Phnom Krom
Tonle Sap
☐ Area illustrated in the main map

Siem Reap ❶

Pronounced "See-em Reep," Siem Reap literally means Siam Defeated, celebrating the 17th-century Khmer victory over the Thai kingdom of Ayutthaya. The town is the capital of Siem Reap Province, located in northwest Cambodia, and has achieved prominence as the main base for people visiting the temples of Angkor and Roluos. As a burgeoning center of tourism with a new airport, Siem Reap features many new hotels and restaurants, and further development is ongoing.

Verdant lawns outside the Grand Hotel d'Angkor (see p245), Siem Reap

Exploring the city

Siem Reap has managed to retain its calm, rural ambience despite becoming increasingly busy catering to millions of visitors every year. Its relaxed, well-equipped setting provides the ideal place to unwind after a day exploring Angkor.

The French-colonial **Grand Hotel d'Angkor**, which stands out regally opposite the Royal Gardens in the northern part of town, has been splendidly restored. The small **Royal Palace**, which is rarely visited by the reigning King Sihamoni, is close by.

South of a statue of Vishnu marking the center of town, Pokambor Avenue runs down the right bank of the Siem Reap River to **Psar Chaa**. This old market is a great place to shop for souvenirs. Nearby, the carefully restored old

VISITORS' CHECKLIST

155 miles (250 km) NW of Phnom Penh. 🚶 ✈ 🚌 from Battambang and Phnom Penh. ℹ *Khmer Angkor Tour Guide Association, (063) 964 347.*

French Quarter is home to some of the most atmospheric restaurants in the Angkor area. For those who wish to explore the area, the banks of the Siem Reap River offer a pleasant stroll. Several blue-painted stilt houses and creaky bamboo waterwheels can be seen here.

Farther south, situated some 6 miles (10 km) away, is the ferry landing on the **Tonle Sap**. The largest freshwater lake in Southeast Asia, it is also a biosphere reserve. The **Krousar Thmey Tonle Sap Exhibition** in the northern outskirts of Siem Reap has displays on the lake, floating villages, and wildlife.

The main monuments at Angkor, the ticket office, and conservatory are all about 4 miles (6 km) north of town. About halfway, at **Wat Thmei**, is a *stupa* displaying the skulls of local Khmer Rouge victims.

🏛 **Krousar Thmey Tonle Sap Exhibition**
On the road to Angkor Wat. **Tel** (063) 964 694. ◯ 8am–6pm daily. ⬤ noon–2pm.

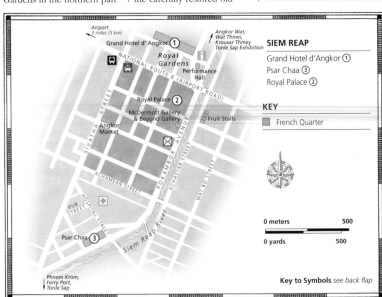

```
                    Airport
                    3 miles (5 km)
        Grand Hotel d' Angkor ①              Angkor Wat,
                                             Wat Thmei,
                  Royal                      Krousar Thmey      SIEM REAP
                  Gardens                    Tonle Sap Exhibition
            NATIONAL ROUTE 6 (AIRPORT ROAD)  Performance        Grand Hotel d'Angkor ①
                                             Hall               Psar Chaa ③
            Royal Palace ②                                      Royal Palace ②
            McDermott Gallery
            & Beyond Gallery        Fruit Stalls                KEY
        Angkor
        Market                                                  ▢ French Quarter
        SIVATHA STREET
                    POKAMBOR AVENUE
                    ACHASVAR STREET
        ACHAMEAN STREET              WAT BO STREET
        PUB
        STREET  HOSPITAL STREET
                                                                0 meters        500
        Psar Chaa ③                                             0 yards         500
            Siem Reap River
        Phnom Krom,
        Ferry Port,
        Tonle Sap                                               Key to Symbols see back flap
```

Visitors enjoying sunset views across Angkor, Phnom Bakheng

Angkor Wat ❷

See pp212–13.

Phnom Bakheng ❸

Just S of Angkor Thom.
☐ *sunrise–sunset daily.* 🎫 *general Angkor ticket.*

The ancient temple complex of Phnom Bakheng sits on a steep hill that rises 220 ft (67 m) above the surrounding plain.

Built by King Yasovarman I (r.889–910) and honoring the Hindu god, Shiva, the Bakheng complex features one of the region's first temple-mountains (*see p214*) – a distinctive style of temple architecture that has become a mainstay of Khmer-style religious buildings. The complex was also surrounded by 109 towers, but most of them are now missing. However, the well-crafted statues of lions, flanking each of the five terraced tiers of the temple, can be seen even today. The central sanctuary, one of five in all, is adorned with several decorative posts and statues of *apsaras* or celestial dancing girls, and *makaras* or mythical sea creatures.

On the east side of the hill, a steep flight of broken stone stairs leads to the summit. The winding path on the south side is safer and is the usual path taken to carry tourists, on elephants, to the top. Here, there are spectacular views over Angkor and the Western Baray. At dusk, the setting sun illuminates the Tonle Sap and the spires of Angkor Wat with an ethereal glow.

Angkor Thom ❹

See pp216–19.

Preah Khan ❺

1 mile (1.6 km) NE of Angkor Thom.
☐ *sunrise–sunset daily.* 🎫 *general Angkor ticket.*

Named for the sacred sword owned by the 9th-century king, Jayavarman II, Preah Khan temple complex was established by Jayavarman VII (r.1181–1215), and functioned as a monastery and religious college. It is also believed to have served as a temporary capital for Jayavarman VII during the restoration of Angkor Thom following the city's sacking by the Kingdom of Champa in 1177.

Statue of a hermit in prayer, Preah Khan

An inscribed stone stele found here in 1939 indicates that the temple, the largest such enclosure in Angkor, was based at the center of an ancient city, Nagarajayacri – *jayacri* means sacred sword in Siamese. The central sanctuary was originally dedicated to the Buddha, but the Hindu rulers succeeding Jayavarman VII vandalized many of the temple's Buddhist aspects, replacing several Buddha images on the walls with carvings of Hindu deities.

Today, the complex extends over a sprawling 141 acres (57 ha), and is surrounded by a 2-mile (3-km) long laterite wall. The premises also have a massive reservoir or *baray*. Access to the central sanctuary, built on a cross-shaped layout, is through four gates, set at the cardinal points of the compass. One of the main highlights at Preah Khan is the Hall of Dancers, so named for the exquisite *apsara* bas-reliefs that line the walls. The shrine of the White Lady, a wife of Jayavarman VII, is still venerated by locals who leave behind offerings of flowers and incense. The most notable temple on the grounds, however, is the Temple of Four Faces, named for the carvings on its central tower.

Like Ta Prohm (*see p220*), Preah Khan is studded with great trees whose creeping roots cover and, in places, pierce the laterite and sandstone structures on which they grow. Yet, unlike Ta Prohm, the complex has undergone extensive restoration. Over the past decade, many of the giant trees here have been felled, and the walls are being painstakingly rebuilt.

Intricately detailed bas-relief of *apsaras* in the Hall of Dancers, Preah Khan

Buddhist monks in front of the Face Tower at the Bayon, Angkor Thom ▷

Angkor Wat ❷

The single largest religious monuments in the world, Angkor Wat literally means "the City which is a Temple." Built during the 12th century by King Suryavarman II (r.1113–50), this spectacular complex was originally dedicated to the Hindu god Vishnu, the Protector of Creation. The layout is based on a *mandala* or sacred design of the Hindu cosmos. A five-towered temple shaped like a lotus bud and representing Mount Meru, the mythical abode of the gods and the center of the universe, stands in the middle of the complex. The outer walls represent the edge of the world, and the moat is the cosmic ocean. Especially outstanding are the intricate carvings that adorn the walls, including a 1,970-ft (600-m) panel of bas-reliefs and around 2,000 engravings of *apsaras* or celestial dancing girls with enigmatic smiles. Angkor Wat, unusually among Khmer temples, faces west and toward the setting sun, a symbol of death.

Highly detailed carvings on the outer walls of the central sanctuary

★ **Central Sanctuary**
Towering over the complex, the Central Sanctuary can be a steep climb. Its four entrances feature images of the Buddha, reflecting the Buddhist influence that eventually displaced Hinduism in Cambodia.

★ **Apsaras**
The carvings of hundreds of sensual apsaras *or celestial dancing girls line the walls of the temple. Holding alluring poses, they are shown wearing ornate jewelry and exquisite headgear.*

For hotels and restaurants in this region see pp244–5 and pp260–61

VISITORS' CHECKLIST

3.7 miles (6 km) N of Siem Reap. ✈ to Siem Reap. 🚌 🚕 ℹ️ *Khmer Angkor Tour Guide Association, Siem Reap, (063) 964 347.* 🕐 5am–6pm daily. 🎫 *general Angkor ticket.* **www**.khmerangkortour guide.com

View of Towers
The five towers of Angkor Wat rise through three levels to a grand central shrine. The entire complex is surrounded by thick walls and a wide moat that represent the outer edge and the ocean of the universe. The view of the temple from the other side of the moat is stunning with its towers reflected in the still water.

Bas-reliefs in the Southern Gallery depict images of King Suryavarman II who initiated the construction of Angkor Wat.

★ **Gallery of Bas-Reliefs**
The southern section of the Western Gallery depicts several scenes from the Hindu epic Mahabharata. *The bas-reliefs here detail images of hundreds of weapon-bearing warriors engaged in furious combat during the Battle of Kurukshetra.*

The Causeway
The wide pathway leading to the temple's main entrance on the west side affords a spectacular view of Angkor Wat's grand exterior. Balustrades carved in the form of nagas *or serpents line both sides of the avenue.*

STAR FEATURES

★ Central Sanctuary

★ Apsaras

★ Gallery of Bas-Reliefs

Architecture

Angkor-period architecture generally dates from Jayavarman II's establishment of the Khmer capital near Roluos *(see p221)* in the early 9th century AD. From then until the 15th century, art historians identify five main architectural styles. The earliest, Preah Ko, is rooted in the pre-Angkorian traditions of Sambor Prei Kuk to Angkor's east and the 8th-century style of Kompong Preah, relics of which are found at Prasat Ak Yum by the West Baray. Khmer architecture reached its zenith during the construction of Angkor Wat, but began declining soon after.

Devada sculpture at Angkor Thom

Pink sandstone library building in the inner enclosure of Banteay Srei

PREAH KO (AD 875–890)

Characterized by a relatively simple temple layout, with one or more square brick towers rising from a single laterite base, the Preah Ko style saw the first use of concentric enclosures

entered via the *gopura* or gateway tower. Another innovation was the library annex, which may have been used to protect sacred fire.

This well-preserved guardian figure *is carved from sandstone and set in the brick outer wall of a sanctuary tower at the 9th-century Lolei Temple of the Roluos Group.*

The eastern causeway of Bakong *runs straight from the main* gopura *to the high central tower. This structure is raised on a square-based pyramid, rising to a symbolic temple-mountain.*

BAKHENG TO PRE RUP (AD 890–965)

The temple-mountain style, based on Mount Meru, evolved during the Bakheng period. Phnom Bakheng *(see p209),* Phnom Krom, and Phnom Bok all feature the classic layout of five towers arranged in a quincunx – a tower at each side, with a fifth at the center. The Pre Rup style developed during the reign of Rajendravarman II (r.944–68). It continues the Bakheng style, but the towers are higher and steeper with more tiers.

Phnom Bakheng *impressively exemplifies the Bakheng style. It was the state temple of the first Khmer capital at Angkor, and dates from the late 9th century. It rises majestically through a pyramid of square terraces to the main group of five sanctuary towers.*

Pre Rup *is distinguished by its size and the abrupt rise of its temple-mountain through several levels to the main sanctuary. The carved sandstone lintels are more finely detailed than in earlier styles. Archaeologists speculate that the structure may have served as a royal crematorium – pre rup means turn the body.*

BANTEAY SREI TO BAPHUON (AD 965–1080)

Represented by the delicate and refined Banteay Srei *(see p220)*, this eponymous style is characterized by ornate carvings of sensuous *apsaras* (celestial dancing girls) and *devadas* (dancers). By the mid-11th century, when Khmer architecture was reaching its majestic apogee, this style had evolved into the Baphuon style, which is distinguished by vast proportions and vaulted galleries. The sculpture of the period shows increasing realism and narrative sequence.

The five-tiered Baphuon *was the state temple of King Udayadityavarman II (r.1050–66). The massive structure was described by 13th-century Chinese traveler Zhou Daguan as "a truly astonishing spectacle, with more than ten chambers at its base."*

Banteay Srei *constructed between 967 and 1000 is known for its fine craftsmanship, evident in the exquisite detail of the bas-reliefs and carved stone lintels.*

ANGKOR WAT (AD 1080–1175)

Art historians generally agree that the style of Angkor Wat *(see pp212–13)* represents the apex of Khmer architectural and sculptural genius. The greatest of all temple-mountains, it also boasts the finest bas-relief narratives. The art of lintel carving also reached its zenith during this period.

Bas-reliefs of Suryavarman II *in the west section of the Southern Gallery portray the king seated on his throne, surrounded by courtiers with fans and parasols. Below him, princesses and women of the court are carried in palanquins. In another fine bas-relief, the king is shown riding a great war elephant.*

An aerial view of Angkor Wat *makes the vast scale and symbolic layout of the complex very clear. Every aspect of Angkor is rich with meaning, the most apparent being the central quincunx of towers rising to a peak, representing the five peaks of the sacred Mount Meru.*

BAYON (AD 1175–1240)

Considered a synthesis of previous styles, Bayon – the last great Angkor architectural style – is still magnificent, but also characterized by a detectable decline in quality. There is more use of laterite and less of sandstone, as well as more Buddhist imagery and, correspondingly, fewer Hindu themes.

The bas-reliefs depicting scenes of battle *at the temple of Bayon in Angkor Thom (see pp216–19) provide a remarkable record of contemporary wars between the Khmer Empire and the Kingdom of Champa. The war resulted in the victory of Khmer King Jayavarman VII in 1181.*

The south gate of Angkor Thom *is surmounted by a large, four-faced carving of the god-king or devaraja, Jayavarman VII. He is depicted as the Bodhisattva Avalokitesvara, gazing somberly in the four cardinal directions for eternity.*

Angkor Thom ❹

Remarkable in scale and architectural ingenuity, the ancient city of Angkor Thom, which means "Great City" in Khmer, was founded by King Jayavarman VII in the late 12th century. The largest city in the Khmer Empire at one time, it is protected by a 26-ft (8-m) high wall, about 7.5 miles (12 km) long, and surrounded by a wide moat. There are five gates to the city – four facing the cardinal directions and an extra one on the east side – all bearing four giant stone faces. Within the city are several ruins, the most celebrated of which is the Bayon, a particularly atmospheric temple at the center of this historic complex.

Rows of gods lining the path to Angkor Thom's South Gate

★ Enigmatic Faces

The temple's central towers are decorated with four huge, mysteriously smiling faces gazing out in the cardinal directions. These are believed to represent the all-seeing and all-knowing Bodhisattva Avalokitesvara as personified by Jayavarman VII himself.

Central Tower

Outer Enclosure

The Western Gallery

A devotee burns incense sticks before a statue of Vishnu, a Hindu god. The idol is thought to date from the time of the founding of the temple, and is installed in the southern section of the Western Gallery, one of the many long galleries surrounding the Bayon.

South Entrance

0 meters	25
0 yards	25

STAR FEATURES

★ Enigmatic Faces

★ Bas-Reliefs on the Southern Gallery

★ Southern View of the Bayon

★ Bas-Reliefs on the Southern Gallery

Carved deep into the walls, the bas-reliefs here feature images from everyday life in 12th-century Angkor. These include depictions of a cockfight, meals being cooked, festival celebrations, and market scenes.

★ **Southern View of the Bayon**
*From a distance, the Bayon appears to be a complicated,
almost erratically structured temple. On closer inspection,
however, its 54 majestic towers and 216 eerie stone sculptures
take a more definite shape – their architectural grandeur
inspiring the visitor with a sense of awe.*

Detail of Devada
The devada *or dancer
differs from the sensual*
apsara *(see p212) and
could be either male or
female. A* devada *is
portrayed in less
alluring postures.*

Bas-reliefs of a
Khmer circus

Inner
Enclosure

East Entrance

THE BAYON
Located in the heart of Angkor Thom, the Bayon is one
of the city's most extraordinary structures, epitomizing the "lost
civilization" of Angkor. This symbolic temple-mountain rises on
three levels, and features 54 towers bearing more than 200 huge,
yet enigmatic stone faces. It is entered through eight cruciform
towers, linked by galleries that were once covered and which are
gradually being restored. These galleries have some of the most
striking bas-reliefs at Angkor, showcasing everyday scenes as well
as images of battles, especially against the Cham.

Khmer Army in Procession
*The bas-reliefs on the Eastern
Gallery provide scenes from the
struggle between the Khmers
and the Cham, which has been
recorded in painstakingly fine
detail. Here, the Khmer king,
seated on an elephant, leads
his army into battle.*

Exploring Angkor Thom

The fortified city of Angkor Thom is spread over an area of nearly 4 sq miles (10 sq km). At its peak, it had a population of around one million. Of the five gateways into the city, the most commonly used is the South Gate, from which a pathway leads straight to the Bayon temple. Beyond this lie the ruins of many other striking monuments, including Baphuon and Phimeanakas. Although most are in a state of disrepair, these colossal, beautifully sculpted structures, adorned with intricate carvings, still reflect the glory and power of the Khmer Empire.

Figure from Terrace of the Leper King

Massive smiling faces gazing into the distance, South Gate

South Gate

The imposing South Gate is the best-preserved of the five gateways into Angkor Thom. Its approach is via an impressive causeway flanked by 154 stone statues, gods on the left side and demons on the right, each carrying a giant serpent.

The South Gate itself is a massive, 75-ft (23-m) high structure, surmounted by a triple tower with four gigantic stone faces facing the cardinal directions. On either side of the gate are statues of the three-headed elephant Erawan, the fabled mount of the Hindu god Indra.

Bayon

Representative of the period's artistic brilliance, the Bayon is the city's most unique temple. Shaped like a pyramid, its two most awe-inspiring features are the several huge calm, smiling faces that adorn its towers, and the fascinating bas-reliefs on its many galleries (*see pp216–17*).

Baphuon

Believed to be one of the grandest of Angkor's temples, Baphuon was built by King Udayadityavarman II in the 11th century. A Hindu temple, its pyramidal mountain form represents Mount Meru, the mythical home of the gods. A central tower with four entrances once stood at its summit, but has long since collapsed.

The temple is approached via a 656-ft (200-m) long raised causeway and has four gateways decorated with elegant bas-relief scenes from Hindu epics such as the *Mahabharata* and *Ramayana* (*Reamker* in Khmer). Inside, spanning the western length of Baphuon, is a huge Reclining Buddha. As the temple was dedicated to Hinduism, this image was probably added later, in the 15th century. The temple has undergone intensive restoration, and a few sections are now open to the public.

Phimeanakas

This royal temple-palace was built during the 10th century by King Rajendravarman II and

added to later by Jayavarman VII. Dedicated to Hinduism, it is also known as the Celestial Palace, and is associated with the legend of a golden tower that once stood here, and where a nine-headed serpent resided. This magical serpent would appear to the king as a woman, and the king would couple with her before going to his other wives and concubines. It was believed that if the king failed to sleep with the serpent-woman, he would die, but by sleeping with her, the royal lineage was saved.

The pyramid-shaped palace is rectangular at the base, and surrounded by a 16-ft (5-m) high wall of laterite enclosing an area of around 37 acres (15 ha). It has five entranceways, and the stairs, which are flanked by guardian lions, rise up on all four sides. There are corresponding elephant figures at each of the four corners of the pyramid. The upper terrace offers great views of the Baphuon to the south.

Preah Palilay and Tep Pranam

Two of the lesser, yet still impressive structures at Angkor Thom, Preah Palilay and Tep Pranam are located a short distance to the northwest of the Terrace of the Leper King.

Preah Palilay dates from the 13th or 14th century and is a small Buddhist sanctuary set within a 164-ft (50-m) square laterite wall. The sanctuary, which is partially collapsed, is entered via a single gateway, and rises to a tapering stone tower. A 108-ft (33-m) long causeway leads to a terrace to the east of the sanctuary, which is distinguished by fine *naga* or serpent balustrades.

Pyramidal exterior of Phimeanakas, Angkor Thom

For hotels and restaurants in this region see pp244–5 and pp260–61

Intricately carved and sculpted bas-reliefs and elephant figures adorning the Terrace of Elephants

Nearby, to the east, lies Tep Pranam, a Buddhist sanctuary built in the 16th century. This was probably originally dedicated to the Mahayana school. Now used as a place of Theravada worship, it features a big sandstone Buddha image, seated in the "calling the earth to witness" *mudra* (posture).

Step-by-step restoration in progress at the Terrace of the Leper King

Terrace of the Leper King

Situated a short walk southeast of Tep Pranam, this small platform dates from the late 12th century. Standing on top of this structure is a headless statue, known as the Leper King. Once believed to be an image of King Jayavarman VII, who, according to legend, had the disease, it is in fact a representation of Yama, the Hindu God of the Underworld. This statue is, however, a replica, as the original was taken for safekeeping to Phnom Penh's National Museum.

The terrace is marked by two walls, both beautifully restored and decorated with exquisite bas-reliefs. Of the two, the inner one is more remarkable, and is covered with figures of underworld

deities, kings, celestial females, *nagas* with five, seven, or nine heads, *devadas, apsaras,* warriors with drawn swords, and strange marine creatures.

The exact function of this terrace, which appears to be an extension of the Terrace of Elephants, is not clear. It was probably used either for royal receptions or cremations.

Terrace of Elephants

Built by King Jayavarman VII, this structure is over 950 ft (300 m) long, stretching from the Baphuon to the connecting Terrace of the Leper King. It has three main platforms and two smaller ones. The terrace was primarily used for royal reviews of military and other parades. The entire terrace is elaborately decorated with almost life-size images of sandstone elephants in a procession and accompanied by mahouts.

There are many images of tigers, lions, serpents, sacred geese, and Garuda, the eagle mount of Vishnu.

North and South Khleang

These two essentially similar buildings are located to the east of the main road running past the Terrace of Elephants. The North Khleang was built toward the end of the 10th century by King Jayaviravarman, and the South Khleang was constructed during the early 11th century by King Suryavarman I (r.1002–50). The main architectural feature of the Khleangs are their sandstone lintels and elegant balustered stone windows. Unfortunately, the original function of the buildings is not yet known. Khleang, which means storehouse, is a modern designation and is considered misleading.

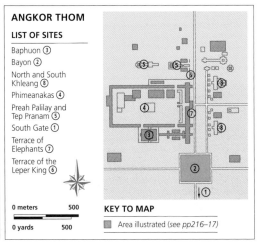

ANGKOR THOM

LIST OF SITES

0 meters 500

0 yards 500

KEY TO MAP

■ Area illustrated (see pp216–17)

Preah Neak Pean 6

2.5 miles (4 km) NE of Angkor Thom.
☐ sunrise–sunset daily. ☑ general
Angkor ticket. ☑ ☐ ☐

One of the most unusual
temples at Angkor, Preah Neak
Pean or Coiled Serpents is a
unique structure dating from
the late 12th century. Like
much else at Angkor, it was
founded by King Jayavarman
VII. Dedicated to Buddhism,
it is located in the middle of
the now dry lake, North Baray.
  The temple is built around
an artificial pond surrounded
by four smaller square ponds,
usually dry except during the
rainy season. In the center is
a circular island with a shrine
dedicated to Bodhisattva
Avalokitesvara. A couple of
intertwined serpents circle its
base, thus giving the temple
its name. To the east of the
island is the sculpted figure of
the horse Balaha, a manifesta-
tion of Avalokitesvara, who,
according to Buddhist mythology, transformed himself into
a horse to rescue shipwrecked
sailors from a sea ogress.
  The pond represents a
mythical lake, Anavatapta,
believed to be the source of
the four great rivers of the
world. They are symbolically
reproduced by four gargoyle-
like heads with spouts for
mouths, from which water
flows into four outer ponds.
The east head is that of a man,
the south a lion, the west
a horse, and the north an
elephant. When the temple
was functioning, Buddhist
devotees would seek the
advice of resident monks,

**Human head-shaped fountainhead
at Preah Neak Pean**

and then bathe in the holy
waters flowing from the spout
of whichever head had been
prescribed by the monk.

Ta Prohm 7

0.6 miles (1 km) E of Angkor Thom.
☐ sunrise–sunset daily. ☑ general
Angkor ticket. ☐ ☐

Perhaps the most evocative
and mysterious of all the temple structures at Angkor, Ta
Prohm, which means Ancestor
of Brahma, was originally a
Buddhist monastery, built
during King Jayavarman VII's
reign. A stone stele at the
complex describes how
powerful the monastery used
to be. At its peak, it owned
more than 3,000 villages, and
was maintained by 80,000
attendants, including 18 high
priests and over 600 temple
dancers. The wealth of the
temple, and of its founder,
Jayavarman VII, is also listed,
and included more than 35
diamonds and 40,000 pearls.

The French started their
archaeological restoration
during the colonial period,
and a deliberate attempt was
made to preserve Ta Prohm
in its existing condition,
limiting restoration, and
cutting down as little of the
dense jungle as possible. As
a result, the temple buildings
remain smothered with the
roots of giant banyan trees,
preserving the atmosphere
that 19th-century explorers
must have experienced.
  The temple sits on the peak
of a hill and has a complex of
stone buildings, surrounded
by a rectangular laterite wall.
The narrow passageways of
the structure, along with huge
kapok trees, provide relief
from the tropical sun, and
link a series of musty,
darkened galleries. The main
entrance is decaying yet
magnificent, and filled with
images of the Buddha that
were recovered from the
ruins. Beyond the gate is the
fascinating Hall of Dancers.
This must-see sandstone
building rests on square
pillars, and is decorated with
false doorways and rows of
intricate *apsara* (celestial
dancing girls) bas-reliefs. To
the west is the main sanctuary,
a simple stone structure distinguished by its jungle setting.

Prasat Kravan 8

2 miles (3 km) E of Angkor Wat.
☐ sunrise–sunset daily. ☑ general
Angkor ticket.

Dating from the early 10th
century, Prasat Kravan was
founded by Harshavarman I
(r.915–23). Comprising five
brick towers, it is one of the
smaller temples in the complex, and was dedicated to
the Hindu god, Vishnu.
  The temple, whose name
means Cardamom Sanctuary,
is chiefly remarkable for its
brickwork and bas-reliefs.
These represent Vishnu, his
consort Lakshmi, Garuda
his eagle mount, *naga* the
serpent, and a number of
other divine attendants.
  The doorways and lintels
of all five towers are made
of sandstone, and that of the

The silk cotton or kapok trees covering Ta Prohm Temple

southernmost tower has a fine image of Vishnu riding his Garuda mount. In the middle of the central tower is a raised stone that was used to receive water for purification rites.

Banteay Srei ❾

19 miles (30 km) km NE of Siem Reap. ○ sunrise–sunset daily. 🎟 general Angkor ticket.

The remote temple complex of Banteay Srei or the Citadel of Women inspires through its exquisitely detailed carving. Executed in pink sandstone, the complex was founded in the second half of the 10th century by Hindu priests, and so, unlike most other monuments in Angkor, is not a royal temple.

Rectangular in shape, and enclosed by three walls and the remains of a moat, the central sanctuary contains ornate shrines dedicated to Shiva, the Hindu God of Destruction. The intricately carved lintels reproduce scenes from the great Hindu epic *Ramayana*. Representations of Shiva, his consort Parvati, the monkey-king Hanuman, the divine goatherd Krishna, and the demon-king Ravana are all beautifully etched. Also exceptional are the elaborate and

Central sanctuary, Lolei Temple, Roluos Group

finely detailed carved figures of gods and goddesses in the recessed niches of the towers in the central sanctuary. The male divinities carry lances and wear simple loincloths. By contrast, the goddesses, with their long hair tied in buns or plaits, are dressed in loosely-draped Indian-style skirts, and almost every inch of their bodies is laden with gorgeous heavy jewelry.

Ancient statue in Banteay Srei

Roluos Group ❿

7 miles (12 km) SE of Siem Reap. ○ sunrise–sunset daily. 🎟 general Angkor ticket.

These ancient temples have borrowed their name from the small town of Roluos. The oldest monuments in the Angkor area, the temples mark the site of Hariharalaya, the very first Khmer capital established by Indravarman I (r.877–89). Three main complexes can be found here. To the north of Highway 6, on the way to Phnom Penh from Siem Reap, is **Lolei**. Founded by Yasovarman I (r.889–910), this temple stands on an artificial mound in the middle of a small reservoir, and is based on a double platform, surrounded by a thick laterite wall. The four central brick

towers have surprisingly well-preserved false doors and inscriptions.

To the south of Lolei stands **Preah Ko** or the Sacred Bull. Built by Indravarman I, this Hindu temple was dedicated to the worship of Shiva. It was built to honor the king's parents, as well as Jayavarman II, the founder of the Khmer Empire. The main sanctuary consists of six brick towers resting on a raised laterite platform. Close by are three statues of the sacred bull Nandi, for whom the temple was named, which are in a remarkably good condition. The motifs on the false doors, lintels, and columns are very well-preserved. They include *kala*, mythical creatures with a grinning mouth and large bulging eyes, *makara*, sea creatures with a trunk-like snout, and Garuda, the eagle mount of the god Vishnu. The temple sits resplendent in its serene rural setting, and is currently undergoing large-scale restoration.

Beyond Preah Ko, the huge mass of **Bakong** cannot be missed. This temple is also dedicated to Shiva, and was founded by Indravarman I in the 9th century. By far the largest monument of the Roluos Group, it is approached by a pathway protected by a seven-headed *naga*, and flanked by guesthouses built for pilgrims. In the center of the complex is an artificial mound representing the mythical Mount Meru, said to be the center of the Hindu world and the abode of the gods. The mount rises in five stages, the first three of which are enhanced by stone elephants on their edges. At the summit rests the square central sanctuary, with four levels and a lotus-shaped tower rising from the middle. The mound is surrounded by eight massive brick towers which, like the rest of Roluos Group, feature finely carved sandstone decorations.

A goddess on the central shrine, inner enclosure, Banteay Srei

Angkor Travel Information

Electric bicycle for rent, Siem Reap

Most visitors to Angkor arrive by air as the large number of international and domestic carriers servicing the country make flying a comfortable and viable option. Local as well as long-distance buses from Vietnam and Thailand provide an affordable alternative. However, though the highway from Phnom Penh has improved, the poor condition of most roads can result in delays and much discomfort in reaching Siem Reap. A more scenic approach is by ferry or boat. Regular hydrofoil services link Siem Reap with Phnom Penh, as well as Siem Reap and Chau Doc *(see p100)* in Vietnam. Moving around within Angkor is easy, with several inexpensive modes of transport to choose from.

Boarding a Bangkok Airways flight, Siem Reap International Airport

WHEN TO GO

The best time to visit Angkor is during the country's cool season, between November and February, although it can still be rather warm for most tourists. Alternatively, during the rainy season between June and November, Angkor is green and relatively cool, if rather wet. At this time, the *barays* (reservoirs) and certain temples such as Preah Neak Pean *(see p220)* overflow with water. It is best to stay away during the hot season between March and May, when temperatures in Angkor can be stifling.

GETTING THERE

There are two international airports in Cambodia – **Phnom Penh International Airport** and **Siem Reap International Airport**. With several national and international airlines offering flights to both Phnom Penh and Siem Reap, visitors will find getting to Angkor easy. Major international airlines

include **Vietnam Airlines, Lao Airlines, Malaysia Airlines, SilkAir, Thai Airways, Bangkok Airways, Jetstar Asia, Eva Airways,** and **Cathay Pacific.** Except for Jetstar Asia, all these airlines operate direct flights to Siem Reap from popular holiday destinations such as Hanoi, Ho Chi Minh City, Kuala Lumpur, Bangkok, and Singapore.

Domestic carrier **Air Asia,** flies from Phnom Penh to Siem Reap on a daily basis. Note that it is not uncommon for flight schedules to change suddenly or even for local airlines to shut down completely. For up-to-date information on air fares,

routes, and flight timings, check with your travel agent.

With the recent opening of border crossings for foreigners wishing to enter Cambodia from Thailand and Vietnam, traveling by bus or taxi is now a feasible and cheaper option. Visitors entering from Vietnam have the choice of up to eight different border crossings. The most popular are from Moc Bai to Bavet and from Chau Doc to Phnom Penh. Several scheduled buses run from Ho Chi Minh City to Phnom Penh. This six-hour journey costs about US$11. From Phnom Penh, you can take a shared taxi or minibus to Siem Reap on a five-hour trip.

Another mode of traveling to Angkor is by ferry or boat. The river border crossing between Cambodia and Vietnam lies on the Mekong River. Boats run from Chau Doc to Phnom Penh at regular intervals; the journey takes three to six hours, with fares ranging from US$17 to US$22. Hydrofoils from Phnom Penh to Siem Reap run daily and are easily available, but the journey can take up to six hours (US$22–US$25). Boat tours also operate from Ho Chi Minh City to Siem Reap. These are, however, more expensive than the other cruises. Some of the well-known agencies offering boat tours include **Pandaw Cruises** and **Victoria Hotels**.

VISAS AND PASSPORTS

A one-month visa for Cambodia is issued on arrival at international airports and land and river border crossings. Tourist visas cost US$20. A passport photograph is required. Visitors who wish to stay longer should apply for an extension in Phnom Penh. Those who overstay their visa are fined US$5 each day.

One of the many tourist buses providing access to Siem Reap

E-visas can be purchased on-line at www.mfaic.gov.kh/evisa for US$25 payable by credit card. They are emailed to and printed by the applicant.

TOURS FROM VIETNAM

There are several reputed travel agencies in both Hanoi and Ho Chi Minh City that arrange tours from Vietnam to Angkor. Although packaged tours are pre-determined, visitors can also draw up personalized itineraries. The prices are usually inclusive of travel costs, sightseeing, and a guide. Visas, departure tax, and entry tickets to Angkor are generally not included.

GETTING AROUND

Transport in Siem Reap and Angkor is readily available and comes in various forms, including bicycles, *motos* (motorbike taxis), minibuses, tuk-tuks, and elephants. A great way to explore Angkor is on a bicycle, available to

Motorcycle taxis are very common in Siem Reap

rent from bike shops and hotels. The most comfortable way to travel is by hiring a car, easily arranged through hotels in town. An air-conditioned car with driver costs between US$25 and US$50 per day depending on the distance and time.

CUSTOMS INFORMATION

Customs procedures tend to be lax, but penalties for violations are strict. The usual prohibitions on importing drugs and pornography apply. Signs warn against

bringing explosives into the country, and you may need to declare if you carry above US$3,000. The most enforced custom regulation is the smuggling of antiquities dating from or before the Angkorian period.

DEPARTURE TAX

For international flights there is a departure tax of US$25 per person. This is, strangely, more expensive than an entry visa. The departure tax for domestic flights is US$18. Both are payable in US dollars.

DIRECTORY

EMBASSIES

Australia
Villa 11, RV Senei Vinnavut Out (St. 254), Phnom Penh. **Tel** *(023) 213 470.* **www**.cambodia. embassy.gov.au

Canada
Canadian interests are managed and represented by the Australian Embassy (see above).

United Kingdom
27–29 St. 75, Phnom Penh. **Tel** *(023) 427 124.* **http://**ukincambodia. fco.gov.uk

United States
1 St. 96, Sangkat Wat Phnom, Phnom Penh. **Tel** *(023) 728 000.* **http://**cambodia. usembassy.gov

Vietnam
436 Monivong Blvd, Phnom Penh. **Tel** *(023) 362 531.*

AIRPORTS

Phnom Penh International Airport
Tel *(023) 890 890.* **www**.cambodia-airports. com/phnompenh/en

Siem Reap International Airport
www.cambodia-airports. com/siemreap/en

AIRLINES

Air Asia
Phnom Penh International Airport. **Tel** *(023) 890 035.* **www**.AirAsia.com

Bangkok Airways
Siem Reap. **Tel** *(063) 965 422/3.* **www**.bangkokair.com

Cathay Pacific
168 Monireth Road, Phnom Penh. **Tel** *(023) 424 300.* **www**.cathaypacific.com

Eva Airways
11–14B St. 205, Phnom Penh. **Tel** *(023) 210 303.* **www**.evaair.com

Jetstar Asia
Siem Reap. **Tel** *(063) 964 388.* **www**.jetstarasia.com

Lao Airlines
114, Hwy 6, Siem Reap. **Tel** *(063) 963 283.* **www**.laoairlines.com

Malaysia Airlines
Siem Reap International Airport. **Tel** *(063) 964 135.* **www**.malaysia airlines.com

SilkAir
313 Sisowath Quay, Phnom Penh. **Tel** *(023) 426 807.* **www**.silkair.com

Thai Airways
294 Mao Tse Tung Blvd, Phnom Penh. **Tel** *(023) 890 292.* **www**.thaiair.com

Vietnam Airlines
342, Hwy 6, Siem Reap. **Tel** *(063) 964 488.* **www**.vietnamairlines. com

BOAT TOURS

Pandaw Cruises
Tel *(012) 939 644 (Phnom Penh).* **Tel** *(090) 371 1235 (Ho Chi Minh City).* **www**.pandaw.com

Victoria Hotels
32 Le Loi St, Chau Doc, Vietnam. **Tel** *(076) 386 5010.* **www**. victoriahotels-asia.com

TOUR COMPANIES

Destination Asia
143 Nguyen Van Troi St, Ho Chi Minh City. **Tel** *(08) 3844 8071.* **www**. destination-asia.com

Hanuman Tourism
310 St. 12, Phnom Penh. **Tel** *(023) 218 396.* **www**. hanumantourism.com

Phoenix Voyages
82–83 St. 7B, Khu A–An Phu/An Khanh, District 2, Ho Chi Minh City. **Tel** *(08) 6281 0222.* **www**. phoenixvoyages.com

Angkor Practical Information

Pharmacy sign in Siem Reap

After years of much unrest, Cambodia is presently undergoing a phase of economic recovery and reinvention. An important part of this process is its tourism industry, which is currently experiencing a major boom. The credit for this is largely due to the rich cultural heritage of Angkor, and the millions of visitors it attracts each year. As a result, the sleepy town of Siem Reap, serving as a gateway to Angkor, has transformed into a bustling tourist town, with lodgings and eateries to suit all pockets. The simple ticket system, easily arranged transport, and new communication facilities have made sightseeing in Angkor a straightforward affair.

Entrance to the Victoria Angkor Hotel, Siem Reap (see p245)

ADMISSION CHARGES AND OPENING HOURS

To gain access to the Angkor complex, visitors need to buy a pass from the booth at Angkor's main entrance (open 5am–6pm daily). The ticketing system in effect here might seem a bit expensive at first glance but offers good value for money, especially because part of the funds collected go toward the preservation of Angkor's many historic monuments.

Three types of passes are available, each allowing entry into all the monuments in the complex except Phnom Kulen, Koh Ker, and Beng Melea, for which extra charges apply. Choices range from a one-day pass for US$20, ideal for a quick walk through the main ruins; a three-day pass for US$40 to be used within one week and sufficient for exploring the prominent temples; and a seven-day pass for US$60 to be used within one month.

A passport-size photograph has to be provided along with the entry fee to create an identity pass. You can carry your own picture or have one taken at the admission booth. Passes must be shown at each site.

TOURIST INFORMATION

The privately-owned **Tourism Information Office** in Siem Reap is housed in a white building on Pokambor Avenue, but is not particularly helpful except for making bookings. More useful, and in the same building, is the **Khmer Angkor**

Tour Guide Association, which offers cars for rent, along with licensed and well informed, English-speaking drivers.

The quarterly publication *Siem Reap Angkor Visitors Guide* provides up-to-date travel-related information to visitors. It includes shopping and transport listings, as well as a detailed list of restaurants and hotels in the area. It is available free of charge at many hotels all over town.

WHERE TO STAY

At one time, accommodation in Siem Reap was scarce and unappealing, but today, new hotels and guesthouses open every month. The variety of lodgings available is wide, with options to suit every budget. From five-star luxury hotels such as Grand Hotel d'Angkor *(see p245)* to a range of family-run hotels with basic conveniences and a selection of well-equipped and reasonably priced guesthouses.

Visitors who have not opted for a pre-booked tour will find plenty of information regarding accommodation at the airport. Many touts also hover around

the airport but it is wise to exercise caution when dealing with them – scam artists are not rare. Most establishments, even down to the humblest guesthouses, will send a car and driver to meet you at the airport. Another easier and often substantially cheaper option is to book online. Note that room rates usually fluctuate between expensive during peak season from November to March, to very cheap during the low season from May to November.

WHERE TO EAT

The assortment and quality of cuisines available in Siem Reap is varied enough to suit all tastes, ranging from Thai, Cambodian, Vietnamese, and Chinese to French, Indian, American, and Italian.

The array of eateries to choose from is also impressive *(see pp260–61)*. There are many reasonably priced restaurants, especially near Psar Chaa. This area is also full of street food vendors, serving local fare. Baguettes, pâté, and good coffee can be found throughout the area.

Guests enjoying a meal at the Red Piano (see p261), Siem Reap

Most guesthouses have small cafés, while the larger hotels boast fine restaurants. Most can pack picnic baskets as well if requested.

PERSONAL HEALTH AND SECURITY

Cambodia is a poor country, and not particularly advanced in health care. In almost any serious situation, it makes sense to be evacuated for treatment to nearby Bangkok. However, with proper precautions most visitors have a safe and healthy stay. Drink only bottled water, eat well-cooked food, avoid ice, and be sure to wash your hands before eating. To avoid dehydration, heat exhaustion, and even heatstroke when visiting Angkor, carry bottled mineral water and wear a hat or headscarf. Avoid going out during the hottest part of the day.

Malaria is present in parts of Cambodia, including Angkor, and travelers can take a prophylactic. Other risks are dengue fever, hepatitis, and rabies. Ask your doctor about immunization requirements before you travel. STDs and AIDS are also prevalent in Cambodia.

Unexploded mines are a serious concern in Siem Reap. Tourists should steer clear of areas off the well-beaten path, and stay close to their guides.

Personal security in Angkor can be taken care of by applying common sense. Avoid dark and remote areas, do not wear too much jewelry or revealing clothes in the case of women, and leave valuable items in the hotel safe. Tourist police and guards are stationed at points throughout the complex.

BANKING AND CURRENCY

The Cambodian currency is the *riel*, worth approximately 4,000 to the US dollar. *Riel* notes come in denominations from 50r to 100,000r, though even the latter is worth only around US$25. However, visitors to Angkor infrequently need to use the *riel* since, for many tourist transactions, the US dollar is the preferred

currency. Failing this, the Thai *bhat* is often acceptable in Siem Reap. Still, it is a good idea to keep some change in *riel* handy for giving small tips or buying very cheap items.

There are several banks in Siem Reap, offering facilities for exchanging currency and cashing traveler's checks. Banking hours are generally 9am–4pm Monday to Friday. Major credit cards are widely accepted, and can be used to obtain a cash advance from a bank. ATMs, courtesy of **ANZ Royal Bank**, are another source of cash.

One of the many banks and money exchanges in Siem Reap

COMMUNICATIONS

The communication network in Angkor is fairly well developed. Making international calls is simple, using either prepaid calling cards for public telephones, or Internet phone services, available in most cyber cafés. It is also possible to call from your hotel, but this is a more expensive option. The area code for Siem Reap is 063.

Internet cafés and Wi-Fi are plentiful and affordable, and there are no government restrictions on Internet access. For postal and courier services, visitors can head to the main post office in town, or agencies such as **DHL** and **EMS**.

DISABLED TRAVELLERS

There are presently virtually no special facilities for disabled travelers anywhere in Angkor. Many of the new luxury hotels, however, are making an effort to become better equipped to meet the needs of those who require special assistance.

DIRECTORY

VISITOR INFORMATION

Khmer Angkor Tour Guide Association
Tel (063) 964 347. **www.** khmerangkortourguide.com

EMERGENCY NUMBERS

Fire
Siem Reap.
Tel (063) 760 133,
(012) 784 464.

Tourist Police
Opposite the main ticket office for Angkor.
Tel (012) 402 424,
(012) 969 991.

MEDICAL CENTERS

Angkor Hospital for Children
PO Box 50, Siem Reap.
Tel (063) 963 409.

Jin Hua International Hospital
Hwy 6, Airport Rd, Siem Reap.
Tel (063) 963 299.

Naga International Clinic
Hwy 6, Airport Rd, Siem Reap.
Tel (063) 964 500.

BANKS

ANZ Royal Bank
566–70 Tep Vong St, Siem Reap.
Tel (023) 726 900.
Siem Reap Airport.
Tel (023) 726 900.
www.anzroyal.com

Cambodia Asia Bank
Corner Sivutha Blvd & Airport Rd at Angkor Holiday Hotel, Siem Reap. *Tel* (063) 964 7412.

Cambodia Commercial Bank
130 Sivatha Rd, Siem Reap.
Tel (063) 965 315.
Siem Reap Airport.
Tel (063) 963 152.

COURIER SERVICES

DHL Express
15A Sivatha St, Siem Reap.
Tel (063) 964 949.

EMS
National Rd 6, Wat Bo, Sala Kamroeuk. *Tel* (063) 765 678.

TRAVELERS'
NEEDS

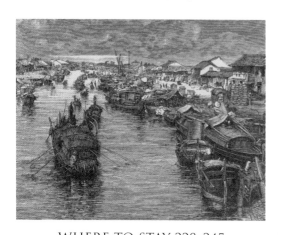

WHERE TO STAY 228–245

WHERE TO EAT 246–261

SHOPPING IN VIETNAM 262–267

ENTERTAINMENT IN VIETNAM 268–271

OUTDOOR ACTIVITIES AND
SPECIAL INTERESTS 272–275

WHERE TO STAY

Accommodations in Vietnam run the gamut from historic boutique hotels and plush resorts to basic guesthouses and cheap inns. Luxury hotels are found in all large cities and beaches, while budget lodgings are available throughout the country. Major hotels offer amenities such as swimming pools, gyms, restaurants, and even nightclubs. Resorts, many of which are concentrated along the central coast, also offer ample opportunities for self-indulgence.

Waiter at Continental Hotel

While budget hotels and guesthouses lack the high-end frills, all but the very cheapest are air-conditioned and have Western-style toilets and hot water. Dormitories are rare and camping almost unheard of, but a new addition is the homestay, where travelers can lodge with a family from the village. Not only does this give you a close-up glimpse into daily life in rural Vietnam, but often also allows you to sample the most delicious and authentic local cuisine.

HOTEL GRADING

There is an official system for grading hotels in Vietnam, but price is the only indication of luxury or the lack thereof. Typically, establishments charging more than US$150 per night would fall into the five-star category in Europe or the US. Keep in mind that overall prices notwithstanding, the same hotel may demonstrate varying standards across rooms, ranging from opulent suites to motel-style quarters.

Also note that there is a distinction between a hotel (*khach san*) and a guesthouse (*nha khach*). While the latter can resemble budget hotels, they have fewer amenities and do not offer room service.

LUXURY HOTELS

A selection of luxury hotels is now available at every major tourist destination in Vietnam. As a result, the country is now popular with more than

The stately façade of the Continental Hotel (*see p58*), Ho Chi Minh City

just the backpacking set – it is also a getaway for the rich and famous. Places like Ho Chi Minh City, Hanoi, Nha Trang, and Mui Ne boast multinational chains such as Sheraton, Hilton, Marriott, Novotel, Sofitel, and Ana Mandara/Six Senses. The Victoria Hotels and Resorts chain offers luxurious and chic accommodation in beautiful buildings and scenic locations. All adhere to international standards in terms of facilities and service, with liveried staff catering to guests' every whim. The rooms are generally spacious and always air-conditioned. Modern conveniences such as a minibar and cable TV are standard. Wi-Fi is also available, though at hugely inflated

rates. The hotels also have a gym on their premises.

Business travelers will find a wide array of facilities. Most of these hotels offer conference halls, with provisions for conference calls, meeting rooms, and Internet services.

Virtually every four- and five-star hotel boasts a spectacular food service, employing skilled international chefs. Their superb restaurants serve gourmet foreign cuisine, including French, Chinese, Japanese, and Italian. Breakfast is an extremely lavish affair, featuring a spread of American, Continental, and Vietnamese fare.

In the evenings, a number of high-end hotels are transformed into glamorous venues for Western-style entertainment. Some boast discotheques, and most provide some kind of musical performance in their lounges every night.

The five-star Fusion Maia Da Nang resort (*see p239*), China Beach

◁ Patrons at a street stall in Hoi An (*see pp124–9*)

RESORT HOTELS

Vietnam is no stranger to elegant resort hotels, which were first introduced to the country by leisure-loving French colonists. A few of these charming old quarters, now substantially upgraded and renovated, still remain. The Sofitel Dalat Palace *(see p237)* in Dalat, for instance, has been converted into a holiday getaway.

The trend, however, is for the development of modernly outfitted resorts, mostly along the extensive coastline. The most luxurious of these are the Evason Ana Mandara *(see p238)* in Nha Trang and the Six Senses Hideaway *(see p238)* in Ninh Hoa. Other resorts do not look very different from any other high-rise hotel, but qualify as resorts on the technicality that they are somewhat isolated from the towns. Particularly affected by tourist-oriented development, both Nha Trang and Phan Thiet have earned reputations as resort towns. Their seaside establishments have all the usual amenities such as a swimming pool, fine restaurants, and, of course, a beautiful, white sand beach. Most also offer a range of adventure activities, including diving and kite-boarding.

A large number of resorts also offer specialized tours and holiday packages. Treks to hill tribe communities are arranged by Sapa's local tour guides and

Pool table adjoining the lobby lounge at Miss Loi's Guesthouse *(see p232)*

operators, while in Hue, the Saigon Morin arranges historic trips down the Perfume River. The Sun Spa Resort *(see p239)* in Dong Hoi promotes health and healing programs. Diet, yoga, aromatherapy, as well as herbal remedies, are just some of the services provided.

GUESTHOUSES AND BUDGET HOTELS

Vietnamese guesthouses generally offer comfortable and clean rooms, with western toilets, hot water, cable TV, and frequently a refrigerator with minibar. They are usually operated by a family who resides within the same building. Extra services may include laundry, breakfast, booking facilities (tours, as well as bus, train, and airplane tickets), luggage storage, bicycle and motorcycle rental, and free Wi-Fi.

In cities that have long been on the tourist map, such as Ho Chi Minh City and Nha Trang,

budget hotels are often clustered together (like in the Pham Ngu Lao neighborhood of Ho Chi Minh City). In these areas, little or no haggling is required. In more out-of-the-way places, hotels and guesthouses are spread out across town and may require some negotiation on the price.

Guesthouses and budget hotels usually expect you to leave your room key at the front desk when you go out. If you do not, the hotel will assume that you are in your room and do not wish to be disturbed, therefore the room will not be cleaned.

A guesthouse or budget hotel room ranges from as little as US$8 in cities like Dalat to US$20 in Ho Chi Minh City. Expect to pay an average of US$10–US$15. A plain room with a fan and no window can be rented for as little as US$6, but such places are casual about cleanliness, and service is non-existent.

HOMESTAYS

Though not very common in Vietnam yet, homestays are growing in popularity at a rapid pace. Currently, they are most easily available in parts of the Mekong Delta, such as Vinh Long *(see p90)*, and in the Northern Highlands. This invaluable experience costs from US$15 per night. It is fairly easy to arrange a homestay through a travel agency in Ho Chi Minh City or Hanoi. **Innoviet**, for one, specializes in customized and themed tours, including homestays. Alternatively, you could contact the local tourist office in the area of interest.

Swimming pool of the French-colonial Saigon Morin *(see p240)*, Hue

The Majestic Hotel *(see p233)* on Dong Khoi Street, Ho Chi Minh City

PRICES

Vietnam offers reasonably priced accommodation options for all. A room in the most upscale resort will not cost anywhere near what it would in most Western countries. In major cities, a room with basic amenities such as a TV and air-conditioning will be available for as little as US$15 a night *(see p229)*, and in smaller towns US$8–US$10. Mid-range hotels average US$40–US$50, and all the luxury of a high-end hotel can be yours for US$150 and up.

Note that most establishments will charge different prices for Vietnamese and foreign tourists and may even vary the price according to the nation of origin of their guests. This is especially true in government-owned hotels.

BOOKING

Advance booking is advisable for visitors traveling during the high season *(see p278)*, especially at major hotels and resorts. Also note that both Ho Chi Minh City and Hanoi receive a steady stream of business travelers throughout the year, and hotels catering to them may be booked solid at any time of year.

While any travel agent can make reservations for you, all high-end hotels have websites offering online booking services. A surprising number of budget hotels also provide this facility. Though some may not have their own websites, most have access to e-mail.

Alternatively, you may contact one of the several reliable accommodation service outfits in operation, such as **Hotels in Vietnam**, **Vietnam Stay**, and **Vietnam Lodging**. All have a website on which they represent a range of hotels, resorts, apartments, and guesthouses. In addition to being efficient and quick, such groups also negotiate with hotels to ensure that you get the best rates.

CHECKING IN

When checking in, guests will normally be asked for their passport, which is then kept by the hotel for the duration of their stay. The hotel needs it to report a guest's presence to the local police. Large establishments in Ho Chi Minh City and Hanoi may simply copy the information and return your passport instead of retaining it during your stay. If your passport has been sent to an embassy for visa renewal, or if you are uncomfortable leaving it with the hotel, a photocopy is usually acceptable.

Legally, a foreigner cannot occupy the same room as a Vietnamese citizen of the opposite sex.

RENTAL APARTMENTS

If you are staying in one part of Vietnam for more than a few weeks, a serviced apartment or condo can be rented if you want to cut back on costs but still live in luxury. There are not many such operations at present, but they are in demand and more companies may start offering the service. One of the best arrangements in the country is **Sedona Suites** in Hanoi and Ho Chi Minh City, which offers stylish, fully furnished individual suites.

A cheaper, if considerably more tiresome, procedure is to go out into the real estate market to rent an apartment. However, this requires a lot of paperwork, and you must

The lush poolside gardens of Ancient House *(see p239)*, Hoi An

register with the local police. It is much easier and cheaper to rent a room in a private home. This allows visitors to experience, first-hand, the day-to-day life of ordinary people of the country. The best place to find such opportunities are on the bulletin boards of backpacker cafés and restaurants. Registration with the local police is still required when renting a room.

Bao Dai's Villas *(see p110)*, Nha Trang

TAXES

All high-end hotels levy a ten percent tax on the room tariff, plus a five percent service charge. Both amounts are displayed on the bill. In budget operations, the taxes are included in the basic charge, and are not reflected on the bill.

BARGAINING

Every hostelry is open to some kind of bargaining if it is not packed to capacity. It is more difficult to lower the price if you book online or on the phone, but once you arrive in person, the published fare is negotiable. If you plan to stay longer than a week, or are willing to take a less desirable room, the price can plummet by as much as 30 percent in a major hotel. Budget hotels will try to oblige and will usually take a few dollars off, but they do not have as much room to maneuver.

TIPPING

Although tipping was not customary in Vietnam, with the advent of tourism, it is now becoming the norm. There is no need to tip in major hotels as there is already a service charge, but if a staff member proves to be extremely obliging and helpful, a gratuity of US$1 is considered generous.

FACILITIES FOR CHILDREN

Although there are virtually no special facilities for kids *(see p280)*, except in top-end hotels, all establishments will welcome them. Most hotels allow children under 12 to share a bed with their parents free of charge. For a small fee, you can rent an extra bed or cot in any decent hotel. Even the more primitive establishments will receive children with open arms, and go all out to ensure that they have a comfortable stay. Virtually any hotel, big or small, grand or cheap, would be willing to arrange for an experienced baby-sitter to watch your children for a reasonable fee.

FACILITIES FOR DISABLED TRAVELERS

Unfortunately, most hotels in Vietnam provide very limited facilities for the disabled *(see p280)*. While the major and newest luxury properties do have wheelchair ramps, elevators, and other special facilities, such considerations are almost non-existent in lesser establishments. Some of the older hotels have tiny French elevators that cannot take in a wheelchair. Most hotels will be glad to help you hire an attendant, although he or she is unlikely to possess any particular qualifications.

DIRECTORY

HOMESTAYS

Innoviet
158 Bui Vien St, Dist.1, HCMC.
Map 2 D5. *Tel (08) 6295 8840.*
www.innoviet.com

BOOKING

Hotels in Vietnam
Hoa Linh Hotel, 35 Hang Bo St,
Hoan Kiem Dist, Hanoi.
Map 2 E3.
Tel (04) 3825 0034.
www.hotels-in-vietnam.com

Vietnam Lodging
216 De Tham St, Dist. 1, HCMC.
Map 2 D5.
Tel (08) 3920 5847/3920 4767.
www.vietnamlodging.net

Vietnam Stay
RAO IBC Building 1A Melims Sq,
Dist.1, HCMC.
Map 2 F4.
Tel (08) 3823 3771.

37 Ly Nam De St, Hoan Kiem Dist,
Hanoi. **Map** 2 D2.
Tel (04) 3747 2597.
www.vietnamstay.com

RENTAL APARTMENTS

Sedona Suites
65 Le Loi Blvd, Dist.1, HCMC.
Map 2 E4.
Tel (08) 3822 9666.

96 To Ngoc Van St, Hanoi.
Tel (04) 3718 0888.
www.sedonahotels.com.sg

Plush, well-appointed interior of Sedona Suites, Ho Chi Minh City

Choosing a Hotel

The hotels in this guide have been selected across a wide price range for the quality of their facilities, location, character, and value. The prices listed are those charged by the hotels, although discounts may be available off season or through travel agencies. The hotels are listed by region, which are further divided into areas or towns.

PRICE CATEGORIES
The following price ranges are for a standard double room, taxes, and service charges per night, during the high season. Breakfast is included.

$ under $20
$$ $20–$50
$$$ $50–$100
$$$$ $100–$150
$$$$$ over $150

HO CHI MINH CITY

CHOLON Arc en Ciel
$$$
52 Tan Da St **Tel** (08) 3855 2550 **Fax** (08) 3855 2424 **Rooms** 86
Map 4 E4
Famously featured in Graham Greene's *The Quiet American*, Arc en Ciel is one of Cholon's historic hotels. The imposing Art Deco facade gives way to a distinctly Chinese-influenced interior, with small but well-equipped rooms in bright colors. It has a rooftop bar and karaoke disco on the third floor.

CHOLON Equatorial
$$$$
242 Tran Binh Trong St **Tel** (08) 3839 7777 **Fax** (08) 3839 0011 **Rooms** 333
Map 4 F3
On the cusp of Districts 1 and 5, the luxurious Equatorial is easily accessible to both Chinatown and Pham Ngu Lao. The rooms are spacious and elegant, and there are non-smoking floors as well. The spa facilities are excellent, and the Chinese and Japanese restaurants are very popular. **www.equatorial.com/hcm**

CHOLON Windsor Plaza
$$$$$
18 An Duong Vuong St **Tel** (08) 3833 6688 **Fax** (08) 3833 6888 **Rooms** 405
Map 4 F4
The ultra-modern design of the Windsor Plaza stands out amid the chaotic bustle of Cholon. In addition to gourmet restaurants, a shopping center, and a spa, the five-star hotel is home to America Discotheque, Vietnam's largest dance venue. The rooms are excellent, with some designed especially for the disabled. **www.windsorplazahotel.com**

DISTRICT 1 Linh Linh Hotel
$
175/14 Pham Ngu Lao St **Tel** (08) 3837 3004 **Fax** (08) 3836 1851 **Rooms** 12
Map 2 D5
Located just off the main thoroughfare, Linh Linh Hotel is quieter and more laid-back than other hotels in the vicinity. The all-suites establishment features discreet sitting areas, spacious baths, as well as wide balconies sporting lots of foliage. The hotel is child-friendly and ideal for families traveling on a budget.

DISTRICT 1 Miss Loi's Guesthouse
$
178/20 Co Giang St **Tel** (08) 3837 9589 **Rooms** 15
Map 2 E5
Situated in a quiet street, just a five-minute walk from the frenetic District 1, Miss Loi's Guesthouse is one of the most popular and charming budget accommodations in the city. The villa-like structure is warmly decorated, and features a koi pond in the spacious lobby. Rooms are cozy and cheerful, and the service is always friendly.

DISTRICT 1 Phoenix 74 Hotel
$
74 Bui Vien St **Tel** (08) 3837 0538 **Fax** (08) 3836 9591 **Rooms** 20
Map 2 D5
This mini-hotel is run by a warm and helpful family who ensure that guests have little to complain about in their house. The rooms are small and sparsely decorated, but those facing the busy street have wide windows offering great views of the action below. Breakfast is simple but authentic. **www.vietnamtourism.com/phoenix74hotel**

DISTRICT 1 An An Hotel
$$
40 Bui Vien St **Tel** (08) 3837 8087 **Fax** (08) 3837 8088 **Rooms** 22
Map 2 D5
Located right in the center of the city, this hotel has spacious rooms. All provide several modern amenities, including cable TV and international telephone lines, though the tariff excludes breakfast and room service. The rooms are cleaned every day. **www.ananhotel.com**

DISTRICT 1 Dong Do Hotel
$$
35 Mac Thi Buoi **Tel** (08) 3827 3637 **Fax** (08) 3824 5763 **Rooms** 26
Map 2 F4
Location is a big factor affecting the price of this hotel, which is within walking distance of the Dong Khoi area. The modern rooms are simple but comfortable, with wooden or tile floors. Each room has free Wi-Fi access and a safe, as well as basics like air-conditioning and satellite TV.

DISTRICT 1 Lac Vien
$$
28/12–14 Bui Vien St **Tel** (08) 3920 4899 **Fax** (08) 320 4900 **Rooms** 36
Map 2 D5
Around 6 miles (10 km) from the international airport, Lac Vien is a convenient place to stay. Rooms are aesthetically decorated and offer several facilities, including 24-hour room service. A pick-up service from the airport is also available. The restaurant has a good variety of dishes from all over Vietnam, and is known for its Western and Asian menus.

Key to Symbols *see back cover flap*

DISTRICT 1 Le Le Hotel [W] $$

171 Pham Ngu Lao St ***Tel*** *(08) 3836 8686* ***Fax*** *(08) 3836 8787* ***Rooms*** *30* ***Map*** *2 D5*

A prominent landmark on busy Pham Ngu Lao, Le Le Hotel is excellent value for money. Although the decor is spare, the rooms are clean, comfortable, and well equipped. Added advantages are baby-sitting facilities, Internet access, and a decent restaurant. A travel agent is stationed in the lobby, and vehicles may be rented for excursions.

DISTRICT 1 Madame Cuc $$

64 Bui Vien St ***Tel*** *(08) 3836 5073* ***Fax*** *(08) 3836 0658* ***Rooms*** *16* ***Map*** *2 D5*

Madame Cuc has won a loyal following over the years, and Number 64 is just one of her five well regarded and consistently excellent guesthouses. The clean decor is complemented by the convivial family atmosphere and great service. Home-cooked meals are included in the price, and free tea and snacks are available all day.

DISTRICT 1 Mogambo Hotel [W] $$

20 Bis Thi Sach St ***Tel*** *(08) 3825 1311* ***Fax*** *(08) 3822 6031* ***Rooms*** *10* ***Map*** *2 F3*

Famous throughout Vietnam for the American-style diner and bar on its ground floor, Mogambo Hotel offers affordable accommodation on its upper floors. The rooms are well equipped, and the bathrooms are a good notch better than those in many other hotels. The ambience is relaxed and the staff friendly.

DISTRICT 1 Huong Sen [W] $$$

66–70 Dong Khoi St ***Tel*** *(08) 3829 1415* ***Fax*** *(08) 3829 0916* ***Rooms*** *76* ***Map*** *2 F4*

Surrounded by shops and restaurants, Huong Sen's central location is its greatest advantage. The exterior is vaguely French-colonial with Asian overtones, and the interior is plush. The restaurant serves a good breakfast, while the rooftop bar and pool are its best features. **www.vietnamtourism.com/huongsen**

DISTRICT 1 Liberty 3 [W] $$$

187 Pham Ngu Lao St ***Tel*** *(08) 3836 9522* ***Fax*** *(08) 3886 4557* ***Rooms*** *61* ***Map*** *2 D5*

Part of the Que Huong chain of hotels, the smart Liberty 3 is the epicenter of the "backpacker district," and is thoroughly modern, both inside and out. Staying here is quite a bargain, with spacious rooms that are well equipped with all mod cons. The restaurant-bar is a pleasant place for a quiet drink and snack. **www.libertyhotels.com.vn**

DISTRICT 1 Continental Hotel [W] $$$$

132–134 Dong Khoi St ***Tel*** *(08) 3829 9201* ***Fax*** *(08) 3829 0936* ***Rooms*** *80* ***Map*** *2 F3*

One of the most atmospheric hotels in Vietnam, the Continental Hotel *(see p58)* is a sight in its own right, featuring classic French-colonial architecture, with arched windows and terraces. Today, it is best known for its atrium garden restaurant and bar. Most rooms are large and modestly decorated. **www.continentalvietnam.com**

DISTRICT 1 Caravelle Hotel [W] $$$$$

19 Lam Son Sq ***Tel*** *(08) 3823 4999* ***Fax*** *(08) 3824 3999* ***Rooms*** *335* ***Map*** *2 F3*

The soaring tower of the historic Caravelle Hotel *(see p58)* dominates Lam Son Square, and the interior is just as impressive, the plush surroundings almost a small neighborhood of polished marble and rich carpet. Rooms are large and tastefully decorated, with every amenity provided. Superb food and service. **www.caravellehotel.com**

DISTRICT 1 Grand Hotel [W] $$$$$

8 Dong Khoi St ***Tel*** *(08) 3823 0163* ***Fax*** *(08) 3827 3047* ***Rooms*** *107* ***Map*** *2 F4*

This historic hotel has been impressing visitors with its grandeur since the 1930s. Easily recognized by its distinctive dome, it is cool and airy, with marble-lined interiors. Rooms are spacious and have an old-world charm. The swimming pool, surrounded by plush gardens, is located in a shady atrium. **www.grandhotel.vn**

DISTRICT 1 Majestic [W] $$$$$

1 Dong Khoi St ***Tel*** *(08) 3829 5517* ***Fax*** *(08) 3829 5510* ***Rooms*** *175* ***Map*** *2 F4*

Overlooking the Saigon River, the Majestic dates back to the early 20th century, and is a gorgeous piece of French-colonial architecture, with an Art Deco interior. It boasts two rooftop bars, one on the fifth floor of the old wing, and one atop the modern wing. While the first has more charm, the latter has a wider view. **www.majesticsaigon.com.vn**

DISTRICT 1 New World Saigon Hotel [W] $$$$$

76 Le Lai St ***Tel*** *(08) 3822 8888* ***Fax*** *(08) 3823 0710* ***Rooms*** *538* ***Map*** *2 E4*

The largest hotel in the city, the New World Saigon has huge interiors, with very high ceilings. The rooms are spacious and comfortable, and the service efficient and friendly. The hotel is home to a number of high-end shops, breakfast is lavish, and the restaurant is said to serve the best Chinese cuisine in town. **www.newworldsaigon.com**

DISTRICT 1 Park Hyatt [W] $$$$$

2 Lam Son Sq ***Tel*** *(08) 3824 1234* ***Fax*** *(08) 3823 7569* ***Rooms*** *252* ***Map*** *2 E3*

The massive yet graceful Park Hyatt dominates one side of Lam Son Square and, although it was built in 2005, has none of the chrome-and-metal swagger of high-rise hotels. Inside, it is all about taste and class, and a colonial-style ambience prevails. Exquisite decor, great service, and superb Italian restaurant. **www.saigon.park.hyatt.com**

DISTRICT 1 Renaissance Riverside [W] $$$$$

8–15 Ton Duc Thang St ***Tel*** *(08) 3822 0033* ***Fax*** *(08) 3823 5666* ***Rooms*** *319* ***Map*** *2 F4*

Run by the Marriott Group, Renaissance Riverside has great views over the river, and is just a minute's walk from Dong Khoi Street. Rooms are spacious, well equipped, and match international standards. The rooftop bar is spectacular, and the main lounge is famous for presenting foreign jazz ensembles. **www.marriott.com**

DISTRICT 1 Rex Hotel
141 Nguyen Hue St **Tel** *(08) 3829 2185* **Fax** *(08) 3829 6536* **Rooms** *286*   **Map** *2 E4*

One of the city's major landmarks, Rex Hotel *(see p60)* appears to be lost in time in terms of style and decor. The rooms are not very large, but the standard of service is high. Evenings are best spent at the rooftop bar from where the best views of the city can be enjoyed. **www.rexhotelvietnam.com**

DISTRICT 1 Sheraton Towers
88 Dong Khoi St **Tel** *(08) 3827 2828* **Fax** *(08) 3827 2929* **Rooms** *470*   **Map** *2 F4*

Located at the heart of Ho Chi Minh City's business district, the twin towers of the Sheraton preside grandly over the surrounding area. Everything about the hotel is huge, be it the lobby, ballrooms, lounges, or the opulent rooms. The chic Level 23 nightclub is a popular hangout for locals as well as expats. **www.starwoodhotels.com/sheraton**

DISTRICT 1 Sofitel Saigon Plaza
17 Le Duan St **Tel** *(08) 3824 1555* **Fax** *(08) 3824 1666* **Rooms** *286*   **Map** *2 E2*

Towering above the diplomatic quarter, the tower of the Sofitel is an easy landmark. Rooms are modern and elegantly decorated, and are both cozy and stylish at the same time. The restaurants have a very good reputation, and the rooftop swimming pool has one of the best views in the city. **www.sofitel.com**

DISTRICT 3 Chancery Saigon
196 Nguyen Thi Minh Khai St **Tel** *(08) 3930 4088* **Fax** *(08) 3930 4088* **Rooms** *96*   **Map** *2 D4*

A Best Western property, Chancery Saigon has a distinctly American feel to it. The rooms are not very large but are comfortably furnished, with a TV, minibar, terraces, and comfortable beds. It also has two restaurants and a cocktail lounge, as well as a popular bakery producing breads, cakes, and cookies. **www.chancerysaigonhotel.com**

PHU NHUAN DISTRICT Mövenpick Hotel Saigon
253 Nguyen Van Troi St **Tel** *(08) 3844 9222* **Fax** *(08) 3844 9198* **Rooms** *278*   **Map** *1 A1*

The headquarters of the CIA during the Vietnam War, the Mövenpick looks a bit like barracks from the outside but feels like a luxurious private estate inside. The hotel is some distance from the city center but close to the airport. Nice rooms, superb Chinese and Japanese restaurants, and an authentic Irish pub. **www.moevenpick-hotels.com**

TAN BINH DISTRICT Novotel Garden Plaza
309B Nguyen Van Troi St **Tel** *(08) 3842 1111* **Fax** *(08) 3842 4370* **Rooms** *193*   **Map** *1 A1*

Ideal for business travelers, Novotel Garden Plaza is a sleek, modern building, just a five-minute taxi ride from the airport, and away from the hustle and bustle of downtown Ho Chi Minh City. Rooms are spacious, with appealing decor and all the modern conveniences. Friendly, efficient service, and popular restaurant and lounge. **www.novotel.com**

AROUND HO CHI MINH CITY

LONG HAI Palace Hotel
11 Nguyen Trai St **Tel** *(064) 386 8364* **Rooms** *120*

A tall, white structure near the tip of the Long Hai Peninsula, the Palace Hotel is one of the most popular and well-priced options in the area. Rooms are large, bright, and well equipped. The lounge is a great place for evening cocktails, and the tennis court becomes a social center in the afternoon.

LONG HAI Anoasis Beach Resort
Domain Ky Van **Tel** *(064) 386 8227* **Fax** *(064) 386 8229* **Rooms** *48*

Truly an oasis, this sprawling, award-winning resort was originally one of Emperor Bao Dai's Villas, and comprises a collection of 30 charming bungalows set amid lush gardens. Rooms are cheerful, with bamboo furniture and spacious bathrooms. A private beach, tennis courts, and child-care facilities are also available. **www.anoasisresort.com.vn**

VUNG TAU Son Thuy Resort
165C Thuy Van St **Tel** *(064) 352 3460* **Fax** *(064) 352 4169* **Rooms** *44*

Facing Back Beach across the road, Son Thuy Resort is a collection of A-frame buildings surrounding a central circular swimming pool, all of which combine to produce a relaxed beach-house ambience. Rooms are up to three-star standards and are ideal for families.

VUNG TAU Palace Hotel
1 Nguyen Trai St **Tel** *(064) 385 6411* **Fax** *(064) 385 6878* **Rooms** *94*

Located in the center of town and within easy walking distance of the hydrofoil dock, the Palace is one of the larger hotels in town. The interior is bright and airy, providing some respite from the tropical heat. Well-equipped rooms, tennis court, and good service. Folk music performances take place here for guests. **www.palacehotel.com.vn**

VUNG TAU Petro House
63 Tran Hung Dao St **Tel** *(064) 385 2014* **Fax** *(064) 385 2015* **Rooms** *53*

An intimate boutique hotel set in a restored French-colonial building, the Petro House has arched windows and terraces, giving it the look of a Mediterranean villa. It comprises well-appointed rooms, as well as service apartments for longer stays. Its well-regarded French restaurant also serves Vietnamese fare.

Key to Price Guide *see p232* **Key to Symbols** *see back cover flap*

MEKONG DELTA AND SOUTHERN VIETNAM

BAC LIEU Thong Nhat Guesthouse

50 Thong Nhat St **Tel** *(0781) 382 1085* **Rooms** *7*

Located near Bac Lieu's busy main bridge, Thong Nhat is fortunately set back from the street, giving it an aura of solitude. The rooms in this small, family-run operation have no decor, but are functional and quite comfortable. The second-story terrace is a pleasant setting for afternoon tea. There is a free laundry service as well.

BAC LIEU Bac Lieu Hotel

4–6 Hoang Van Thu St **Tel** *(0781) 382 2437* **Fax** *(0781) 382 3655* **Rooms** *70*

Easily recognizable by its high, glass facade, Bac Lieu Hotel is arguably the best in town. Although it purports to be a three-star hotel, rooms range from the bare minimum, with only a bed and fan, to large and comfortable, with all the amenities. Both car and motorbike rentals are available, and the Bac Lieu Tourist office is next door.

BEN TRE Hung Vuong

166 Hung Vuong Rd **Tel** *(075) 382 2408* **Fax** *(075) 381 0911* **Rooms** *40*

Situated on the waterfront and near the center of town, Hung Vuong is the best located hotel in Ben Tre, and offers excellent value for money. It boasts a very modern design, with high ceilings and spacious rooms, many of which overlook the river. The central tennis courts can be used late into the night.

CAN THO Saigon-Can Tho

55 Phan Dinh Phung St **Tel** *(0710) 382 5831* **Fax** *(0710) 382 3288* **Rooms** *42*

Close to the main market and a string of restaurants along the riverside, Saigon-Can Tho has simple but well-decorated rooms, equipped with a TV, minibar, in-house movies, and music. Recreational facilities include table tennis and billiards, while the rooftop bar specializes in traditional Vietnamese music. **www.saigoncantho.com.vn**

CAN THO Phuong Dong

62 30 Thang 4 St **Tel** *(0710) 381 2199* **Fax** *(0710) 382 0133* **Rooms** *46*

The centrally located Phuong Dong is one of the first in town to claim international hotel status. Although it is somewhat bland in terms of character, it is popular with business travelers and tourists alike, and has most of the amenities of a three-star hotel. Its better rooms are spacious and decorated in modern European style.

CAN THO Victoria Can Tho

Cai Khe Ward **Tel** *(0710) 381 0111* **Fax** *(0710) 382 9259* **Rooms** *92*

A top international-class resort, the riverside Victoria Can Tho is located on the Cai Khe Peninsula, facing the town. The lovely colonial-style building is surrounded by lush gardens, which can be seen from the rooms, all of which are spacious and beautifully decorated with wooden furniture. **www.victoriahotels-asia.com**

CHAU DOC Song Sao

12 Nguyen Huu Canh St **Tel** *(076) 356 1777* **Fax** *(076) 386 8820* **Rooms** *25*

Set on one of the town's quieter streets, Song Sao is a relatively classy yet inexpensive mini-hotel. The interior has a clean and modern East Asian design, with potted plants and rattan trim. Rooms, many with balconies, are plainly but pleasantly decorated, and all have a TV and minibar. The restaurant is well regarded, and serves Vietnamese fare.

CHAU DOC Nui Sam

Vinh Te Village **Tel** *(076) 386 1666* **Fax** *(076) 386 1600* **Rooms** *21*

Situated at the bottom of Sam Mountain *(see p100)*, this tile-roofed, two-story building offers good value to families with small children with its four-bed family rooms. All rooms have balconies and are well equipped with a TV and minibar. The restaurant specializes in local dishes, and there is a small bar. Secure basement parking.

CHAU DOC Victoria Chau Doc

32 Le Loi St **Tel** *(076) 386 5010* **Fax** *(076) 386 5020* **Rooms** *92*

The imposing Victoria Chau Doc dominates the riverbank on the southern outskirts of town. The interior is airy, with high ceilings and stylish furnishings. Rooms are elegant and those facing the river offer breathtaking views. Luxury package holidays and tours are also on offer. **www.victoriahotels-asia.com**

CON DAO ISLAND ATC Hotel

8 Ton Duc Thang St **Tel** *(064) 383 0345* **Fax** *(064) 383 0111* **Rooms** *8*

Built in the early 20th century, the ATC was originally a French villa. Today, it is a cluster of cottages nestled in a well-kept and creatively tended garden. Rooms are decorated with tropical woods, wicker, and rattan. Amenities are few but adequate, and the family who operates the hotel is very hospitable.

CON DAO ISLAND Saigon-Con Dao

18 Ton Duc Thang St **Tel** *(064) 383 0336* **Fax** *(064) 383 0335* **Rooms** *33*

Located on the Con Dao archipelago's main island of Con Son and set near the beach, this secluded resort comprises seven renovated French villas. Rooms are modest but tasteful, and equipped with all necessities. The grounds, which feature two tennis courts, are meticulously maintained. An air of serenity prevails. **www.saigoncondao.com**

HA TIEN Ha Tien Hotel
36D Tran Hau St **Tel** *(077) 395 2093* **Rooms** *32*

In the heart of the action, on the riverside, Ha Tien's nicest hotel offers comfortable but simple carpeted rooms with wooden furnishings. The hotel boasts all the basics, including satellite TV and air-conditioning, plus a large restaurant and a small spa with sauna and Jacuzzi.

MY THO Chuong Duong Hotel
10, 30 Thang 4 St **Tel** *(073) 387 0875* **Fax** *(073) 387 4250* **Rooms** *27*

The architecture of the elegant waterfront Chuong Duong Hotel, with its whitewashed walls, arches, and tiled roof, recalls the Mediterranean. The rooms are spotlessly clean, large, and spare without looking austere. All the usual amenities are provided, and the restaurant is quite good *(see p253)*.

PHU QUOC ISLAND Hong Tuyet
14 Bach Dang St **Tel** *(077) 384 8879* **Fax** *(077) 384 6248* **Rooms** *9*

Built in the mini-hotel style, with four levels, Hong Tuyet is just a few meters from the airport, making it a convenient place to stay. The rooms in this unassuming little hotel, though spare, are spacious and functional with satellite television and minibar; all street-facing ones have balconies. Service is first rate, including child-care arrangements.

PHU QUOC ISLAND Tropicana Resort
Duong To, Long Beach **Tel** *(077) 384 7127* **Fax** *(077) 384 7128* **Rooms** *30*

A tranquil beach hideaway, Tropicana Resort comprises a collection of charming thatch-roofed bungalows knitted together by brick trails weaving through well-tended lawns. Rooms are spacious and comfortable. The hotel also arranges scuba diving and snorkeling excursions, as well as fishing trips. **www.northvalleyroads.com/tropicana**

PHU QUOC ISLAND Saigon Phu Quoc Resort
1 Tran Hung Dao Beachside Blvd **Tel** *(077) 384 6999* **Fax** *(077) 384 7163* **Rooms** *90*

Only 10 minutes from the airport, but in an idyllic world of its own, this luxurious seaside resort is composed of low-slung, terraced villas surrounding the circular swimming pool. Offers lovely rooms, recreational facilities, good service, and great beaches. Tours and watersports can be arranged in-house. **www.sgphuquocresort.com.vn**

RACH GIA Hung Tai
E11 Thu Khoa Huan St **Tel** *(077) 387 7508* **Fax** *(077) 387 7508* **Rooms** *15*

A pink three-story building on the corner of the central market, Hung Tai is close to much of the town's action. The rooms are utilitarian but have all the necessary amenities, even though the beds feature the delta region's customary thin mattresses. There is a small bar and a decent restaurant. Spacious and safe parking area.

RACH GIA Phuong Hoang
6 Nguyen Trung Truc St **Tel** *(077) 386 6525* **Fax** *(077) 386 6525* **Rooms** *20*

Overlooking the south bank of the Cai Lon River, Phuong Hoang is close to the town center but far enough to be more quiet and peaceful. The architecture and decor are simple and pleasing. Rooms are on the small side but clean and well appointed, with very good baths and comfortable beds. Staff are very friendly.

SOC TRANG Phong Lan I
124 Dong Khoi St **Tel** *(079) 382 1619* **Fax** *(079) 382 3817* **Rooms** *16*

With wide terraces running the width of the building, the somewhat boxy Phong Lan I is centrally located, offering nice views of the river. The rooms are uninspiring but a good bargain for the price. The restaurant serves seafood, specializing in local favorites such as fried river fish and fish soup. Also has a small karaoke bar with a dance floor.

SOC TRANG Phong Lan II
133 Nguyen Chi Thanh St **Tel** *(079) 382 1757* **Fax** *(079) 382 3451* **Rooms** *28*

An old building dating back to the French-colonial era, Phong Lan II features broad terraces and a penthouse on the topmost floor. The place shows its age but wears it gracefully enough from the outside, although the rooms are rather indifferently appointed. The restaurant is satisfactory. The sauna services are well above average.

TRA VINH Cuu Long
999 Nguyen Thi Minh Khai St **Tel** *(074) 386 2615* **Fax** *(074) 386 6027* **Rooms** *52*

Located in a quiet area on the outskirts of town, Cuu Long is an unremarkable structure but still offers the best comforts among all the hotels in town. Rooms are well appointed with a TV, minibar, and simple yet charming bamboo furnishings. Those facing the street have pleasant balconies, while larger rooms have tubs as well as showers.

VINH LONG Phuong Hoang I Hotel
2H Hung Vuong St **Tel** *(070) 382 5185* **Rooms** *12*

This backpacker hotel in the center of town has spacious, clean rooms with air-conditioning. The staff are friendly and speak good English. An affiliated property a few doors down offers more rooms when this place is fully booked. Internet access is also available at the sister hotel.

VINH LONG Cuu Long
No. 1, 1 May Rd **Tel** *(070) 382 3656* **Fax** *(070) 382 3848* **Rooms** *34*

Overlooking the river, the glass facade of Cuu Long's central tower, flanked by terraced wings, rises up eight stories. The interior is bright and airy, with very modern, minimalist furnishings. Rooms are similarly spacious and simple, with a TV, minibar, and complimentary fruit basket. Also has tennis courts and billiard tables, as well as a karaoke bar.

SOUTH CENTRAL VIETNAM

BUON MA THUOT Thang Loi $$

1 Phan Chu Trinh St **Tel** *(050) 385 7615* **Fax** *(050) 385 7622* **Rooms** *40*

Located right in the heart of Buon Ma Thuot, conveniently next door to the Daklak Tourist office and a 24-hour ATM machine, Thang Loi's rooms have little aesthetic appeal but are spacious and have en suite bathrooms and satellite TV. The large restaurant is quite popular locally, and serves Vietnamese as well as some international dishes.

DALAT Dreams Hotel $$

151 Phan Dinh Phung St **Tel** *(063) 383 3748* **Fax** *(063) 383 7108* **Rooms** *13*

An enduringly popular budget establishment, this family-run hotel has smallish rooms, but its cleanliness, cheerful decor, and amenities more than make up for it. Extremely helpful English-speaking staff, delicious breakfast, and free Internet access are some of the highlights. Dreams Hotel also has an annexe located at 164B Phan Dinh Phung St.

DALAT Dalat Hotel Du Parc $$$

7 Tran Phu St **Tel** *(063) 382 5777* **Fax** *(063) 382 5666* **Rooms** *140*

Established in the 1930s, the restored hotel was originally the French-run Hotel du Parc. Still redolent of the colonial era, and with clean, well-equipped rooms (no air-conditioning since it is not really needed in Dalat), this fine mid-range hotel is one of best options in town. Excellent restaurant. **www.hotelduparc.vn**

DALAT Dalat Palace $$$$$

12 Tran Phu St **Tel** *(063) 382 5444* **Fax** *(063) 382 5666* **Rooms** *43*

One of the most opulent hotels in Vietnam, Dalat Palace is quite reasonably priced for the quality it offers. Completed in 1922, it has retained its colonial grandeur, combining it with the best Southeast Asian hospitality. The rooms are splendidly decorated, with heavy drapes, fireplaces, and antiques. A golf course is right next door. **www.dalatpalace.vn**

KONTUM Dakbla Hotel $

2 Phan Dinh Phung St **Tel** *(060) 386 3333* **Fax** *(060) 386 3336* **Rooms** *42*

Even the best hotels in Kontum do not have a great many facilities, but the Dakbla, which is designed to reflect local Bahnar architectural style, has character. The rooms are clean with all basic amenities, the staff friendly and efficient, the restaurant passable, and there is a helpful tourist office in the lobby on the ground floor.

MUI NE BEACH Mui Ne Backpackers $

88 Nguyen Dinh Chieu St **Tel** *(062) 384 7047* **Rooms** *20*

Mui Ne Backpackers (formerly Vietnam-Austria House) was one of the first places in Mui Ne to offer accommodation. Bungalows, dorm beds, and hotel-style rooms are available. The hostel maintains a homely feel at backpacker prices, despite the 4- and 5-star resort setting that has developed around it. **www.muinebeach.net**

MUI NE BEACH Mia Resort Mui Ne $$$

24 Nguyen Dinh Chieu St **Tel** *(062) 384 7440* **Fax** *(062) 384 441* **Rooms** *30*

Formerly a sailing club, Mui Ne's premier boutique resort is part of one of the oldest fine-dining resort groups in Vietnam. Its Sandals Restaurant *(see p251)* is critically acclaimed and Storm Kiteboarding, one of the most respected centers for the sport in Mui Ne, is found here. Exquisite tropical gardens and superb beach location. **www.sailingclubvietnam.com**

MUI NE BEACH Coco Beach $$$

58 Nguyen Dinh Chieu St **Tel** *(062) 384 7111* **Fax** *(062) 384 7115* **Rooms** *34*

With a choice of either wooden cabins or two-room villas, Coco Beach is one of the most attractive and comfortable resorts on Mui Ne Beach. The rooms are bright and cheery with all modern conveniences, except a TV. Other facilities include a library service, playground, and a travel service. **www.cocobeach.net**

MUI NE BEACH Pandanus Resort $$$$

Mui Ne, Phan Thiet **Tel** *(062) 384 9849* **Fax** *(062) 384 9850* **Rooms** *134*

If you want the ambience of Mui Ne's lush coconut groves, red-sand dunes, and fisherman's culture, but long for a sense of solitude and privacy, try this upscale resort behind Mui Ne Village. An express highway links the resort directly to the Sea Links Golf Club. **www.pandanusresort.com**

MUI NE BEACH Seahorse Resort & Spa $$$$

7 miles (11 km) from Ham Tien **Tel** *(062) 384 7507* **Fax** *(062) 384 7774* **Rooms** *90*

This luxurious resort maintains a boutique feel thanks to the exotic, spacious landscaping and personal attention to each guest. A lavish buffet breakfast is served each morning. Facilities include kite-boarding and windsurfing lessons, Wi-Fi, tennis courts, childcare, and a beachside restaurant. **www.seahorseresortvn.com**

NHA TRANG Sao Mai Hotel $

99 Nguyen Thien Thuat St **Tel** *(058) 352 6412* **Rooms** *20*

One of the best budget options in town. The large, tidy rooms open onto shared balconies and have hot water, a fridge, TV, and air-conditioning (or fans, if preferred). The owner, photographer Mai Loc, leads excellent motorbike tours of central Vietnam. The hotel also offers one of the cheapest motorbike rentals in town at just US$3 per day.

NHA TRANG Nha Trang Lodge $$$

42 Tran Phu St **Tel** *(058) 352 1500* **Fax** *(058) 352 1800* **Rooms** *120*

A good middle-range option, Nha Trang Lodge is on the marine drive overlooking the bay and islands. The rooms are pleasant and provide all the usual facilities, with most affording superb views over the sea. The business center offers 60 minutes of free Internet time, and the travel agency can arrange and confirm flights. **www.nhatranglodge.com**

NHA TRANG Evason Ana Mandara Spa $$$$$

Tran Phu Blvd **Tel** *(058) 352 2222* **Fax** *(058) 352 5828* **Rooms** *78*

Fronting its own stretch of the beach, the Ana Mandara, set amid tropical gardens and fountains, is extremely luxurious. Its Six Senses Spa is quite famous, and the rooms are set in 17 beautiful bungalows. The two restaurants serve high-standard Vietnamese and international cuisine. **www.sixsenses.com**

NHA TRANG Melia Sunrise Hotel $$$$$

12–14 Tran Phu St **Tel** *(058) 382 0999* **Fax** *(058) 382 2866* **Rooms** *123*

This glamorous high-rise hotel dominates the marine drive and is just a stone's throw from the beach. Stylish and luxurious, the interior is all marble and glass, with elaborate chandeliers and a large circular, ornamental pool. Rooms are elegant and most offer spectacular views. Several fine restaurants. **www.sunrisehotelvietnam.com**

NHA TRANG Vinpearl Resort $$$$$

7 Tran Phu St, Vinh Nguyen **Tel** *(058) 359 8188* **Fax** *(058) 359 8147* **Rooms** *485*

The largest and most luxurious resort in Nha Trang, the Vinpearl has just about every luxury, business, and sports facility imaginable. Set on the Hon Tre Island, a 10-minute boat ride from the mainland, it is well decorated, with wooden and rattan furniture. **www.vinpearlland.com**

NINH HOA Six Senses Hideaway Ninh Van Bay $$$$$

Ninh Van Bay **Tel** *(058) 352 4268* **Fax** *(058) 372 8223* **Rooms** *55*

The ultra-luxurious Six Senses really is a "hideaway," since it can only be reached by a 20-minute boat journey from Ninh Hoa. Quite simply, the boutique resort has every luxury imaginable, set against a stunning backdrop of mountains, and facing a white sand beach with a coral reef nearby. **www.sixsenses.com**

PHAN RANG Ho Phong Hotel $

363 Ngo Gia Tu **Tel** *(068) 392 0333* **Fax** *(068) 383 7717* **Rooms** *30*

Affordable convenience is the theme of Ho Phong. Just off the highway, it is right on the edge of downtown, with easy access to good cafés and the central market. The hotel offers good value for money, with bright, comfortable rooms, all with TVs and some with balconies.

PHAN THIET Novotel Ocean Dunes & Golf Resort $$$$

1A Ton Duc Thang **Tel** *(062) 382 2393* **Fax** *(062) 382 5682* **Rooms** *135*

Granting easy access to Ocean Dunes Golf, the Novotel is the only reason to stay in Phan Thiet rather than nearby Mui Ne Beach. Private balconies have beautiful views, whether they face the sea or the golf course and mountains. Nightly live music, a spa, watersports facilities, and tennis courts are some of the amenities. **www.novotel.com**

QUANG NGAI My Khe Resort $

Tinh Khe St **Tel** *(055) 368 6111* **Fax** *(055) 368 6064* **Rooms** *12*

This resort on a beautiful stretch of My Khe Beach is the ideal place to stay if visiting Quang Ngai. Situated 11 miles (17 km) north of town, it is truly tranquil and the beach is often deserted. The rooms are bright and clean, the staff friendly, and the restaurant serves a variety of Vietnamese dishes and great seafood.

QUY NHON Quy Nhon Hotel $$

8 Nguyen Hue St **Tel** *(056) 389 2401* **Fax** *(056) 389 1162* **Rooms** *43*

Perhaps the best lodging in Quy Nhon town, this large and spacious hotel is well located near the city beach, but apart from being clean and relatively quiet, it has little in the way of atmosphere. The rooms are bland but adequate. The restaurant, however, serves some delicious Vietnamese specialties. Facilities include a sauna.

QUY NHON Life Resort Quy Nhon $$$$

Ghenh Rang, Bai Dai Beach **Tel** *(056) 384 0132* **Fax** *(056) 384 0138* **Rooms** *63*

Located by the beach 10 miles (16 km) south of town, this is the best place to stay and pamper yourself in the Quy Nhon area. Spectacular architecture, reminiscent of a Cham temple, houses just about every luxury, including a spa offering a wide range of treatments, yoga, tai chi, and general relaxation. **www.life-resorts.com**

CENTRAL VIETNAM

BA NA HILL STATION Ba Na Resort $

100 Bach Dang St **Tel** *(0511) 379 1000* **Rooms** *45*

Located right on the summit of Ba Na Hill, this resort offers fine views and cool, clear mountain air to breathe. Accommodation is in a combination of decently equipped hotel rooms and private bungalows, and the large restaurant serves Vietnamese food that even the locals relish. **www.banahills.com.vn**

Key to Price Guide *see p232* **Key to Symbols** *see back cover flap*

CHINA BEACH Furama Resort Danang

68 Ho Xuan Huong St **Tel** *(0511) 384 7333* **Fax** *(0511) 384 7666* **Rooms** *198*

One of the most plush beach resorts in Vietnam, the Furama is only a 10-minute drive from central Danang. Maintaining a tranquil and exclusive air, it boasts a private stretch of beach, beautiful rooms, and splendid views. Recreational facilities range from watersports to billiards, and the restaurant is highly recommended. **www.furamavietnam.com**

CHINA BEACH Fusion Maia Da Nang

Son Tra–Dien Ngoc Coastal St **Tel** *(0511) 396 7999* **Fax** *(0511) 396 7888* **Rooms** *87*

Located on the outskirts of Da Nang, Fusion Maia is a luxurious resort offering world-class facilities. With a fabulous restaurant, lavish breakfast buffet, unlimited spa treatments included with all rooms, private pools with each bungalow, and a sunken, black granite bathtub in each room, you won't want to leave. **www.fusionmaiadanang.com**

DANANG Modern Hotel

186 Bach Dang St **Tel** *(0511) 382 0113* **Fax** *(0511) 382 1842* **Rooms** *40*

Spotlessly clean and comfortable at a budget price, the Modern Hotel is well located in the heart of downtown Danang, and offers most amenities, including cable TV and en suite bathrooms. The restaurant serves Vietnamese, Chinese, and international cuisine. Other facilities include air and train ticket reservation, sauna, and a karaoke bar.

DANANG Royal Hotel

17 Quang Trung St **Tel** *(0511) 382 3295* **Fax** *(0511) 382 7279* **Rooms** *60*

On par with international three-star standards, the Royal has large, well-appointed rooms, all of which come equipped with ADSL Internet service. Facilities include a fine restaurant serving an eclectic range of cuisines, karaoke bar, nightclub, travel agency, as well as car rentals. **www.royaldananghotel.com.vn**

DANANG Saigon Tourane

5 Dong Da St **Tel** *(0511) 382 1021* **Fax** *(0511) 389 5285* **Rooms** *82*

One of the largest and best-equipped hotels in Danang, the Saigon Tourane is located by the Han River. Rooms are spacious, with subtle, aesthetic decor, and have all the modern conveniences, including cable TV. A large and breezy rooftop restaurant serves Vietnamese and international cuisine. **www.saigontourane.com.vn**

DONG HA Hieu Giang

138 Le Duan St **Tel** *(053) 385 6856* **Fax** *(053) 385 6859* **Rooms** *31*

Dong Ha is relatively off the trodden tourist trail and, as a result, the hotels in town are fairly limited. Hieu Giang is reckoned the best of the bunch. Although the rooms are on the drab side, they are perfectly adequate for an overnight stay, being clean and equipped with cable TV. The restaurant serves good simple food at reasonable prices.

DONG HOI Cosevco Nhat Le

16 Quach Xuan Ky St **Tel** *(052) 384 0088* **Fax** *(052) 384 0392* **Rooms** *44*

The largest hotel in downtown Dong Hoi, the riverfront Cosevco Nhat Le is rather nondescript. Rooms are plain but clean, with all the usual amenities, including cable TV. The restaurant serves good Vietnamese and passable international fare. Additional facilities include a sauna, as well as tennis courts.

DONG HOI Sun Spa Resort

My Canh, Bao Ninh **Tel** *(052) 384 2999* **Fax** *(052) 384 2555* **Rooms** *234*

The most luxurious accommodation between Hue and Hanoi, the Sun Spa Resort is surrounded by water on three sides making for a very attractive setting. The bright and charming rooms have all the trimmings of a top-quality resort, including cable TV, laptop portals, and Jacuzzi. **www.sunsparesortvietnam.com**

HOI AN Cua Dai Hotel

18A Cua Dai St **Tel** *(0510) 386 2231* **Fax** *(0510) 386 2232* **Rooms** *24*

Located on the road to Cua Dai beach, this budget hotel offers attractive, colonial-style rooms and friendly service. The lush gardens contain some rare and beautiful plants and trees, and are an ideal place to relax. Guests can make free use of the hotel's bicycles for exploring the surrounding areas. **www.cuadai-hotel.com**

HOI AN Thanh Xuan (Long Life) Hotel

30 Ba Trieu St **Tel** *(0510) 391 6696* **Fax** *(0510) 391 6697* **Rooms** *20*

An appealing, modern hotel located a short distance to the north of Hoi An, Thanh Xuan offers just about the best rates for this level of service in town. Rooms are airy, bright, and cheery, the staff helpful, the restaurant service excellent, and facilities include a travel agency, car hire, and free bicycle hire. **www.longlifehotels.com**

HOI AN Ancient House

377 Cua Dai St **Tel** *(0510) 392 3377* **Fax** *(0510) 392 3477* **Rooms** *52*

This lovely resort, comprising new villas built to emulate traditional Hoi An architecture, makes for a pleasurable stay. Set around beautiful gardens and ponds, the rooms are stylish, and a nightclub, beauty salon, sauna, and spa add to the overall charm. Bicycle hire and shuttle to the Old Quarter is free of charge. **www.ancienthouseresort.com**

HOI AN Hoi An Riverside Resort

175 Cua Dai St **Tel** *(0510) 386 4800* **Fax** *(0510) 386 4900* **Rooms** *62*

Comprising a cluster of modern villas in French-colonial style, by the bank of a small river, this boutique resort is one of the most attractive and serene in the area. Just about everything is on offer, including a baby-sitting service, boutiques, an art gallery, spa, valet service, and billiards room. A lovely getaway from it all.

HOI AN Life Resort Hoi An

1 Pham Hong Thai St **Tel** *(0510) 391 4555* **Fax** *(0510) 391 4515* **Rooms** *94*

Just a 5-minute walk from Hoi An's historic old town, this luxurious riverside resort has plush rooms, fine food, and a large swimming pool right by the river. Unexpected bonuses include visa processing, air ticket confirmation, a travel agency, free daily newspapers, and foreign currency exchange and child-care facilities. **www.life-resorts.com**

HOI AN Victoria Hoi An Beach Resort and Spa

Cam An Beach **Tel** *(0510) 392 7040* **Fax** *(0510) 392 7041* **Rooms** *104*

This magnificent upscale resort has just about every facility available, plus a great deal of charm. In addition to the usual five-star services, there is a library, a free shuttle service to the Old Quarter, volleyball and badminton courts, elephant rides on the beach, and child care, amusement, and watersports facilities. **www.victoriahotels-asia.com**

HUE Thuan Hoa

7 Nguyen Tri Phuong St **Tel** *(054) 382 3340* **Fax** *(054) 382 2470* **Rooms** *69*

Situated in the heart of the French Quarter, Thuan Hoa is spacious, clean, friendly, and reasonably priced, with an attractive garden and pleasant, well-equipped rooms. Additional services include baby-sitting, a travel agency, sauna, tennis court, as well as car and bike rentals.

HUE Le Loi Hotel

2 Le Loi St **Tel** *(054) 382 4668* **Fax** *(054) 382 4527* **Rooms** *199*

Close to the railway station, Le Loi is quite a bargain considering the relatively superior services and amenities offered. The standard rooms have all the usual conveniences plus an en suite shower, while suites have bathtubs and balconies. The large restaurant serves well-prepared Vietnamese and international cuisine. **www.greenhotel-hue.com**

HUE Saigon Morin

30 Le Loi St **Tel** *(054) 382 3526* **Fax** *(054) 382 5155* **Rooms** *183*

Built in 1901, this grande dame of Hue hotels is set round a large and attractive courtyard filled with shady trees. The old colonial rooms are truly vast, and the bathrooms packed with every luxury, including jars of bath salts. Traditional music and dance shows accompany the alfresco dinner at the Royal Cuisine Restaurant. **www.morinhotel.com.vn**

HUE Century Riverside

49 Le Loi St **Tel** *(054) 382 3390* **Fax** *(054) 382 3394* **Rooms** *135*

This grand hotel is set on the south side of the Perfume River, with fine views across to the Citadel. Rooms are richly decorated, and come with complimentary fruit, tea, and coffee. The hotel's Imperial Restaurant specializes in Hue's royal cuisine, and also hosts traditional Vietnamese cultural performances. **www.centuryriversidehue.com**

HUE La Residence Hotel & Spa

5 Le Loi St **Tel** *(054) 383 7475* **Fax** *(054) 383 7476* **Rooms** *122*

Possibly the best hotel in town, this restored building, once the French governor's residence, offers lovely views of the river and Citadel. Boasts opulent rooms, with four-poster beds and antique furniture, as well as suites, with themes ranging from birds to ancient Egypt. The period feel is offset by state-of-the-art amenities. **www.la-residence-hue.com**

LANG CO BEACH Lang Co Beach Resort

Loc Hai Commune, Lang Co **Tel** *(054) 387 3555* **Fax** *(054) 387 3504* **Rooms** *88*

Modeled on a highly decorative Hue architectural theme, and located on one of Vietnam's best beaches, Lang Co Beach Resort is home to both delightful, balconied villas and standard rooms, all with good views and equipped with every comfort. Facilities include a beauty salon, sauna, and tennis courts. **www.langcobeachresort.com.vn**

VINH Phu Nguyen Hai

81 Le Loi St **Tel** *(038) 384 8429* **Fax** *(038) 383 2014* **Rooms** *25*

Widely held to be the best budget hotel in Vinh, Phu Nguyen Hai has big, clean, well-equipped rooms, helpful staff, and a restaurant that serves quality Vietnamese cuisine at very reasonable prices. Conveniently located in the heart of town, the hotel is only a few meters from the main bus station.

HANOI

FRENCH QUARTER Lotus Guesthouse

42V Ly Thuong Kiet St **Tel** *(04) 3826 8642* **Fax** *(04) 3934 4197* **Rooms** *10*   **Map** 2 E4

The range of facilities provided by the cozy Lotus Guesthouse explains its popularity among backpackers the world over. This bed-and-breakfast features en suite rooms with a mini-fridge and cable TV. The location is good, the staff very helpful, and the café offers a pleasant place to hang out with other travelers.

FRENCH QUARTER De Syloia

17A Tran Hung Dao St **Tel** *(04) 3824 5346* **Fax** *(04) 3824 1083* **Rooms** *33*   **Map** 2 F5

A pleasant, medium-sized hotel in the heart of downtown Hanoi, De Syloia is within easy walking distance of many major sightseeing destinations. Spacious, attractive rooms with all mod cons, a choice of in-house films, and a baby-sitting service. Cay Cau Restaurant *(see p258)* offers a wide choice of delectable dishes. **www.desyloia.com**

Key to Price Guide *see p232* **Key to Symbols** *see back cover flap*

FRENCH QUARTER Guoman Hotel $$$$

83A Ly Thuong Kiet St **Tel** *(04) 3822 2800* **Rooms** *154* **Map** *2 D4*

A deservedly popular hotel catering primarily to business travelers, with a wide range of facilities, including Jacuzzi, and a choice of four restaurants. Rooms are very well equipped, while the staff are friendly and fluent in English. The location is convenient for both shopping and the railway station.

FRENCH QUARTER Melia Hotel $$$$

44B Ly Thuong Kiet St **Tel** *(04) 3934 3343* **Fax** *(04) 3934 3344* **Rooms** *238* **Map** *2 E4*

This upscale establishment is all about serious style and luxury. Boasts gracious, elegant bedrooms, and an exceptional breakfast. Features a helipad on the roof, an outdoor swimming pool on the third floor, and a band playing in the lobby every evening. The restaurants serve fine Vietnamese and Mediterranean cuisine. **www.meliahanoi.com**

FRENCH QUARTER Zephyr Hotel $$$$

4 Ba Trieu St **Tel** *(04) 3934 1256* **Fax** *(04) 3934 1262* **Rooms** *44* **Map** *2 E4*

A pleasant boutique hotel, the Zephyr is very well located, and about as central as it is possible to get in downtown Hanoi. Friendly and efficient, with a homely atmosphere. Facilities include a bar and lounge on the eighth floor, which offers fantastic views across nearby Hoan Kiem Lake. Good Vietnamese cuisine. **www.zephyrhotel.com.vn**

FRENCH QUARTER Hilton Hanoi Opera $$$$$

1 Le Thanh Tong St **Tel** *(04) 3933 0500* **Fax** *(04) 3933 0530* **Rooms** *269* **Map** *2 F5*

An extraordinarily elegant structure built to mirror the Opera House next door, the Hilton Hanoi Opera offers superb service and every conceivable amenity. The opulent rooms, many featuring silk drapes and artwork by local artists, are furnished in Vietnamese style, and have splendid views over the city. **www.hanoi.hilton.com**

FRENCH QUARTER Sofitel Legend Metropole Hotel $$$$$

15 Ngo Quyen St **Tel** *(04) 3826 6919* **Fax** *(04) 3826 6920* **Rooms** *363* **Map** *2 F4*

The Sofitel Legend Metropole *(see p162)*, restored to its original splendor, is the one of the most atmospheric hotels in the city. The rooms are soundproofed and lavishly equipped, while the bathrooms feature generous bathtubs. Le Beaulieu *(see p258)* is arguably the best French restaurant in Hanoi. **www.sofitel.com**

OLD QUARTER Camellia Hotel II $

13 Luong Ngoc Quyen St **Tel** *(04) 3828 3583* **Fax** *(04) 3824 4277* **Rooms** *26* **Map** *2 E2*

The first of a group of four budget mini-hotels with the same management, Camellia Hotel II offers friendly and efficient service, decent accommodation, and tour services across the country, all at rock-bottom rates. The hotel staff will redirect visitors to another branch if they are full, as is often the case. Free Internet access.

OLD QUARTER Prince Hotel I $

51 Luong Ngoc Quyen St **Tel** *(04) 3828 0155* **Fax** *(04) 3828 0156* **Rooms** *14* **Map** *2 E2*

With a second branch at 42B Hang Giay, Prince Hotel I caters to the discerning budget traveler. Rooms offer IDD telephones, mini-fridge, cable TV, coffee- and tea-making facilities, en suite bathrooms with hair dryers, Wi-Fi Internet, and a free pick-up from the airport for those staying for more than three days. **www.princehotelhanoi.com**

OLD QUARTER Venus Hotel $

10 Hang Can St **Tel** *(04) 3826 1212* **Fax** *(04) 3824 6010* **Rooms** *10* **Map** *2 E2*

At the bottom end of the price range in the Old Quarter, the Venus is nevertheless good value for money, with clean rooms offering a TV, air-conditioning, and a mini-fridge. A downside is that the building is far from attractive, and the rooms at the back are windowless. On the upside, the price includes a substantial breakfast.

OLD QUARTER Anh Dao $$

37 Ma May St **Tel** *(04) 3826 7151* **Fax** *(04) 3828 2008* **Rooms** *40* **Map** *2 E2*

A mini-hotel conveniently located in the heart of the Old Quarter, Anh Dao offers comfortable rooms with good facilities at very reasonable rates. It is advisable to book a superior or deluxe room at a marginally higher price, as some standard rooms do not have windows.

OLD QUARTER Classic I Hotel $$

22A Ta Hien St **Tel** *(04) 3826 6224* **Fax** *(04) 3828 1727* **Rooms** *36* **Map** *2 E2*

A clean and comfortable hotel with all the standard amenities, plus a helpful and friendly, English-speaking staff. There is free Internet access for guests on the first floor, and a small restaurant that serves mainly breakfast. A tour service in the lobby can arrange trips around Hanoi or anywhere in the north.

OLD QUARTER Classic Street Hotel $$

41 Hang Be St **Tel** *(04) 3825 2421* **Fax** *(04) 3934 5920* **Rooms** *15* **Map** *2 E3*

The rooms in this popular mini-hotel are well equipped, clean, and also have cable TV and en suite bathrooms. The staff are amiable and helpful, and rates are very reasonable for the level of comfort provided. The management clearly appreciates kitsch art, and paintings on ceramics hang on the bathroom walls, giving the hotel a quirky charm.

OLD QUARTER Hong Ngoc Hotel I $$

39 Hang Bac St **Tel** *(04) 3926 0322* **Fax** *(04) 3926 1600* **Rooms** *25* **Map** *2 E3*

This little hotel has more frills, airs, and graces than most other budget lodgings, as is evident from the "imperial-style" beds and the mother-of-pearl chairs. The entire establishment is non-smoking. The small restaurant serves tasty Vietnamese, Chinese, and international food, also unusual by local budget hotel standards.

OLD QUARTER Sunshine 1 Hotel
42 Ma May St **Tel** *(04) 3926 1559* **Fax** *(04) 3926 1558* **Rooms** *12* — **Map** *2 E2*

Among the better of Hanoi's Old Quarter budget lodgings, Sunshine Hotel features ordinary but fairly spacious and comfortable rooms; all bathrooms have bathtubs. Distinguished by an Italian restaurant, as well as a tour agency that can arrange travel anywhere in Vietnam. Free Internet access, and friendly staff. **www.hanoisunshinehotel.com**

OLD QUARTER Win Hotel
34 Hang Hanh St **Tel** *(04) 3828 7371* **Fax** *(04) 3824 7448* **Rooms** *10* — **Map** *2 E3*

A very pleasant and reasonable mini-hotel, just a 5-minute stroll from the northern shore of Hoan Kiem Lake. The rooms are all en suite and equipped with amenities such as minibar, cable TV, IDD phone, and hair dryer. If visiting Hanoi in the cold winter months, the heating facilities here are a very definite advantage.

OLD QUARTER Lucky I Hotel
12 Hang Trong St **Tel** *(04) 3825 1029* **Fax** *(04) 3825 1731* **Rooms** *50* — **Map** *2 E3*

Not quite the boutique hotel it purports to be, Lucky I Hotel is still a surprisingly charming and well-decorated place. Rooms have all standard amenities, service is good, the free breakfast is tasty, and if the hotel is full guests can pray that Lucky II at nearby 46 Hang Hom Street lives up to its name and has room for them. **www.luckyhotel.com.vn**

OLD QUARTER Queen Travel Hotel
65 Hang Bac St **Tel** *(04) 3826 0860* **Fax** *(04) 3826 0300* **Rooms** *10* — **Map** *2 E3*

Rather upmarket for an Old Quarter budget hotel, the slightly higher prices at this hotel are good value for money. Features aesthetic antique decorations and extremely comfortable rooms, with the option of a Jacuzzi for an extra US$5. Also has a carp-filled pond and a rooftop garden with fine views of the old city. **www.azqueentravel.com**

WEST OF HOAN KIEM LAKE Spring Hotel
38 Pho Au Trieu St **Tel** *(04) 3826 8500* **Fax** *(04) 3826 0038* **Rooms** *16* — **Map** *2 D3*

A budget hotel with a great deal of style and a warm, homely atmosphere. Fine views of St. Joseph's Cathedral, and easy access to the trendy shops and restaurants around Nha Tho Street and the Old Quarter. Facilities may be limited, but rooms are spotlessly clean, well furnished, and, best of all, have balconies. Helpful, English-speaking staff.

WEST OF HOAN KIEM LAKE Thu Giang
5A Tam Thuong St **Tel** *(04) 3828 5734* **Rooms** *7* — **Map** *2 D3*

One of the first budget hotels to open in Hanoi, this remarkably versatile hotel has rooms ranging from US$3 to US$16, some with air-conditioning and some with a fan. It offers Internet access, DVD rental, airport pick-up by arrangement, and well-trained staff. Second location at 35A Hang Dieu Street.

WEST OF HOAN KIEM LAKE Church Hotel
9 Nha Tho St **Tel** *(04) 3928 8118* **Fax** *(04) 3828 5793* **Rooms** *20* — **Map** *2 E3*

Aimed chiefly at Western visitors, Church Hotel is small, simple, clean, friendly, and aesthetically decorated. The location, close to Hanoi Cathedral, a stone's throw from the lake, and just a short stroll from the Old Quarter, is superb. Surrounded by some of the best boutiques, restaurants, and art shops in town.

WEST OF HOAN KIEM LAKE Dragon Hotel
48 Xuan Dieu St **Tel** *(04) 3829 2954* **Fax** *(04) 3829 4745* **Rooms** *30*

Overlooking the tranquil lake, the Dragon, with its over-the-top facade and decor, is anything but quiet-looking. A friendly place, it offers ornate rooms, as well as apartments and suites for longer stays. Features fishponds, a pleasant patio, and an open-air restaurant serving Vietnamese and international cuisine. **www.hoteldragon.vn**

WEST OF HOAN KIEM LAKE Sheraton Hanoi
K5 Nghi Tam, 11 Xuan Dieu Rd **Tel** *(04) 3719 9000* **Fax** *(04) 3719 9001* **Rooms** *299*

A 15-minute drive from downtown Hanoi, the Sheraton stands in splendid isolation on a small peninsula projecting into the gleaming Ho Tay. The hotel has everything from panoramic views and the most luxurious rooms imaginable, to a wide range of fine local and international cuisines. Facilities for disabled guests. **www.sheraton.com/hanoi**

WEST OF HOAN KIEM LAKE Hanoi Daewoo
360 Kim Ma St **Tel** *(04) 3831 5000* **Fax** *(04) 3831 5010* **Rooms** *411* — **Map** *1 A3*

The 15-story, marble-laden Daewoo has joined Hanoi's upper-end hotels. Steeped in opulence, it has every convenience and luxury, including an impressive collection of Vietnamese art hanging on the walls, and the largest swimming pool in the city. Superb Italian, French, Chinese, and Japanese cuisine. **www.hanoi-daewoohotel.com**

WEST OF HOAN KIEM LAKE Hanoi Horison
40 Cat Linh St **Tel** *(04) 3733 0808* **Fax** *(04) 3733 0888* **Rooms** *250* — **Map** *1 A3*

A luxurious hotel, Hanoi Horison is very convenient for visiting the Temple of Literature *(see pp166–7)* and several of Hanoi's best museums. Top quality facilities, including high-speed Internet access in all rooms, doctor on call, three restaurants serving Vietnamese, French, and Chinese fare, as well as a lobby bar and casino. **www.swiss-belhotel.com**

WEST OF HOAN KIEM LAKE Nikko Hanoi
84 Tran Nhan Tong St **Tel** *(04) 3822 3535* **Fax** *(04) 3822 3555* **Rooms** *260*

Exclusive and stylish, the Japanese-owned Nikko Hanoi is aimed primarily at business customers and, accordingly, has one of the best-equipped business centers in town. It also offers luxurious rooms with all amenities, state-of-the-art spa, and sauna. The Japanese restaurant is perhaps the best in Hanoi.

Key to Price Guide *see p232* **Key to Symbols** *see back cover flap*

WEST OF HOAN KIEM LAKE Sofitel Plaza $$$$$

1 Thanh Nien St **Tel** *(04) 3823 8888* **Fax** *(04) 3829 4283* **Rooms** *317* **Map** *1 B1*

This high-rise palace overlooking Ho Tay offers all the luxuries and services synonymous with the Sofitel brand. All rooms have panoramic views through floor-to-ceiling windows, and are equipped with all the amenities you'd expect. Excellent restaurant, three stylish bars, and a nightclub. **www.sofitel.com**

NORTHERN VIETNAM

BA BE NATIONAL PARK Ba Be National Park Guesthouse $

National Park Headquarters **Tel** *(0281) 389 4126* **Fax** *(0281) 389 4026* **Rooms** *60*

A large and pleasant building surrounded by forested karst hills, this is a pleasant place to wake up in, especially as breakfast is served on the large, open, first-floor veranda, with good views of the park. There is a restaurant, but it is often closed, though food can be ordered in advance. Rooms are clean and quiet.

BAC HA Sao Mai Hotel $$

Ban Pho Rd **Tel** *(020) 388 0288* **Fax** *(020) 388 0288* **Rooms** *40*

The best hotel in Bac Ha, and with the best restaurant, this establishment has three wings – two wooden buildings and an older concrete one. The rooms in the wooden buildings are better value and more attractive. The large restaurant is open all day and attracts many walk-in guests. Food is Vietnamese and Western.

CAO BANG Huong Thom $

91 Kim Dong St **Tel** *(026) 385 5888* **Fax** *(026) 385 6228* **Rooms** *11*

A clean, perfectly adequate, but uninspiring hotel, which is still about the best value this dusty northern town has to offer. Rooms at the back overlook the Bang Giang River and Cao Bang's giant war memorial. In winter, the air-conditioners double as heaters, which is an advantage as Cao Bang is one of the coldest places in Vietnam.

CAT BA ISLAND Noble House $$

1/4 St, Cat Ba Town **Tel** *(031) 388 8363* **Fax** *(031) 388 8570* **Rooms** *5*

Centrally located and just a short walk from the pier, this is one of the nicer places to stay in Cat Ba Town. The rooms are clean, large, and well equipped, and offer fine views south across the harbor. The restaurant is quite good and serves reasonably priced Vietnamese and international food.

CAT BA ISLAND Holiday View $$$

1/4 St, Cat Ba Town **Tel** *(031) 388 7200* **Fax** *(031) 388 7208* **Rooms** *120*

A high-rise development on the eastern side of the marina overlooking the harbor, Holiday View is clean, efficient, and probably about the best Cat Ba has to offer in terms of service, if not charm. The restaurant serves Vietnamese and Western dishes, and specializes in fresh seafood. **www.holidayviewhotel-catba.com**

DIEN BIEN PHU Khach San Cong Ty Bia $

No. 17 Ward 28 St **Tel** *(023) 382 4635* **Fax** *(023) 382 5576* **Rooms** *10*

Also known as the Beer Hotel as it stands next to a small brewery, this hotel is Dien Bien Phu's best known budget establishment. The rooms are clean though facilities are limited to TV and a hot shower. Breakfast is provided but other meals will have to be eaten at one of the restaurants in town.

HAIPHONG Harbour View $$$$$

4 Tran Phu St **Tel** *(031) 382 7827* **Fax** *(031) 382 7828* **Rooms** *122*

An elegant and stylish hotel, with an atmospheric colonial feel, Harbour View is the best accommodation in Haiphong, and excellent value for money. Although there is no real view of the harbor, the rooms are plush and spotlessly clean, the service impeccable, and the cuisine excellent. **www.harbourviewvietnam.com**

HALONG CITY Heritage Halong $$

88 Halong St, Bai Chay **Tel** *(033) 384 6888* **Fax** *(033) 384 6999* **Rooms** *101*

One of the most upscale hotels in the city, Heritage Halong offers subtle and tastefully furnished rooms, all of which come equipped with every facility. Some rooms have splendid views over the bay. The hotel tour agency can arrange boat tours, a hotel doctor is on call, and the property also has a discotheque. **www.heritagehalonghotel.com**

HALONG CITY Novotel Ha Long Bay $$$$

Halong Rd, Bai Chay **Tel** *(033) 384 8108* **Fax** *(033) 369 6808* **Rooms** *214*

This four-star hotel is close to all the major local attractions. It offers lavish, modern interiors and bountiful amenities such as Wi-Fi, 24-hour security, and disability-friendly facilities. The outdoor pool with swim-up bar overlooks the bay. All rooms have panoramic bay windows and splendid views. **www.novotelhalongbay.com**

HALONG CITY Saigon Halong Hotel $$$$

168 Halong Rd, Bai Chay **Tel** *(033) 384 5845* **Fax** *(033) 384 5849* **Rooms** *228*

With six separate categories of rooms and suites, this stylish hotel caters to business travelers as well as tourists. It has three restaurants and two bars serving Vietnamese, Chinese, and international cuisine. The Panorama Restaurant claims to be the highest in Halong City, with majestic views across the bay. **www.saigonhalonghotel.com**

HALONG CITY Huong Hai Junk

⊞ ▤ Ⓦ　$$$$$

1 Vuon Dao St, Bai Chay **Tel** *(033) 384 5042* **Fax** *(033) 384 6263* **Rooms** *61*

Spread over nine junks, the Huong Hai offers a luxurious way to experience Halong Bay *(see pp182–4)*. The boats leave the city daily around noon and head off into the bay, where they anchor amid limestone karsts as the sun sets. Dine on board with seafood specialties. Rooms are well appointed, with great views. **www.halongdiscovery.com**

MAI CHAU VALLEY Mai Chau Guesthouse

▤　　$

Mai Chau Village **Tel** *(018) 385 1812* **Rooms** *4*

A simple wooden house on the high street, this guesthouse offers minimal facilities, but the White Thai family who runs the place is friendly. Food can be cooked by arrangement and eaten alone or with the owners. Mosquito nets and bedrolls are provided for sleeping on the floor. Lights usually go out early, but the local white liquor is a good soporific.

NINH BINH Ngoc Anh Hotel

▤ ▤　$

30 Luong Van Tuy St **Tel** *(030) 388 3768* **Fax** *(030) 388 3761* **Rooms** *10*

Ngoc Anh offers simple but reliably clean and comfortable accommodation with all the basics such as hot water, air-conditioning, a fridge, and cable TV. Some rooms have balconies, and multiple-occupancy rooms are also available. Little English is spoken here but the hotel staff are friendly and as helpful as possible.

NINH BINH Viet Hung Hotel

▤ ⊞ ▤ Ⓦ　$

150 Tran Hung Dao St **Tel** *(030) 387 2002* **Fax** *(030) 388 0247* **Rooms** *15*

Well located in the commercial heart of Ninh Binh and close to the market, this is a pleasant family establishment where, although little English is spoken, the staff are helpful. The restaurant serves good and cheap Vietnamese food and Western breakfasts. The owner can arrange trips to the various attractions out of town.

SAPA Son Ha Guesthouse

▤ ⊞ Ⓦ　$

25 Fansipan Rd **Tel** *(020) 387 1273* **Rooms** *15*

Attractive budget accommodation, with large, comfortably furnished rooms upstairs, which afford good views across the valley towards Mount Fansipan *(see p196)*. A bonus is that the rooms have fireplaces, which makes them especially cozy in the cold winter months. The restaurant downstairs serves Vietnamese and Western food.

SAPA Sapa Goldsea

▤ ⊞ ▤ Ⓦ　$$

58 Fansipan Rd **Tel** *(020) 387 1869* **Fax** *(020) 387 2185* **Rooms** *34*

Looking over to the Muong Hoa Valley, Sapa Goldsea is a cozy and comfortable establishment with very helpful English-speaking staff. The cable TV works – which is not always the case in town – and rooms have good heaters, a real boon in winter. Ethnic minority guides available for tours. **www.sapagoldsea-hotel.com.vn**

SAPA Topas Ecolodge

⊞ Ⓦ　$$$$$

24 Muong Hoa, Cau May **Tel** *(020) 387 2404* **Fax** *(020) 387 2405* **Rooms** *25*

On a hill just out of Sapa, this lovely resort consists of 25 granite bungalows, with wonderful views across the valley and of the river below. The rooms are very well appointed, and guests can relax on their own private veranda to enjoy the vista. A restaurant serves good Vietnamese and Western food in a stilt house. **www.topas-eco-lodge.com**

SAPA Victoria Sapa

⊞ ⊞ ▤ Ⓦ ⊞　$$$$$

Hoang Dieu St **Tel** *(020) 387 1522* **Fax** *(020) 387 1539* **Rooms** *77*

Modeled on a Swiss chalet, Victoria Sapa is easily the area's most luxurious hotel. Even getting there can be a royal experience, as the exclusive Victoria Express private train whisks guests from Hanoi in a manner reminiscent of the Orient Express. Return rail fares start at US$90. Food at the restaurant is superb. **www.victoriahotels-asia.com**

SON LA Trade Union Hotel

▤ ⊞ ▤ Ⓦ　$

No. 4, 26/8 St **Tel** *(022) 385 2804* **Fax** *(022) 385 5312* **Rooms** *100*

Despite its rather dreary name, this old-fashioned, state-run establishment is probably the best place to stay in Son La. It features large, clean rooms, an excellent restaurant serving Vietnamese cuisine – no international dishes – and bathrooms with plenty of hot water. The staff in traditional White Thai garb add to the pleasant atmosphere.

ANGKOR

SIEM REAP Babel Guesthouse

▤ ⊞ ▤ ⊞　$

Wat Bo Rd **Tel** *(063) 965 474* **Rooms** *23*

This guesthouse is good value for money with spotless white rooms, large bathrooms, and full-size baths. There are pleasant spots in the tropical gardens to relax in and the place, although basic, is welcoming. The staff are friendly and can speak both English and French.

SIEM REAP Earthwalkers

⊞ ⊞ ▤ ⊞　$

Sala Kanseng Village, Sangkat No. 2 **Tel** *(012) 967 901* **Rooms** *20*

One of the original backpacker haunts, Earthwalkers now represents amazing value with a block of rooms overlooking its swimming pool. It also has a dormitory. The food is fresh and varied and the crowd friendly. Staff can help with trips to the temples of Angkor. **www.earthwalkers.no**

Key to Price Guide *see p232* **Key to Symbols** *see back cover flap*

SIEM REAP Ivy Guesthouse

West off Pokambor Ave, near the river **Tel** *(012) 800 860* **Rooms** *17*

An intimate travelers' guesthouse with pretty gardens, hammocks, and pleasant rooms, some with air-conditioning, Ivy Guesthouse offers great value for money and is only a 5-minute walk from the center of town. The food here is delicious and the staff are very hospitable.

SIEM REAP Rosy's Guesthouse

74, Phum Slor Kram **Tel** *(063) 965 059* **Rooms** *15*

This attractive old villa is run by a Western couple and offers great value, with Wi-Fi, TVs, and DVD players in all rooms (air-conditioning is optional). Rosy's Guesthouse has plenty of hammocks to relax in in the lounging area. The staff are friendly and always ready to help patrons. **www.rosyguesthouse.com**

SIEM REAP Dead Fish Tower Inn

Sivatha Blvd at Dead Fish Plaza **Tel** *(016) 330 821* **Rooms** *35*

This strangely named inn is a well established place with clean, comfortable rooms. Much of its charm comes from its quirkiness: there is a crocodile pool, and guests receive a free welcome head massage. The lively restaurant, offering Thai and Khmer dishes, hosts traditional Cambodian dance shows. **www.deadfishtower.com**

SIEM REAP Eight Rooms

138/139 Streoung Thmey Village, Svydangkum Commune **Tel** *(063) 969 788* **Rooms** *8*

A gay-friendly, stylish flashpacker (affluent backpacker) option, Eight Rooms offers clean rooms, a relaxing roof terrace, and free pick-up facility from the airport. Wi-Fi is available in the lobby and garden. The staff are friendly and helpful. **www.ei8htrooms.com**

SIEM REAP Mysteres d'Angkor

235 Phum Slorkram **Tel** *(063) 963 639* **Rooms** *23*

Situated in a traditional, wooden Khmer house, Mysteres d'Angkor is a tranquil French-run boutique hotel, which has tastefully decorated rooms and a lovely pool surrounded by decking and lush gardens. The hotel has a friendly bar and restaurant, bicycles for rent, and provides a laundry service. **www.mysteres-angkor.com**

SIEM REAP Victoria Angkor Resort and Spa

Central Park, PO Box 93145 **Tel** *(063) 760 428* **Rooms** *130*

One of the best-loved hotels in Siem Reap, Victoria Angkor Resort and Spa is a beautiful old Colonial villa, favoring lavish Colonial interiors, with fine cuisine, old-world service, and swimming pool. A short distance from the temples of Angkor, it looks out on to the Royal Park. **www.victoriahotels.asia**

SIEM REAP Amansara

262 Krom 8, Phum Beong Don Pa **Tel** *(063) 760 333* **Fax** *(063) 760 335* **Rooms** *12*

This 1960s designed hotel is easily the most exclusive accommodation in the city. The Amansara has a small collection of rooms, each of which has its own hot tub and pool. An exquisite hotel, it is favored by A-list celebrities seeking low-key privacy. **www.amanresorts.com**

SIEM REAP Apsara Angkor

Route 6, Airport Rd **Tel** *(063) 964 999* **Fax** *(063) 964 567* **Rooms** *168*

Just about everything is on offer at the Apsara Angkor. The rooms feature wooden floors and are exquisitely decorated with colorful Khmer silks. Facilities include poolside Internet access, a 24-hour on-call doctor, baby-sitting services, special facilities for the disabled, and free airport pick-up, among others. **www.apsaraangkor.com**

SIEM REAP FCC Angkor

Pokambor Ave **Tel** *(063) 760 280* **Fax** *(063) 760 281* **Rooms** *31*

A byword for style in Cambodia, the FCC fuses contemporary cool with elegant Indochinese decor, open-plan restaurants, and stylish bars. This is all coupled with an inviting pool and minimalist, fresh rooms. The FCC also enjoys a lovely riverfront location. **www.fcccambodia.com**

SIEM REAP Hotel De La Paix

Sivatha Blvd **Tel** *(063) 966 000* **Fax** *(063) 966 001* **Rooms** *107*

Regarded as a chic space, this Art Deco hotel has a centerpiece courtyard crowned by a banyan tree, which is surrounded by a bar and fashionably sparse rooms finished in dark wood. The staff are courteous and the spa superb. The hotel also has a great New York deli that serves delicious snacks. **www.hoteldelapaixangkor.com**

SIEM REAP La Résidence d'Angkor

River Rd **Tel** *(063) 963 390* **Rooms** *62*

Set among lush manicured gardens, this hotel has stylish wood and laterite rooms, each with their own hot bath or Jacuzzi along with Wi-Fi. The hotel's spa is excellent. Staff can arrange tours to the temples, and bicycles are also available for rent. **www.residencedangkor.com**

SIEM REAP Raffles Grand Hotel d'Angkor

1 Charles de Gaulle St, Khum Svay Dang Kum **Tel** *(063) 963 888* **Rooms** *120*

The epitome of Colonial style and contemporary service, the Raffles Grand Hotel d'Angkor has hosted a number of illustrious guests including Charles De Gaulle, Charlie Chaplin, and Bill Clinton. The hotel also has several restaurants and an outstanding spa. **www.raffles.com**

WHERE TO EAT

The Vietnamese are passionate about eating, which means that fresh ingredients and experienced cooks are bountiful. Whether you are looking for a quick bite or a full meal, you will find an amazing variety of eating venues throughout the country, from pushcarts, roadside stalls, and sidewalk cafés to pizzerias and gourmet restaurants. Washing down tasty treats is easy as well, with hot tea or cold beer never too far away. The best news is that the prices are extremely reasonable, as the country's eclectic and innovative culinary repertoire offers a range of delicious options to suit every budget. Increasingly, this also includes Western-style fast food, and there are plenty of Italian, American, and Indian restaurants now located in big cities and towns. The most reliable places to find well prepared international food are high-end restaurants catering to foreign tourists and expats, while good Vietnamese fare is easily available everywhere.

Platters of delicacies

Terrace overlooking the Hoan Kiem Lake at Thuy Ta café (see p259), Hanoi

RESTAURANTS

Eateries with trained waiters, printed menus, and starched napkins are found mainly in the major cities, as well as in big hotels and resorts.

Sit-down restaurants offering Vietnamese food often specialize in a particular type of dish. One of the most common is *bun thit nuong*, where grilled, marinated meat (most commonly beef or pork) is served on a bed of rice noodles, fresh herbs, and pickled vegetables, with a sweet and spicy fish-sauce broth. *Banh xeo* is a flavorful rice or cornflour pancake stuffed with pork, seafood, and beansprouts, and served with a sweet and sour fish-sauce broth. *Lau* is a fragrant broth that is placed on a stove in the center of the table. It is eaten communally, and diners can add a selection of vegetables, herbs, noodles, and meat as desired.

Chinese restaurants are also common, while Vietnam's surfeit of cafés ensures that freshly baked baguettes, hot coffees, and fruit juices are never far away. American-style diners, pizzerias, and fast-food chains such as KFC have emerged in Hanoi, Ho Chi Minh City, and major tourist destinations, and some major hotels and restaurants offer European *haute cuisine*.

COM AND PHO

A restaurant that serves an ample portion of rice along with meat and vegetables is called a *quan com*. *Com* is the Vietnamese word for rice. It is usually a humble affair, often seating as few as half a dozen people. The food is displayed in a glass case at the front, and one need only point to what appeals. Meats, either grilled, braised, or stewed, and fish in some kind of sauce are common, as are braised bamboo shoots, grilled eggplant, fried greens, and tofu preparations.

Pho (see p248), Vietnam's national noodle soup dish, often features in small, family-run eateries. The unmistakable star anise aroma of *pho* will announce it even if a sign does not. *Pho* is typically served with beef or chicken. Fresh herbs and a variety of condiments are added according to taste.

STREET FOOD

Vietnam has a long and rich tradition of street food. Vendors in all cities and towns patrol the streets with baskets of delicious snack foods such as tamarind pods,

Freshly prepared food being sampled at an outdoor eatery, Hue

Patrons at Highlands Coffee, a popular coffee chain

pastries, baguette sandwiches, sticky rice, or fresh fruits. Some cooks carry savory or sweet treats wrapped in banana leaves, which are then steamed or roasted. Pushcarts can carry entire kitchens, typically offering *pho*, fried noodles, tofu preparations, and *chao*, a rice porridge also known as congee. The best part is that the food is cooked in front of your eyes. Some vendors carry their food in a yoke slung across their shoulder. They may offer anything from dry snack foods to fresh fruits and vegetables, while some even carry a small stove with which to prepare a hot meal on the spot.

BEER GARDENS AND BIA HOI

Especially plentiful in the south, where the weather never turns cold, beer gardens are open-air restaurants that can vary in size from a few dozen tables to seemingly acres. They are always promoting one beer or another, and the brand can change every week. The staple fare offered here is grilled meat, served with piles of greens. Rice wrapper *(see p95)* is provided, and used to roll the food into tasty bundles, which are then dipped in piquant dipping sauces.

Bia hoi, literally fresh beer, is a specialty of Hanoi. Often likened to draught beer, though a more accurate term might be microbrew or even homebrew, this refreshing drink is free of preservatives and costs only pennies per glass. Dedicated *bia hoi* bars abound and are usually hole-in-the-wall pubs, frequented mostly by local men. Foreign visitors can also join the crowd, and these joints can be a way to experience the country's bar culture.

VEGETARIAN OPTIONS

There are very few exclusively vegetarian restaurants in the country, but those wishing to avoid red meat will find it easy to do so. A wide selection of fish, poultry, and vegetables is always available wherever you go. However, if you are a vegan or a very strict vegetarian, be aware that *nuoc mam*, the much-beloved fermented fish sauce, finds its way into most meals. While most restaurateurs are aware of vegetarian practice, and quite willing to make accommodations, it is, nevertheless, necessary for vegetarians to be vocal and specific about their dietary needs and requirements.

Bottle of Saigon Beer

PRICES

Food will probably be the least expensive item on your budget. Even a full meal in a hotel can cost less than US$15 per head, though imported alcohol can easily quadruple the price. Taxes on wine can be ruinous, but imported spirits are more manageable, and beer imported from the Southeast Asia region is quite reasonable. Budget travelers eschewing alcohol and dining largely in smaller restaurants or on street food can eat fairly lavishly for as little as US$6 a day.

EATING CUSTOMS

Unlike at the Western table, meals in Vietnam are not served in a succession of courses. Dishes are brought to the table as they are ready. The usual practice is to order one different dish per person, plus one for the table. Diners then proceed to sample each others' dishes liberally, relishing the sharing as much as the food. Table manners *(see p281)* are simple to follow. Just enjoy yourself and let everybody know that you are. Enthusiastic dining and loud conversations are the norm.

TIPPING

While tipping has not always been customary in Vietnam, it has become common in better restaurants and backpacker areas with the advent of modern tourism. If service is good, a 10 percent tip is appreciated. Do not tip if service is poor. In upscale hotels and restaurants, a 5 percent charge is usually levied. However, you may wish to offer a small tip in addition to that small fee.

Chic exterior of a French-style café in Ho Chi Minh City

Flavors of Vietnam

Over the course of history Vietnam has absorbed many culinary influences but has still managed to preserve its own distinct cuisine. The long period of Chinese domination left its mark on Vietnamese cooking, not least in the use of chopsticks, soy sauce, and bean curd. Western tastes were also imported during French colonial rule, notably coffee, bread, and dairy products. In the south, Indian, Khmer, and Thai influences are apparent in a cuisine that features coconut and aromatic curries.

Bunches of mint, basil, and coriander

Woman preparing food at a market stall in Hoi An

Vietnamese cuisine relies on herbs and spices – especially coriander, mint, ginger, lemon grass, and spring onions – and fish sauce. Rice *(see p95)*, however, is Vietnam's staple. Its significance is even reflected in the language; for example, the most common greeting *(Ban an com chua?)* literally translates as "Have you eaten rice yet?" There is a vast vocabulary referring to various types of rice, the individual stages of the process of planting, growing and harvesting, as well as a plethora of expressions for meals prepared from rice. It accompanies every meal: for everyday consumption the Vietnamese use *gao te* (ordinary, non-sticky rice), while special occasions such as anniversaries, festivals, and votive offerings call for *gao nep* (glutinous sticky rice). Ground rice is the basis of a wide range of products including noodles, cakes, and

THE CUISINE

The fertile deltas of the Red River in the north and the Mekong River in the south guarantee Vietnam's supply of rice. The country's long coastline, rivers, ponds, and lakes provide a plentiful stock of fish and seafood, while the tropical climate means that fruit and vegetables grow in abundance.

Pomelo

Durian

Bananas

Rambutans

Limes

Mangosteens

A selection of tropical fruit found throughout southeast Asia

LOCAL DISHES AND SPECIALTIES

There are three main regions in Vietnamese cuisine. The north with its cooler climate has a simple cooking style. Exotic meats, including dog, are delicacies, and snake wine is widely available. Central Vietnam boasts a rich vegetarian tradition as well as the sophisticated imperial cuisine of the former royal capital Hue.

Garnish for *pho*

The southern regions benefit from richer tropical produce.

Pho, a traditional noodle soup, captures the essence of Vietnamese cooking. This humble dish originated in the north but has become the nation's favorite dish. With slices of raw beef that cook in a bowl of hot broth, *pho* is a nutritious meal in itself. The quality of the soup can vary; connoisseurs prefer to come late to *pho* stalls to benefit from a stronger broth.

Pho *This classic dish combines white noodles, slices of beef, and spring onions in a rich broth.*

Fish drying in the sun for use in *nuoc mam*, Nha Trang

and snacks. Stalls that are packed with people sitting around on plastic seats are likely to serve the tastiest dishes. *Pho* (noodle soup), *banh xeo* (pancake), and filled baguettes are favorite snacks.

A typical sight on the streets of Vietnam is a woman carrying a long pole with a basket on each side. These are filled not only with ingredients, such as noodles, herbs, meat, and vegetables, but also with bowls, chopsticks, and a charcoal stove, making them portable kitchens that can produce remarkable feasts.

rice paper, while distilled rice is used to make rice wine and liquors.

Vietnam's long Buddhist tradition has been responsible for the popularity of a vegetarian cuisine perfected over centuries. Especially renowned is the vegetarian cooking of Hue, which is the country's traditional center of Buddhism. Here, Vietnamese women are skilled in offering sumptuous feasts that include vegetarian versions of famous dishes with meat replaced by beancurd or mushrooms.

Among the more unusual aspects of Vietnamese cuisine is the consumption of exotic meats such as frogs, snakes, sparrows, snails, and turtles. Some restaurants even serve wild species, such as porcupine, despite these being officially banned.

STREET FOOD

Com binh dan (popular food) or *com bui* (dusty food) refers to street food. Almost everywhere you go in Vietnam, you will be only a few paces away from a stall serving mouth-watering meals

Street vendor selling baguettes in Ho Chi Minh City

Cahn Chua Ca *A hot and sour soup usually made with pineapple, catfish, and plenty of chili.*

Banh Xeo *A pork and prawn pancake often wrapped in a lettuce leaf and served with a tangy lime and chili dip.*

Cha Ca *Originating from Hanoi, this dish features fried fish, noodles, dill, peanuts, and* nuoc cham.

Choosing a Restaurant

The restaurants in this guide have been selected, as far as possible, for their excellent food, ambience, and location. However, in the remote parts of Vietnam, few restaurants can be recommended using this criteria. In such cases, convenient places that offer at least good value have been suggested. The restaurants are all listed by region.

PRICE CATEGORIES
The following price ranges are the equivalent of a meal for two made up of a range of dishes, including service tax but no alcohol.

$ Under $5
$$ $5–$10
$$$ $10–$20
$$$$ $20–$30
$$$$$ Over $30

HO CHI MINH CITY

CHOLON Café Central An Dong   📋 V $$$$
Windsor Plaza Hotel, 18 An Duong Voung St **Tel** *(08) 3833 6688*   **Map** *4 F4*

Located in the Windsor Plaza Hotel *(see p232)*, this café-cum-bar is open from 6am until midnight. The generic coffee-shop decor is forgiven when one is presented with the superb international buffet featuring more than 150 dishes. The price goes down on weekends, and the set lunch is a mere US$10.

DISTRICT 1 Bun Cha Hanoi   📋 🖼 $
26/1 Le Thanh Ton St **Tel** *(08) 3827 5843*   **Map** *2 F3*

A unique Hanoi-style barbecue dish, *bun cha* consists of grilled pork served along with a dish of vegetables, typically lettuce, bean sprouts, and cucumber, as well as a portion of rice vermicelli. A typical establishment of its sort, this very popular but unadorned eatery is furnished with tiny tables and chairs that fill up as soon as they are vacated.

DISTRICT 1 Bo Tung Xeo   📋 V $$
31 Ly Tu Trong St **Tel** *(08) 3825 1330*   **Map** *2 E3*

Set in a beer garden-like setting, this is one of the most enduring and festive eateries in town. It gets its name from the house specialty, *bo tung xeo* – barbecued beef dish. A brazier is brought to the table and patrons cook their own beef on it, a very enjoyable ritual. The Hanoi-style fried fish and fresh dill preparation, *cha ca (see p249)* is also served.

DISTRICT 1 Mi Keo Soi Trung Hoa   📋 $$
86 Bis Le Thanh Ton St **Tel** *(08) 3827 4407* **Fax** *(08) 3827 4408*   **Map** *2 E4*

A popular place with both expatriates and locals for lunch and dinner, the delicious noodles at Mi Keo Soi Trung Hoa are freshly made by hand in full view of diners, and served with grilled pork and a bowl of broth. Side dishes include spring rolls, dumplings, and a variety of dim sum. The simple decor does not distract from the food.

DISTRICT 1 Pho 24   📋 📋 V $$
5 Nguyen Thiep St **Tel** *(08) 3822 6278* **Fax** *(08) 3821 7244*   **Map** *2 F4*

Vietnam's quintessential street food has been taken indoors, cleaned up, and air-conditioned at Pho 24. The restaurant claims to earn its name from "24 ingredients and 24 hours of preparing the choicest beef" to make the nourishing *pho* soup. Chicken *pho* is also available.

DISTRICT 1 Sozo   📋 V $$
176 Bui Vien St **Tel** *(095) 870 6580*   **Map** *2 D5*

A purveyor of American-style pastries, bagels, chocolate-chip cookies, cinnamon rolls, and coffee, Sozo doubles as a training facility for local street children. To help them out of poverty and helplessness, children and young people are taught to bake, balance the books, and conduct all the tasks necessary to run a business. Free Wi-Fi service.

DISTRICT 1 Asian Kitchen   📋 🖼 V $$$
185/22 Pham Ngu Lao St **Tel** *(08) 3836 7397*   **Map** *2 D5*

Down a narrow alley off the main street, Asian Kitchen is a well priced little restaurant, with a pleasant beach-style decor. It specializes in a wide range of Vietnamese dishes. Pork cooked in a clay pot is the signature dish, and an array of vegetarian options are also available. A great selection of American hit songs of the 1950s and '60s to listen to.

DISTRICT 1 Black Cat   📋 📋 V $$$
13 Phan Van Dat St **Tel** *(08) 3829 2055*   **Map** *2 F4*

Operated by an American expat and his Vietnamese wife, Black Cat serves the best burgers in town, along with a Tex-Mex menu that never disappoints. The sorbets and smoothies, made from local fruits, are legendary. The walls are papered with images of Vietnamese cities and the full bar serves the tallest gin and tonic anywhere in town.

DISTRICT 1 Bourbon Street   📋 📋 $$$
123 Le Loi St **Tel** *(08) 3914 2183* **Fax** *(08) 3914 2184*   **Map** *2 E4*

A bit of New Orleans in downtown Ho Chi Minh City, the sparse decor belies the quality of food in this homage to the cuisine of the Mississippi Delta. Cajun and Tex-Mex favorites dominate the menu, including jambalaya, gumbo, baby back ribs, steaks, fajitas, buffalo wings, and an all-you-can eat salad bar. Good selection of imported beers.

Key to Symbols *see back cover flap*

DISTRICT 1 Cool Saigon

30 Dong Khoi St **Tel** *(08) 3829 1364* **Fax** *(08) 3824 7708* **Map** *2 F4*

Serving classic Vietnamese dishes, the interestingly decorated Cool Saigon lives up to its name. The bottom level represents a Vietnamese village, complete with an in-house creek and waterwheel, while the second floor is a more formal dining room. Dishes include sumptuous spring rolls, grilled meats, and a variety of noodle dishes.

DISTRICT 1 Original Bodhi Tree

175/4 Pham Ngu Lao St **Tel** *(08) 3837 1910* **Fax** *(08) 3837 1238* **Map** *2 D5*

Down a little side street known as "Pagoda Alley," the Original Bodhi Tree is one of the best-known vegetarian restaurants in the city, and is frequented by a clientele of foreigners. The Vietnamese menu is enlivened with a bit of Italian and Mexican. The paintings on the walls are for sale, and the proceeds go to benefit poor children.

DISTRICT 1 Red Dot

15/17 Phan Van Dat **Tel** *(08) 3822 6178* **Map** *2 F4*

One of the few air-conditioned restaurants in the area, the decor of Red Dot *(see p270)* recalls an Italian *piazza*, complete with a playing fountain. Several restaurants claim Mexican flavor, but this is one of the rare few with any authority and authenticity. Great tortillas, enchiladas, and of course, burritos. The fish tacos are especially good.

DISTRICT 1 Tan Hai Van

162 Nguyen Trai St **Tel** *(08) 3839 9617* **Map** *2 D5*

This happening Chinese restaurant is a magnet for the hip young people of Ho Chi Minh City who flock here in great numbers to enjoy the matchless dim sum. The more exotic options on the menu include crunchy, fried duck tongues and shark fin soup. The outside tables are buzzing when most other places are closed.

DISTRICT 1 Vietnam House

93–95 Dong Khoi St **Tel** *(08) 3829 1623* **Fax** *(08) 3829 8076* **Map** *2 F4*

Vietnam House is the place to go for traditional Vietnamese delicacies in an atmosphere of French-inspired elegance. Spread across three floors, the best tables are on the street level, where visitors can watch the city go by as they tuck into crisp spring rolls. Enjoy a cocktail with great music playing in the background.

DISTRICT 1 Wrap and Roll

62 Hai Ba Trung St **Tel** *(08) 3822 2166* **Map** *2 F3*

At Wrap and Roll diners can create their own meal at their table. All dishes except soups are brought to the table "disassembled." Patrons take the meat, fish, vegetables, and herbs of their choice and wrap them up into rolls of rice paper. Dipping sauces and good wines complete the meal.

DISTRICT 1 Sandals Restaurant

93 Hai Ba Trung St **Tel** *(08) 3827 5198* **Map** *2 F3*

This fine-dining venue is also one of Saigon's most stylish nightspots. Soft earth tones are complemented by a beautifully furnished wood and bamboo interior. Enjoy Asian fusion cuisine on one of three floors, including the street-level bar, a top spot to be seen and for people-watching, and the private dining suite.

DISTRICT 1 Xu Restaurant and Lounge

71–75 Hai Ba Trung St **Tel** *(08) 3824 8468* **Fax** *(08) 3824 8469* **Map** *2 F3*

An ultra-modern space with an attached bar/lounge, Xu features cushy low-lying seats, subtle lighting, and a range of exotic cocktails. The fare is "New Vietnamese," which is classic Vietnamese preparations such as wraps and rolls served with a bit of European or California flair. Service is excellent and the wine list extensive.

DISTRICT 1 Bonsai Cruises

Bach Dang Pier at foot of Nguyen Hue St **Tel** *(090) 880 0775* **Map** *2 F4*

The best and newest of four floating restaurants that take guests on a nightly dinner cruise on the Saigon River. The food is both Western and Vietnamese, served buffet style. There is always seafood in both styles, German sausages with mustard, Vietnamese noodles, as well as a fine wine list. Dancing every night to the live band.

DISTRICT 1 Camargue

16 Cao Ba Quat St **Tel** *(08) 3824 3148* **Fax** *(08) 3823 2828* **Map** *2 F3*

The stylish Camargue is set in a restored French-colonial villa, and the best place to dine here is on its picturesque open-air terrace above the main bar. Oysters, cheese, and wine are flown in daily from Paris, and steaks, roasts, and seafood dominate the menu. All dishes are prepared in classic French style, with the saucier's art much in evidence.

DISTRICT 1 Maxim's

13–17 Dong Khoi St **Tel** *(08) 3829 6676* **Map** *2 F4*

One of the oldest restaurants in town, Maxim's *(see p269)* goes back to the French-colonial era. The elegant formal dining room surrounds a stage on three sides where a string quartet plays most nights. Western classical and cabaret performances also take place occasionally. The food is mainly classic Vietnamese served with flair.

DISTRICT 3 Mai Thai

13 Ton That Thiep St **Tel** *(08) 3821 2920* **Map** *2 F4*

One of the more popular of the several Thai restaurants in town, Mai Thai is richly decorated in colorful Thai fabrics, adding to its cheerful ambience. With one of the best-priced menus to be had in District 3, the tasty set lunch is an especially good bargain. The friendly staff help the place get unusually high marks for service.

DISTRICT 3 Tandoor   🗐📖 🇻   ⑤⑤⑤
103 Vo Van Tan St **Tel** *(08) 3930 4839* **Fax** *(08) 3930 4125*   **Map** *1 C4*

One in a chain of a growing number of Indian restaurants, covering both Ho Chi Minh City and Hanoi. All the usual North Indian suspects are on the menu, including flat breads, kebab meats grilled in a *tandoor* or clay oven, as well as vegetarian specialties. These spicy treats can be washed down with chilled beer.

DISTRICT 3 Texas Barbeque   🗐📠   ⑤⑤⑤⑤
206 Pasteur St **Tel** *(08) 3825 1142* **Fax** *(08) 3823 1468*   **Map** *2 D3*

This restaurant lives up to its name and is popular with expatriates. The ribs, steaks, and brisket combos arrive in huge portions, while side orders such as corn on the cob, french fries, coleslaw, and BBQ beans could also make a meal. Inside, the spare decor is bright and airy, and out on the patio it is downright festive.

DISTRICT 3 Au Lac Do Brazil   📖🎵📑   ⑤⑤⑤⑤⑤
238 Pasteur St **Tel** *(08) 3820 7157* **Fax** *(08) 3820 7682*   **Map** *1 C2*

High ceilings, tilework, and starched white table linen add an atmospheric Brazilian touch to this restaurant specializing in red-meat preparations. The pièce de résistance is *churrasco*, piles of roasted and grilled meats, which are brought to the table on skewers and spits, and carved by staff wielding flashing, sword-like blades.

DISTRICT 10 Anh Thien   🗐   ⑤
251 Dao Duy Tu St **Tel** *(08) 3853 2182*   **Map** *4 E3*

Nothing much to look at from the outside, Anh Thien is a little hideaway which claims to have the juiciest beef steak in the city. Many people seek out this eatery when they crave a juicy steak at a very low price. The meat is cooked in the kitchen, and is then set on a sizzling platter with grilled onions and pats of butter. Simple but delicious.

AROUND HO CHI MINH CITY

LONG HAI Le Belvedere   🏨 🇻   ⑤⑤⑤
Anoasis Beach Resort, Domain Ky Van **Tel** *(064) 386 8227*

Perched on a hilltop overlooking the Anoasis Resort and the beach beyond, most tables of Le Belvedere are on a covered patio that catches the sea breeze. The international menu includes Italian pastas, Greek salad, a selection of filling sandwiches, as well as Vietnamese favorites such as grilled pork and braised vegetables.

VUNG TAU Good Morning Vietnam   🏨 🇻   ⑤⑤
6 Hoang Hoa Tham St **Tel** *(064) 385 6959*

Despite the lack of serious competition in Vung Tau, this outlet of the famous chain offers great service and quality pasta dishes, pizzas, and other Italian favorites, all prepared by an imported Italian chef. Pizzas are the main draw at this open-air restaurant on the corner of the town square, between Front and Back beaches.

VUNG TAU Plein Sud   🗐🏨🇻   ⑤⑤⑤⑤
152A Ha Long Rd **Tel** *(064) 351 1570*

The charming Plein Sud seems to have been plucked from the south of France and transported whole to Vietnam. A charming terrace surrounds the structure, which is set in a grove of trees near the beach. The wood-fired oven serves up smoky pizzas, roasted meats, and seafood, as well as fair French bread. Decent selection of wines.

MEKONG DELTA AND SOUTHERN VIETNAM

BAC LIEU Bac Lieu Restaurant   🗐📖🇻   ⑤⑤⑤
Bac Lieu Hotel, 4–6 Hoang Van Thu St **Tel** *(0781) 382 2437* **Fax** *(0781) 382 3655*

Located on the ground floor of the eponymous hotel *(see p235)*, this large restaurant features an attractive Chinese-style decor, with round tables and friendly service. The menu is full of traditional Vietnamese claypot dishes, crisp stir fries, seafood preparations, and an array of noodle dishes. Note that the restaurant tends to close early.

CAN THO Nam Bo   🗐🏨🇻   ⑤⑤⑤
50 Hai Ba Trung St **Tel** *(0710) 382 3908* **Fax** *(0710) 381 2024*

Occupying a former French-colonial villa, complete with lazy ceiling fans and a surrounding garden, Nam Bo offers a choice of dining indoors or on the upper terrace during good weather. In addition to standard Vietnamese dishes, the restaurant offers international favorites such as pizzas, sandwiches, salads, and soups.

CAN THO Spices   🏨📖🇻   ⑤⑤⑤⑤⑤
Victoria Can Tho Hotel, Cai Khe Ward **Tel** *(0710) 381 0111* **Fax** *(0710) 382 9259*

Located in the luxurious Victoria Can Tho Hotel *(see p235)*, Spices is decorated in a traditional delta theme, with the option to dine either inside or out on the terrace facing the river. The menu is international, with a selection of Italian dishes, an American-style barbecue buffet, as well as standard Vietnamese fare, including whole fried fish.

Key to Price Guide *see p250* **Key to Symbols** *see back cover flap*

CAO LANH Tu Hao   🗐 $$$

Intersection of Dien Bien Phu and Nguyen Hue Sts **Tel** *(067) 385 2589*

Across the river from town but easily reached by taxi, Tu Hao is a plain but comfortable and welcoming place that has been run by the same family for generations. A meat-eater's restaurant, specializing in grilled meats of all kinds, the menu includes somewhat unusual items, including rats and snakes.

CHAU DOC Lam Hung Ky   🗐 V $$

71 Chi Lang St **Tel** *(076) 386 6745*

An unassuming but pleasant restaurant, Lam Hung Ky is located across the main market, and is a good stop for lunch; near enough yet apart from the swirl and bustle of shopping. The menu serves Vietnamese fare laced with Chinese touches such as a bit of soy sauce, lots of ginger, and the high heat and oil type of stir fry. Soups are good.

CHAU DOC Bassac   🖩 🗐 V $$$

Victoria Chau Doc Hotel, 32 Le Loi St **Tel** *(076) 386 5010* **Fax** *(076) 386 5020*

Named after Bassac River on whose bank it sits, this elegant restaurant's decor harks back to the colonial era, with the uniformed waiters and hushed atmosphere adding to the effect. The menu features locally farmed duck and fish prepared in Vietnamese style. Sandwiches, burgers, and pizza also available. Pleasant views from the terrace.

CON DAO ISLAND Poulo Condore   🖩 🗐 V $$$

Saigon Con Dao Resort, 18 Ton Duc Thang St **Tel** *(064) 383 0366*

One of the few polished sit-down restaurants on the island, Poulo Condore offers the option of dining al fresco in the garden, with the salty sea breeze adding piquancy to the meal. Seafood is the house specialty, and the menu reflects the regional variations in northern, central, and southern Vietnamese cuisine.

HA TIEN Xuan Thanh   🗐 V $$$

20 Tran Hau St **Tel** *(077) 385 2197*

Across from the central market, Xuan Thanh is a clean, cheerful little restaurant serving traditional Vietnamese fare, as well as some Western items such as sandwiches and pasta. *Lau* or hotpot *(see p249)*, swimming with fresh ingredients, is a specialty, as are deep-fried catfish and many stir-fried dishes, including squid.

MY THO Chuong Duong Restaurant   🗐 🖩 V $$$

10 St 30I4, Ward 1 **Tel** *(073) 387 0875* **Fax** *(073) 387 4250*

With a capacity of 500, this restaurant in the Chuong Duong Hotel *(see p236)* is right on the riverbank, the spacious dining terrace looking out on the water. The menu, heavy on fish and seafood, features competently prepared Vietnamese as well as Chinese dishes. Portions are generous, and the restaurant is a popular venue for local functions.

PHU QUOC ISLAND An Thai Café   🗐 🖩 V $$$

Khu Pho 3 St, An Thoi **Tel** *(077) 384 4307*

A popular place for lunch, dinner, as well as coffee and cocktails, An Thai Café is set on a second-floor "bungalow" with an A-shaped frame roof and open walls, providing an excellent view and cooling sea breezes. The menu is heavy on seafood prepared in Vietnamese style and several Western fast-food items such as sandwiches and burgers.

PHU QUOC ISLAND Minh Tri   🗐 🖩 V $$$

DC Tran Hung Dao – Khu St 1 **Tel** *(077) 384 8829*

Located on Long Beach in a garden-like setting with two levels, the ground level of Minh Tri is a sprawling expanse of tables and chairs, some of it under a roof and others shaded by trees. Tables on the upper deck look out over the whole scene. Seafood specialties include elephant snail, eel, and squid, as well as a full range of meats and soups.

PHU QUOC ISLAND Saigon Restaurant   🖩 V $$$

Saigon Phu Quoc Resort, 1 Tran Hung Dao St, Duong Dong **Tel** *(077) 384 6999* **Fax** *(077) 384 7163*

On a low hill overlooking the sea, most of this 150-seat restaurant is on a covered deck that catches a good breeze, and offers an inspiring view. The decor is simple and cheerful, and specialties include a staple of Vietnamese meats, fish, noodles, and soup, as well as deliciously fresh sushi and sashimi.

RACH GIA Hai Au   🗐 🖩 🗐 V $$$

2 Nguyen Trung Truc St **Tel** *(077) 386 3740*

With fine views over the river, Hai Au is spread over two levels, with a spacious patio area that is furnished with Mediterranean-style tables and parasols. Although the surprisingly decent wine list features mostly French wines, the food is purely Vietnamese. House specialties are hotpot and a wide variety of seafood and freshwater fish dishes.

SOC TRANG Quan Com Hung   🗐 $$$

Mau Than 74–76 St **Tel** *(079) 382 2268*

A plain, unpretentious little place, Quan Com Hung is one of the most popular eateries in town. It specializes in a variety of rice dishes, but the hotpot, also known as steamboat, is the most enjoyable to eat. A brazier is brought to the table with a pot of broth. Diners then place ingredients of their choice in the broth and cook to taste.

VINH LONG Thien Tan   🗐 V $$

56/1 Pham Thai Buong St **Tel** *(070) 382 4001*

Like most restaurants in the delta, not much attention is paid to the decor, but fortunately, quite the opposite holds true for the food. The barbecued meat dishes are tasty, although most patrons may think it prudent to pass on the roasted field rat. Flavorful poultry and fish cooked in clay and bamboo are also available here and well worth trying.

SOUTH CENTRAL VIETNAM

BUON MA THUOT Dam San Hotel Restaurant

$$$

212 Nguyen Cony Tru St **Tel** *(0500) 385 1234* **Fax** *(0500) 385 2309*

The most elegant restaurant in Buon Ma Thuot, the Dam San's dining room is an opulent banquet hall often hired out for weddings and other events. Fare is predominantly Vietnamese and Chinese but there are some foreign options too. The hotel is just a few miles from downtown and the restaurant is open to non-guests.

DALAT Au Lac

$$$

71 Phan Dinh Phung St **Tel** *(063) 382 2025*

Fresh vegetables such as carrots, avocados, and greens abound in Dalat, and the vegetarian restaurant Au Lac does all these succulent ingredients justice, serving them in Western, Vietnamese, and Chinese preparations, with mounds of rice and noodles. Even MSG and smoking are frowned upon, so this place is a boon for health-conscious backpackers.

DALAT Café V

$$$

1/1 Bui Xui Thuan St **Tel** *(063) 352 0215*

Run by an American-Vietnamese couple, the cuisine at this budget café consists of an eclectic mix of Vietnamese and Mexican cuisine. Surprisingly authentic, the menu features burritos, nachos, chimichangas, refried beans, tortillas, and even Italian pizza. These filling treats can be accompanied by Dalat wine, cold beer, or even a margarita or two.

DALAT Long Hoa

$$$

No.6, 3/2 St **Tel** *(063) 382 2934*

An old favorite with both locals and tourists, Long Hoa serves good-quality Vietnamese dishes, with emphasis on the hotpots and stir fries of southern cuisine. A small selection of Continental dishes, particularly sautées and soups are on offer as well. Several varieties of local beer as well as strong locally grown coffee. Live piano music occasionally.

DALAT Le Café de la Poste

$$$$

Tran Phu St **Tel** *(063) 382 5444*

This cozy French-colonial café and diner located between Du Parc and Dalat Palace hotels serves an elaborate western-style breakfast buffet from 6am until 10pm. Lunches and dinners feature simple American, French, Italian, and Asian dishes presented with gourmet flair. The setting is charming, with posters from the colonial era.

DALAT Le Rabelais

$$$$$

Dalat Palace, 12 Tran Phu St **Tel** *(063) 382 5444*

The most sophisticated, and indeed expensive, dining venue in Dalat, Le Rabelais offers exquisite French cuisine and an extensive wine list. The staff are knowledgeable, the French-colonial architecture lovely, and the setting sumptuous. Guests are expected to dress smartly and may enjoy a nightcap in the piano room where live music is played nightly.

KONTUM Dakbla Restaurant

$$$

Dakbla Hotel, 2 Phan Dinh Phung St **Tel** *(060) 386 3333*

Kontum is not really known for its fine dining, and the restaurant of the Dakbla Hotel *(see p237)* is about as good as it gets. It is clean, with a pleasant terraced area, and offers friendly service, good eggs, baguettes, *pho*, and coffee for breakfast. The collection of local ethnic minority artifacts decorating the walls add color to the surroundings.

MUI NE BEACH Joe's Café

$$

139B Nguyen Dinh Chieu St **Tel** *(062) 374 3447*

Joe's is the original 24-hour hangout with soft couches, cozy nooks, movies, and great Western comfort food. Run by an American, Joe, and his Vietnamese wife, Thao, the café has become the heart of Mui Ne. The all-day breakfasts, Bobby Brewers coffee, pizzas, and baguette sandwiches are immensely popular. Great wine list too.

MUI NE BEACH Rung (Forest)

$$$

7 Nguyen Dinh Chieu St, Han Tien Ward **Tel** *(062) 384 7589*

Gourmet Vietnamese and seafood dishes served in an exotic atmosphere by the seafront. The setting is a garden filled with ethnic crafts of all kinds, and the food is served on tables made of tree trunks cut into sections. Live traditional Vietnamese music in the evenings, and children, who love the setting, are welcome.

MUI NE BEACH Shree Ganesh

$$$$

57 Nguyen Dinh Chieu St, Han Tien Ward **Tel** *(062) 374 1330*

This popular eatery, part of a chain of North Indian and tandoori restaurants, is a welcome addition to Mui Ne's gastronomic scene. The rustic decor, balcony seating on the upper floor, and Indian pop music make for a lively setting. There's a vast range of lamb, chicken, and seafood curries, as well as numerous vegetarian choices.

MUI NE BEACH Champa

$$$$$

Coco Beach Resort, 58 Nguyen Dinh Chieu **Tel** *(062) 384 7111*

Set beside a swimming pool and surrounded by tropical gardens, this excellent restaurant in Coco Beach Resort *(see p237)* is presided over by an accomplished French chef. On offer are a range of rich imported foods as well as local seafood prepared in classic French style. A big plus is the range of pastries and desserts on offer. Closed on Mondays.

Key to Price Guide *see p250* **Key to Symbols** *see back cover flap*

NHA TRANG Da Fernando $$$

96 Nguyen Thien Thuat St **Tel** *(058) 222 9102*

The finest of half-a-dozen Italian restaurants in town, Da Fernando is Italian-owned and run by the former manager of Good Morning Vietnam Mui Ne. Located in a quiet and modest setting, the restaurant churns out authentic comfort food prepared from the heart. Pizzas, pasta dishes, and risottos are real delights.

NHA TRANG Lanterns Vietnamese Restaurant and Cooking Classes $$$

72 Nguyen Thien Thuat St **Tel** *(058) 247 1674*

Though their roots are humble, the staff and owners of Lanterns have used the restaurant as an opportunity to train disadvantaged local children in the culinary arts. In the process, they have created a popular fine-dining experience with authentic yet refined Vietnamese cuisine – try the BBQ beef, seafood hotpot, or the fish cooked in a clay pot.

NHA TRANG Rainbow Divers $$$

90A Hung Vuong St **Tel** *(058) 352 4351*

Scuba diving works up an appetite, so when Vietnam's top dive shop began serving some of Nha Trang's best food, opening a restaurant seemed the logical progression. Whether you come for burgers and pizza, Australian steaks and meat pies, or a jumbo mug of coffee and free Wi-Fi, Rainbow Divers provides a cozy break from the surf and sun.

NHA TRANG Ana Pavilion $$$$

Ana Mandara Resort, Tran Phu St **Tel** *(058) 352 2222*

Under the management of a New Zealand chef, this seaside restaurant offers sumptuous seafood and Vietnamese fusion cuisine. Open all day, it's a great place for a lavish breakfast, while the generous seafood lunch buffets are a real bargain. Dinner is *à la carte*, with a reasonable selection of wines and plenty of imported cold beer on tap.

NHA TRANG Louisiane Brewhouse $$$$

Lot 29, Tran Phu St **Tel** *(058) 352 1948*

The swankiest restaurant and microbrewery in Central Beach is also one of the most expensive spots in town. The open-air setting with on-the-beach and poolside seating is exotic and reminiscent of an upscale resort. The menu includes Vietnamese seafood and sushi, steaks, burgers, and a large selection of pastries. Try the delicious ginger ale.

QUANG NGAI Cung Dinh Restaurant $$$$

5 Ton Duc Thang St **Tel** *(055) 381 8555*

Enjoy Quang Ngai and Hue specialties in gazebos overlooking the Tra Khuc River. Staff here are friendly and fast, and many of them speak English. Among the unmissable dishes on the menu are *don*, a soup made with snails, *ram bap*, tiny corn spring rolls, and the delectable Emperor Seafood Salad.

QUY NHON Seafood 2000 $$$

1 Tran Doc St **Tel** *(056) 381 2787*

The most popular seafood restaurant in Quy Nhon for its friendly ambience, reasonable rates, and absolutely prime location overlooking Quy Nhon Bay. Seafood 2000 offers grilled giant prawns, barbecued squid, fresh lobster (when available), shark steak, a delicious seafood hotpot reminiscent of *bouillabaisse*, cold beer, and no pretensions.

CENTRAL VIETNAM

BA NA HILL STATION Ba Na Restaurant $$$

100 Bach Dang St **Tel** *(0511) 382 8262*

A huge restaurant capable of seating around 200 people, this resort restaurant caters almost exclusively to local Vietnamese tourists. It has an extensive menu of Vietnamese dishes but little in the way of international food. Good choice of local and imported beers, but only local Dalat wine. Barbecues are popular in the evening for dinner.

CHINA BEACH Loi Restaurant $$$

My Khe Beach **Tel** *(0511) 383 1088*

Located right on the beach, this is a fine place to drink cold beer and eat grilled prawns while looking out over the waters of the South China Sea. Patrons are assured of the freshness of the seafood as most creatures destined to be dinner are kept alive in tanks for inspection. Specialties include grilled clams in spicy tomato sauce. Lobster is great too.

DANANG Bread of Life $$

Cnr of Bach Dang and Dong Da Sts **Tel** *(0511) 356 5185*

This expatriate oasis is managed by an American family and staffed almost entirely by the deaf as part of a program to break cultural trends and help them lead self-sufficient, independent lives. The American comfort food served is deliciously authentic, from the burgers and pizzas to the baked macaroni and traditional Thanksgiving dinners.

DANANG My Hanh $$$

265 Nguyen Van Thoai St **Tel** *(0511) 394 0994*

This huge restaurant can seat 200, and even so, it almost always seems to be completely full. Since the clientele are mainly locals, that is as good a recommendation as one can get. The house specialty is every sort of seafood, and the quality is superb. Prices are not listed, however, as they vary from day to day. Ask before placing your order.

DANANG Apsara
222 Tran Phu St **Tel** *(0511) 356 1409*

A large, well-appointed restaurant near the famous Cham Museum, Apsara draws inspiration from Cham culture, which influences its appealing decor as well as the gardens that flaunt a replica Cham tower. The food is all Vietnamese, however, and really very good. An extensive menu specializing in seafood keeps the place busy.

DONG HOI Anh Dao
56 Quang Trung St **Tel** *(052) 382 0889*

Although it is not exactly remarkable, Anh Dao is nevertheless the best restaurant in town. What it offers is clean surroundings, polite service, and a good range of Vietnamese dishes, mainly prepared in northern and central styles. Not much English is spoken, but if in doubt, it is considered acceptable to go to the kitchen and point.

HOI AN Brother's Café
29 Phan Boi Chau St **Tel** *(0510) 391 4150*

Located by the banks of the river in the former French Quarter, this delightfully restored colonial building is one of the best and most charming restaurants in town. Patrons have the option of dining indoors or in the secluded garden. The Vietnamese food is delicious, and the presentation exquisite. Offers an excellent wine list, and daily changing set meals.

HOI AN Good Morning Vietnam
102 Nguyen Thai Hoc St **Tel** *(0510) 391 0227*

Housed in an antique house, and popular with tourists and locals alike, Good Morning Vietnam is an authentic Italian chain specializing in wood-fired oven pizzas with all types of toppings – the fresh seafood is highly recommended. Crisp salads for starters and sinful chocolate concoctions for dessert. Branches in Ho Chi Minh City, Mui Ne, and Nha Trang.

HOI AN Mango Room
111 Nguyen Thai Hoc St **Tel** *(0510) 391 0839*

Sophisticated fusion cuisine in an attractive setting prepared by a Viet Kieu, or overseas Vietnamese, who has returned from the USA as a successful restaurateur. Beef, prawn, and seafood specialties combine Vietnamese influence with Californian and Mexican, with surprisingly delicious results. Good selection of wines and cocktails.

HOI AN Nhu Y
2 Tran Phu St **Tel** *(0510) 386 1527*

One of the oldest and best sidewalk restaurants in Hoi An, the Nhu Y specializes in local specialties such as *cao lau*, a unique pork and noodle concoction, and "white rose" or rice-flour dumplings stuffed with shrimp. The staff are friendly and attentive, the restaurant attractively furnished, and the illustrated menu is helpful. Cooking lessons on offer.

HOI AN Tam Tam Cafè & Bar
110 Nguyen Thai Hoc St **Tel** *(0510) 386 2212*

A great little restaurant specializing in French and Italian cuisine, with a few Vietnamese dishes thrown into the mix. The setting is as appealing as the food. An attractively restored pastel yellow building with balcony seating, the colonial feel is palpable. Ice-cold beer is always available, and wine is served on request. Free Wi-Fi.

HOI AN Thanh
76 Bach Dang St **Tel** *(0510) 386 1366*

Set in a beautiful, old Sino-Vietnamese house by the Thu Bon River, this excellent little restaurant serves Chinese and unique Hoi An delicacies, including the famous *cao lau* noodles mixed with slices of pork, bean sprouts, and croutons. The dish has to be prepared with water from Hoi An's Ba Le Well to be just right. Wine available on request.

HUE La Boulangerie Française
47 Nguyen Tri Phuong St **Tel** *(054) 383 7437*

Without a doubt, this is one of the finest French bakeries in Vietnam. The delicate pastries, blueberry tarts, cakes, and fresh breads that come out of the oven look, smell, and taste amazing. The café is linked to a charity that trains disadvantaged street kids to become pastry chefs and bakers. Open all day, but best at breakfast time.

HUE Lac Thanh/Lac Thien/Lac Thuan
6 Dinh Tien Hoang St **Tel** *(054) 352 7348*

These strange, indeed almost legendary, Hue establishments, are owned and staffed entirely by a mute family of great charm. The food is wonderful, especially the crispy beef noodles, but the atmosphere is somewhat let down by the graffiti left on the walls by legions of backpackers. Ice-cold Huda beer – a Hue brand – is always on tap.

HUE Ong Tao
134 Ngo Duc Ke St **Tel** *(054) 352 2037*

Good central Vietnamese cuisine is the house specialty, though there's plenty from Ho Chi Minh City and Hanoi to choose from as well. The owner is an amiable and knowledgeable Hue resident who offers useful insights on the city's imperial cuisine. As usual, the seafood is excellent, the beef succulent, and the chicken a little tough at times.

HUE Tropical Temple
5 Chu Van An St **Tel** *(054) 383 0716*

Close to the Perfume River, this establishment offers a choice of either dining in the eponymous tropical garden or the air-conditioned space indoors. Dishes are Franco-Vietnamese fusion cuisine, often presented with great sizzling, skewered flamboyance. Delectable desserts with a Vietnamese touch and an adequate wine list.

Key to Price Guide *see p250* **Key to Symbols** *see back cover flap*

HUE Le Parfum

□ V ☲ $$$$

La Residence Hotel & Spa, 5 Le Loi St **Tel** *(054) 383 7475*

Located in the plush La Residence *(see p240)*, Le Parfum is run by a German chef who has helped make it one of Hue's finest dining establishments. Elegant and sophisticated, it is the best place for Western cuisine, particularly Central European specialties. Large portions, a good wine list, and a fine choice of desserts. Lovely views of Hue Citadel.

LANG CO BEACH Thanh Tam

▦ □ $$$

Thanh Tam Resort, Lang Co Beach **Tel** *(054) 387 4456*

Part of the Thanh Tam Seaside resort, this is the best restaurant in Lang Co and enduringly popular with tour groups passing through. The outdoor terrace restaurant looks directly down onto the South China Sea, so it's no surprise that seafood is the specialty. The hotel's swimming and showering facilities can be used for free once food is ordered.

HANOI

EAST OF HOAN KIEM LAKE Ly Club

♫ □ V ☲ $$$$

51 Ly Thai To St **Tel** *(04) 3936 3069*   **Map** 2 F4

Set in an attractive colonial villa, the plush Ly Club is impressively creative in terms of both decor and food. French and Vietnamese specialties are prepared with great style, and guests can choose between exotic appetizers such as caviar on a sweet potato crêpe or scallops served with chopped apples. Live traditional music redolent of Imperial Hue.

FRENCH QUARTER Pho 24

▤ □ V $$

26 Ba Trieu St **Tel** *(04) 3936 1888*   **Map** 2 E4

As the name suggest, Vietnam's most famous noodle dish, *pho*, is justly celebrated at Pho 24 *(see p250)*. Usually a streetside snack eaten for breakfast or late at night, *pho* can be eaten in the air-conditioned comfort of this chain restaurant at any time of the day, and in normal-sized chairs rather than the tiny plastic stools favored by street vendors.

FRENCH QUARTER Alfresco

□ V $$$

23 Hai Ba Trung St **Tel** *(04) 3826 7782*   **Map** 2 E4

A great place in the heart of downtown Hanoi, Alfresco specializes in Western-style comfort food. Under Australian management, the selection is large and portions equally so. Ribs, burgers, pizza, steak, french fries, baguette sandwiches, memorable salads, and mouthwatering desserts. All washed down with cold beer or the excellent coffee.

FRENCH QUARTER Au Lac Café

▦ □ V $$$

57 Ly Thai To St **Tel** *(04) 3825 7870*   **Map** 2 F4

Close to the iconic Sofitel Metropole Hotel *(see p241)*, this charming café-bistro offers good Vietnamese, fusion, and international cuisine in a restored French villa with a small patio garden. The seafood dishes are especially good, and the house specialties include tamarind and chili pepper sauces to stimulate the taste buds. Very good value for money.

FRENCH QUARTER Cay Cau

▦ ♫ □ V $$$

De Syloia Hotel, 17A Tran Hung Dao St **Tel** *(04) 3933 1010*   **Map** 2 F5

An adjunct of the classy De Syloia Hotel *(see p240)*, Cay Cau is a tasteful Vietnamese restaurant, with a long menu of delicious dishes at surprisingly reasonable prices. There's also quite an extensive choice of desserts – unusual in a Viet establishment – including cheesecakes, tarts, and other rich fare. Live music performances are held every evening.

FRENCH QUARTER Emperor

▦ □ V ☲ $$$

18B Le Thanh Tong St **Tel** *(04) 3826 8801*   **Map** 2 F5

A restored French-colonial villa and a Vietnamese stilt house jointly preside over a central courtyard at the aptly named Emperor, which specializes in Hue's imperial cuisine. Beautifully prepared and elegantly presented dishes include delights such as "dragon eggs," bird's nest soup, and fried soft-shell crabs with tamarind. Good choice of wines.

FRENCH QUARTER Hoa Sua

▦ □ V $$$

28A Ha Hoi St **Tel** *(04) 3942 4448*   **Map** 2 E5

Set in a renovated French villa, this unusual establishment is run as a culinary training school for orphans on a nonprofit basis. Under French management, it serves delicious French and Vietnamese fare at very reasonable prices, and also has a special menu for children. Try the pork in caramel sauce followed by a fluffy mille-feuille pastry for dessert.

FRENCH QUARTER Il Grillo

□ ☲ $$$

116 Ba Trieu St **Tel** *(04) 3822 7720*   **Map** 2 E5

Fine traditional Italian food can be enjoyed at the popular Il Grillo. Other than a wide range of pastas, Italian favorites not usually found in stand-alone Vietnamese restaurants are available here, including veal *carpaccio*, *parma con melone*, porcini mushrooms, and rich desserts such as *zabaglioni* and tiramisu. Good wine list, cozy decor, and attentive service.

FRENCH QUARTER Indochine

▦ ♫ □ V ☲ $$$

16 Nam Ngu St **Tel** *(04) 3942 4097*   **Map** 1 C4

A fine restaurant set amid a complex of restored colonial villas and a shady courtyard, Indochine is one of the longest-established restaurants in Hanoi. The Vietnamese menu is extraordinarily extensive, detailing more than 100 dishes, including banana flower salad and fried squid stuffed with pork. Live traditional music on Tuesdays and Thursdays.

FRENCH QUARTER San Ho

🎵📋🍽 $$$

58 Ly Thuong Kiet St **Tel** *(04) 3934 9184*   **Map** *2 D4*

One of the best-known and most successful seafood restaurants in Hanoi, the aquarium-lined San Ho offers a choice of *à la carte* or set-meal dining at reasonable prices. The cuisine is primarily Vietnamese, with Chinese overtones, and chilled beer rather than wine is the standard accompaniment. Live piano music plays every evening.

FRENCH QUARTER Classico Café and Restaurant

📶🅥 $$$$

68 Quan Su **Tel** *(04) 3941 2327*   **Map** *2 D4*

One of the north's finest Italian restaurants, Classico is a hidden gem. The fare includes Italian mainstays such as pasta, lasagne, gnocchi, and seafood; the New York-style pizzas are heavy on toppings. Both the indoor and outdoor seating areas are elegant, and the private museum of ancient Dong Son relics inside the restaurant is a delight.

FRENCH QUARTER Le Beaulieu

📋🍽 $$$$

Sofitel Metropole Hotel, 15 Ngo Quyen St **Tel** *(04) 3826 6919*   **Map** *2 F4*

Simply as good as French food gets in Hanoi, Le Beaulieu is a jewel in Hanoi's culinary crown. Finest imported beef, fresh seafood, delicately spiced sauces, creamy desserts, and an impressive wine list are just some of the highlights. The famed buffet lunch features trolleys piled high with European cheese of all varieties. Knowledgeable, attentive staff.

FRENCH QUARTER Spices Garden

📶📋🅥🍽 $$$$

Sofitel Metropole Hotel, 15 Ngo Quyen St **Tel** *(04) 3826 6919*   **Map** *2 F4*

A fantastic restaurant in the Sofitel Metropole Hotel *(see p241)*, Spices Garden is tended to by a French executive chef who brings the most excellent Vietnamese, French, and fusion food to the table. The buffet selection at lunch would do credit to the very best restaurants in Europe, and unexpectedly includes an impressive array of cheese.

HAI BA TRUNG DISTRICT Wild Rice

📋🅥 $$$

6 Ngo Thi Nham St **Tel** *(04) 3943 8896*   **Map** *2 E5*

Set in a fine restored colonial building, Wild Rice is surprisingly modern inside although the waitresses wear traditional *ao dai*. The chef plays cleverly on classic Vietnamese food, adding deft French, Japanese, and Chinese touches. Spring rolls with banana and shrimp, braised eggplant with pork, and many other unusual preparations.

OLD QUARTER Little Hanoi

📋🅥 $$

21–23 Hang Gai St **Tel** *(04) 3928 5333*   **Map** *2 E3*

A friendly and convenient little eatery located right in the heart of the bustling Old Quarter, Little Hanoi specializes in baguette sandwiches, fried chicken, desserts, and ice creams. The *Chon* or Weasel coffee *(see p263)* is made from beans that have passed through the animal's digestive tract. The idea is a bit distasteful but the coffee delicious.

OLD QUARTER Thu Huyen

📋 $$

36 Hang Giay St   **Map** *2 D2*

Frequented by few Westerners but very popular with locals, Thu Huyen is a bustling, grubby, and strangely appealing little restaurant, serving a wide variety of excellent Vietnamese dishes at very cheap rates, along with tall glasses of cold *bia hoi (see p247)*, a national institution which is at its best and most authentic in Hanoi's Old Quarter.

OLD QUARTER Cha Ca La Vong

📋📋 $$$

14 Cha Ca St **Tel** *(04) 3825 3929*   **Map** *2 E2*

A legendary restaurant, Cha Ca La Vong *(see p156)* serves only one dish – *cha ca* or fried fish – prepared using a recipe that has been perfected here. The fish is steeped in a marinade of galangal, saffron, fermented rice, and fish sauce, and then placed into a rich, oily stew, along with fresh chives and dill. Served on noodles and sprinkled with peanuts.

OLD QUARTER Green Tangerine

📶📋🍽 $$$

48 Hang Be St **Tel** *(04) 3825 1286*   **Map** *2 E3*

A fine restaurant in a fantastic setting, Green Tangerine is housed in a whimsical building that appears to combine French-colonial and tube-house architecture. The French cuisine, with Vietnamese undertones, is a treat for the eyes and the palate. Smoked salmon stuffed with pistachios, scallops and watercress, ice cream with chili – it's all here.

OLD QUARTER Tandoor

📋🅥 $$$

24 Hang Be St **Tel** *(04) 3824 5359*   **Map** *2 E3*

A good Indian restaurant, Tandoor *(see p252)* is a popular chain serving curries, kebabs, and a whole gamut of dishes from the country. It is popular with the Indian community – Hanoi's Indian connection dates back to the French-colonial period when Tamils from the then French territory of Pondicherry moved to Vietnam to open clothing businesses.

OLD QUARTER Tassili

📋🍽 $$$

78 Ma May St **Tel** *(04) 3828 0774*   **Map** *2 E2*

This Algerian-run restaurant serves couscous, hummus, excellent tender lamb, lightly spiced but intensely flavorful soups, *merguez*, a type of sausage, and a wide range of other Mediterranean specialties inspired by Lebanese, Greek, and Italian culinary traditions. Great wine list, attentive service, and a mellow, laid-back ambience.

TAY HO DISTRICT Restaurant Bobby Chinn

📋🅥 $$$$$

77 Xuan Dieu St **Tel** *(04) 3719 2457*   **Map** *2 E4*

TV show host Bobby Chinn serves the most imaginative Southern Californian and Asian fusion food in the city. He closed his famous restaurant on Hoan Kiem Lake in early 2009 and opened this small venue until a larger location can be found. Creative cocktails and an extensive wine list. Expensive but well worth it.

Key to Price Guide *see p250* **Key to Symbols** *see back cover flap*

WEST OF HOAN KIEM LAKE Mediterraneo Italian Restaurant ⛱ ☰ [V] $$$

23 Nha Tho St ***Tel*** *(04) 3826 6288* ***Map*** *2 E3*

The name says it all – good Mediterranean food with a distinct Italian trattoria vibe, this appealing restaurant is conveniently close to Hanoi Cathedral and the trendy restaurants and art boutiques around Nha Tho. Mediterranean specialities include moussaka and a range of pastas and pizzas. Wine is available.

WEST OF HOAN KIEM LAKE Moca Café ☰ [V] $$$

14–16 Nha Tho St ***Tel*** *(04) 3825 6334* ***Map*** *2 E3*

Designed to look rather like a stripped-down warehouse loft, Moca is a trendy café that draws plenty of customers to savor its wide range of international cooking, with dishes ranging from Mexican to Bengali. Good local as well as imported coffee, draught beer, a selection of wines and juices, plus a decent choice of desserts at reasonable prices.

WEST OF HOAN KIEM LAKE Thuy Ta 💳 ⛱ [V] $$$

1 Le Thai To St ***Tel*** *(04) 3828 8148* ***Map*** *2 F3*

Set right on the northwestern shore of Hoan Kiem Lake, Thuy Ta is something of a lakeside institution. Boasting fine views across the water, this eatery serves international cuisine, with good fast food such as baguettes and burgers, as well as an extensive range of cakes, pastries, and ice creams. Good coffee too – a great place to take a break.

WEST OF HOAN KIEM LAKE Brother's Café ⛱ ☰ [V] $$$$

26 Nguyen Thai Hoc St ***Tel*** *(04) 3733 3866* ***Map*** *1 C3*

Hanoi has more than its share of fine restaurants set in delightfully restored French-colonial villas, and this is one of the best. The range of Hanoi-style delicacies include *bun cha*, a tasty meatball and fish sauce preparation. Buffet lunches are served indoors or on the veranda under sunshades. Excellent value barbecue buffets for dinner.

WEST OF HOAN KIEM LAKE Vine Wine Boutique Bar and Café ☰ [V] $$$$$

1A Xuan Dieu St ***Tel*** *(04) 3719 8000*

A rather good restaurant out by Hanoi's increasingly upmarket Ho Tay, serving a selection of well-prepared and tasty Vietnamese, Thai, Japanese, and Italian dishes. It is not called Vine Wine Boutique for nothing – it probably has one of the most extensive wine lists in Hanoi, and the bottles are attractively arrayed in racks around the walls.

NORTHERN VIETNAM

BAC HA Cong Phu 💳 $$$

By Bac Ha Bus Station ***Tel*** *(020) 388 0254*

One of a very small handful of eating places in Bac Ha, Cong Phu is a backpacker joint that has convenient English-language menus, with pencils to hand so diners just tick the boxes. Simple dishes such as spring rolls, roasted pork, and fried rice are available. There may not be the widest range of culinary choices but it's as good as it gets in Bac Ha.

CAT BA ISLAND Flightless Bird Café 💳 $$$

Cat Ba Harbor

The somewhat strange name of this café-cum-bar is explained by the fact that it is under joint Vietnamese and New Zealand management. Generally closed during the day, it comes alive in the evening as people gather to drink beer or cocktails, and indulge in international snack foods. Dart boards, movies, and a sound system help to entertain.

CAT BA ISLAND The Green Mango [V] 💳 $$$

Block 4, 1–4 St ***Tel*** *(031) 388 7151*

Easily the best restaurant in Cat Ba, The Green Mango is an extraordinary find in this little seaside town. Decorated tastefully, it offers a variety of dishes featuring Vietnamese, Western, and fusion cuisine, the seafood being particularly succulent. Dishes range from prawn on sugarcane to British-style fish 'n' chips. Also serves beer, wine, and cocktails.

DIEN BIEN PHU Lien Tuoi 💳 ☰ $$$

27 Muong Thanh St ***Tel*** *(023) 382 4919*

Although there are few good eating establishments in Dien Bien Phu, Lien Tuoi has a few fairly tasty items on its menu. The cuisine is Sino-Vietnamese, with a tendency towards wild game meats such as deer and boar, and includes a variety of fish dishes, wholesome, piping-hot steamboat, sweet-and-sour chicken, as well as spring rolls.

HAIPHONG Com Viet 💳 ⛱ $$

4 Hoang Van Thu St ***Tel*** *(031) 384 1698*

A small eatery set in a pleasant courtyard, Com Viet offers simple Vietnamese meals and snacks, with an emphasis on rice-based dishes and local seafood. The ubiquitous noodles and spring rolls are also available, but you may have to point and order, as the establishment doesn't see many non-Vietnamese customers. The atmosphere is relaxed.

HAIPHONG Thien Nhat Chie 💳 ☰ $$$

18 Tran Quang Khai St ***Tel*** *(031) 382 1018*

One of the best restaurants in Haiphong, Thien Nhat Chie specializes in a surprisingly impressive range of Japanese dishes. As expected, fresh seafood features prominently on the menu, and the sushi and sashimi are not bad at all. Imported Asahi beer for those who wish to complete the Japanese casual-dining experience.

HALONG CITY Asian Restaurant 💳 🍴 📋 $$$

Vuon Dao St, Bai Chay ***Tel*** *(033) 364 0028*

One of the best among the many restaurants clustered near the waterfront along Vuon Dao or Hotel Street, this Asian Restaurant serves a wide range of tasty and reasonably priced Vietnamese food, as well as good cold beer to wash it all down with. The owner speaks English and German, and the menus are bilingual.

HALONG CITY Bien Mo Floating Restaurant 🍴 📋 ☂ $$$

35 Ben Tau St, Hong Gai ***Tel*** *(033) 382 8951*

If it swims and is edible, it will be on the menu of this upmarket floating restaurant. Lobster, giant prawns, squid, cuttlefish, shark, and grouper are all as fresh as it gets. The dishes are well prepared and presented with style, but of course, a small premium must be paid for the experience of dining on the waters of the bay.

MAI CHAU VALLEY Mai Chau Guesthouse 💳 🍴 $

Mai Chau Village ***Tel*** *(0218) 386 7262*

Mai Chau is at the very heart of White Thai territory, and the local fare available at the Mai Chau Guesthouse *(see p244)* includes sticky rice made into neat balls, which are then dipped in a selection of spicy condiments, served with fish sauce, dried fish, grilled chicken, and salads made with beef or buffalo.

NINH BINH Hoang Hai 💳 $$$

36 Truong Han Sieu St ***Tel*** *(030) 387 5177*

Probably the best dining option in Ninh Binh, Hoang Hai is quite an interesting little restaurant. A long deck raised on stilts makes the most of the cool evening air. Offers good seafood and the steamboat here is a must-try. The staff are friendly, and can speak a little bit of English.

SAPA Baguette and Chocolat 💳 [V] ☂ $$$

Thac Bac St ***Tel*** *(020) 387 1766*

This stylish establishment is a place of indulgence for those with a sweet tooth. Big breakfasts, pasta, and pizza are on offer, but above all, the wide selection of cakes and sweets will undoubtedly help to fill out the calorie-deprived traveler seeking some Western comfort food as a change from healthy, low-fat Vietnamese cuisine.

SAPA Bon Appetit 💳 $$$

25 Xuan Vien St ***Tel*** *(020) 387 2927*

A cozy, comfortable, and centrally located restaurant aimed squarely at the overseas tourist market, this is a good place for large Western breakfasts, hamburgers and fries, stuffed baguette sandwiches, pasta, and nourishing stews. There is a good range of standard Vietnamese food available too, and the service is friendly and swift.

SAPA Delta 💳 $$$

33 Cau May St ***Tel*** *(020) 387 1799*

Probably the best, as well as the longest-running Italian restaurant in Sapa, Delta serves wood-fired oven pizzas, a wide range of pastas, fresh veal, chicken breast in mushroom sauce, hot minestrone, and other nutritious soups. Beer, wine, cocktails, and coffee complement the menu.

SAPA Mimosa 💳 🍴 $$$

64 Sapa, Cay Mau St ***Tel*** *(020) 387 1377*

A cheap and good Sapa standby that involves climbing a long flight of concrete steps off Cay Mau Street – just the thing to raise an appetite. Set in a comfortable and well-appointed old house, the restaurant also offers al fresco seating on the terrace. Specialties are an unusual mix of Western international fare and local wild game dishes.

SON LA Long Phuong 💳 $$

Thinh Doi St ***Tel*** *(022) 385 2339*

Son La restaurants aren't plentiful or exceptional, but they are cheap. The local specialty is *de* or goat meat, *lau de* or mutton hotpot, and *tiet canh*, a delicacy consisting of congealed goat's blood sprinkled with chopped peanuts and green shallots. Not much English is spoken, and it may be necessary to point at the items on the menu.

ANGKOR

SIEM REAP Common Grounds 💳 ♿ [V] ☂ $

Behind the Center Market ***Tel*** *(063) 965 687*

A clean, air-conditioned café with modern amenities such as free and speedy Wi-Fi. Also on offer is a dizzying array of cakes, brownies, soups, salads, sandwiches, fresh juices, coffees, and teas. All profit from this excellent eatery directly supports NGO projects in Cambodia.

SIEM REAP El Camino Taqueri 💳 ♿ [V] $

The Passage, Siem Reap ***Tel*** *(092) 207 842*

This trendy Mexican bar does some very appetizing, authentic Mexican snacks such as tacos, fajitas, nachos, guacamoles, and chimichangas. The decor is more urban chic than rural charm, with mosaic walls to stare at while guzzling deliciously prepared margaritas.

Key to Price Guide *see p250* **Key to Symbols** *see back cover flap*

SIEM REAP Temple Balcony
St 8, Old Market area **Tel** *(015) 999 909*

Set above the lively Temple Bar, this airy balcony restaurant is one of Pub Street's most popular haunts and a meeting point for travelers. Each night, there are traditional *apsara* dances between 7:30 and 9:30pm. The food comprises tasty Khmer, Thai, and Western dishes. Wi-Fi is available here.

SIEM REAP Terrasse Des Eléphants
Sivatha Blvd, Old Market area **Tel** *(063) 965 570*

A hotel restaurant, the Terrasse Des Eléphants is set in a Colonial-style building among gardens bursting with flowers. The menu offers both Khmer and international cuisine, from chicken *amok* (steamed catfish in coconut curry) and beef curry in milk to burgers and steaks. The bar complements the restaurant and is ideal for an evening cocktail.

SIEM REAP The Soup Dragon
Old Market area **Tel** *(063) 964 933*

This hole in the wall has bags of atmosphere and plaudits for its Vietnamese food, particularly its *pho* (noodle soup) and fresh spring rolls. There are also moderately priced entrées and soups, as well as a range of wok-fried dishes. Open-air seating is available on two floors, but the rooftop section offers a cooler place for diners.

SIEM REAP Viroth's
Wat Bo Rd **Tel** *(012) 778 096*

Garnering great reviews for his distinctive *amok* (steamed catfish in coconut curry) dishes and modern take on Khmer food, Chef Viroth draws a regular crowd of discerning diners to his stylish garden terrace, which also has indoor seating. The restaurant is as well known for the excellent service as it is for the delicious food.

SIEM REAP Café Central
Old Market area **Tel** *(017) 692 997*

Siem Reap's most famous café is a great place to unwind with a latte and a Western-style sandwich in contemporary, exposed brick surroundings. The menu features many Western favorites: fish and chips, soups and salads, pizzas, pastas, a big selection of burgers, and even a children's menu. Free Wi-Fi for all diners.

SIEM REAP Café Indochine
Sivatha Blvd **Tel** *(012) 804 952*

Set in an old wooden building, this lovely restaurant is popular with tour groups for its consistently tasty cuisine, a blend of Asian and European dishes. On the menu are spring rolls (fresh and fried), savory salads, spicy Thai soups and bouillabaisse, curries, *amok*, and a variety of meat and vegetable dishes.

SIEM REAP Dead Fish Tower
Sivatha Blvd **Tel** *(063) 963 060*

This restaurant is a great place to sample fine Thai cuisine. The Khmer menu excels with dishes such as *amok* (steamed catfish in coconut curry) and ginger chicken. The dining area is curiously multi-tiered, but guests enjoying a cocktail bucket need to be careful, as there is little to break an accidental fall. Open daily from 7am to 1am.

SIEM REAP FCC Angkor
Pokambor Ave **Tel** *(063) 760 283*

The sister of FCC in Phnom Penh, the FCC Angkor has more space and style than its counterpart, but perhaps lacks its effervescence. The building is set amid manicured lawns, beside a swimming pool. The dining room is delightful, with an attractive bar and open kitchen. The menu ranges from Western comfort food to Asian fusion dishes.

SIEM REAP Funky Monkey
Pokambor Ave **Tel** *(017) 824 553*

This bar-cum-restaurant packs a punch with terrific style-your-own burgers, Pop Art decor, and an extensive cocktail menu. There are also vegetarian burgers on offer. A friendly and fun alternative to more sober dining, the establishment is particularly known for its quiz night, held on Thursdays.

SIEM REAP Khmer Kitchen
The Passage, behind Bar St **Tel** *(063) 964 154*

Occupying an unpretentious building, the ever-busy Khmer Kitchen offers simple, hearty fare. The eclectic menu of Thai and Khmer staples features a variety of soups, stir-fries, curries, and spring rolls. Try the baked pumpkin or the beef *lok lak*. The staff speak English and service is friendly. Open from 10am to 10pm daily.

SIEM REAP Red Piano Restaurant
Pub St **Tel** *(063) 963 240*

Patronized by Angelina Jolie during the making of *Tomb Raider*, the Red Piano is set in a lovely old villa. This is a lively place with sidewalk, indoor, and veranda seating. The food is predominantly Western, offering favorites such as pastas and steaks. There is also a selection of Asian dishes on the menu.

SIEM REAP Hotel De La Paix
Sivatha Blvd **Tel** *(063) 966 001*

One of the most stylish places to eat, this Khmer restaurant is reached via the stylish Arts Lounge Bar and ends by a beautiful boddhi tree in the courtyard. On offer is exquisite, seasonal Khmer cuisine presented with great finesse. There is also a range of salads, sandwiches, baguettes, and paninis.

SHOPPING IN VIETNAM

Until a few decades ago, the most memorable thing about a Vietnamese store was the emptiness of its shelves. Today, the scene has changed dramatically, as shops all across the country are overflowing with a variety of products, including distinctive conical hats, fine silk, designer clothes, colorful lamps, delicate ceramic ware, and elegantly carved bamboo furnishings – all available at affordable rates. Perhaps

Painting with intricate work

the most coveted of all goods are the traditional wares, such as exquisitely embroidered textiles, handicrafts, and jewelry made by Vietnam's ethnic minorities. While upmarket malls are present in major cities, the local markets and the shopping streets and districts of Hanoi and Ho Chi Minh City are the best places to shop. However, Hoi An, with its amazing array of lacquerware, apparel, and crafts is the ultimate shopper's paradise.

Textiles for sale in a White Thai village, Mai Chau

OPENING HOURS

Most city shops open at about 8am and do not close until late in the evening at 8pm or 9pm. The newer malls and department stores in big cities open by 10am and close as late as 10pm. Keep in mind that staff tend to start shutting down an hour before the posted closing time. The traditional markets, such as Ben Thanh *(see p66)* in Ho Chi Minh City and Dong Xuan *(see p158)* in Hanoi, generally operate from sunrise to sunset. Some of these offer a thriving night market on the street outside as well, which runs until midnight. Virtually all retail operations operate seven days a week. However, during Tet *(see pp28–9)*, some shops shut for a few days, while others open later than usual.

HOW TO PAY

Though the Vietnamese *dong* (VND) is the only legal tender in the country, nobody would refuse a US dollar. In areas that are very popular with visitors, especially the more expensive districts, most shops prefer to quote prices in dollars rather than *dong*. The reason being that dollars are more profitable for sellers than the *dong* because of its fluctuating exchange rate. Hence, as the buyer, always try and pay in *dong* as it will be cheaper.

Major credit cards are accepted in high-end shops, hotels, and restaurants in big cities and major resort towns.

However, in small towns and villages, as well as at local bus stations, markets, street food stalls, and other such places, only cash is accepted.

RIGHTS AND REFUNDS

As a rule, all sales are final. Though some department stores in big cities may offer a return policy, by and large, once money, goods, or any services have changed hands, there is no going back. Some goods, especially electronic items such as cell phones, do come with a guarantee. But even here, it covers replacement, not refund.

BARGAINING

Unless you are in an upscale shop, mall, or national book store chain, the asking price of goods is not necessarily the final price. Except for food and drink, which have smaller margins, the rate quoted is twice or even more than what the merchant is willing to settle for. As such, be prepared to bargain.

Effective negotiation requires three things. First and most importantly is a pleasant attitude, even a sense of humor. Remember that this is not just a commercial transaction, it's a social encounter. Secondly, be ready to spend some time. You cannot get the price down from US$50 to US$25 easily. A transaction of that magnitude can take up to ten minutes. And lastly, try walking away. At times, this prompts a drastic reduction in price.

Huge selection of handbags at a shop in Binh Tay Market, Ho Chi Minh City

Gleaming exterior of the exclusive Diamond Plaza, Ho Chi Minh City

DEPARTMENT STORES AND MALLS

Luxury shopping malls and department stores are now present in most big cities. **Vincom Shopping Center**, in Ho Chi Minh City, is the country's largest retail center, with international brands and foreign fast food chains. Another high-end shopping mall is **Diamond Plaza**, which also boasts a movie theater and bowling alley.

Nearby is **Parkson**, a classy, four-story department store, boasting brands such as Nike, Guess, Estée Lauder, and Mont Blanc among others. It also has a supermarket and several eateries. The centrally located **Tax Trading Center** hosts numerous stores, and offers better prices than most, and **Zen Plaza**, with six floors of outlets and cafés, is ideal for anything from clothing to furniture and artifacts. Close by is **Saigon Shopping Center**, with a supermarket, book store, and numerous toy and electronics stores. In the Cholon district, **An Duong Plaza** has many stores offering a range of goods, including a wide variety of Asian items.

In Hanoi, **Trang Tien Plaza** is an international level shopping center, hosting several brands, both foreign and local, while **Big C Thang Long** supermarket is not just a great place to buy quality foodstuffs. This two-story mall has goods ranging from fresh food to appliances, garments, home decorations, and electronics. The first four floors of the massive **Vincom City Towers** are a hub for shopping and entertainment. It also has a food court that serves an eclectic selection of international cuisine.

MARKETS AND STREET VENDORS

While modern malls are cropping up in large cities, the traditional markets are still the best places to shop. They are considerably cheaper, and ideal stopping points to absorb the city's atmosphere. The biggest markets in Ho Chi Minh City are Ben Thanh (*see p66*) in District 1 and Binh Tay (*see p71*) in Cholon. Both carry an amazing selection of products, from clothing and groceries to appliances and furnishings. For imported foods, drinks, personal items, accessories, and much more, the **Old Market** is worth a visit.

In Hanoi, Dong Xuan Market (*see p158*) is a favorite among visitors, and carries a vast array of household goods, as well as clothing, souvenirs, and more. For a great selection of fabrics, visit **Hang Da Market**. You can also get clothes tailored here.

One of the most charming markets in Vietnam is in Hoi An (*see pp124–8*). While the day market teems with clothes, lacquer and ceramic ware, silk, footwear, and handicrafts, the night market is ideal for a fascinating evening stroll.

In addition to local markets, the streets are overflowing with shops selling souvenirs, kitchenware, counterfeit goods, and clothes.

Colorful lamp shop, Dong Khoi, Ho Chi Minh City

SHOPPING STREETS AND DISTRICTS

All the streets in Hanoi's Old Quarter (*see pp156–7*) are named after the products once sold there. For example, Ma (paper) Street offers paper goods, Hon Gai (hemp) Street has rows upon rows of silk shops, Chieu (mats) Street has rush mats and bamboo blinds, and Thiec (tin) Street offers tin and glass items, as well as mirrors. Although the placement of products on these streets is not so strict today, they remain excellent places to browse the wide range of goods at bargain prices.

The main shopping district in Ho Chi Minh City is Dong Khoi (*see pp56–7*), with a huge selection of outlets selling clothing, antiques, arts and crafts, and home furnishings.

COUNTERFEIT GOODS

Counterfeit goods can be bought on almost any street corner in Vietnam. Articles for sale include Rolex watches, army dog tags, Zippo cigarette lighters with regimental markings, and DVDs, CDs, and video games.

COFFEE AND TEA

Vietnamese coffee is unique, and comes in a wide selection of flavors, including vanilla, anise, and chocolate. There are three varieties of coffee – Arabica, Robusta, and Weasel. While Arabica is the most expensive and richest, Robusta is cheaper. Weasel is also an expensive coffee made from coffee cherries eaten and defecated by *chon,* Vietnamese weasels. Vietnamese tea is a green tea scented with lotus flower. The best place to buy coffee or tea is at markets such as Ben Thanh in Ho Chi Minh City or Dong Xuan in Hanoi. Street vendors also sell them but overcharge.

Collection of bright and colorful crafts and artifacts, Hoi An

ARTS AND CRAFTS

Traditional arts and crafts are produced almost everywhere in Vietnam. Exquisitely embroidered linen, intricately carved artifacts and figurines, colorful silken lanterns, as well as stylized paintings are just some of the specialties available. For fine textiles, especially good quality, hand-embroidered silk by French and Japanese artists, visit Chi Vang in Hanoi. Also check out **Tan My** for gorgeous, hand-embroidered tablecloths, throws, and quilts. **Lan Handicrafts** also carries fine textiles, made by people with disabilities specifically for this non-profit outlet. A similar operation in Hoi An is at Hoa-Nhap Handicrafts. Dong Khoi district in Ho Chi Minh City is home to many silk merchants, such as **Bao Nghi**, which also carries linen and other fabrics.

Hill-tribe handicrafts made by ethnic minorities are available in Ho Chi Minh City at **Sapa** outlet, which offers a range of handwoven clothing, embroidered silks, and footwear. In Hanoi, **Craft Link**, **Viet Hien**, and **Craft Window** offer a wide selection of handicrafts, while in Hoi An, **House of Traditional Handicrafts** and Handicraft Workshop (see p128) are good. For pottery, tableware, and silk lamps, walk through Hoi An's streets, which are lined with many shops selling such items. Some great ceramics – tea sets, vases, and bowls – are available at **Em Em** in Ho Chi Minh City.

Hanoi Gallery is a good place to buy modern art. In Ho Chi Minh City's District 1, **Dogma** carries political art and **Galerie Quynh** showcases contemporary works by leading local and foreign artists. **Que Noi Gallery** in Hoi An is worth visiting.

CLOTHING

Decorative souvenir statue

Hoi An is the most popular place to buy clothes in all of Vietnam. Boutiques here can copy any outfit from any international fashion magazine in a few hours, and at one-third of the cost at home. The most stylish outlet, with extremely high quality goods and service, is **Yaly Couture**. They can also make a range of shoes, mostly women's. For cloth purchases and simple tailoring, check out the **Hoi An Cloth Market**. For silk outfits, try **Khaisilk Boutique**, while **Bao Khan Tailors** specialize in custom-made formal wear. You can also visit **VN Colour**, **Gia Thuong**, and **Thang**.

Dressmaker taking measurements of a client at a shop in Hoi An

In Hanoi, **Khai Silk** gets rave reviews, especially for formal attire, while **Ha Noi Silk** can tailor suits in 24 hours. For an excellent row of silk shops, walk down Hang Gia Street. Traditional clothing and silver jewelry can be found at **La Boutique and The Silk**. In Ho Chi Minh City, **H&D Tailors** make outfits for men, and women can get an *ao dai*, a traditional Vietnamese dress, made at **Ao Dai Si Hoang**. Check out **Creation** for custom-made outfits.

FURNITURE

Furniture is regarded as an art form in Vietnam. Most of what is available is finely wrought hardwood, often inlaid with mother of pearl or richly carved. Special orders are gladly taken, and most shops also arrange to ship your purchases home. In Ho Chi Minh City, **Furniture Outlet** offers some of the best pieces and prices, while Tien An carries light furniture, specializing in bamboo chairs, cabinets, and grass mats. **Do Kim Dung** features a line of cast-and-wrought iron furniture, and **The Lost Art** offers antique pieces and reproductions. In Hanoi, **Viet Hien** carries a range of furnishings. And in Hoi An, **Kim Bong Carpentry** can make furniture to order from a photograph.

LACQUERWARE AND CERAMICS

Vietnam is famous for its lacquerware and ceramics, such as decorative pieces, tea sets, vases, bowls, plates, trays, and paintings to name a few. Some lacquer products feature an amazingly delicate inlay of eggshells or mother of pearl, while several ceramic pieces bear intricate designs. Jewelry boxes are also commonly rendered in lacquer. In Ho Chi Minh City, the noteworthy **Nga Shop** carries works by renowned designer Michele de Alberts. **Quang's Ceramics** in Hanoi has a splendid collection, and Le Duan Street also has some good shops. In Hoi An, there are many such shops selling traditional Vietnamese goods.

DIRECTORY

DEPARTMENT STORES AND MALLS

An Duong Plaza
18 An Duong Vuong St,
Cholon, HCMC.
Map 4 F4.
Tel (08) 3832 3288.

Big C Thang Long
222 Tran Duy Hung St,
Hanoi.

Diamond Plaza
34 Le Duan St,
Dist. 1, HCMC.
Map 2 E3.
Tel (08) 3822 5500.
www.diamondplaza.
com.vn

Parkson
35 bis 45 Le Than Ton St,
Phuong Ben Nghe,
HCMC. **Map** 2 E3.
Tel (08) 3827 7636.

Saigon Shopping Center
65 Le Loi St,
Dist. 1, HCMC.
Map 2 E4.
Tel (08) 3829 4888.
www.keppelland.com.sg

Tax Trading Center
39 Le Loi St,
Dist. 1, HCMC.
Map 2 F4.
Tel (08) 3821 6475.

Trang Tien Plaza
24 Hai Ba Trung St,
Hanoi.
Map 2 E4.

Vincom City Towers
191 Ba Trieu St, Hanoi.
Map 2 E5.
Tel (04) 3974 9999.
www.vincomjsc.com

Vincom Shopping Center
72 Le Thanh Ton St,
Dist. 1, HCMC.
Map 2 E3.
Tel (08) 3936 9999.
www.vincomcenter.com

Zen Plaza
54 Nguyen Trai St,
Dist. 1, HCMC.
Map 2 D5.
Tel (08) 3925 0339.

MARKETS

Hang Da Market
Cnr. of Hang Ga
and Doung Thanh Sts,
Hanoi.
Map 2 D2.

Old Market
Cnr. of Ham Nghi and
Ton That Dam Sts,
Dist. 1, HCMC.
Map 2 F4.

ARTS AND CRAFTS

Bao Nghi
127 Dong Khoi St, Dist.1,
HCMC.
Map 2 F4.
Tel (08) 3823 4521.

Craft Link
43 Van Mieu St, Hanoi.
Map 1 B4.
Tel (04) 3843 7710.
www.craftlink.com.vn

Craft Window
97 Nguyen Thai Hoc St,
Hanoi.
Map 1 C3.

Dogma
43 Ton That Thien St,
Dist. 1, HCMC.
Map 2 E4.
Tel (08) 3821 8019.

Em Em
38 Mac Thi Buoi St,
Dist. 1, HCMC.
Map 2 F4.
Tel (08) 3829 4408.

Galerie Quynh
65 De Them St, Dist. 1,
HCMC. **Map** 2 D5.
Tel (08) 3836 8019.
www.galeriequynh.com

Hanoi Gallery
110 Hang Bac St, Hanoi.
Map 2 E3.

House of Traditional Handicrafts
41 Le Loi St, Hoi An.
Tel (0510) 386 2164.

La Gai Handicrafts
103 Nguyen Thai Hoc St,
Hoi An.
Tel (0510) 391 0496.

Lan Handicrafts
36 Phan Phu Tien,
Hanoi. **Map** 1 B4.
Tel (04) 3843 8443.

Que Noi Gallery
87 Hung Vuong St,
Hoi An.
Tel (0510) 386 1792.

Sapa
223 De Tham, Dist. 1,
HCMC. **Map** 2 D5.
Tel (08) 3836 5163.

Tan My
66 Hang Gai St, Hanoi.
Map 2 E3. *Tel (04) 3825
1579.* www.tanmy
embroidery.com.vn

Viet Hien
8B Ta Hien St, Hanoi.
Map 2 E2.
Tel (04) 3826 9769.

CLOTHING

Ao Dai Si Hoang
135 Namky Khoi Nghia,
Dist. 1, HCMC.
Map 2 E3.
Tel (08) 3993 8040.

Bao Khan Tailors
37 Phan Dinh Phung St,
Hoi An.
Tel (0510) 391 0757.

Creation
105 Dong Khoi St,
Dist. 1, HCMC. **Map** 2 F4.
Tel (08) 3829 5429.

Gia Thuong
41 Nguyen Thai Hoc St,
Hoi An.
Tel (0510) 386 1816.

H&D Tailors
76 Le Lai St, Dist. 1,
HCMC. **Map** 2 D5.
Tel (08) 3824 3517.

Ha Noi Silk
Sofitel Plaza, 1 Thanh
Nien Rd, Hanoi. **Map** 2
E3. *Tel (04) 3716 3062.*
www.hanoisilkvn.com

Hoi An Cloth Market
Cnr. of Tran Phu and
Hoang Dieu Sts, Hoi An.

Khai Silk
121 Nguyen Thai Hoc St,
Hanoi. **Map** 1 C3.
Tel (04) 3747 0583.
www.khaisilkcorp.com

Khaisilk Boutique
Hoi An Riverside Resort,
Cua Dai Rd, Hoi An.
Tel (0510) 386 4800.
www.khaisilkcorp.com

La Boutique and The Silk
40 Hang Trong St, Hanoi.
Map 2 E3.
Tel (04) 3928 5368.

Thang
66 Tran Phu St,
Hoi An.
Tel (0510) 386 3173.

VN Colour
79 Nguyen Thai Hoc St,
Hoi An.
Tel (0510) 391 0827.

Yaly Couture
358 Nguyen Duy Hieu St,
Hoi An.
Tel (0510) 391 4995.
www.yalycouture.com

FURNITURE

Do Kim Dung
42 Mac Thi Buoi St,
Dist. 1, HCMC.
Map 2 F4.
Tel (08) 3822 2539.

Furniture Outlet
3B Ton Duc Thang St,
Dist. 1, HCMC.
Map 2 F2.
Tel (08) 3827 2728.

Kim Bong Carpentry
108 Nguyen Thai Hoc St,
Hoi An.
Tel (0510) 3862 279.

The Lost Art
18 Nguyen Hue St,
Dist. 1, HCMC.
Map 2 F4.
Tel (08) 3827 4649.

Viet Hien
See Arts and Crafts.

LACQUERWARE AND CERAMICS

Nga Shop
61 Le Thanh Ton St,
Dist. 1, HCMC.
Map 2 F3.
Tel (08) 3825 6289.

Quang's Ceramics
95 Ba Trieu St,
Hanoi.
Map 2 E5.
Tel (04) 3945 4235.

What to Buy in Vietnam

Sprawling traditional markets, sidewalk hawkers, and even the odd shopping mall in Vietnam offer a wide range of attractive and unique items. Almost anything wearable is usually a good bargain, be it clothing, footwear, or jewelry, while handicrafts such as ceramics, basketry, lacquerware, and even paintings by local artists make splendid souvenirs. The most distinctive items on sale are the exquisite hand-embroidered goods and silver jewelry of the hill peoples. In direct contrast, but just as tempting, are the surfeit of counterfeit products found just about everywhere.

Pretty silk bag in Hanoi

Hand-dyed silks of the White Tai decorated with distinctive patterns

Clothes, Shoes, and Accessories

The traditional ao dai *is surely the best pick for women. The two-piece is available in cotton, silk, and synthetics in a variety of colors. Vietnam also offers affordable clothing ranging from cotton T-shirts to silk dresses and designer wear – often good value compared to the West. Vietnamese-style silk shirts and trousers are also tailored cheaply and quickly. Stoles and scarves embroidered or woven by hill peoples are well worth every* dong.

Richly embroidered bags of the Red Dao minority

Finely woven stoles with beaded tassles

Flip-flops with bright designs

Tailored silk dress with a Chinese collar

Lacquerware

The Viets learned to harvest lacquer from sumac trees about 2,000 years ago, and even today, the country offers the most beautiful lacquer souvenirs. Even the simplest boxes, vases, and jewelry are transformed into exquisite objets d'art once they have been covered in lacquer – a process that takes months to complete. The lacquer is generally applied on a wooden base, and is usually painted or embellished with intricate inlay work.

Bowl glazed with brightly dyed lacquer

Spice jars painted with traditional motifs

Pencil case with mother-of-pearl inlay work

Lacquerware inlaid with eggshells

Mariners' compass set with zodiacal symbols

Lacquered jewelry box, with carvings of birds and leaves

Ceramics

From giant pots to tiny teacups, Vietnamese potters create beautiful and useful ceramic artifacts, which are sold throughout the country. Most renowned are the items created by the artisans in Bat Trang near Hanoi. The area is known for the quality of its white clay, and the unique glazing styles, such as "ancient pearl glaze" and "indigo-blue flower glaze," which evolved here over the centuries.

Hand-painted ceramic elephants

Chinese-style, blue-and-white porcelain jar

Huge vases with swirling floral designs over ivory glaze

Paintings

Vietnam is fast becoming a draw for art collectors. Watercolors and oils are found almost everywhere, but most exquisite are the unique lacquer and silk paintings. The finest art is found in the cultural hubs of Hanoi, Hoi An, and Hue.

Silver Jewelry of the Hill Peoples

Silver is a traditional symbol of wealth among many hill peoples. Antique earrings, chunky pendants, and bangles are commonly available in shops in major towns and villages. Ornate silver belts worn by women are especially attractive.

A colorful painting by a contemporary artist

Traditional Red Dao headdress

Selection of silver earrings

Rattan trays used for serving

Wooden fruit bowls

Traditional Vietnamese conical hat

Wicker serving tray with ceramic handles

Painted cosmetic box

Bamboo, Rush, Leaves, and Grass

Woven with great skill into interesting shapes and sizes, grass and rush mats are used as mattresses, seating, and curtains in Vietnam. Wicker trays and bowls are popular, as are embroidered bamboo window blinds and kitchenware. The traditional non la *or conical hats are found everywhere, often made from thick dried palm leaves. In Hue, the hats often reveal subtly painted designs when held up to the light.*

Brightly painted wicker Tet mask

ENTERTAINMENT IN VIETNAM

The cultural climate in Vietnam is more vibrant, exciting, and promising than ever. Traditional music and theater, first performed centuries ago, are being strongly promoted through cultural festivals held all around the country. Although the nation's rich artistic heritage draws international audiences, major cities also offer night clubs and modern multiplexes. Stately concert halls stage opera recitals, even as local pop stars belt out the latest ballads on makeshift stages. Ho Chi Minh City's midnight curfew is over, and a surfeit of bars and nightclubs tempt with live music and expertly mixed cocktails until the early hours of the morning. Water puppetry thrives in Hanoi, and so does jazz. Turntables and techno beats are common in small cities. Betting is legal but only on greyhounds and horses. With its many contrasts and contradictions, Vietnam offers a heady mix of entertainment options to all.

Retired pop singer
Ho Quynh Ha

Three of the leading lifestyle publications in Vietnam

INFORMATION

The official monthly magazine of the National Administration of Tourism, *Travellive* is packed with travel and lifestyle news from around the country, as is Vietnam Airlines' in-flight magazine *Heritage*. For maximum coverage of leisure and lifestyle issues and events, as well as up-to-date listings, pick up *The Word* and *Asia Life* monthly magazines, or *Time Out* for the city of your interest. Found free of charge in many restaurants, bars, and hotels, *Vietnam Pathfinder* has reviews and travel and culture stories from around the country. The national English-language newspaper, *Viet Nam News*, and the monthly *Saigon Times* feature sections dedicated to upcoming events in both Ho Chi Minh City and Hanoi.

BOOKING TICKETS

Buying tickets in advance is not yet the norm in Vietnam, but most hotels are very helpful, and will either book your tickets or purchase them in advance for you. Online booking is rare but **Ticket Vietnam** is an up-and-coming service. It is usual for most Vietnamese and visitors to buy tickets on arrival at the show's venue.

TRADITIONAL THEATER, MUSIC, AND DANCE

Traditional music, dance, and theater are inextricably linked in Vietnam, and one is usually incomplete without the other. Even as the nation races head-long toward modernization, these performing arts have been given great impetus by tourism and still thrive.

Hanoi is regarded as the cultural heart of Vietnam. Among other things, it is the birthplace of the nation's most delightfully idiosyncratic theatrical format, water puppetry *(see p159)*. The best place to see this unique art form, where marionettes enact wildly colorful tales on a watery stage, is the Thang Long Water Puppet Theater *(see p158)* at the **Kim Dong Theater** in Hanoi. The Museum of Vietnamese History *(see p61)* in Ho Chi Minh City holds daily performances, and **Binh Quoi Tourist Village** also includes water puppet shows in its range of cultural events.

Various forms of theatrical arts are popular in Vietnam. The nation's traditional theater *(see pp24–5)* can be categorized into three primary dramatic modes, *hat boi, hat cheo,* and *cai luong*. All three types are sung – *hat* means sing – and are distinctly operatic in form. Characterized by extravagant costumes and makeup, as well as highly stylized acting, *hat boi* or *tuong* is clearly influenced by Chinese theater but is Vietnamese in flavor.

A pared-down and simplified version of *hat boi* is *hat cheo*. Similar to operetta, this also focuses on high drama and tragedy, but is leavened with humor. *Cai luong*, in contrast, originated in the early 20th century and is somewhat like a Broadway musical. The stage is elaborately decorated, and every scene is rife with melodrama. Regardless of the story or song lyrics, it features a set number of tunes representing emotions such as happiness,

Elaborately costumed puppets, Water Puppet Theater, Hanoi

sadness, suspicion, and so on. Avid theatergoers know all the melodies by heart.

Today, traditional theater enjoys more widespread popularity in Hanoi than anywhere else in the country. *Hat cheo* performances are staged regularly in **National Cheo Theater**, while **Chuong Vang Theater** maintains focuses mainly on *cai luong*. On weekends, Den Ngoc Son *(see p160)* presents excerpts from *hat cheo* plays. Also check the local listings for theater performances at the Temple of Literature *(see pp166-7)*. In Ho Chi Minh City, **Hoa Binh Theater** stages several excellent renditions of traditional plays.

Apart from opera, Vietnam's classical music features both vocal and instrumental compositions. Once subject to the strict regulations and conventions of Hue's imperial court, formal music got a new lease of life under French-colonial rule. Three styles – *bac* (northern), *trung* (central), and *nam* (southern) – eventually emerged. Vietnamese chamber music employs string, percussion, and woodwind instruments, creating a distinctive sound. When used for traditional theater, brass is included in the orchestra to add dramatic resonance to the sound. Musicians play often in Ho Chi Minh City's Reunification Hall *(see p61)* but their performances do not follow a set schedule. Like Hanoi and Ho Chi Minh City, most cities and towns have prominent cultural centers and theaters. In Hoi An, the **Traditional Arts Theater** hosts musical recitals and plays almost every night. **Classical Opera Theater** in Danang and Hue's Biennial Arts festival, held in June every even-numbered year, keep ancient Vietnamese drama, dance, and music alive. Also in Hue, the Hon Chen Temple *(see p148)* presents music and dance performances and recitals in the third and seventh lunar

Traditional music performance in Ho Chi Minh City

Actor in full cai luong regalia

months. Nha Trang's **Vien Dong Hotel** has a nightly program showcasing ethnic minority music and dance.

CONTEMPORARY MUSIC AND CONCERTS

Vietnam's most celebrated concert halls are the Opera House *(see p162)* in Hanoi and the Municipal Theater *(see p58)* in Ho Chi Minh City. They present orchestral music, Western and Asian opera, as well as pop music concerts. The **Conservatory of Music** in Ho Chi Minh City is home to the local symphony, and hosts classical music, opera, and jazz recitals regularly.

Given the country's balmy weather, the Vietnamese are extremely fond of outdoor concerts. In Ho Chi Minh City, the scenic **Van Hoa Park** is very popular, while Hanoians enjoy their favorite crooners around Hoan Kiem Lake *(see p160)*. Most of these shows feature Vietnamese pop music, and on occasion, a chorus line dance by women in their traditional *ao dai*. Although these performances may be an acquired taste for most foreigners, the festive atmosphere is extremely infectious. Sports stadiums, such as Ho Chi Minh City's **Military Region 7 Stadium**, are also common concert venues. Young Vietnamese turn up in great numbers to watch the local stars perform live.

Certain restaurants, bars, and fashion houses in Ho Chi Minh City and Hanoi also present lively concerts fairly often. These events are announced in the local media, but hotel concierges are also good sources of information. **Maxim's Dinner Theater**, one of the oldest such venues in Ho Chi Minh City, can be relied on for a fine meal and an enjoyable show. It showcases everything from string quartets and pop music to Vietnamese folk songs and the latest local rock acts.

MODERN THEATER

Although there are many fine and ambitious playwrights producing insightful dramas and comedies, modern theater is a connoisseur's art in this country. Plays, usually in Vietnamese, are generally staged in small, tucked-away theaters. One good venue for foreigners is the **Ho Chi Minh City Drama Theater**, where local works are presented with English subtitles. Hanoi's **Youth Theater** is one of the best theater operations in the country. Its director, Le Hung, studied his craft in Moscow where he was inspired by Stanislavsky and Brecht. He now brings those teachings to bear on contemporary Vietnam. Many plays performed by the repertory group have been written by Le himself, while others are adaptations of works by Vietnamese and foreign playwrights. Most interesting are the modernized versions of *hat cheo*, which are staged occasionally.

The exterior of the ultra-cool Q Bar, Ho Chi Minh City

MOVIES

Vietnamese movies are occasionally dubbed or subtitled for an English-speaking audience. Some movie halls in Hanoi, such as the **National Cinema Theater** and **Cinematheque**, are noteworthy venues for locally produced art and foreign-language films. In all major cities, **Megastar Cineplex** features the latest international releases. Foreign films are also very popular in smaller towns, although they are mostly seen on pirated video CDs and DVDs.

NIGHTCLUBS, DISCOS, AND BARS

Even in the first few years of Vietnam's economic reforms or *doi moi*, it seemed that the only legal hedonistic pursuit available in Ho Chi Minh City was nursing a tepid beer in a backpacker hangout. Today, the city's nightlife is picking up at an encouraging pace. **Hien and Bob's Place**, one of the oldest bars around, set an example for a slew of other intimate little watering holes.

While many bars in Ho Chi Minh City seem to come and go almost on a weekly basis, some old favorites such as **Apocalypse Now** are still going strong. This is the most famous nightclub in Vietnam and has a branch in Hanoi as well. Ho Chi Minh City's backpacker district, in and around Pham Ngu Lao Street, boasts a string of dingy bars and lively clubs. Among them, **163 Cyclo Bar** is the most upscale, with a great view of the street. For a quiet drink one can head for **Bach Duong**, a coffee bar that usually plays Vietnamese music. Both **California Pizza Works** and **Red Dot** provide cold beers along with filling bites to eat. Newer to the scene is **Blue Gecko**, a popular bar, complete with a pool table and dart board. **Lucky Café** allows you to watch sports on its large screen as you down your beer. **Car Men Bar** is famous for its wooden walls and flamenco music, while the **Rainforest Discotheque** boasts a decor that matches its name.

Greater sophistication can be found at rooftop bars in Dong Khoi Street's posh hotels such as Rooftop Garden at the Rex *(see p60)*. Live bands play music as guests watch the city go by below. The same goes for Saigon Saigon in the Caravelle *(see p58)*, **Bellevue Bar**, and **Saigon Pearl**. **Q Bar**, set in the same building as the Municipal Theater *(see p58)*, is a trendy and happening spot, while for an evening of mellow live jazz, few venues can match the atmospheric **Sax n Art**.

Hanoi may not be quite as glamorous as Ho Chi Minh City but its inhabitants know how to enjoy themselves. Tiny places where the local beer *bia hoi (see p247)* is the specialty are very popular. For those who want to avoid the rough and ready, **Restaurant Bobby Chinn** is a hip hangout with great wine, shisha, and the celebrity chef himself. Classical music on piano and violin is played at **O.V. Club**, while **Seventeen Saloon** is all about the Wild West. **Relax Bar** is a great place to do just that.

Most interesting, though, is Hanoi's thriving jazz scene. A shifting network of clubs can be tracked through the local media, but the top spot is the superb **Jazz Club** where local sax master Quyen Van Minh jams almost every night.
In Hoi An, **Tam Tam Café & Bar** *(see p256)* has a decor redolent of old Indochina, but a hip DJ spins at night. The **Amsterdam Bar** specializes in dry gin and succulent snacks.

Nha Trang's **Louisiane Brewhouse** is a great place to spend an afternoon or evening, while **La Bella Napoli** serves the only glass of grappa in town. One of the best hangouts here is the **Sailing Club**, a laid-back bar by day and hip dance club by night. In Hue, the **DMZ Bar** oozes old-world charm, while the **Why Not Bar** is perfect for a long cocktail.

Karaoke clubs are generally fronts for prostitution and are best avoided as the government is currently cracking down on these bars.

SPECTATOR SPORTS

Without doubt, football is the national passion. Local teams and leagues are revered, and the country seems to come to a halt for the World Cup. Most major matches take place at **Thong Nhat Stadium** in Ho Chi Minh City and **My Dinh National Stadium** in Hanoi. Following a close second is badminton, which the Vietnamese enjoy playing even more than they like to watch the national champions.

Gambling is an integral part of Vietnamese customs and culture but is mostly illegal in the country. However, the state-run lottery, the **Saigon Racing Club**, and **Lam Son Stadium**, where greyhounds race, are above board.

A horse race in progress at the famous Saigon Racing Club

DIRECTORY

BOOKING TICKETS

Ticket Vietnam
www.ticketvn.com

TRADITIONAL THEATER, MUSIC, AND DANCE

Binh Quoi Tourist Village
1147 Xo Viet Nghe Tinh St, Binh Thanh Dist, HCMC.
Tel (08) 3898 8599.

Chuong Vang Theater
72 Hang Bac St, Hanoi.
Map 2 E3.
Tel (04) 3826 0374.

Classical Opera Theater
155 Phan Chu Trinh St, Danang.
Tel (0511) 356 1291.

Hoa Binh Theater
240 Ba Thang Hai St, Dist. 10, HCMC. **Map** 1 A5.
Tel (08) 3865 5215.

Kim Dong Theater
57B Dinh Tien Hoang St, Hanoi. **Map** 2 E3.
Tel (04) 3824 9494.

National Cheo Theater
Khu Van Cong Mai Dich Tu Liem St, Hanoi.
Tel (04) 3764 3280.

Traditional Arts Theater
75 Nguyen Thai Hoc St, Hoi An.
Tel (0510) 386 1159.

Vien Dong Hotel
1 Tran Hung Dao St, Nha Trang.
Tel (058) 352 3608.

CONTEMPORARY MUSIC AND CONCERTS

Conservatory of Music
112 Nguyen Du St, Dist. 1, HCMC. **Map** 2 D4.
Tel (08) 3824 3774.

Maxim's Dinner Theater
13,15,17 Dong Khoi St, Dist. 1, HCMC. **Map** 2 F4.
Tel (08) 3829 6676.

Military Region 7 Stadium
2 Pho Quang St, Tan Binh, HCMC.

Van Hoa Park
115 Nguyen Du St, Dist. 1, HCMC. **Map** 2 D3.

MODERN THEATER

Ho Chi Minh City Drama Theater
30 Tran Hung Dao St, Dist. 1, HCMC. **Map** 2 E5.
Tel (08) 3836 9556.

Youth Theater
11 Ngo Thi Nham St, Hanoi. **Map** 2 E5.
Tel (04) 3943 4673.

MOVIES

Cinematheque
22A Hai Ba Trung St, Hanoi. **Map** 2 E4.
Tel (04) 3936 2648.

Megastar Cineplex
www.megastar.vn

National Cinema Theater
87 Lang Ha St, Hanoi.
Map 1 A3.
Tel (04) 3514 1791.

NIGHTCLUBS, DISCOS, AND BARS

163 Cyclo Bar
163 Pham Ngu Lao St, Dist. 1, HCMC. **Map** 2 D5.
Tel (08) 3920 1567.

Amsterdam Bar
Life Resort, 1 Pham Hong Thai St, Hoi An.
Tel (0510) 391 4555.

Apocalypse Now
2 C Thi Sach St, Dist. 1, HCMC. **Map** 2 F3.
Tel (08) 3825 6124.

25C Hoa Ma St, Hanoi.
Tel (04) 3971 2783.

Bach Duong
28 Phan Dinh Phung St, Hanoi. *Tel (04) 3733 8255.*

Bellevue Bar
Majestic Hotel, 1 Dong Khoi St, Dist. 1, HCMC.
Map 2 F4.
Tel (08) 3829 5514.
www.majesticsaigon.com

Blue Gecko
31 Ly Tu Trong, Dist. 1, HCMC. **Map** 2 E3.
Tel (08) 3824 3483.

California Pizza Works
25B Tran Cao Van St, Dist. 1, HCMC. **Map** 2 D2.
Tel (08) 3827 9682.

Car Men Bar
8 Ly Tu Trong St, Dist. 1, HCMC.
Tel (08) 3829 7699.

DMZ Bar
60 Le Loi St, Hue.
Tel (054) 382 3414.
www.dmzbar.com.vn

Hien and Bob's Place
43 Hai Ba Trung St, Dist. 1, HCMC.
Map 2 F3.
Tel (08) 3823 0661.

Jazz Club
31 Luong Van Cam St, Hanoi. **Map** 2 E3.
Tel (04) 3828 7890.

La Bella Napoli
60 Hung Vuong St, Nha Trang.
Tel (058) 352 7299.

Louisiane Brewhouse
Lot 29, Tran Phu St, Nha Trang. *Tel (058) 352 1948.*

Lucky Café
224 De Tham St, Dist. 1, HCMC. **Map** 2 D5.
Tel (08) 3836 7277.

O. V. Club
15 Ngo Quyen St, Hoi An.
Tel (04) 3733 0808.

Q Bar
7 Lam Son Sq, Dist. 1, HCMC. **Map** 2 F3.
Tel (08) 3823 3479.
www.qbarsaigon.com

Rainforest Discotheque
5–15 Ho Huan Nghiep St, Dist. 1, HCMC.
Map 2 F3.
Tel (08) 3821 8753.

Red Dot
15/17 Phan Van Dat St, Dist. 1, HCMC. **Map** 2 F4.
Tel (08) 3822 6178.

Relax Bar
60 Ly Thuong Kiet St, Hanoi.
Tel (08) 3942 4409.

Restaurant Bobby Chinn
77 Xuan Dieu St, Hanoi.
Map 2 E4.
Tel (04) 3719 2460.
www.bobbychinn.com

Saigon Pearl
Palace Hotel, 56–66 Nguyen Hue St, Dist. 1, HCMC. **Map** 2 F4.
Tel (08) 3829 2860.
www.palacesaigon.com

Sailing Club
72 Tran Phu St, Nha Trang. *Tel (058) 382 6528.* www.sailingclub vietnam.com

Sax n Art
28 Le Loi, Dist. 1, HCMC. **Map** 2 E3.
Tel (08) 3822 8472.
www.saxnart.com

Seventeen Saloon
98B Tran Hung Dao St, Hanoi. **Map** 2 D4.
Tel (04) 3942 6822.

Tam Tam Café and Bar
110 Nguyen Thai Hoc, Hoi An.
Tel (0510) 386 2212.

Why Not Bar
21 Vo Thi Sau St, Hue.
Tel (054) 382 4793.

SPECTATOR SPORTS

Lam Son Stadium
15 Le Loi St, Vung Tau.
Tel (064) 380 7309.

My Dinh National Stadium
Hoa Lac St, Tu Liem Dist, Hanoi.

Saigon Racing Club
2 Le Dai Hanh St, Dist. 11, HCMC.
Map 3 C2.
Tel (08) 3962 4319.

Thong Nhat Stadium
138 Dao Duy Tu St, Dist. 10, HCMC.
Map 4 E3.
Tel (08) 3855 7865.

OUTDOOR ACTIVITIES AND SPECIAL INTERESTS

With its misty mountain tops, tropical forests, gushing rivers, and increasingly cosmopolitan cities, Vietnam today is a playground for a range of activities. The country's relatively undeveloped coastline stretches for hundreds of miles, and is a water lover's dream, with secluded beaches, pristine bays, and an untrammeled surf. Trekkers and nature enthusiasts are drawn to the impressive network of national parks, mountain trails, and nature walks, while cyclists embrace the opportunity to explore the terrain or ride

Footballer on Vung Tao beach

on uncrowded roads all the way from Hanoi to Ho Chi Minh City. Catering to the needs of millions of international visitors, luxury golf clubs have cropped up in all the major cities and resort towns. Food lovers can exercise their palates on one of the many culinary holidays, savoring the imperial cuisine of Hue and the exotic fruit of Mekong Delta as they go along. With so many activities to choose from, Vietnam is a multifaceted country with something that fits the interests and budget of most visitors traveling here.

Divers preparing to go under, Nha Trang

DIVING, SNORKELING, AND SWIMMING

The best developed location for diving in Vietnam is the resort town of Nha Trang *(see pp108–11)*, which is home to several competent specialists offering equipment, boats, and instructors for crash courses. **Rainbow Divers** is the oldest and most trusted operation for aquatic activities here, and has a number of branches in diving locales throughout the country. Nha Trang has many other reliable outfits in operation, including **Sailing Club Divers**. About 37 miles (60 km) north of town, **Whale Island Resort** is an increasingly popular location for both diving and snorkeling. Located farther south, Phu Quoc Island *(see p101)* and Con Dao Island *(see p98)* are blessed with shallow coral reefs, and are primed to become serious competitors to Nha Trang. At the moment, Phu Quoc and

Con Dao are both relatively unspoiled, and much cheaper than Nha Trang. Rainbow Divers is the sole operator in these places. Hoi An *(see pp124–8)*, with its string of fishermen's islands about an hour's boat ride from shore, provides excellent diving opportunities in Central Vietnam. One-, two-, and three-day trips to these islands can be organized by **Cham Island Diving Center**.

Most beaches along the coast from Danang *(see p134)* to Nha Trang offer stretches of water ideal for swimming. Among the safest is Mui Ne Beach *(see p106)*, where the undercurrents are weakest. Swimming facilities are also available in cities, as most hotels allow the use of their pools for a small sum. In Ho Chi Minh City, Grand Hotel *(see p233)* offers one of the cheapest rates for a day at its pool, while the International Club has a pool, sauna, steam room, and gym available for less than US$10 per day. In Hanoi, the swimming pools in **Army Hotel** and **Thang Loi Hotel** are affordable to use. Water parks such as Dam Sen *(see p71)* in Ho Chi Minh City, **Ho Tay Water Park** in Hanoi, as well as the **Phu Dong Water Park** in Nha Trang are all good for a nice dip.

SURFING, KITE-BOARDING, AND WINDSURFING

Although few Vietnamese surf, many foreign visitors take advantage of the superb, if not terribly huge waves at China Beach *(see p133)*. Surfing boards can be rented locally.

Kite-boarding has caught on in a big way at Mui Ne, which is now the site of an annual international competition in the sport. The calm sea and strong winds provide perfect conditions. **Jibe's Beach Club** offers kite-boarding package holidays. The popularity of windsurfing is also escalating. Two operations for both kite-boarding and windsurfing are **Storm Kiteboarding** and **Windchimes**.

Windsurfers riding the gentle waves of the South China Sea, Mui Ne

KAYAKING

Kayaks, still something of a novelty in Vietnam, were first introduced at Halong Bay *(see pp182–4)*, and soon proved to be ideal for exploring the islands, coves, and caves of the area. While visitors are free to wander the waters on their own, it is wise to contract with a specialist tour agency. Reliable outfits include old favorites Sinh Café *(see p281)* and **Buffalo Tours**, both of which arrange kayaking holidays. Also recommended is **Handspan Adventure Travel**, known for keeping to small groups and using its own vehicles and guides. **Green Trail Tours** organizes kayaking tours in Halong Bay as well as at Ba Be Lake *(see p200)* and the Mekong Delta.

Kayaking in the crystal clear waters of Halong Bay

GOLF

Once regarded by Communist Party stalwarts as a decadent and bourgeois pastime, golf is becoming popular in Vietnam. Once the domain of the expatriate community, golf clubs are now frequented by a growing number of local Vietnamese enthusiasts. While club memberships are quite expensive, guest fees are not so steep.

Courses are clustered around Ho Chi Minh City, Mui Ne, Danang, Dalat, and Hanoi. **Rach Chiec Driving Range** is about a 10-minute drive north of the city center, and is more economical than most venues. **Vietnam Golf and Country Club** is a top-class facility, with two floodlit 18-hole courses that enable guests to play at night.

In Hanoi, you can practice your swing at **Lang Ha Driving Range**, while an hour west of the city is the exclusive **King's**

The luxuriant expanse of the beachside Ocean Dunes golf course, Phan Thiet

Island Golf Course. The most popular courses, though, are in and around Dalat *(see p114–16)*. Two extremely stylish golf clubs are **Dalat Palace**, established during the French-colonial era, and Phan Thiet's **Ocean Dunes**, designed by Nick Faldo. **Sea Links** in Mui Ne is one of the country's most luxurious courses.

TREKKING

The sheer topographic variety found in Vietnam makes it a mecca for trekkers. You can choose between nature walks on national park trails or go on a hike on mountain slopes, adventurous romps through densely foliaged forests, and long strolls along the beaches.

The northern mountainous area around Sapa *(see pp196–7)* is one of the most popular trekking areas with visitors and locals alike, served by many tour agencies such as **Topas Adventure**, **Exotissimo**, and **Footprints**. Both take pride in their hands-on style, and provide local guides, who make useful ambassadors when approaching ethnic villages.

National parks are also ideal for trekking expeditions, with tended trails and some basic infrastructure. Cat Ba National Park *(see p189)* has one of the most challenging hiking trails in the park system. It winds its way through 29 miles (18 km) of jungle, right up to the summit of one of the park's highest hills. Sturdy shoes, a plastic raincoat, and plenty of water are essential. It is advisable to hire a guide. Any nearby hotel can make the necessary arrangements. Not all trails in Cuc Phuong National Park *(see p193)*

are marked, so it is best to take a guide. The longest walk here is a five-hour trek to the village of Kanh, where one can stay the night and go rafting on Buoi River. A 5-mile (8-km) trek takes hikers deep into the forest to a huge tree said to be 1,000 years old. Shorter hikes include a nice walk through the botanical garden and to the Primate Rescue Center, while another leads to a cave where prehistoric artifacts were discovered.

Some of the most impressive trails are in Bach Ma National Park *(see p136)*. Summit Trail leads to the top of Bach Ma Mountain or White Horse Mountain, so named for the streaks of white cloud often seen at its summit. The stunning views are well worth the steep climb. The Five Lakes Cascade Trail takes hikers by a series of enchanting waterfalls through the park, and is filled with rare flora and fauna. Alternatively, the Rhododendron Trail lives up to its name during spring when it is cloaked in flowers.

A section of the Five Lake Cascade Trail, Bach Ma National Park

CYCLING

The best way to get a feel of the "real" Vietnam is on a bicycle. The route between Hanoi and Ho Chi Minh City has become the Holy Grail for many cyclists. Highway 1 has become congested and is also susceptible to flooding, so the preferred route these days is Highway 14. While it lacks the ocean breeze of the coastal route, it is still very picturesque.

The Mekong Delta region offers easy riding on flat roads. Views here are beautiful, especially at rice harvest time. In the Central Highlands, mountain cycling is taking off, though there are no dedicated trails at present. The condition of the roads along the southern route can vary; however, the many rivers and bridges on the way provide scenic stopovers. **Veloasia** organizes customized cycling tours to remote parts of the country, as does the excellent Bangkok-based **SpiceRoads**. However, try to avoid long-distance tours in the northern mountains in winter as the roads can be slippery and quite dangerous. For cycling in Dalat and the South Central Highlands, try **Phat Tire Ventures**.

Cyclists planning to travel independently should bring their own gear – rented bikes can be unreliable. If the bike breaks down, there are several bicycle repair shops along the way. You will also have to be vigilant of your possessions.

Cyclists exploring the streets of Hoi An

Martial arts instructor practising in a park, a common sight

MARTIAL ARTS

Martial arts are an important part of the cultural, athletic, and social mix in Vietnam. Many forms are practised here, including the indigenous *vo dao*, the origins of which go back around 2,000 years. Like judo, it turns the opponent's strength against him or her, and like kung fu, includes a wide vocabulary of blows. Weapons such as cudgels, swords, and axes can also be incorporated into the practitioner's repertoire. You can take a course or just watch a class at **Nam Huynh Pagoda** in Ho Chi Minh City. Another martial art that is indigenous to Vietnam is *sa long cuong*. It stresses the principles of mind over matter, and flexibility over rigidity. Lessons are given at the **Youth Culture House of HCMC** in Ho Chi Minh City.

Various other combative arts such as judo, aikido, and kung fu can be practised at **Phu Tho Stadium** in Ho Chi Minh City for a minimal fee. Those who are only interested in watching the art can do so for free as well. In some of the city's parks, particularly in the Cholon district, it is common to see martial arts instructors practising in full-swing. In Hanoi, taekwondo – a style of unarmed combat for self-defence – is the most popular martial art, and the renowned **GTC Club** in Hanoi is one of the best places to practice.

BIRD-WATCHING

Before the appearance of avian influenza, Vietnam was fast becoming a prime destination for bird-watching enthusiasts. The country is also an important breeding ground for many migratory birds, and the more common birds can be spotted everywhere. At one time, tour agencies were beginning to include specialized tours in their itineraries, and information was easy to come by in tourist offices. Currently, one can only hope that the bird flu situation improves soon and visitors can once again enjoy Vietnam's feathered fauna.

Fresh ingredients and spices awaiting preparation, Hue

CULINARY HOLIDAYS

Vietnam is home to one of the most interesting cuisines in the world. While culinary tours can be expensive, most epicures swear by them. New York-based **Absolute Asia** offers a luxury tour that starts in Ho Chi Minh City, moves on to Hoi An *(see pp124–8)* and Hue *(see pp138–44)*, and wraps up in Hanoi. In little more than a week, it lets you sample the basic styles of Vietnamese cooking. Cookery classes can be another option. Many hotels offer courses, one of the best being Madame Thi Kim Hai's at the Sofitel Metropole Hotel *(see p162)* in Hanoi. This half-day course takes you on a trip to the market and then back to the kitchen to prepare the ingredients in northern style. Another interesting course to take a look at is **Miss Vy's Cooking Class** in Hoi An.

SPAS

Some of Vietnam's best spas are part of luxurious hotel complexes, like the Six Senses Hideaway Ninh Van Bay *(see p238)* in Ninh Hoa. However, other, smaller spas are also making a mark, such as the **Thap Ba Hot Springs** *(see p110)* in Nha Trang, and **Tam Spa** and **Forester Spa** in Mui Ne.

Water villas on the beach at the Six Senses Hideaway Ninh Van Bay, Ninh Hoa

DIRECTORY

DIVING, SNORKELING, AND SWIMMING

Army Hotel
33C Pham Ngu Lao St, Hanoi. **Map** 2 F4.
Tel (04) 3826 5541.

Cham Island Diving Center
88 Nguyen Thai Hoc St, Hoi An. *Tel (0510) 391 0782.*

Ho Tay Water Park
614 Lac Long Quan St, Hanoi. *Tel (04) 3718 4175.*

Phu Dong Water Park
Tran Phu St, Nha Trang.

Rainbow Divers
90A Hung Vuong St, Nha Trang. *Tel (058) 352 4351.*

Sailing Club Divers
72–74 Tran Phu St, Nha Trang. *Tel (058) 352 2788.*

Thang Loi Hotel
Yen Phu St, Ho Tay, Hanoi. *Tel (04) 3823 8161.*

Whale Island Resort
2 Me Linh St, Nha Trang. *Tel (058) 351 3871.*

SURFING, KITE-BOARDING, AND WINDSURFING

Jibe's Beach Club
90 Nguyen Dinh Chieu St, Mui Ne, Phan Thiet. *Tel (062) 384 7088.*

Storm Kiteboarding
24 Nguyen Dinh Chieu St, Mui Ne, Phan Thiet. *Tel (062) 384 7442.* **www.** stormkiteboarding.com

Windchimes
Saigon Mui Ne Resort, Mui Ne, Phan Thiet.
Tel (090) 972 0017.

KAYAKING

Buffalo Tours
Hanoi. *Tel (04) 3828 0702.* **www.buffalotours.com**

Green Trail Tours
Hanoi. *Tel (04) 3754 5268 (ext. 101).* **www. greentrail-indochina.com**

Handspan Adventure Travel
Hanoi. *Tel (04) 3926 0581.* **www.handspan.com**

GOLF

Dalat Palace
Phu Dong Thien Vuong St, Dalat. *Tel (063) 382 1201.*

King's Island Golf Course
Dong Mo Lake, Ha Tay. *Tel (034) 368 6555.*

Lang Ha Driving Range
16A Lang Ha St, Hanoi. *Tel (04) 3835 0908.*

Ocean Dunes
1 Ton Duc Thang St, Phan Thiet. *Tel (062) 382 1995.*

Rach Chiec Driving Range
An Phu Village, Dist. 9, HCMC. *Tel (08) 389 6756.*

Sea Links Golf & Country Club
Nguyen Dinh Chieu St, Mui Ne, Phan Thiet.

Tel (062) 374 1741. **www.sealinksvietnam. com**

Vietnam Golf and Country Club
Long Thanh My Village, Thu Duc, HCMC. *Tel (061) 3351 1812.*

TREKKING

Exotissimo
26 Tran Nhat Duat St, Hanoi. **Map** 2 E2. *Tel (04) 3828 2150.* **www.exotissimo.com**

Footprints
6 Le Thanh Tong St, Hanoi. **Map** 2 F5. *Tel (04) 3933 2844.* **www. footprintsvietnam.com**

Topas Adventure
2 To Ngoc Van St, Hanoi. **Map** 1 C1. *Tel (04) 3715 1005.* **www.topastravel.vn**

CYCLING

Phat Tire Ventures
73 Truong Cong Dinh St, Dalat. *Tel (063) 382 9422.* **www.phattireventures. com**

SpiceRoads
www.spiceroads.com

Veloasia
283/20 Pham Ngu Lao St, Dist. 1, HCMC.
Map 2 D5.
Tel (08) 3837 6766.
www.veloasia.com

MARTIAL ARTS

GTC Club
A3 Ngoc Khanh St, Hanoi. *Tel (04) 3846 3095.*

Nam Huynh Pagoda
29 Tran Quang Khai St, Dist. 1, HCMC.
Map 1 C1.

Phu Tho Stadium
1 Lu' Gia St, Dist. 11, HCMC. **Map** 3 C2.
Tel (08) 3866 0156.

Youth Culture House of HCMC
4 Pham Ngoc Thach St, Dist. 1, HCMC.
Map 2 E3.
Tel (08) 3829 4345.

CULINARY HOLIDAYS

Absolute Asia
www.absoluteasia.com

Miss Vy's Cooking Class
Cargo Club, 107 Nguyen Thai Hoc St, Hoi An. *Tel (0510) 391 0489.* **www.restaurant-hoian.com**

SPAS

Forester Spa
65A Nguyen Dinh Chieu St, Mui Ne, Phan Thiet.
Tel (062) 374 1317.

Tam Spa
9A Nguyen Dinh Chieu St, Mui Ne, Phan Thiet.
Tel (062) 374 1114.

Thap Ba Hot Springs
25 Ngoc Son St, Nha Trang.
Tel (058) 383 0090.
www.thapbahotspring. com.vn

SURVIVAL
GUIDE

PRACTICAL INFORMATION

Vietnam today is a top tourist destination, drawing an ever increasing number of visitors each year. Although the country opened up to tourism during the mid-1990s, it is only now that infrastructure and related facilities are gradually improving for the millions of tourists visiting each year. All major cities offer accommodations ranging from budget guesthouses to five-star hotels. Most towns and cities also have a range of restaurants catering to varying tastes and budgets. Almost the entire coastline is

Tourist with a street vendor

now open to tourist development and new resorts continue to crop up all the time. The white sand beaches and the spectacular coral reefs add to the beauty. Remote areas such as the northern mountains are still relatively undeveloped – a virtue perhaps – but not too difficult to access given the proliferation of travel agencies in most cities. Government-run outfits are not known for their helpfulness, but there are several reliable private tour operators who can arrange organized trips in most parts of this scenic and beautiful country.

WHEN TO GO

The temperature and rainfall patterns in Vietnam fluctuate widely from region to region *(see pp34–5)*. Hence, visitors should make their itineraries according to the area they plan to visit, taking care to avoid the worst of the monsoon. The south gets its heaviest rainfall between May and November, while in the north, May to August are the wettest months. However, as these rainy months are in the off-season, it can work out much cheaper to visit. But bear in mind it can be uncomfortable and inconvenient due to flooding and low visibility.

If you want to participate in major holidays such as Tet *(see pp28–9)*, the period from December to February is best, although prices are higher. For better weather and fewer crowds, the period from March to May is the best time to visit.

A balmy January afternoon at Phan Thiet *(see p106)*

WHAT TO TAKE

There is very little that cannot be bought in Vietnam's towns and cities, and at cheaper rates than back home. Villages and more remote areas are not likely to offer the same range of options though. In general, it is advisable to wear a wide-brimmed hat and carry lots of sunblock, while a collapsible umbrella is a must for rainy months. It is also a good idea to keep a Swiss army knife, a torch and batteries, and a mosquito repellent handy.

The best clothing for the south's warm, tropical climate is pale, lightweight colored cotton or silk. Shoes should be light in weight as you will probably need to walk a lot. In the north, especially in the highlands, nights are cold and day temperatures can fall quite low. Travelers should wear layers to trap body heat in order to keep warm.

ADVANCE BOOKING

The peak flying season to Vietnam is from December to February. During this time, thousands of Viet Kieu or overseas Vietnamese flock back to their homeland to spend Christmas and Tet with their families. Make reservations for this period at least three months in advance. Some travelers avoid this crush by entering overland from either Laos or Cambodia, but most countries in Southeast Asia

experience the same holiday rush. Several reliable travel agencies can take care of the bookings *(see p281 & p291)*. It is also wise to book your accommodation well in advance during this period, especially if you plan to stay in a high-end hotel. However, budget accommodations usually present no problem.

Posters advertising specialized tours offered by a travel agency

VISAS AND PASSPORTS

Most travelers to Vietnam must possess a valid passport and visa, whether entering by air, land, or sea. Citizens from a number of surrounding countries may receive visa waivers on arrival, of varying lengths. Visas to Vietnam are

A trader passport being inspected at the Chinese border

issued only by Vietnamese embassies and are best applied for through a travel agency. A procedure is now in place for granting visas on arrival. This process is usually carried out by local travel agencies.

A standard tourist visa is valid for only 30 days but can be extended 3 times. Those wishing to stay longer may make the brief journey to Phnom Penh, Cambodia, where they can apply for a new visa at the Vietnamese embassy. It takes two days to process. A business visa can be issued for up to six months in Phnom Penh, though officially the limit is three months. A multiple-entry visa, for both tourist and business purposes, can be applied for at an extra cost.

IMMUNIZATION

Several vaccinations have been recommended by the World Health Organization (WHO) for anyone traveling in Southeast Asia. The list of diseases that one needs to be immunized against includes hepatitis A and B, tetanus, rubella, measles, mumps, diphtheria, and typhoid. Malaria has been eradicated from most of the country, but it is still present on Phu Quoc Island and Highland areas. Drug recommendations for malaria can vary depending on time, terrain, weather, and even the breed of mosquito. It is best to consult your family doctor or the WHO in advance when traveling to this region.

Dengue fever is now a serious problem in Vietnam, as in many of the surrounding countries. Unfortunately, there is currently no vaccination to protect against it. The virus is transmitted by mosquito and the best form of prevention is the use of repellent and nets.

Be aware that the quality of medical facilities and other health care in Vietnam, especially in smaller towns and rural areas, can be very poor. Patients may also be refused treatment if they are unable to provide proof in advance that they can pay their medical fees. For further information on personal health, see pages 282–3.

CUSTOMS INFORMATION

Once attended by much red tape and strictness, customs regulations are now fairly straightforward in Vietnam. Visitors are allowed to bring in one liter of alcoholic beverages and 200 cigarettes with them. Any foreign currency and jewelry must be declared.

Upon arrival, a customs form has to be filled in, a yellow copy of which will be handed back to you. While few foreign visitors are searched, items deemed culturally offensive or sensitive can be seized, including pornography, CDs, video tapes, and any material considered critical of the government. The website of the **Vietnam Embassy** in the United States is a useful source of up-to-date information on customs regulations.

DIRECTORY

EMBASSIES

Australia
8 Dao Tan St, Hanoi.
Map 2 F3.
Tel (04) 3831 7755.
www.vietnam.embassy.gov.au

Cambodia
71 Tran Hung Dao St, Hanoi.
Map 2 D5.
Tel (04) 3942 4788.

Canada
31 Hung Vuong St, Hanoi.
Map 1 B3.
Tel (04) 3734 5000.
www.canadainternational.gc.ca/
vietnam

France
57 Tran Hung Dao St, Hanoi.
Map 2 E5.
Tel (04) 3943 7719.
www.ambafrance-vn.org

Laos
22 Tran Binh Trong St, Hanoi.
Map 1 D5.
Tel (04) 3942 4724.

United Kingdom
31 Hai Ba Trung St, Hanoi.
Map 2 E4.
Tel (04) 3936 0500.
http://ukinvietnam.fco.gov.uk/en

United States
7 Lang Ha St, Hanoi.
Tel (04) 3831 4590.
http://vietnam.usembassy.gov

CUSTOMS INFORMATION

Vietnam Embassy in the United States
www.vietnamembassy-usa.org

Group of tourists posing before Ho Chi Minh Mausoleum *(see p165)*

Neon-lit sign and logo of Saigon Tourist, Ho Chi Minh City

TOURIST INFORMATION

Vietnam's hospitality industry is still developing. The two official sources of information and assistance, **Saigon Tourist** and **Vietnam Tourism**, have improved greatly over the past few years and have very useful websites. However, they are both state-owned enterprises that expect to make a profit by operating hotels and arranging tours. Independent travel agents and tour operators (see also p291 & p293) are better and more service-oriented if you need help in planning your own itinerary, or if you want the benefits of a customized package tour. While there are a few dubious enterprises in business (namely the open tour bus companies), most service providers are reliable and knowledgeable.

ADMISSION CHARGES

Most museums, zoos, and botanical gardens charge a modest entry fee, which is usually US$1 or less. Until recently, a two-tiered pricing system was enforced, in which the price for foreigners could be five times that paid by the locals. This practice has been done away with officially, but is still prevalent in places. Most pagodas do not charge an admission fee, though a donation box is always prominently displayed.

FACILITIES FOR THE DISABLED

Unfortunately, facilities for the disabled are quite rare in this country, especially for those who use a wheelchair. Though the sidewalks are wide, it is quite difficult to maneuver a wheelchair along them as many street vendors have set up shop there, while others use them for parking their two-wheelers. There appear to be wheelchair ramps on every block, but these are actually meant for motorbike access. Elevators are not very common, and toilets for the disabled are virtually unheard of. Nonetheless, even though they should be ready for some discomfort, disabled travelers with special needs should not be deterred by these infrastructural shortcomings. Many high-end hotels and resorts are now well equipped to accommodate the disabled, while travel agents can hire an assistant, albeit not always a qualified one, for those who require one. With planning and the help of specialist agencies such as **Accessible Journeys** and **Society for Accessible Travel and Hospitality**, inconveniences can be minimized.

FACILITIES FOR CHILDREN

Children are adored by all and welcomed almost everywhere in this family-oriented nation. The sight of parents traveling with small children is common here, and diapers, baby food, and other child-care products are readily available, especially in bigger cities. All restaurants are child friendly; however, most do not offer any special menus. Some foods may be spicy for kids, but ice cream, yogurt, and fresh fruit are always on offer. There is little in the way of special accommodation for children, but many hotels have rooms furnished with three or more single beds.

LANGUAGE

With its range of tonal variations, Vietnamese can be a very hard language to learn. Fortunately, many people, especially those who want to sell goods or services to foreigners, speak a smattering of English. It is often fractured, and, at times, difficult to understand, but since Vietnamese is written in the Roman alphabet, most vendors can write what they need to say.

All the major airlines, banks, and hotels have some staff that speak adequate English. In rural areas, it is wise to travel with an interpreter or guide who can be hired for as little as US$10 a day.

Multilingual sign at a temple

ETIQUETTE

Vietnamese etiquette is strict but generally easy to comply with. As a rule, smile a lot, do not raise your voice, and never point at people. If you need to beckon or attract someone's attention, make sure that your palms are facing downwards before you gesture to them. It is also important to remember that losing your temper is counterproductive. The Vietnamese are more likely to respond to your grievances when they are addressed politely.

When meeting and greeting, shaking hands is customary. Do not touch anybody on the head as that is considered the repository of the soul. That said, most Vietnamese are tactile individuals. People of the same sex walk arm in arm, pat each other on the shoulder, and hold

Sacred pagoda, please donot wear short clothes   Welcome

Pagoda sign asking visitors to dress modestly

Travelers relaxing and enjoying a meal at a pavement café

hands. This does not extend to people of the opposite sex unless the couple is married. It is very common for locals to swoop down on foreign babies, often pinching their cheeks or even cuddling them. Some visitors may find this perturbing, but there is only affection behind such spontaneous displays. In apparel, it is not unusual to see a man wearing just a pair of loose-fitting shorts. Most women dress modestly. Always keep in mind that the Vietnamese are very particular about propriety, especially in places of worship. At such sites, you should dress appropriately, with arms and legs covered. At the table, it is good manners to wait for the oldest person there to start the meal, unless you are the guest of honor. Never stab food with chopsticks or set them upright in a bowl of food, as that is a funerary practice. It is normal to eat with noisy gusto as an expression of appreciation for the food. Note that although you may be invited to dine in someone's home, guests are usually entertained in restaurants. See page 247 for additional advice on table manners and customs, as well as tipping.

PHOTOGRAPHY

Most places in Vietnam are photogenic. Good-quality camera equipment, film, and memory cards are easily and cheaply available in Ho Chi Minh City, Hanoi, and other large cities. Film processing

is easy and inexpensive. Note that photography is restricted in military areas and around police stations. It is also safer to request permission before taking pictures of religious sites or of people, especially the ethnic minorities.

TIME AND CALENDAR

Tourist taking a photograph

Vietnam is seven hours ahead of Greenwich Mean Time (GMT), 15 hours ahead of Pacific Standard Time (PST), and 12 hours ahead of Eastern Standard Time (EST). Although the Western Gregorian calendar is used for official and commercial requirements, the lunar calendar is still used for religious purposes such as calculating the dates of festivals.

MEASUREMENTS

The metric system has been in use since the French era. Some basic conversions from the US Standard to metric are:
1 inch = 2.54 centimeters
1 foot = 30 centimeters
1 mile = 1.6 kilometers
1 ounce = 28 grams
1 pound = 454 grams
1 US quart = 0.947 liter
1 US gallon = 3.6 liters

ELECTRICITY

As is common throughout the region, the electrical current in Vietnam is 220 volts. Most wall sockets accommodate French-style rounded pins as well as American-style flat pins. Hotel staff usually have adaptors on hand but they can also be found at any shop

carrying domestic goods. Still, to be on the safe side, it is a good idea to bring along your own adapter. Charge your laptop and cell phone batteries daily as power outages are not uncommon, especially in small and remote towns.

DIRECTORY

TRAVEL AGENCIES AND TOURIST INFORMATION

Ann Tours
77 Pham Hong Thai, Hanoi.
Map 2 D1.
Tel (04) 3715 0950.
58 Ton That Tung St, Dist. 1, HCMC. **Map** 1 C5.
Tel (08) 3833 2564.
www.anntours.com

Saigon Tourist
23 Le Loi St, Dist. 1, HCMC.
Map 2 E4.
Tel (08) 3829 2291.
www.saigon-tourist.com

Sinh Café
14 Cua Bac St, Hanoi. **Map** 2 E2.
Tel (04) 3926 1568.
246 De Tham St, Dist. 1, HCMC.
Map 2 D5.
Tel (08) 3836 7338.
www.sinhcafe.com

TNK Travel Vietnam
216 De Tham St, Dist. 1, HCMC.
Map 2 D5.
Tel (08) 3920 4766.
www.tnktravelvietnam.com

Tuan Travel
130 Bui Vien, Dist. 1, HCMC.
Map 2 D5. *Tel* (091) 813 3165.
www.tuantravel.com

Vietnam Tourism
80 Quan Su St, Hanoi.
Map 2 D4. *Tel* (04) 3942 3760.
www.vietnamtourism.com

DISABLED SERVICES

Accessible Journeys
www.disabilitytravel.com

Disability World
www.disabilityworld.com

Mobility International USA
www.miusa.org

Royal Association for Disability and Rehabilitation
www.radar.org.uk

Society for Accessible Travel & Hospitality
www.sath.org

Personal Security and Health

Pharmacy sign in Ho Chi Minh City

Vietnam is one of the safest places to travel in the world. In addition to a very authoritarian government, the country boasts a generally law-abiding society. Visitors can roam most streets at night without fear, although common-sense rules do apply. Sadly, petty crime is on the increase in big cities. Although violent crime is rare, it does happen. The Vietnamese are fastidiously clean, and while street food is safe enough, it is better to stick to bottled water. Healthcare facilities, however, are still lacking. With few ambulances or well-equipped emergency rooms, it is wise to carry travel insurance with a good medevac (medical evacuation) provision.

GENERAL PRECAUTIONS

Though traveling in Vietnam is considered to be quite safe, there are some basic precautions that should be followed. Since petty crimes such as bag-snatching and pick-pocketing are prevalent in larger cities such as Ho Chi Minh City and Nha Trang, avoid carrying large sums of money or wearing much jewelry. It is advisable to keep part of your cash, any traveler's checks, and passport in a hidden money belt, and leave a portion of your valuables in your hotel's safe. Secure your cameras and purse when out walking or on a motorbike ride, as motorbike-mounted thieves have been known to pull up alongside, snatch such items, and drive on.

Another basic safety rule is to avoid venturing into unfamiliar areas at night. Do not accept coffee invitations from stangers in Downtown Saigon as Filipino Mafia prey upon tourists in this way. It is also important to take photocopies of your passport, travel insurance, departure card, and other relevant documents. In case of theft or loss, these copies will aid replacement.

There is a growing HIV problem in Vietnam, and sexual transmission has taken over intravenous transmission as the main cause of its spread. In 2000, UNAIDS estimated that there were 280,000 HIV-positive people in the country; the number is thought to have more than doubled since.

Traffic policeman *(left)* **and general policeman** *(right)* **in uniform**

TOURIST POLICE

In addition to the traffic and general police forces, Vietnam's tourist police are stationed at popular tourist sites. However, their presence is generally just for show, and they may not be able to help in an emergency. Generally, the police presence is unobtrusive and scant. In any dealing with the police, be polite. If you are robbed, the police might help you file a report for insurance purposes, but they often refuse. You may need an interpreter.

HOSPITALS AND MEDICAL FACILITIES

Most Western-operated and up-to-date medical facilities in the country are located in Ho Chi Minh City and Hanoi. If you fall ill in a small town, do try and get to one of these two cities. However, though the hospitals and clinics here are sufficient for daily needs and minor surgery, they might lack the drugs, equipment, or expertise for more complicated cases. The same holds true for dental care. If you are seriously injured, then it is better to leave Vietnam and go to major destinations such as Bangkok, Hong Kong, or even Singapore.

Most pharmacies in Hanoi and Ho Chi Minh City now stock a wide variety of drugs, but do check the expiry date before buying. If you require some specific medicine, do remember to carry a sufficient supply from home.

TRAVEL INSURANCE

A general travel insurance policy is a good idea in most places, but especially in this part of the world. Make sure that in addition to illness and injury, it covers theft as well. Most importantly, it should cover medical evacuation in case of an emergency.

FOOD- AND WATER-BORNE DISEASES

The most common ailments are diarrhoea, dysentery, and giardiasis, all of which are food-related. Each of these is treatable with antibiotics, and preventable by following some

One of the many well-stocked fresh fruits stalls found throughout Vietnam

general safeguards. Wash your hands thoroughly before each meal, eat only at clean places, which offer well-cooked food or prepare the food in front of you, and peel fresh fruit yourself. Street food isn't always risky, although due caution as well as judgement should be used. Care is also needed when eating at a buffet or using room service even in five-star hotels.

If your normal diet is bland, do keep in mind that food in Vietnam can be extremely spicy. This simple change of diet can lead to an upset stomach for some. Always carry pills such as Tums and Pepto Bismol for indigestion.

To prevent water-borne diseases such as typhoid and cholera, stick to bottled water, easily available everywhere, or well-boiled water. Drinking tea is usually safe as the water is traditionally brought to a full boil at the time of preparation.

HEAT

During summer, it can become exceedingly hot in Vietnam. It is important to stay hydrated if you are traveling in this warm and humid weather. Always carry plenty of water, and remember to drink it at regular intervals. To protect yourself from heat stroke, wear a hat, sunglasses, and loose-fitting clothes. Use a good sunscreen to avoid getting sunburns.

INSECT BITES & INFECTIONS

A mosquito bite may lead to dengue or, less frequently, malaria, two potentially serious diseases that a few precautions can prevent. The disease-carrying mosquitos are more active at dusk or dawn, and to avoid getting bitten, apply a repellent and sleep under a mosquito net. Rooms with fans or air-conditioning usually don't have mosquitos. Take a prophylactic for malaria if visiting jungle areas or the Mekong, but seek advice from a doctor first.

Carry your own disinfectant ointment and bandages as

wounds can become infected relatively easily in this climate, and should be kept clean.

BIRD FLU

Bird flu was a major problem in 2005, but Vietnam is now relatively free from the threat as a result of large-scale vaccinations of millions of birds, and swift culling of infected flocks. Temples, however, do keep caged birds, often wild, for release as a form of prayer. These birds are best avoided.

UNDETONATED EXPLOSIVES

Leftover or unexploded bombs and artillery shells are still a matter of some concern in areas such as the DMZ *(see p149)*. All major tourist areas have been cleared of these dangers. Should you go off-the-beaten path and see anything that looks like a rocket or bomb, do not touch it. Walk away carefully and inform the authorities.

A female visitor strolling along Vietnam's streets with a child

WOMEN TRAVELERS

It is not at all unusual to see a foreign woman traveling alone. They may be stared at in some rural areas, more out of curiosity than hostility or predation. The Vietnamese are hospitable people, and female tourists can find themselves invited home to dinner or even a sleepover with the family. Avoid skimpy clothes as they attract unwanted attention. Normal precautions should be taken at night.

DIRECTORY

EMERGENCY NUMBERS

Ambulance, nationwide
Tel 115.

Fire, nationwide
Tel 114.

Police, nationwide
Tel 113.

MEDICAL RESOURCES

Centers for Disease Control
www.cdc.gov

Vietnam Family Medical Practice
www.vietnammedicalpractice.com

World Health Organization
www.who.int/ith

GAY AND LESBIAN TRAVELERS

Utopia
www.utopia-asia.com

GAY AND LESBIAN TRAVELERS

Vietnam's societal attitudes towards homosexuality have changed drastically over the last decade. An influx of western culture has led to a more tolerant attitude and Ho Chi Minh City now has a thriving gay scene. For more information, consult websites such as **Utopia**.

PUBLIC TOILETS

Public toilets are rare. Even in Ho Chi Minh City, only the central part of town has attended pay toilets, costing about US 10 cents. Hoi An has the largest number of public toilets per capita. Mainly you will find squat toilets, often squalid, with little privacy. Bring your own toilet paper but don't flush it or you will block the plumbing.

Men's public toilet sign

Banking and Currency

In all major Vietnamese cities, as well as towns of appreciable size, financial services are abundant. Traveler's checks can be cashed at banks, and well-established hotels accept them as payment. Shopkeepers are also happy to accept US dollars. While currency exchanges and Automatic Teller Machines (ATMs) are common in most towns and cities, this is not yet the case in remote areas. Remember to carry a sufficient amount of Vietnamese currency when traveling to such places, although you will never be more than a few hours' journey from a banking facility of some kind.

Withdrawing money from an ANZ Automatic Teller Machine

BANKS AND BANKING HOURS

Vietnam's leading banks are **Vietcombank** and **Sacombank**, while the most common international banks are **ANZ** and **HSBC**. All maintain offices and ATMs throughout the country, and are connected to the Plus ATM network. Going to a bank for currency exchange or credit card withdrawal is more time consuming than an ATM or private exchange.

While it can vary marginally in different cities and banks, banking hours are generally from 8am to 5pm, Monday to Friday, with some banks closing at midday for lunch. Most private currency exchanges set their own hours.

ATM SERVICES

In 1999, there were only two ATMs in the country, both in Hanoi. Now they are found virtually everywhere there is a bank. All provide instructions in Vietnamese and English, and are available 24 hours a day. Money is issued only in the Vietnamese currency, calculating dollar withdrawals at the daily official rate of exchange. An unlimited number of withdrawals may be made in a day, but each is limited to 2,000,000 *dong*, with a fee for each withdrawal, usually between US$2 and US$5. Larger withdrawals can be arranged with a bank teller. If you are planning to stay in Vietnam for more than a few months, consider opening your own account. Though the red tape involved can be daunting, it will make financial transactions smoother for you.

CHANGING MONEY

The process of changing cash has improved over the past few years, but a long wait at banks is still the norm. The process is faster at a private exchange, although the rates are not as good. In fact, the best rates are given by gold and jewelry shops, but they offer no security against short-changing or counterfeit bills. With the proliferation of ATMs in most cities, however, many travelers opt simply to use their debit cards instead.

CREDIT AND DEBIT CARDS

Although credit and debit cards are not widely accepted in Vietnam's smaller towns, plastic is almost as useful as dollars and *dong* in larger cities, especially Ho Chi Minh City and Hanoi. Airlines, travel agents, upmarket hotels and restaurants, as well as upscale shops catering to tourists, are all glad to accept major credit cards such as MasterCard and Visa. If needed, you can also get a cash advance at the bank drawn on your credit card.

CURRENCY

The *dong*, abbreviated to VND or d, is the Vietnamese unit of currency. Though it is not "official," US dollars are accepted almost everywhere, especially in tourist zones. Always ensure that these notes are in mint condition. It is also advisable to always keep some *dong* notes (preferably in smaller denominations) and coins at hand for day-to-day expenditure. Bear in mind that the *dong* cannot be converted outside Vietnam.

TRAVELER'S CHECKS

Encashing and using traveler's checks is not the best option in Vietnam, though it is a good idea to carry a few in case of an emergency. They can be cashed in at leading banks and exchanges, as well as at airlines and high-end hotels for a small commission. If lost, it is likely that you will need to go to a major city to have them replaced.

A branch of Vietcombank, a reliable option for currency exchange

Banknotes

Vietnamese banknotes are circulated in denominations of 500d, 1,000d, 2,000d, 5,000d, 10,000d, 20,000d, 50,000d, 100,000d, and 500,000d. All notes bear Ho Chi Minh's visage, and notes from 10,000d upward are made of polymer. Denominations under 1,000d are being phased out.

500,000 dong

100,000 dong

50,000 dong

200,000 dong

20,000 dong

10,000 dong

5,000 dong

200 dong   500 dong   1,000 dong   2,000 dong

5,000 dong

5,000 dong

Coins

In 2004, the Vietnamese government introduced 200d, 500d, 1,000d, 2,000d, and 5,000d coins in order to facilitate the phasing out of banknotes of the same denomination. Perceived by many as merely a gimmick, some shops and street vendors won't accept them because they are heavy and easily lost.

DIRECTORY

BANKS

ANZ Bank
11 Me Linh Sq, Dist. 1, HCMC. **Map** 2 F4. **Tel** (08) 3829 9319.
14 Ly Thai To St, Hanoi. **Map** 2 F3. **Tel** (04) 3825 8190. www.anz.com/vietnam/en/personal

HSBC Bank
235 Dong Khoi St, Dist. 1, HCMC. **Map** 2 F4. **Tel** (08) 3829 2288. www.vn.hsbc.com

Sacombank
278 Nam Ky Khoi Nghia St, Dist. 3, HCMC. **Map** 1 C2. **Tel** (08) 3932 0420. www.sacombank.com

Vietcombank
29 Ben Chuong Duong St, Dist.1, HCMC. **Map** 2 F5. **Tel** (08) 3823 0311.
2 Hang Bai St, Hanoi. **Map** 2 E4. **Tel** (04) 3934 3472. www.vietcombank.com.vn

Communication

SIM card by VinaPhone

Once considered archaic and mostly unreliable, the communications network in Vietnam has improved dramatically over the years. It is now possible to make an international call or send an e-mail or a fax from all but the most remote of locations. Nearly everybody has a cell phone. Public phones, on the other hand, are quite limited, but usually more dependable. The country also provides easy access to the Internet, with hotels and cafés offering the service. Major international publications are available in all big cities, and locally published English magazines and newspapers are growing in number. The postal system is efficient and staffed by helpful people, though courier services are generally preferred for faster delivery. The post office remains strictly censored, however, and all parcels are inspected before being sent.

Small yet reliable cyber café found all over Ho Chi Minh City

Public telephone booth at a street corner in Ho Chi Minh City

INTERNATIONAL AND LOCAL TELEPHONE CALLS

International calls can easily be made from most hotels, but are usually very expensive, as are local calls, though to a lesser extent. The best place to make international calls is from the post office. Callers also have the option of reversing the charges to major destinations.

Another option for making international calls is to use the budget-friendly Voice Over Internet Protocol (VoIP). This economic service enables users to make calls via the Internet. Dial 1717 plus 00, followed by the country code, the area code, and then the telephone number. A prepaid option using the 1717 calls facility is also available, for which you need to purchase a 1717 card, which is available at most telecommunication outlets.

In contrast, domestic calls are much more affordable. Vietnam made changes to its phone system in 2008, adding an extra digit (usually a 3) to all landlines. Most places now have seven-digit numbers, plus a three- or four-digit area code. Exceptions include Ho Chi Minh City, Haiphong, and Hanoi. The landline service is usually reliable, but a long-distance connection can have much disturbance and static. Most shops offer a cheap telephone service. Look out for a blue sign: *dien thoai cong cong* (public telephone).

Cell phones are very popular in Vietnam, and they are cheaper than in the West. Network services and sending text messages is also cheap. If you are staying for more than a few weeks, the best option is to purchase a SIM card from VinaPhone or MobiFone for your cell phone. All cell numbers have a 10-digit number provided by the operating company.

INTERNET FACILITIES

Today, even the smallest towns in Vietnam boast Internet facilities. In fact, at places where foreigners congregate, Internet facilities are ubiquitous. Most modern hotels provide Wi-Fi (Wireless Internet connection) in their rooms and so do some backpacker hostelries as well. Many bars and restaurants also offer Wi-Fi, which is useful for laptop and cell phone users. Dedicated Internet cafés are available but not as popular as a few years ago. They are often crowded, and most are not air-conditioned, so the combination of body heat, machine heat, and warm weather can be uncomfortable. Places that offer air-conditioned facilities normally display signs to that effect.

POSTAL SERVICES

No matter where you are in Vietnam, you will not be far from a post office. The Vietnamese are enthusiastic letter writers and gift senders, so the postal service plays an important role in daily life. Most post offices are open until late, typically from 8am to 9pm, seven days a week. The staff are usually very helpful and willing clerks help wrap parcels and fill out customs forms, and will even stick stamps for you. Vietnamese stamps do not always have adhesive backs, and a pot of glue and a brush is needed. The postal delivery process, though not very speedy, is reliable. However, be aware that all parcels will be opened and inspected

Pair of colorful Vietnamese stamps

before they are mailed. Letters posted from Hanoi or Ho Chi Minh City usually take five to ten days to reach the US and other Western nations, while parcels can take a few days more. Post from a small town, and bound for foreign shores, can take a month to reach the international departure system.

Postal rates more or less match what they are in the rest of the world. A postcard to the US or Europe will cost just about half a dollar. *Poste restante* is available in major cities such as Hanoi and Ho Chi Minh City at a nominal charge. For faster delivery, well-known courier companies such as **DHL**, **Federal Express**, and **UPS** are available. However, parcels sent by courier can be detained and searched by the authorities. The same is true for packets with CDs and photographs, which may be intercepted for further scrutiny.

Some international and national newspapers available in Vietnam

NEWSPAPERS AND MAGAZINES

A selection of international publications, both English and French, are available in most prominent hotels and at news-stands in major cities. These include newspapers such as *International Herald Tribune*, *Le Monde*, and *Bangkok Post*, as well as magazines such as *Time* and *Newsweek*. Many bars in Ho Chi Minh City and Hanoi stock newspapers for use by their patrons. The most widely read English language newspaper is *Viet Nam News*. It is a useful paper for cultural

happenings, and the Sunday edition has a leisure magazine. For further information on upcoming events and up-to-date listings, you can check publications such as *Saigon Times* and *The Guide*.

All media is censored by the government, and journalists who have criticized the authorities have been imprisoned for "abusing freedoms."

TELEVISION AND RADIO

Vietnamese television and radio – VTV and Voice of Vietnam respectively – are both government operated, consisting mainly of news, soap operas, Viet Pop music, and films. However, most of the hotels now offer a range of popular international TV channels including Cinemax, CNN, HBO, BBC, Star TV, Singapore's News Asia, and MTV. Sports stations are also favored, especially during the soccer season.

VIETNAMESE ADDRESSES

Addresses in Vietnam are quite straightforward: number, street, and city. In Ho Chi Minh City, the district number is also added after the street. Addresses with a slash, such as 120/5 Nguyen Trai Street, means that you have to go to No. 120 on this street, and then find building No. 5 in the alley next to it. Also note that the same street

begins new numbering upon entering a new district, and that the Vietnamese word for street, *pho* or *duong*, comes at the start of the street name.

USEFUL DIALING CODES

- For international calls, dial 00, then the country code, the area code, and then the number.
- Some country codes are: USA and Canada 1; Australia 61; UK 44; New Zealand 64; and France 33.
- To call Vietnam from abroad, dial 011, then 84, followed by the city code and the number.
- To speak to the international operator, just dial 00.
- For any kind of directory assistance, call 1080.
- To speak to the domestic operator, dial 0. This number may change according to the service provider for your cell phone. Customer assistance is available in English as well as Vietnamese. You may have to wait for some time to get to the instructions in the English language.

Cell phone calling cards by VinaPhone

TRAVEL INFORMATION

Most visitors fly to Vietnam. The country's domestic air transport system is good and getting better. The safety record is admirable, while the flights are mostly on time, and well connected to the main tourist destinations. Visitors from the US and Europe usually arrive via Bangkok or Hong Kong. From Cambodia, traveling by boat along the Mekong River is a scenic option. With the opening of several border crossings, many travelers opt to enter Vietnam by train, car, or bus from China, Laos, or Cambodia. The cheapest, often the quickest, and the most convenient way to get around the country is by the long haul bus system and the Open Tour bus. And for the independent traveler, a car with a driver is relatively inexpensive. Locally, metered and motorcycle taxis are the preferred modes of transport.

Symbol of Vietnam Airlines

New arrivals outside Ho Chi Minh City's busy Tan Son Nhat airport

ARRIVING BY AIR

Of all three international airports in Vietnam, Ho Chi Minh City's Tan Son Nhat is by far the busiest. Hanoi's Noi Bai Airport and Danang International are also major airports. **Vietnam Airlines**, the country's official international carrier, operates direct flights from many destinations across the world, such as Paris, Beijing, San Francisco, Sydney, Siem Reap, Bangkok, and Singapore. Many prominent international airlines also service Vietnam, including **Air France**, **Cathay Pacific**, **Thai Airways**, **Malaysia Airlines**, **Qantas**, **Lufthansa**, **Japan Airlines**, and **Singapore**

Airlines to name a few. A trans-Pacific journey from the USA takes over twenty hours, while from Europe, the trip takes less time.

AIR FARES

The cost of flying to Vietnam varies with airline, the season, and your travel agent. The average cost from the North American West Coast is about US$1,500 return fare; prices are equivalent from Europe. The busiest and most expensive time to travel to Vietnam is from December to February, when many families are flying in to celebrate Tet *(see pp28–9)*. Discounted tickets are usually available during the off-season. Check for any special deals being offered by airlines flying into the country.

ON ARRIVAL

The arrival system in Vietnam is now more efficient and streamlined. While on the plane, passengers are handed an immigration form and a customs form to fill out. These need to be submitted, along with your passport, at the airport's immigration counter. A yellow copy of the customs form is handed back to you. For the time being, this form does not need to be presented upon departure, as was previously the case.

GETTING FROM THE AIRPORTS

Ho Chi Minh City's Tan Son Nhat is the biggest and best-equipped airport in Vietnam. Both arrivals and departures are handled in a quick and efficient manner. Note that at this airport, you must go through security checks during arrival and departure. The airport is 3 miles (5 km) from the center of the city. A metered taxi can be hired from the authorized taxi service, which is located near the currency exchange counter at the airport. Avoid any drivers offering flat rates. Minibuses are also available for transport to the city as are shuttle pick-ups, which can be provided by the hotels on request. Be prepared for large

Airport taxi, a convenient mode of transport

AIRPORTS	[i] INFORMATION	DISTANCE FROM CITY CENTER	AVERAGE TAXI FARE	AVERAGE JOURNEY TIME
Tan Son Nhat, Ho Chi Minh City	(08) 3848 5383	3 miles (5 km)	US$9	10 minutes
Danang International	(0511) 383 0339	1 mile (1.6 km)	US$2	5 minutes
Noi Bai Airport, Hanoi	(04) 3886 6674	20 miles (35 km)	US$15	45–60 minutes

Tourists loading luggage into a bright-yellow, metered Vina Taxi

crowds outside the terminal as people come not only to pick up their family members, but also to watch passengers and planes arrive and depart.

Hanoi's Noi Bai Airport is the farthest from the city center, and it can take more than 45 minutes by taxi to get into town. All transport service operators, including metered taxis and minibuses, are located outside the terminal. Airport taxis offer the most convenient means to get downtown. Look for the line of empty taxis and hire a prepaid taxi from the airport. This will cost about US$15. The cheapest way to get to the city center is by taking the number 7 city bus which departs every 15 minutes. It takes an hour to reach the city, and stops when requested on its way to Hoan Kiem Lake (*see p160*). Another affordable option is the Vietnam Airlines shuttle bus, which costs about US$3, and is supposed to take all its passengers to the airlines' office on Trang Thi Street. Some drivers also drop off passengers at their hotels if requested. Note that you are not required to pay any toll taxes on the way to or from the airport.

Located at the western edge of town, Danang International is the smallest of the three international airports. There is only one terminal, with a small part of it dedicated to international flights. The taxi service outside the terminal offers fixed and inexpensive rates for a ride into the city.

DEPARTURE TAX

Visitors no longer need to pay departure tax when leaving the country as the tax is now included in airline ticket fares. Costs can vary depending on which airport is being used and the season in which you are traveling.

ARRIVING VIA LAND OR WATER

Vietnam shares land borders with three countries – China, Laos, and Cambodia. With new border crossings opening to foreigners (presently there are three with China, six with Laos, and eight with Cambodia), more independent travelers are taking the land route.

From China, you can enter Vietnam by car, bus, or train. The popular Friendship Pass, located at Dong Dang, is open to rail and road traffic, and is the busiest crossing between the nations. A bi-weekly train, connecting Beijing to Hanoi, makes a brief stop at this pass. The other two border crossings are at Lao Cai (*see p197*) and Mong Cai. Open only to motor vehicles, they are less popular routes.

The crossings from Laos are Lao Bao, west of Dong Ha; the popular Cau Treo; Nam Can; Cha Lo; Na Meo; and Bo Y. The first three are open only

to motor vehicles. Crossing by bus can be extremely time-consuming. Visitors are advised to fly in from Laos.

Entry from Cambodia is easy and usually hassle free (*see pp222–3*). The Moc Bai crossing is the busiest, being only about two hours from Ho Chi Minh City. Many buses run daily between the two countries. The Vinh Xuong border near Chau Doc offers a more scenic approach to Vietnam. Tourists can travel along the Mekong River, taking in the view from a boat or a luxury ship. Six other, more remote, crossings are less often used.

DIRECTORY

AIRLINES

Air France
1 Ba Trieu St, Hanoi. **Map** 2 E4.
Tel (04) 3824 7066.
www.airfrance.fr

Cathay Pacific
49 Hai Ba Trung St, Hanoi.
Map 2 D4. *Tel* (04) 3826 7298.
www.cathaypacific.com

Japan Airlines
63 Ly Thai To St, Hanoi.
Map 2 F4. *Tel* (04) 3826 6693.
www.jal.co.jp

Lufthansa
19–25 Nguyen Hue St, Dist. 1,
HCMC. **Map** 2 F4. *Tel* (08) 3829 8529. www.lufthansa.com

Malaysia Airlines
49 Hai Ba Trung St, Hanoi.
Map 2 D4. *Tel* (04) 3826 8820.
www.malaysiaairlines.com

Qantas
4 Pham Ngu Lao St, Hanoi.
Map 2 F4. *Tel* (04) 3933 3026.
www.qantas.com.au

Singapore Airlines
17 Ngo Quyen St, Hanoi.
Map 2 F4. *Tel* (04) 3826 8888.
www.singaporeair.com

Thai Airways
44B Ly Thuong Kiet St, Hanoi.
Map 2 E4. *Tel* (04) 3826 7921.
www.thaiair.com

Vietnam Airlines
1 Quang Trung St, Hanoi.
Map 2 E4. *Tel* (04) 3943 9660.
www.vietnamairlines.com.vn

An airport bus traveling through the streets of Ho Chi Minh City

Getting Around Vietnam

With the rapid development of Vietnam's infrastructure, the country's internal transport system is improving at a fast pace, and becoming more convenient and affordable. Railway lines run from Ho Chi Minh City to Hanoi, connecting several cities en route, before passing on into China. Reasonably comfortable and inexpensive trains are the most efficient mode of transport. Long-distance buses are popular with backpackers, but most can be uncomfortable after a few hours, although the more expensive express buses are comparatively luxurious. Most popular is the Open Tour bus system, which links major centers. For quick travel between major cities, the airline system is great, while ferries and hydrofoils connect some ports. Travelers can also hire a motorbike or a car and driver.

Passengers boarding a train at Ho Chi Minh City's railway station

DOMESTIC AIRLINES

The four domestic airlines are Vietnam Airlines (see pp288–9), **Jetstar Pacific Airlines**, **Vietnam Air Service Company (VASCO)**, and **Indochina Airlines**. Vietnam Airlines and VASCO are owned by the state. The former is the major carrier, servicing the entire nation; VASCO operates in much of southern Vietnam. Jetstar Pacific is partly owned by the state and serves the six largest cities, while Indochina Airlines serves the three international airports in Ho Chi Minh City, Hanoi, and Danang.

PLANE TICKETS, FARES, AND RESERVATIONS

Tickets can be purchased at the airlines' booking offices in major cities or at the reservation counter at the airport. An English-speaking attendant is usually on duty. Any of the many travel agents throughout Vietnam can also arrange air travel, and their prices are usually no more than what you would pay at the airline office. You can also book tickets at the travel desk of some of the better hotels, or even through some diving operators and select souvenir shops.

Domestic fares are usually under US$150 excluding baggage fees. A departure tax of about US$2 is included in the price. It is a good idea to make advance reservations if planning to travel during the peak season, from December to February.

RAILROAD NETWORK

The railroad network services almost the entire length of the country. It mainly follows the coast from Ho Chi Minh City to Hanoi, with stops at several big cities along the way. From Hanoi, a few lines connect to Halong Bay (see pp182–4), Sapa (see pp196–7), and China. The running times vary, but the fastest transit between Ho Chi Minh City and Hanoi is about 33 hours. Trains commonly run late but, curiously, can also sometimes arrive early. Even-numbered trains run from north to south, while odd-numbered trains run in the opposite direction. Although trains connecting Hanoi to Ho Chi Minh City are called Reunification Expresses, no train is actually named so.

TRAINS

Most passenger trains in Vietnam are fairly affordable, clean, and reasonably comfortable, if not really luxurious. All the carriages are air-conditioned. Four classes of tickets are on offer here: Hard Seat, which is basically a wooden bench; Soft Seat, a cushioned recliner in a carriage with a TV; Hard Sleeper, which is a compartment with six bunks; and Soft Sleeper, a private compartment with four bunks and a lockable door. Meals and snacks are available in all classes for an extra charge. Passengers may also alight at stops to buy food. Long-distance trains have a dining car, and vendors bearing a variety of drinks and snacks roam the trains.

TRAIN TICKETS, FARES, AND RESERVATIONS

Tickets can be purchased at the stations, as well as through travel agents (see p281) and good hotels. Note that some travel agents are limited to single destination tickets, and cannot take you beyond certain points. Other agents may have more ticket options. Check the stations, the **Vietnam Railways** website, and with travel agents for up-to-date schedules. Train fares do not exceed US$70 with the exception of the Victoria Service from Hanoi to Sapa. Be sure to make advance bookings if traveling during popular Vietnamese holidays.

A long-distance bus awaiting departure, Mien Tay bus terminal

Travelers buying tickets at Mien Tay bus terminal, Ho Chi Minh City

BUSES

The advent of new and clean express buses has made bus travel the preferred means of getting around for visitors traveling between major cities. The vehicles are more expensive than their non-express counterparts and local minibuses, but are faster, safer, and more comfortable. Their chief disadvantage, however, is the karaoke machine most of them carry. In addition to the regularly scheduled buses, another viable option is the chartered minibus. Most travel agents and hotels can arrange one to carry up to 16 passengers for out-of-town trips.

The Open Tour bus or coach travels between major destinations and is a popular and quick method of transportation for tourists. Many tourist cafés such as the Sinh Café *(see p281)* run these services. Tickets are one-way, cheap and flexible, and allow stop-offs as well.

BUS TICKETS AND FARES

Bus fares are low, with the Ho Chi Minh City–Hanoi routes ranging from US$45 to US$60. The ticketing and scheduling system, however, can be maddeningly complex. Tickets can be bought on the day of travel or before, but a station can sell tickets only to certain destinations, and connecting routes complicate the matter even more. It is usually best to make arrangements via an agent or hotel.

RENTING A CAR OR MOTORBIKE

If you choose to rent a car, you must also hire a driver licensed in Vietnam. A car plus driver costs between US$65 and US$120 per day. The price varies with the distance you expect to cover and the amount of fuel needed. The driver takes care of his own meals and lodgings on trips lasting more than a day.

Legally, a license is required to rent a motorbike but is rarely asked to be shown. If you want to get around by motorbike, it is best to hire a motorcycle taxi, locally called *xe om* or a Honda *om*. Depending on the distance you expect to travel, it should cost upward of US$10 per day. A helmet is required by law.

BOATS AND FERRIES

Boats sail all the way from Ho Chi Minh City to Chau Doc at the Cambodian border on the Mekong. The river trip takes two days on a slow boat, and one day on a fast boat. There

Cruise liner moored at a Saigon River harbor

are also some ferries to Phu Quoc Island *(see p101)* from Rach Gia, and to many points among the islands of Halong Bay. Hydrofoils, which are run by reliable companies such as **Vina Express**, operate regular services between Ho Chi Minh City and Vung Tau *(see p76).*

DIRECTORY

AIRLINES

Indochina Airlines
www.indochinaairlines.vn

Jetstar Pacific Airlines
www.jetstar.com

VASCO
www.vasco.com.vn/en

TRAIN STATIONS

Danang Station
202 Haiphong St,
Danang.
Tel (0511) 382 3810.

Hanoi Station
120 Le Duan St, Hanoi.
Map 1 C4.
Tel (04) 3942 3433.

Saigon Station
1 Nguyen Thong St,
Dist. 3, HCMC.
Map 1 A3.
Tel (08) 3843 6528.

Vietnam Railways
www.vr.com.vn/english

BUS STATIONS

Cholon Station
86 Trang Tu St, Cholon,
HCMC. **Map** 3 C5.
Tel (08) 3855 7719.

Gia Lam Station
Gia Thuy Long Bien St,
Hanoi. **Tel** (04) 3873 0083.

Giap Bat Station
6 Giai Phong St, Hanoi.
Tel (04) 3864 1422.

Kim Ma Station
Cnr. of Nguyen Thai Hoc
& Giang Vo Sts, Hanoi.
Map 1 A3.
Tel (04) 3845 2846.

Mien Dong Station
292 Dinh Bo Linh, Binh
Thanh Dist, HCMC.
Tel (08) 3899 4056.

Mien Tay Station
395 Dinh Duong Vuong St,
Binh Chanh Dist, HCMC.
Tel (08) 3877 6593.

BOAT AND FERRY TERMINALS

Danang Port
26 Bach Dang St, Danang.
Tel (0511) 382 2513.

Haiphong Port
8A Tran Phu St, Haiphong.
Tel (031) 3383 6109.

Vina Express at Bach Dang Jetty
Ton Duc Thang St, Dist. 1,
HCMC. **Map** 2 F4.
Tel (08) 3829 7892.

TRAVEL AGENCIES

Kangaroo Café
18 Bao Khanh St, Hanoi.
Map 2 E3.
Tel (04) 3877 6593.

Le Lai Air Ticket Agency
80 Le Lai St, Dist.1,
HCMC. **Map** 2 D5.
Tel (08) 3925 3391.

Local Transportation

The public transport system in Vietnam is still in its nascent stage, although it does vary from city to city. The most convenient and safest mode of transport for travelers is by metered taxis. The local bus network is not a viable or reliable option as the buses are crowded, noisy, unsafe, and highly erratic. Probably the quickest and cheapest way to get around is by motorbike taxis, known as *xe oms* or Honda *oms*. The streets of Ho Chi Minh City especially are overflowing with them. Foreign visitors may rent both motorbikes and cars to drive. Though banned in 2009 and not very safe in busy streets, cyclos still service tourist areas in Ho Chi Minh City and Hanoi.

Honda *om*, a convenient mode of transport

they are an inexpensive form of transport, the number of buses servicing the cities is insufficient. In addition, most are slow and lack facilities such as air-conditioning.

Minibuses are available for hire at affordable rates, and can be arranged for by most hotels and travel agencies. Small groups of tourists or families can easily rent one for day trips, and even for a one- or two-day excursion out of town.

GETTING AROUND HANOI AND HO CHI MINH CITY

The best way to explore both Ho Chi Minh City and Hanoi – the latter especially so – is on foot. Though Ho Chi Minh City is a great urban sprawl spread across many miles, each of its districts is walkable in itself. Hanoi's old quarter, on the other hand, is a charming little neighborhood, the length and breadth of which can be easily walked in a day.

A cyclo is a bicycle-like contraption where passengers sit in front of the driver, who pedals them through alleys and city streets. A popular mode of transport for visitors wishing to explore Ho Chi Minh City, Hanoi, Hue, and other centers of tourism, cyclos were also engrained in Vietnamese culture. They were used to transport both passengers and heavy loads of goods between markets, shops, and homes throughout Vietnam's colonial and modern history. Unfortunately, in modern-day Vietnam, the streets are crowded with speeding motorbikes and automobiles, and the cyclo has become a traffic hazard. It is still possible to ride cyclos in some tourist areas, but not necessarily advised.

A faster yet affordable way of getting around, especially in Ho Chi Minh City, is on a Honda *om*, known as *xe om* in Hanoi. These are

motorbike taxis on which the passenger rides pillion, and can be found in large numbers throughout the cities. In major tourist areas, men on motorbikes offer their services at almost every corner. If you are not approached, simply stand on the sidewalk and try to wave down a passing bike. Sooner or later, one will stop for you. A typical fare is about US 60 cents per half-a-mile (1 km). Fares, however, vary from district to district, and will depend largely on your negotiating skills.

BUSES AND MINIBUSES

City buses in Vietnam are not only uncomfortable to ride, but also woefully inadequate, a fact acknowledged even by the government. Although

Metered taxis, operated by various companies in major cities

METERED TAXIS

Until recently, taxis were a rarity on the streets of Vietnam's cities. Where they did exist, they were privately owned, borrowed, or rented cars with negotiable fares. Today, taxis are everywhere

Tam Hanh, a reputable intercity bus company operating in South Vietnam

Heavily congested streets of Ho Chi Minh City

DIRECTORY

TAXI SERVICES – HANOI

Airport Taxis
Tel (04) 3873 3333.

City Taxis
Tel (04) 3822 2222.

Hanoi Taxis
Tel (04) 3853 5353.

TAXI SERVICES –
HO CHI MINH CITY

Airport Taxis
Tel (08) 3844 6666.

Mai Linh Taxis
Tel (08) 3822 2666.

Vina Taxi
Tel (08) 3811 1111.

TOUR COMPANIES

A to Z Queen Café
65 Hang Bac St, Hanoi. **Map** 2
E3. *Tel (04) 3826 0860.*

Buffalo Tours
See p275.

Explorer Tours
2 Tran Thanh Tong, Hanoi.
Map 2 F5. *Tel (04) 3972 1607.*

Kim Travel
270 De Tham St, Dist. 1, HCMC.
Map 2 D5. *Tel (08) 3920 5552.*

Saigon Tourist
See p281.

Sinh Café
See p281.

TNK Travel
216 De Tham St, Dist. 1, HCMC.
Map 2 D5. *Tel (08) 3920 4766.*

in most cities, and virtually all are metered. The government acknowledges that even the most reputable taxi companies rig their meters or cheat customers by taking longer routes. Fares generally start at just under US$1 but vary according to company and location. Always watch the meter closely and demand the correct change. Many drivers falsely claim they have none.

RULES OF THE ROAD

The number one rule of the road is never yield to the temptation to hire a car and drive it yourself. It is simply not advisable for foreigners to hire self-drive cars as the traffic can get very chaotic at times. Renting a motorbike for getting around is relatively safer, although it would be wise to observe and familiarize yourself with the general flow and movement of traffic, usually erratic, for a few days first. Also keep an eye out for livestock on the road.

For the average tourist, the main consideration is how to cross the street. There are few traffic lights, and those that do exist are often considered to convey an advisory rather than a compulsory message. Watch the locals step out into traffic and follow their lead, first waiting for four-wheeled vehicles to pass, and then walking slowly and steadily through a sea of two-wheelers. Don't hesitate or stop suddenly as drivers will not be able to predict your movement and you will risk a collision.

Motorbike riders are required to wear helmets at all times. Only two people are allowed to ride on a motorbike. However, this law is enforced somewhat inconsistently and, at times, blatantly ignored.

Honda *om* or *xe om* motorbikes available for rent

ORGANIZED TOURS

Organized day trips, as well as one- and two-day group tours are very common. In addition to being convenient, they can also, at times, work out cheaper depending on the size of your group. There are numerous companies in both Hanoi and Ho Chi Minh City offering such tours. Since costs can vary extensively, it would be a good idea to check with a few tour companies for the best deal available. Most trips from Ho Chi Minh City are to the Cu Chi Tunnels *(see p73)* and Mekong Delta, while from Hanoi, tours frequently lead to Halong Bay *(see pp182–4)* and Sapa *(see pp196–7)*.

Tour bus making a stop in front of the Thang Long Water Puppet Theater

General Index

Acknowledgments

Dorling Kindersley would like to thank the many people whose help and assistance contributed to the preparation of this book.

Contributors
Andrew Forbes has a BA in Chinese and a PhD in Chinese History. He has lived in Chiang Mai, Thailand, for the past 20 years, where he is editor of CPA Media (www. cpamedia.com). He has visited Vietnam on an annual basis over the past decade.

Richard Sterling is a travel writer of long standing in the greater San Francisco area. He holds the Lowell Thomas Award for travel literature. He has written extensively on Vietnam and travels annually in the region.

Fact Checkers
Adam Bray, Nam Nguyen, Nick Ray

Proofreader
Shahnaaz Bakshi

Indexer
Jyoti Dhar

DK London
PUBLISHER Douglas Amrine
PUBLISHING MANAGERS Jane Ewart, Scarlett O'Hara, Kate Poole
MANAGING EDITOR Kathryn Lane
PROJECT EDITOR Ros Walford
PROJECT ART EDITORS Gadi Farfour, Kate Leonard
DESIGN AND EDITORIAL ASSISTANCE Alexandra Farrell, Emer FitzGerald, Fay Franklin, Anna Freiberger, Rhiannon Furbear, Camilla Gersh, Jacky Jackson, Priya Kukadia, Maite Lantaron, Hayley Maher, Catherine Palmi, Marianne Petrou, Ellen Root, Sands Publishing Solutions, Janis Utton
SENIOR CARTOGRAPHIC EDITOR Casper Morris
DTP DESIGNER Natasha Lu
PICTURE RESEARCH ASSISTANT Rachel Barber
DK PICTURE LIBRARY Romaine Werblow
DIGITAL MEDIA TEAM Fergus Day
PRODUCTION CONTROLLER Louise Daly

Additional Photography
Simon Bracken, Adam Bray, Eric Crichton, Tim Draper, Robin Forbes, Ken Findlay, Frank Greenaway, Colin Keates, Dave King, David Mager, Ian O'Leary, David Peart, Roger Smith, Kavita Saha, Kim Taylor, Álvaro Velasco, Jerry Young.

Special Assistance
Dorling Kindersley would like to thank the following for their assistance: Ton Sinh Thanh, and Nguyen Luong Ngoc, Embassy of the Socialist Republic of Vietnam in New Delhi, India; Pham Ngoc Minh, Buffalo Tours Vietnam; and all the other museums, churches, hotels, restaurants, shops, galleries and sights too numerous to thank individually.

Cartography credits
Base mapping for Ho Chi Minh City and Hanoi derived from Netmaps.

Picture Credits
a = above; b = below/bottom; c = center; f = far; l = left; r = right; t = top.

The Publishers are grateful to the following individuals, companies, and picture libraries for permission to reproduce their photographs:

4CORNERS IMAGES: Amantini Stefano 2-3.

AKG-IMAGES LTD: 49c; Amelot 6-7; François Guénet 267cr.

ALAMY: A.M. Corporation 5tl, 130bl, 181tr; Arco Images 18bl; Bill Bachmann 65tc; Oliver Benn 105br, 114cl; Blickwinkel 18cb, 97crb, 201crb; Tibor Bognar 90tl; Jon Bower 215tr, 216ca, 220bl; Rachael Bowes 45bl; Paul Carstairs 23br; Rob Cousins 3c, 17b; FLPA 182tl; Glow Images 24tl, 26clb, 267bc; Alex Griffiths 23cr, 192clb; Gavin Hellier 205t; Henry Westheim Photography 20tr, 201cla; Hornbil Images Pvt Ltd 19clb; Jeremy Horner 95ca; Imagebroker 99cra, 214crb; ImageState 39t, 146-7; Index Stock 166cla; Ingo Jezierski 32cr; Jon Arnold Images 12, 14tl, 47crb, 60tl, 152, 202-3, 204bl; Elmari Joubert 182bc; E.J. Baumeister Jr 25br; Christian Kober 25tr; Serge Kozak 63br; Kevin Lang 25bl, 28bl, 50crb, 99crb, 120,166br; Barry Lewis 29bl; Mary Evans Picture Library 40br, 203c; Neil McAllister 127crb, 128br, 160tl, 167tl, Chris McLennan 159c, 160cr; Nic Cleave Photography 214bl; David Osborn 18clb; Papilio 97clb; Edward Parker 193tr; Photobyte 199bl; Photofrenetic 19ca, 98c; Photoz.at 129bl; Pictorial Press Ltd 59crb; Christopher Pillitz 276-7; Nicholas Pitt 273tr; Popperfoto 44tr, 45crb; Royal Geographical Society 50cla; Marcus Wilson-Smith 19cra; Stephen Frink Collection 190bl; The Photolibrary Wales 90bl; Tribaleye Images/J. Marshall 179b; Ian Trower 24bc; Visual Arts Library (London) 37br; Andrew Woodley 114tr, 196bl; WorldFoto 192cla.

ARDEA.COM: Jean Paul Ferrero 201c; Masahiro Iijima 201bl; Jean Michel Labat 19br; ASIAN EXPLORERS: Timothy Tye 215tl.

ADAM BRAY ©2008: 116tr, 174ca, 292br.

THE BRIDGEMAN ART LIBRARY: Archives Charmet/Private Collection *The arrival of French troops in the Bay of Haiphong in June 1884* (colour litho), Vietnamese School (19th century) 42tl; Archives Charmet/ Bibliotheque Nationale, Paris, France *The Tours Congress, Ho Chi Minh* (1890-1969) from 'L'Humanite', December 1920 (b/w photo) 169cra; JULIET BUI: 98tr.

CORBIS: 19bc, 273cl; Asian Art & Archaeology, Inc 37c; Bettmann 43br, 44cl, 44bc, 44bl, 45tl, 45tr, 45c, 45clb, 45crb, 46bl, 46br, 151crb, 169cr, 169bl; Christophe Boisvieux 28br, 29cra, 30bl, 249c; Corbis Sygma/J.P. Laffont 46clb, /Jacques Langevin 46tr, /Les Stone 279br, /Orban Thierry 169br; Natalie Fobes 20br, 33tl; Owen Franken 74cla, 183cr; Michael Freeman 104cl, 132cl; Philippe Giraud 156cla; Robert van der Hilst 249tl; Jeremy Horner 99clb; Hulton-Deutsch

Collection 42cb, 169cl; Catherine Karnow 20-21c, 28tl, 182cla, 186-7, 269cb; Charles & Josette Lenars 38tc; Christophe Loviny 215cr; Wally McNamee 45br; Kevin R. Morris 209tl, 218br; David A. Northcott 19c; Tim Page 31bl, 32tl, 119br; Papilio/John R. Jones 20cla, 25cla, 25cra, 41tc; Steve Raymer 13b, 21tl, 21tr, 25cr, 30tc, 166cra, 169cla, 279tl; Reuters/Dien Bien Phu Museum 43crb; Roman Soumar 72tl; Keren Su 19fcra; Luca Tettoni 275tr; Brian A. Vikander 63tl; Nevada Wier 24cra, 29crb, 30cr, 31tl; Alison Wright 198clb; Michael S. Yamashita 99bl; Zefa/Gary Bell 190cla.

CPA MEDIA: 22bl, 38clb, 40c, 42bc, 43tc, 44crb; Jim Goodman 24tr, 24br, 29cr; David Henley 22tl, 23cl, 23clb, 29clb, 135cl, 135c.

DAVID J. DEVINE: 44tl. FUSION MAIA DA NANG RESORT: 228bl.

FRANK LANE PICTURE AGENCY LIMITED: Colin Marshall 178.

GETTY IMAGES: AFP/Hoang Dinh Nam 24cla; Asia Images/Martin Puddy 192tr; Iconica/John W. Banagan 103b; Photographer's Choice/John W. Banagan 97cl; Planet Observer/Universal Images Group 11tr; Riser: Astromujoff 10bl; Robert Harding World Imagery: 18cra, Robert Francis 111crb, 248cl, Occidor Ltd 199br; The Image Bank/Peter Adams 16bl; Time Life Pictures/Larry Burrows: 44-5c, Stringer 44clb; Stone/Simeone Huber 210-11.

HOTEL CONTINENTAL SAIGON: 57tr, 228cr.

TRAN LINH: 32br.

LONELY PLANET IMAGES: John Banagan 4br, 92-3, 102, 112-3, 226-7; Anders Blomqvist 48-9, 153b, 206bl; Alain Evrard 19cla; Mason Florence 84, 164tl; Kraig Lieb 118tl; Craig Pershouse 193bl; Peter Ptschelinzew 40tl; Patrick Ben Luke Syder 23cla.

MARY EVANS PICTURE LIBRARY: 7c, 22tr, 22clb, 36, 43bl, 227c, 277c.

MASTERFILE: Pierre Arsenault 18cla, 85b.

NATUREPL.COM: Jeff Foott 18c; David Kjaer 136c; Pete Oxford 201cr; NGOC: 29cla; NGOC DONG HA NAM CO.

LTD: 267clb, 267cb, 267fclb, 267bc; PHONG T. NGUYEN: 24clb, 24crb, 25cl. MICK PALARCZYK: 9br; PETER PHAM: 198br; PHOTOGRAPHERSDIRECT.COM: Images & Stories 198tr; Jamie Marshall Photography 199tl; Peter Schickert 193tl; Steve MacAulay Photography 199tr; tanchouzuru.com 51cr; Tanya D'Herville Photography 9cl.

PHOTOLIBRARY: Oxford Scientific Films/Mary Plage 77br.

REUTERS: Larry Downing 47tc, 47bc; Kham 78tc; Nguyen Huy Kham 20clb.

SEDONA SUITES HANOI: 231br.

STARS & STRIPES: Photograph by John Olson - "Cu Chi, South Vietnam, November, 1967: Colt .45 and flashlight in hand, wearing a gas mask, "tunnel rat" Sp4 Richard Winters of 2nd Battalion, 27th Infantry, 25th Infantry Division cautiously lowers himself into a 1,000-foot-long Viet Cong tunnel found in Vietnam's "Iron Triangle" 73cra; SWRIGHT.SMUGMUG.COM: Steven L. Wright 95bl.

SUN GROUP CORPORATION: 133t.

TERRA GALLERIA PHOTOGRAPHY: Q.T. Luong 65br, 151tr.

LOUIS VUITTON: 57tl.

WIKIPEDIA.COM: Public Domain 39 bc; WORLD PICTURES: Eur 184b; Stuart Pearce 101bl.

Front Endpaper: ALAMY: Jon Arnold Images c, tr; Kevin Lang cla; FRANK LANE PICTURE AGENCY LIMITED: Colin Marshall tl; LONELY PLANET IMAGES: John Banagan cr; Mason Florence bl.

Cover Picture Credits
Front - ALAMY IMAGES: Charles Bowman. Back - AWL IMAGES: Danita Delimont Stock tl; DORLING KINDERSLEY: Bethany Dawn bl, Tim Draper clb, Frank Grace cla. Spine - ALAMY IMAGES: Charles Bowman t.

All other images © Dorling Kindersley
For further information see: www.dkimages.com

SPECIAL EDITIONS OF DK TRAVEL GUIDES

DK Travel Guides can be purchased in bulk quantities at discounted prices for use in promotions or as premiums. We are also able to offer special editions and personalized jackets, corporate imprints, and excerpts from all of our books, tailored specifically to meet your own needs.

To find out more, please contact:
(in the United States) **SpecialSales@dk.com**
(in the UK) **travelspecialsales@uk.dk.com**
(in Canada) DK Special Sales at **general@ tourmaline.ca**
(in Australia)
business.development@pearson.com.au

Phrase Book

Vietnamese belongs to the Mon-Khmer group in the Austroasiatic family of languages. Besides Standard Vietnamese, which is spoken in the Hanoi area, there are several other dialects, the most important being those of the central and southern regions. These differ mainly in phonetics (for example, they have fewer tones than standard Vietnamese) and lexicology, but not grammar.

For centuries, Chinese (*chu han*) was the official language for administration and education as there was no written form of Vietnamese. Later, a special script called *chu nom* was developed to record the native language. By the 17th century, a romanized script, *quoc ngu*, was devised by Roman Catholic missionaries in southeast Asia as a simple way of transcribing Vietnamese *(see p41)*. With the arrival of the French, *quoc ngu* was officially introduced. Despite early opposition to the new script, perceived to be an instrument of colonial rule, the fact it that was relatively easy to learn gradually won over its critics.

The Six Tones

Vietnamese is a complex tonal language, which means that words are pronounced at varying levels of pitch. Standard Vietnamese has six tones, which are marked by special diacritics usually positioned above the vowel.

Tone can affect the meaning of words dramatically. For example, *ma* has six meanings depending on the pitch at which it is delivered. Accents indicate the tone of each syllable in the following chart:

Ma (ghost)	High, level tone
Mà (but)	Low (falling), level tone
Mã (horse)	Rising broken tone with a glottal stop
Mả (grave)	Falling-rising tone
Má (Cheek)	Rising tone
Mạ (rice seedling)	Sharp falling tone, heavy glottal stop

Kinship Terms

Words denoting family relationships, known as "kinship terms," are used when people address each other. The choice of expression depends on gender, age, social status, and the relationship and degree of intimacy between the speakers. The most common terms are:

Anh (older brother) to address a young male.

Chị (older sister), female equivalent of **anh**.

Em (younger sibling) to address someone younger than you.

Ông (grandfather) to address an older man, formal and respectful, similar to Sir in English.

Bà (grandmother) to address an older woman, formal and respectful.

Cô similar to Madam in English.

Guidelines for Pronunciation

Most of the consonants are pronounced as in English, except the following:

d	as in Zoo (in the north); as in You (in the south)
đ	as in Down
gi	as in Zoo (in the north); as in You (in the south)
kh	aspirated K
ng	nasal n, as in learniNG
ngh	nasal n, as in learniNG
nh	as in KeNYa
r	as in Zebra
t	as in Top
th	as in Top
tr	as in CHop
x	as in See

Vowels are pronounced as follows:

a	as in bAsk
â	as in σ but shorter
ă	as in hUt
e	as in End
ê	as in hEllo
i	as in Ink
o	as in lOng
ô	as in bAll
σ	as in liOn
u	as in pUt
ư	as in mountAIn

Communication Essentials

Hello!	**Xin chào!**
Goodbye!	**Tạm biệt!**
Yes/no	**Vâng/không**
I understand	**Tôi hiểu**
I don't understand	**Tôi không hiểu**
I don't know	**Tôi không biết**
Thank you	**Cám ơn!**
Do you speak English?	**Anh/chị có biết tiếng Anh không?**
I can't speak Vietnamese	**Tôi không biết tiếng Việt**
Sorry/Excuse me!	**Xin lỗi!**
Not at all	**Không dám**
Come in please!	**Mời anh/chị vào!**
emergency	**Cấp cứu**
police	**Công an**
ambulance	**Xe cấp cứu**
fire brigade	**Cứu hỏa**

Useful Phrases

My name is …	**Tên tôi là …**
What is your name?	**Tên anh/chị là gì?**
How do you do/ pleased to meet you	**Rất hân hạnh được gặp anh/chị**
How are you?	**Anh/chị có khỏe không?**
What work do you do?	**Anh/chị làm nghề gì?**
How old are you?	**Anh/chị bao nhiêu tuổi?**
What nationality are you?	**Anh/chị là người nước nào?**
What is this?	**Đây là cái gì?**
Is there … here?	**Ở đây có… không?**
Where is …. ?	**…. ở đâu?**
How much is it?	**Cái này giá bao nhiêu?**
What time is it?	**Bây giờ là mấy giờ?**
Congratulations	**Chúc mừng**
Where is the restroom/toilet?	**Phòng vệ sinh ở đâu?**
Where is the British Embassy?	**Đại sứ quán Anh ở đâu?**

Useful Words

I	**tôi**
man	**đàn ông**
woman	**đàn bà**
family	**gia đình**
parents	**bố mẹ/cha mẹ /ba má**
father	**bố/cha/ba**
mother	**mẹ/má/mạ**

younger brother	**em trai**
older brother	**anh trai**
younger sister	**em gái**
older sister	**chị**
big/small	**to/nhỏ**
high/low	**cao/thấp**
hot/cold	**nóng/lạnh**
good/bad	**Tốt/xấu**
young/old	**trẻ/già**
old/new	**cũ/mới**
expensive/cheap	**đắt/rẻ**
here	**đây**
there	**kia**
What?	**gì?**
Who?	**ai?**
Where	**(ở) đâu?**
Why?	**(tại) sao?**
How? What is it like?	**thế nào?**

Money

I want to change US$100 into Vietnamese currency.	**Tôi muốn đổi 100 đô la Mỹ ra tiền Việt.**
exchange rate	**tỷ giá hối đoái**
I'd like to cash these travelers' checks.	**Tôi muốn đổi séc du lịch này ra tiền mặt.**
bank	**ngân hàng**
money/cash	**tiền/tiền mặt**
credit card	**thẻ tín dụng**
dollars	**đô la**
pounds (sterling)	**bảng**
Vietnamese dong	**đồng (Việt Nam)**

Keeping in Touch

I'd like to make a telephone call.	**Tôi muốn gọi điện thoại.**
I'd like to make an international phone call.	**Tôi muốn gọi điện thoại quốc tế.**
mobile phone	**máy điện thoại di động**
telephone enquiries	**chi dẫn điện thoại**
public phone box	**trạm điện thoại công cộng**
area code	**mã (vùng)**
post office	**bưu điện**
stamp	**tem**
letter	**thư**
registered letter	**thư bảo đảm**
address	**địa chỉ**
street	**phố**
town	**thành phố**
village	**làng**

Shopping

Where can I buy…?	**Tôi có thể mua …. ở đâu?**
How much does this cost?	**Cái này giá bao nhiêu?**
May I try this on?	**Tôi mặc thử có được không?**
How much?	**Bao nhiêu?**
How many?	**Mấy?**
expensive/cheap	**đắt/rẻ**
to bargain	**mặc cả**
size	**số, cỡ**
colour	**màu**
black	**đen**
white	**trắng**
blue	**xanh da trời**
green	**xanh lá cây**
red	**đỏ**
brown	**nâu**
yellow	**vàng**
grey	**xám**
bookstore	**hiệu sách**
department store	**cửa hàng bách hóa**
market	**chợ**
pharmacy	**hiệu thuốc**
supermarket	**siêu thị**
souvenir shop	**cửa hàng lưu niệm**
souvenirs	**đồ lưu niệm**
lacquer painting	**tranh sơn mài**
painting on silk	**tranh lụa**
wooden statue	**bức tượng gỗ**
silk scarf	**khăn lụa**
tablecloth	**khăn trải bàn**
tray	**khay**
vase	**lọ hoa**

Sightseeing

travel agency	**công ty du lịch**
Where is the international ticket office? (plane)	**Phòng bán vé máy bay quốc tế ở đâu?**
Vietnam Airlines	**Hãng hàng không Việt Nam**
beach	**bãi**
bay	**vịnh**
ethnic minority	**dân tộc ít người**
festival	**lễ hội**
island	**hòn đảo**
lake	**hồ**
forest, jungle	**rừng**
mountain	**núi**
river	**sông**
temple	**đền**
museum	**bảo tàng**
pagoda	**chùa**
countryside	**nông thôn**
cave, grotto	**hang**

Getting Around

train station	**nhà ga**
airport	**sân bay**
air ticket	**vé máy bay**
bus station	**bến xe búyt**
ticket	**vé**
one-way ticket	**vé một lượt**
return ticket	**vé khứ hồi**
taxi	**tắc xi**
car rental	**thuê xe ô tô**
car	**xe ô tô**
train	**xe lửa**
plane	**máy bay**
motorbike	**xe máy**
bicycle	**xe đạp**
cyclo	**xích lô**
How long does it take to get to…?	**Đi …. mất bao lâu?**
Do you know …. road?	**Anh/chị có biết đường …. không?**
Is it far?	**Có xa không?**
Go straight.	**Đi thẳng.**
turn	**rẽ**
left	**trái**
right	**phải**
passport	**hộ chiếu**
visa	**thị thực**
customs	**hải quan**

Accommodations

hotel	**khách sạn**
guesthouse	**nhà khách**
room (single, double)	**phòng (đơn, đôi)**
air conditioning	**máy lạnh**
passport number	**số hộ chiếu**

Eating Out

I'd like to book a table for two.	**Tôi muốn đặt trước một bàn cho hai người.**
waiter	**người phục vụ**
May I see the menu?	**Cho tôi xem thực đơn**
Do you have any special dishes today?	**Hôm nay có món gì đặc biệt không?**
What would you like to order?	**Anh/chị muốn gọi gì?**
Can I have the bill, please?	**Anh/chị cho hóa đơn**
I am a vegetarian.	**Tôi ăn chay.**
tasty/delicious	**ngon/ngon tuyệt**
spicy (hot)	**cay**
sweet	**ngọt**
sour	**chua**

bitter	**đắng**	rice	**gạo**
breakfast	**bữa ăn sáng**	rice (cooked)	**cơm**
chopsticks	**đôi đũa**	glutinous rice	**gạo (cơm) nếp**
knife	**dao**	non-glutinous rice	**gạo (cơm) tẻ**
fork	**nĩa**	salad	**xà lách**
spoon	**thìa**	salt	**muối**
to drink	**uống**	snail	**ốc**
to eat	**ăn**	spring rolls	**nem rán (chả giò)**
hungry/thirsty	**đói/khát**	starter	**(món) khai vị**
restaurant	**hiệu ăn, nhà hàng**	soup	**xúp**
western food	**món ăn Âu**	soy sauce	**tương**
Vietnamese specialties	**đặc sản Việt Nam**	stir-fried beef with	**bò xào mắm**
		mushrooms	
		sugar	**đường**

Food

		Vietnamese noodle	**phở**
apple	**táo**	soup	
banana	**chuối**	vegetables	**rau**
bamboo shoots	**măng**		
bean sprouts	**giá**		
beef	**thịt bò**		

Drinks

bread	**bánh mì**	tea	**trà, chè**
butter	**bơ**	coffee (white coffee)	**cà phê (cà phê sữa)**
cake	**bánh ngọt**	water	**nước**
chicken	**(thịt) gà**	fruit juice	**nước quả,**
coconut	**dừa**		**nước trái cây**
crab	**cua**	mineral water	**nước khoáng**
dessert	**(món) tráng miệng**	milk	**sữa**
duck	**vịt**	soft drinks	**nước ngọt**
eel	**lươn**	beer	**bia**
egg	**trứng**	wine	**rượu vang**
fish	**cá**	glass	**cốc**
fish sauce	**nước mắm**	bottle	**chai**
frog	**ếch**		
fruit	**hoa quả, trái cây**		
ginger	**gừng**		

Health

ice	**đá**	What is the matter	**Anh/chị bị**
ice cream	**kem**	with you?	**làm sao?**
lemon	**chanh**	fever	**sốt**
lemongrass	**xả**	accident (traffic)	**tai nạn (giao thông)**
lobster	**tôm hùm**	acupuncture	**châm cứu**
mandarin orange	**quít**	ambulance	**xe cấp cứu**
mango	**xoài**	antibiotics	**thuốc kháng sinh**
menu	**thực đơn**	allergy	**dị ứng**
milk	**sữa**	blood	**máu**
mushrooms	**nấm**	blood pressure	**huyết áp**
meat	**thịt**	(high/low)	**(cao/thấp)**
(well done,	**(tái, vừa, chin)**	cough	**ho**
medium, rare)		diabetes	**bệnh đái đường**
noodles	**mì, miến**	diarrhea	**đi ngoài**
noodle soup beef/	**phở bò/gà**	dizzy	**chóng mặt, hoa mắt**
chicken		doctor	**bác sĩ**
onion	**hành**	ear	**tai**
papaya	**đu đủ**	flu	**cúm**
peach	**đào**	food poisoning	**ngộ độc thức ăn**
pepper	**hạt tiêu**	headache	**đau đầu**
pork	**thịt lợn, thịt heo**	heart	**tim**
potato (sweet potato)	**khoai tây (khoai)**	hospital	**bệnh viện**
prawn	**tôm**	hygiene	**vệ sinh**
rambutan	**chôm chôm**		

insomnia	**mất ngủ**	8:45	**tám giờ bốn mươi**
illness	**bệnh**		**lăm phút/chín giờ**
injection	**tiêm**		**kém mười lăm**
malaria	**bệnh sốt rét**		**(phút)**
medicine	**thuốc**	10:15	**mười giờ mười**
operate	**mổ**		**lăm phút**
pharmacy	**cửa hàng thuốc**	12:00	**mười hai giờ**
prescription	**đơn thuốc**	morning	**buổi sang**
sore throat	**viêm họng**	midday	**buổi trưa**
temperature	**sốt**	afternoon	**buổi chiều**
tetanus injection	**tiêm phòng uốn ván**	evening	**buổi tối**
Vietnamese traditional	**thuốc Nam**	night	**đêm**
medicine			
tooth	**răng**		
toothache	**đau răng**	**Numbers**	
		1	**một**
Time and Season		2	**hai**
		3	**ba**
minute	**phút**	4	**bốn**
hour	**giờ**	5	**năm**
day	**ngày**	6	**sáu**
week	**tuần**	7	**bảy**
month	**tháng**	8	**tám**
year	**năm**	9	**chín**
Monday	**(ngày) thứ hai**	10	**mười**
Tuesday	**(ngày) thứ ba**	11	**mười một**
Wednesday	**(ngày) thứ tư**	12	**mười hai**
Thursday	**(ngày) thứ năm**	15	**mười lăm**
Friday	**(ngày) thứ sáu**	20	**hai mươi**
Saturday	**(ngày) thứ bảy**	21	**hai mươi mốt**
Sunday	**Chủ nhật**	24	**hai mươi bốn/**
season	**mùa**		**hai mươi tư**
spring	**mùa xuân**	25	**hai mươi lăm**
summer	**mùa hè/mùa hạ**	30	**ba mươi**
fall	**mùa thu**	40	**bốn mươi**
winter	**mùa đông**	50	**năm mươi**
dry season	**mùa khô**	100	**một trăm**
rainy season	**mùa mưa**	101	**một trăm linh**
rain (it is raining)	**mưa (trời mưa)**		**(lẻ) một**
wind	**gió**	105	**một trăm linh**
sunny	**nắng**		**(lẻ) năm**
weather	**thời tiết**	200	**hai trăm**
warm/cold	**ấm/lạnh**	300	**ba trăm**
lunar calendar	**Âm lịch**	1,000	**một nghìn/**
solar calendar	**Dương lịch**		**một ngàn**
Vietnamese New Year	**Tết Nguyên đán**	10,000	**mười nghìn/**
What time is it?	**Bây giờ là mấy giờ?**		**mười ngàn**
8:30	**tám giờ rưỡi**	1,000,000	**một triệu**

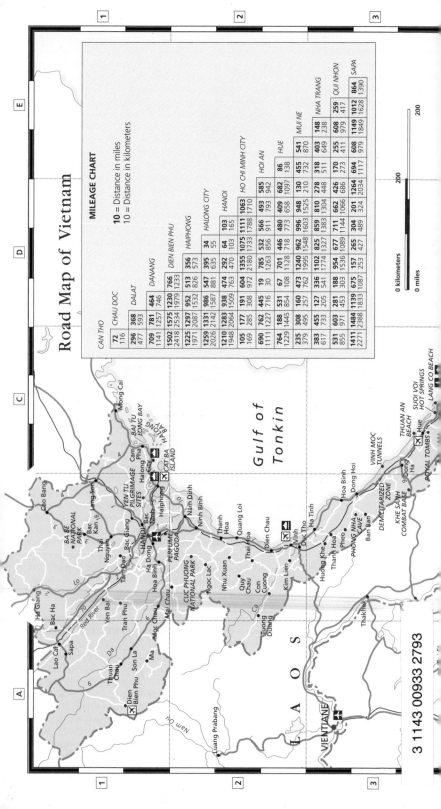

Road Map of Vietnam

3 1143 00933 2793